ROSARIO + VAMPIRE
Season II

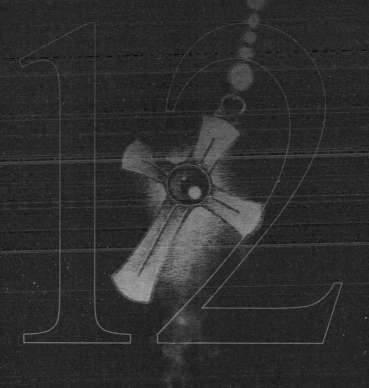

12

AKIHISA IKEDA

ROSARIO + VAMPIRE Season II

12 Contents & Story

Tsukune Aono accidentally enrolls in Yokai Academy, a high school for monsters! After befriending the school's cutest girl, Moka Akashiya, he decides to stay...even though Yokai has a zero-tolerance policy towards humans (a *fatal* policy). Tsukune survives with the help of his News Club friends—Moka (Vampire), Kurumu (Succubus), Yukari (Witch) and Mizore (Snow Fairy).

Just as Tsukune and his friends begin contemplating their future after they graduate, they are attacked by Fairy Tale, an organization bent on destroying the human world by reviving Alucard, the First Ancestor of the Vampires. When Fairy Tale kidnaps Moka, Tsukune and their friends train rigorously under Tohofuhai, one of the three Dark Lords, then infiltrate the Hanging Garden, the enemy's fortress. As their friends fall one by one, Kurumu and Mizore manage to find Moka, only to be defeated by Aqua, Moka's elder sister. The shock of seeing her two friends' defeat breaks the final seal binding Moka to reveal...her true self?!

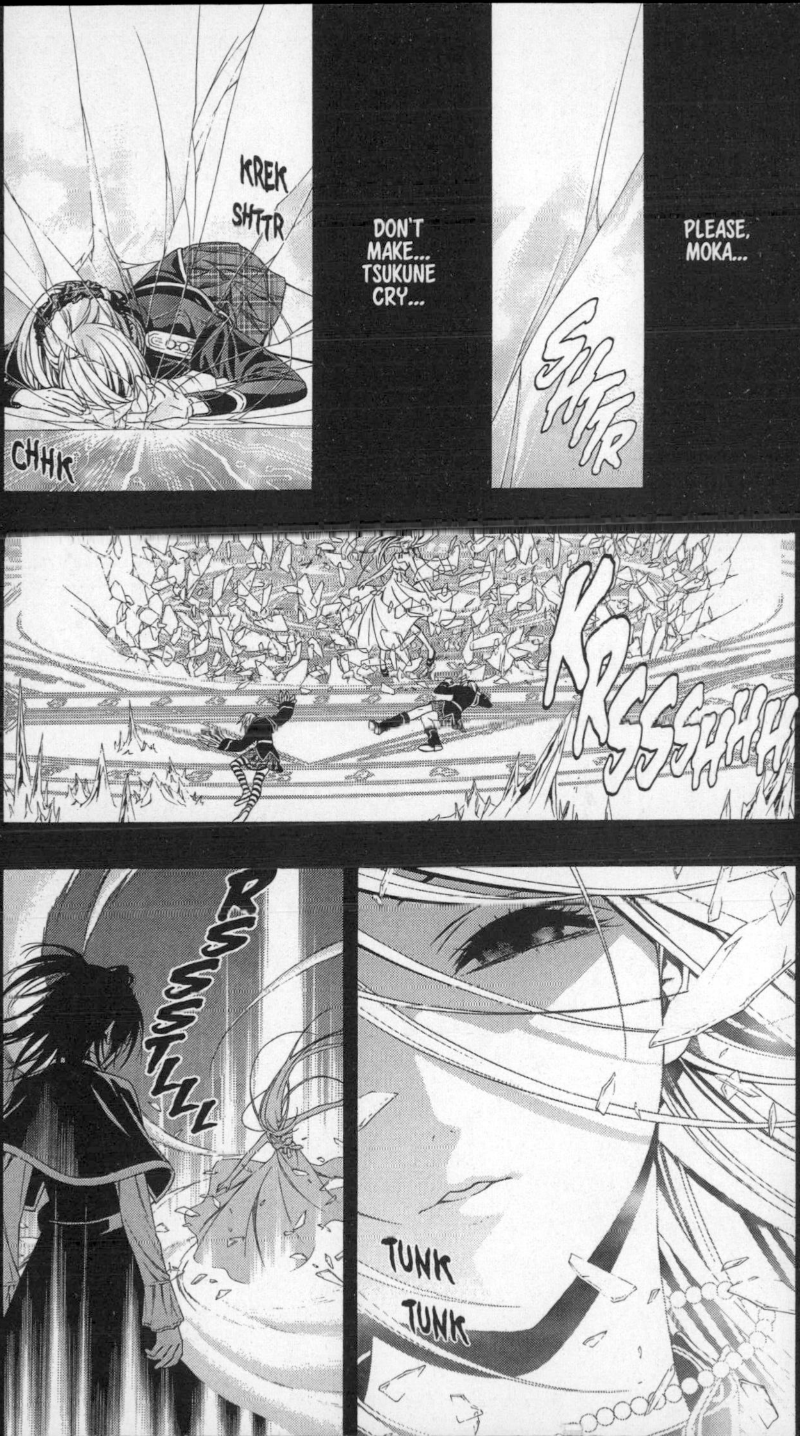
PLEASE, MOKA...
DON'T MAKE... TSUKUNE CRY...
KREK
SHTTR
CHHK
KRSSSHHH
TUNK
TUNK
RSSSTLLL

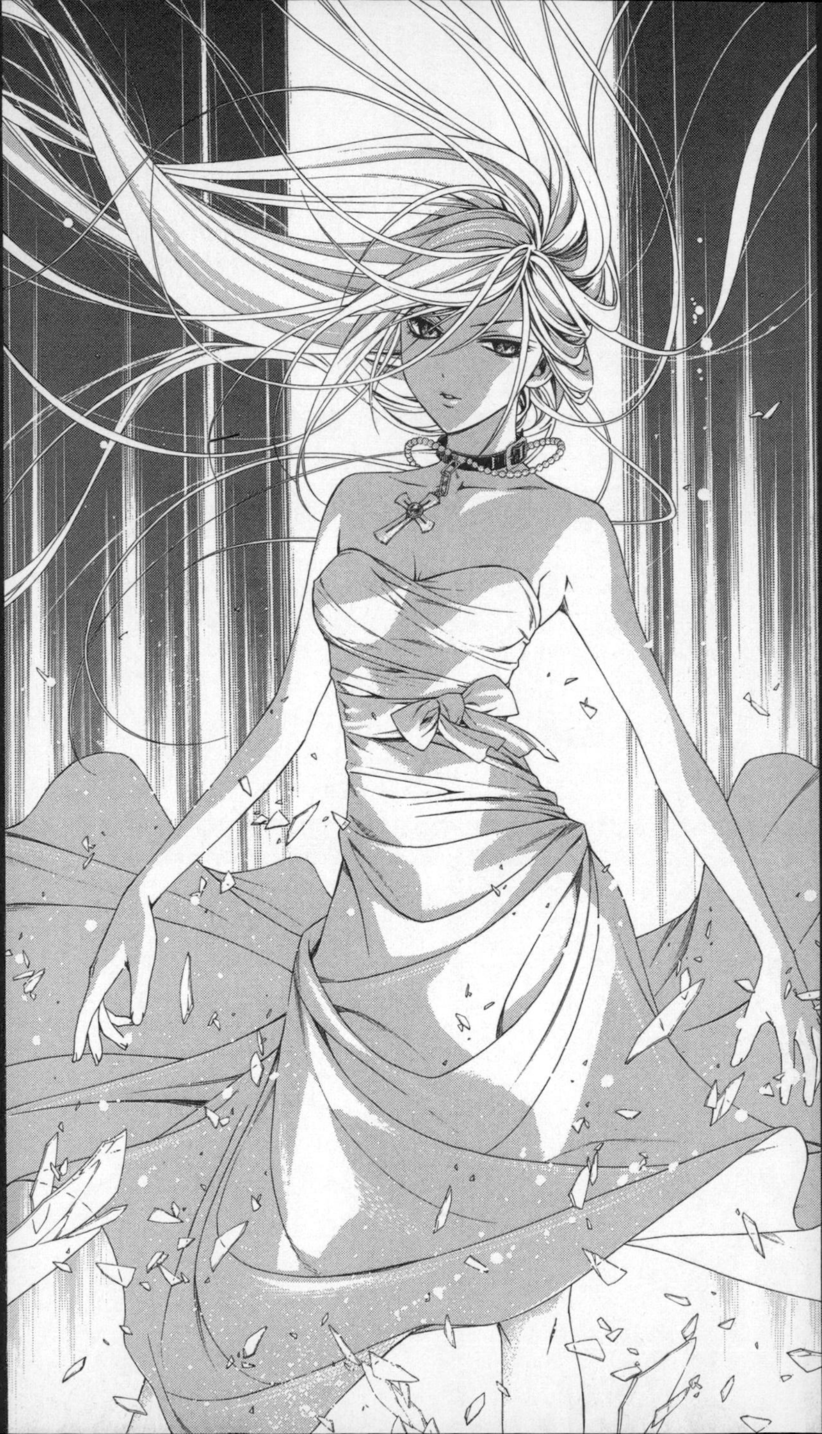

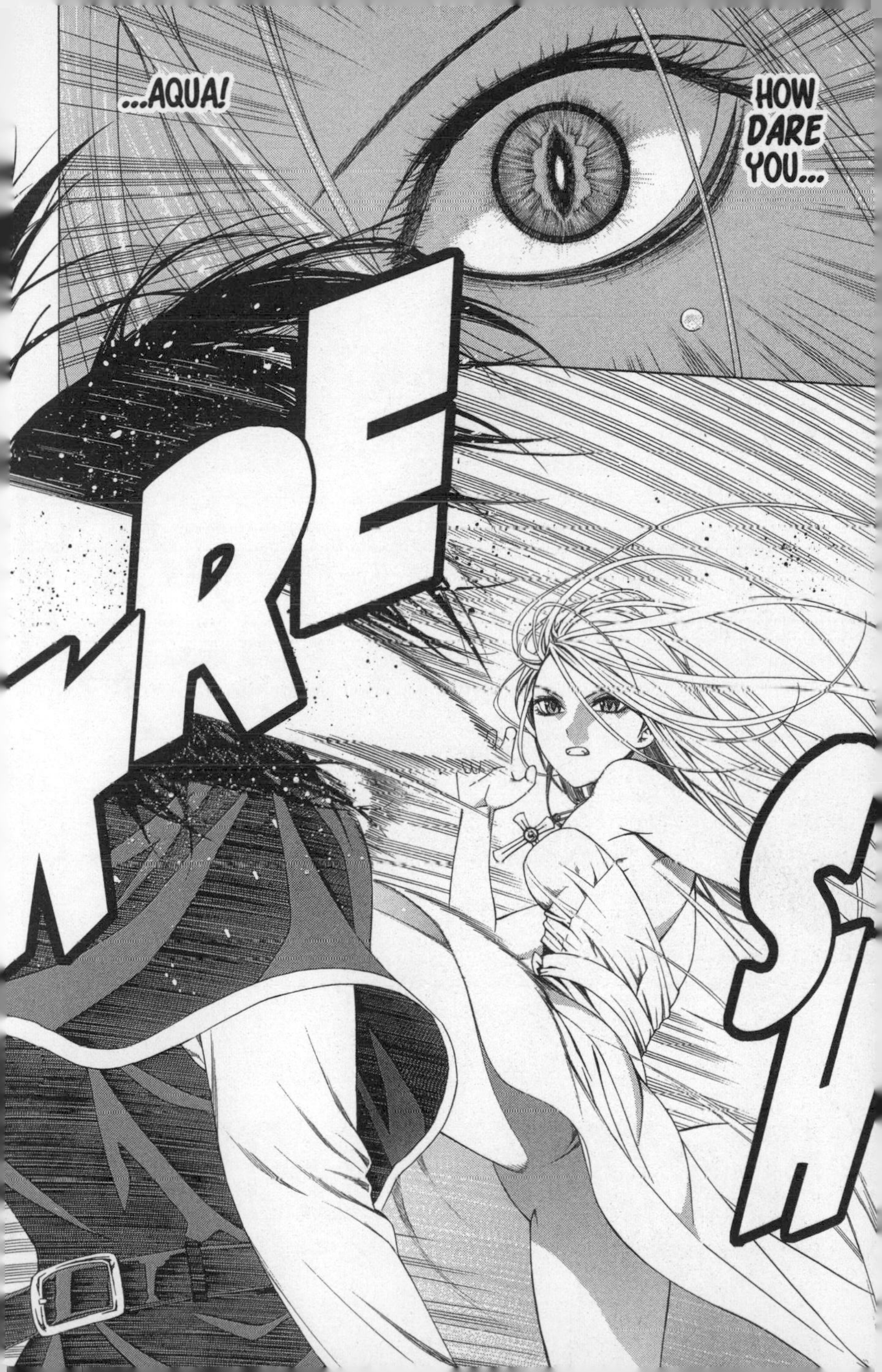
HOW DARE YOU...
...AQUA!

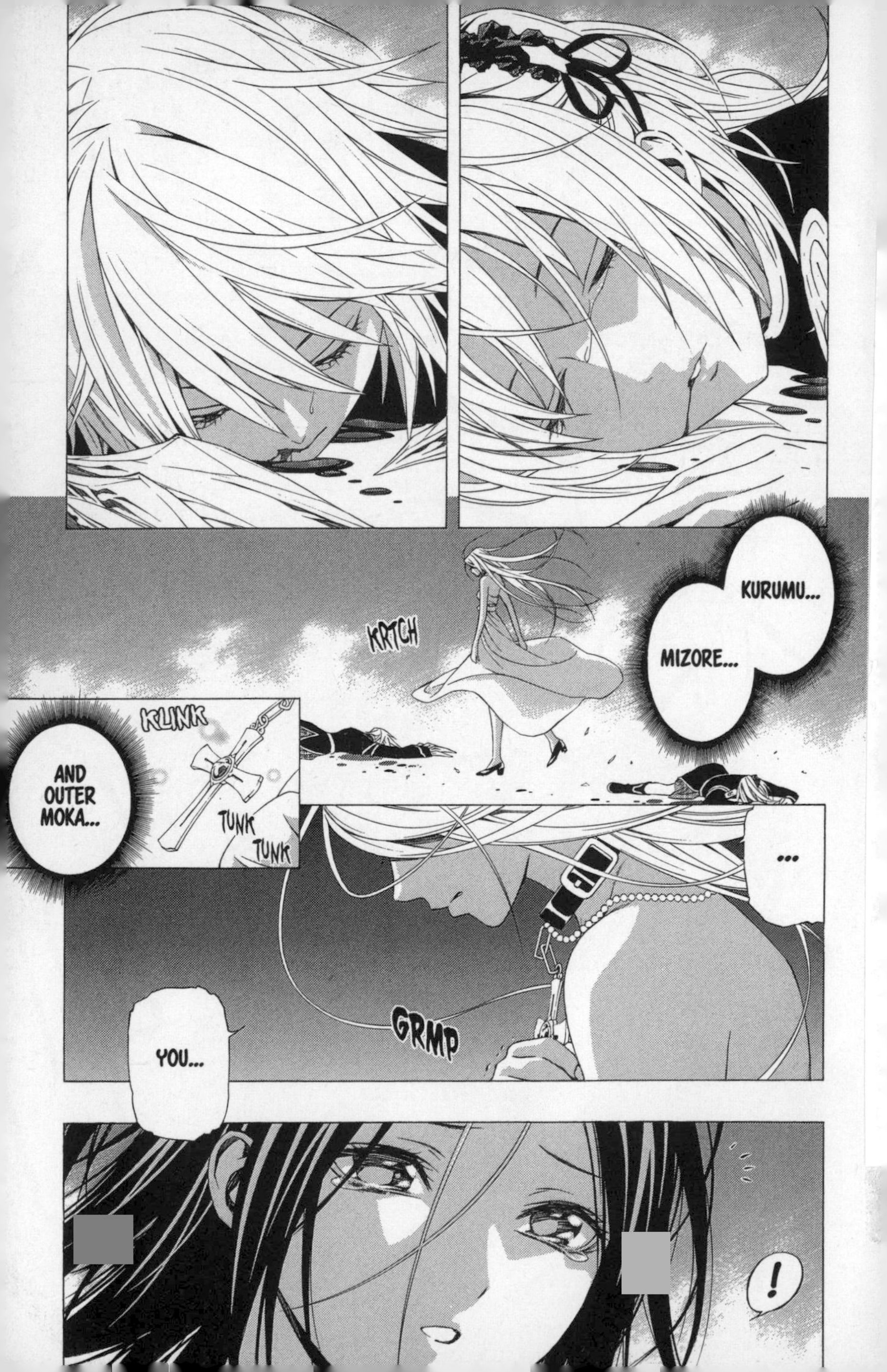
KURUMU...
MIZORE...
KRTCH
AND OUTER MOKA...
KLINK
TUNK TUNK
...
GRMP
YOU...
!

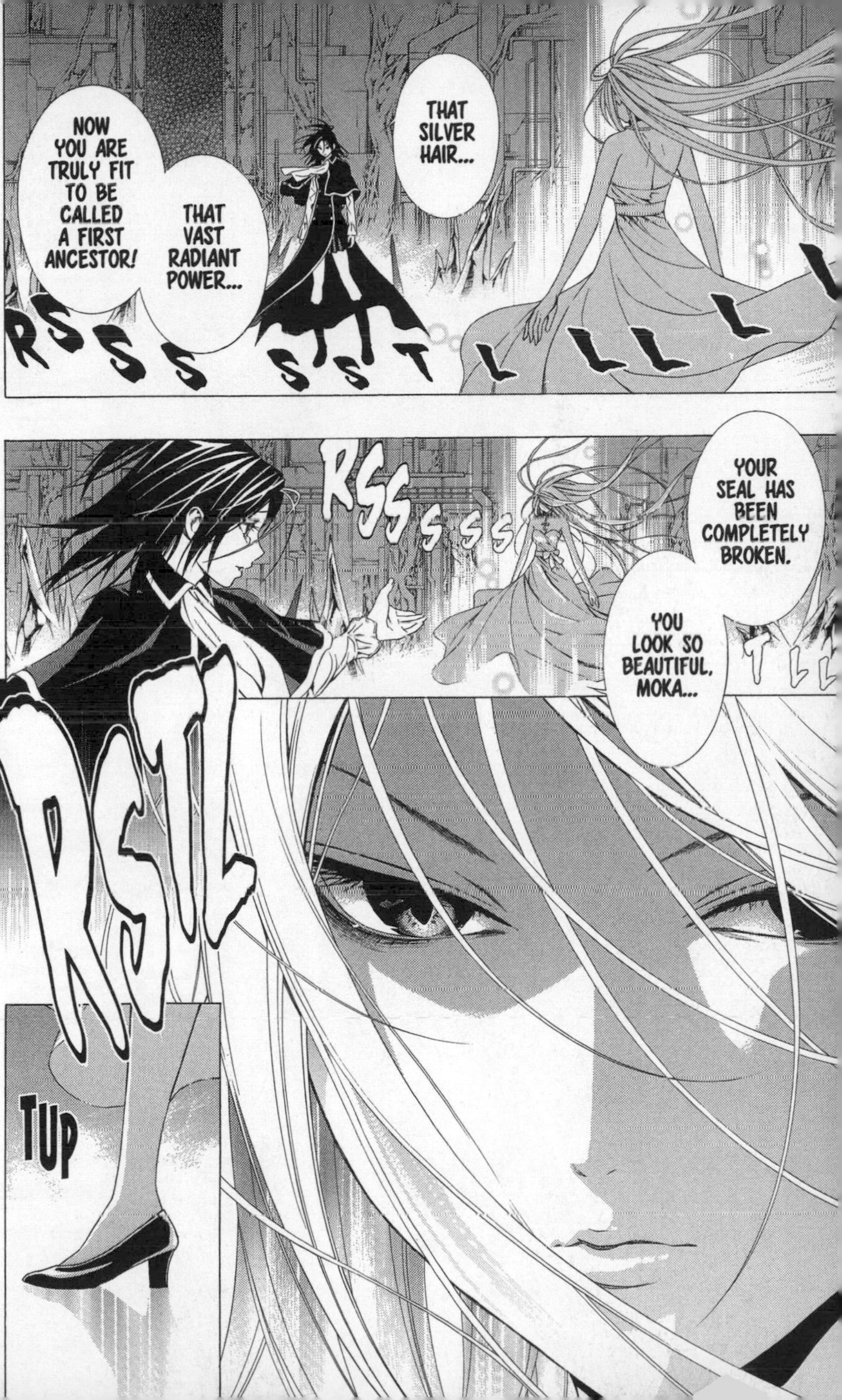
THAT SILVER HAIR...
THAT VAST RADIANT POWER...
NOW YOU ARE TRULY FIT TO BE CALLED A FIRST ANCESTOR!
RSSSSSTLLLLL
YOUR SEAL HAS BEEN COMPLETELY BROKEN.
YOU LOOK SO BEAUTIFUL, MOKA...
RSSSSSS
TLL
RSTL
TUP

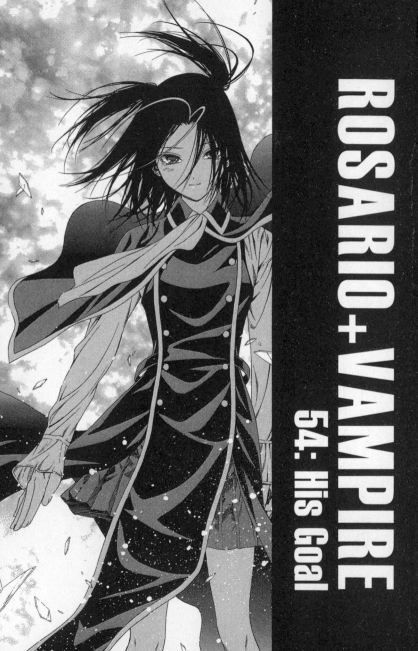

ROSARIO+VAMPIRE

54: His Goal

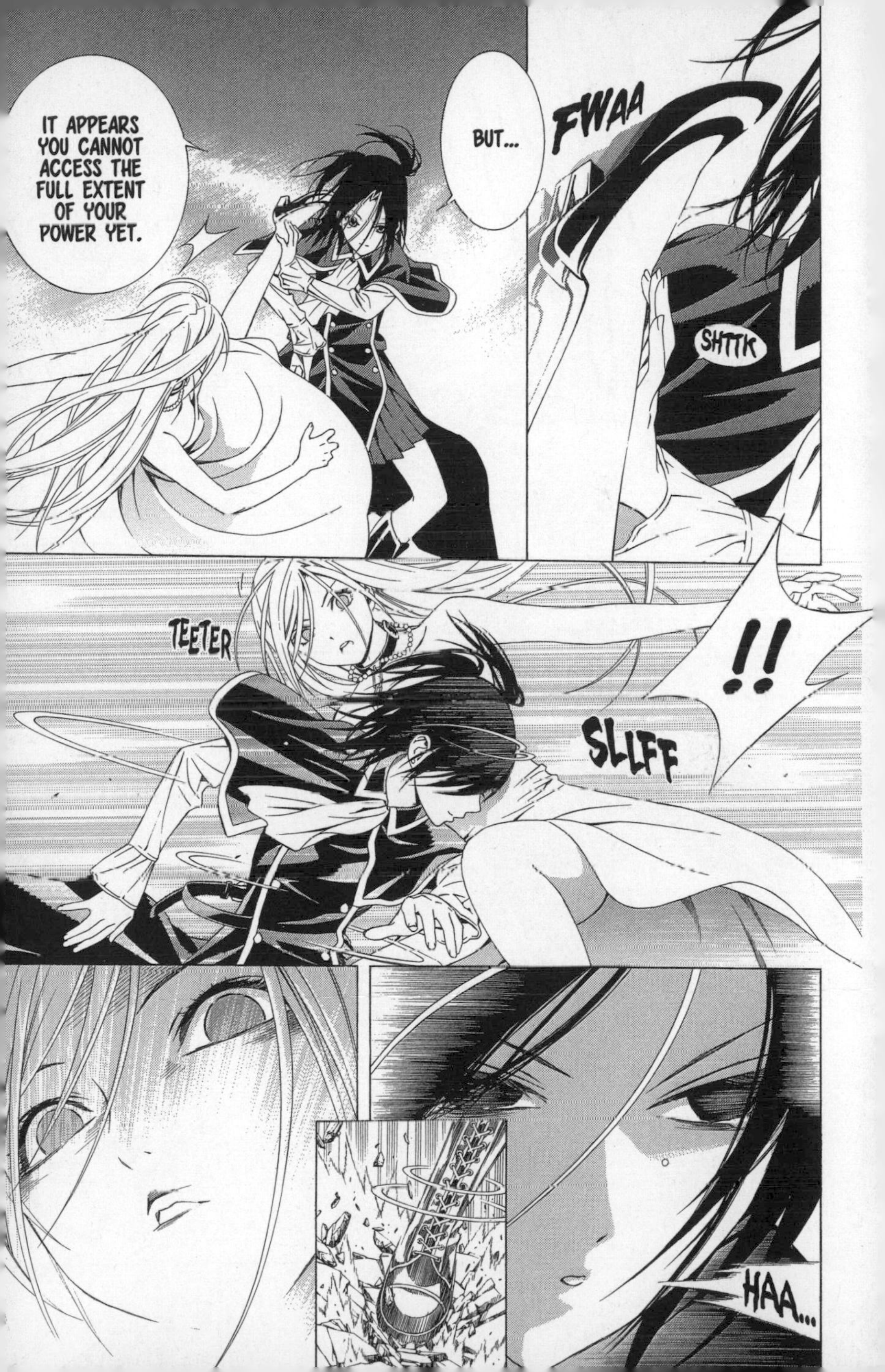
FWAA
SHTTK
BUT...
IT APPEARS YOU CANNOT ACCESS THE FULL EXTENT OF YOUR POWER YET.
!!
SLLFF
TEETER
HAA...

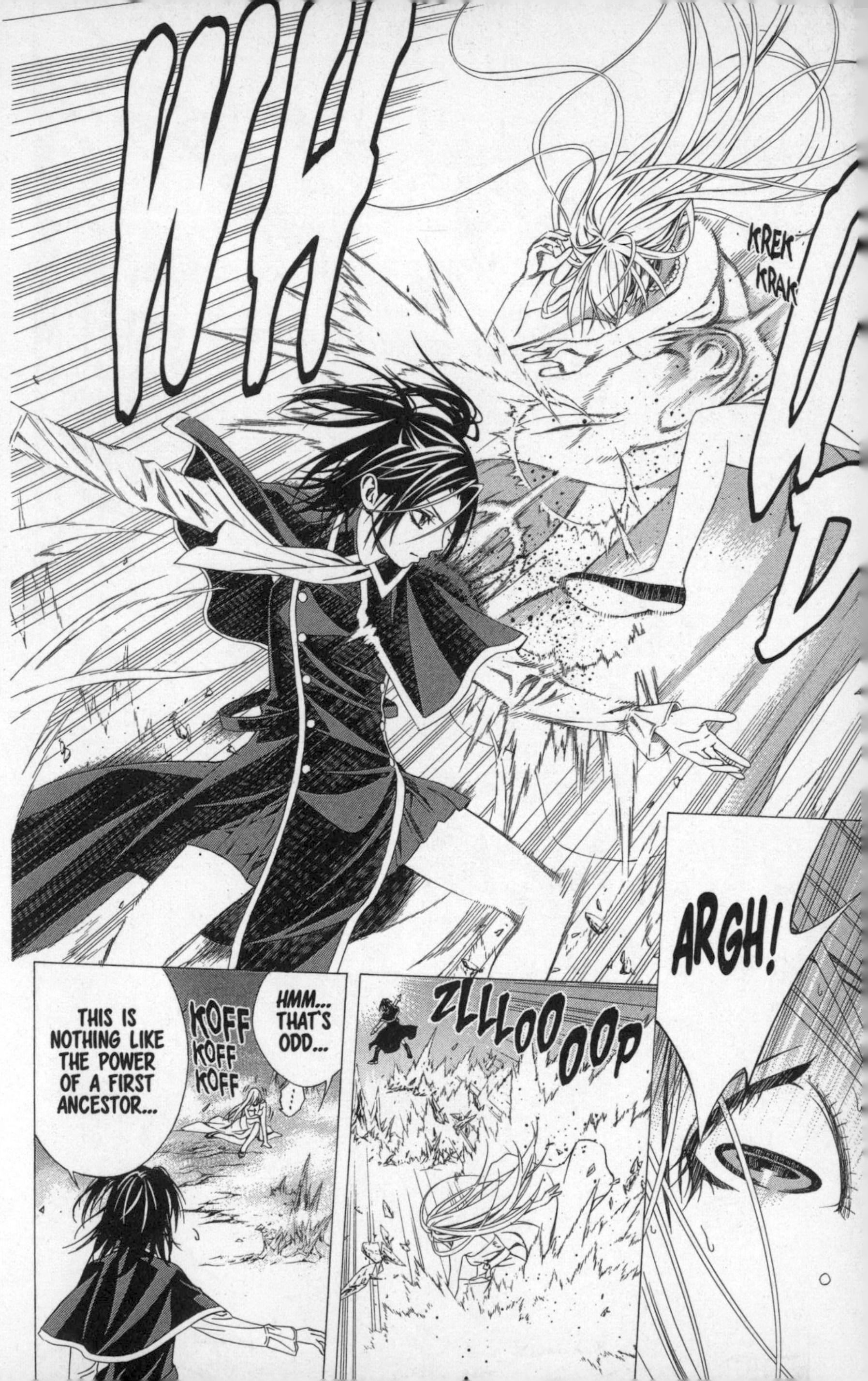
KREK
KRAK
ARGH!
ZLLLOOOOOP
HMM... THAT'S ODD...
KOFF KOFF KOFF
...
THIS IS NOTHING LIKE THE POWER OF A FIRST ANCESTOR...

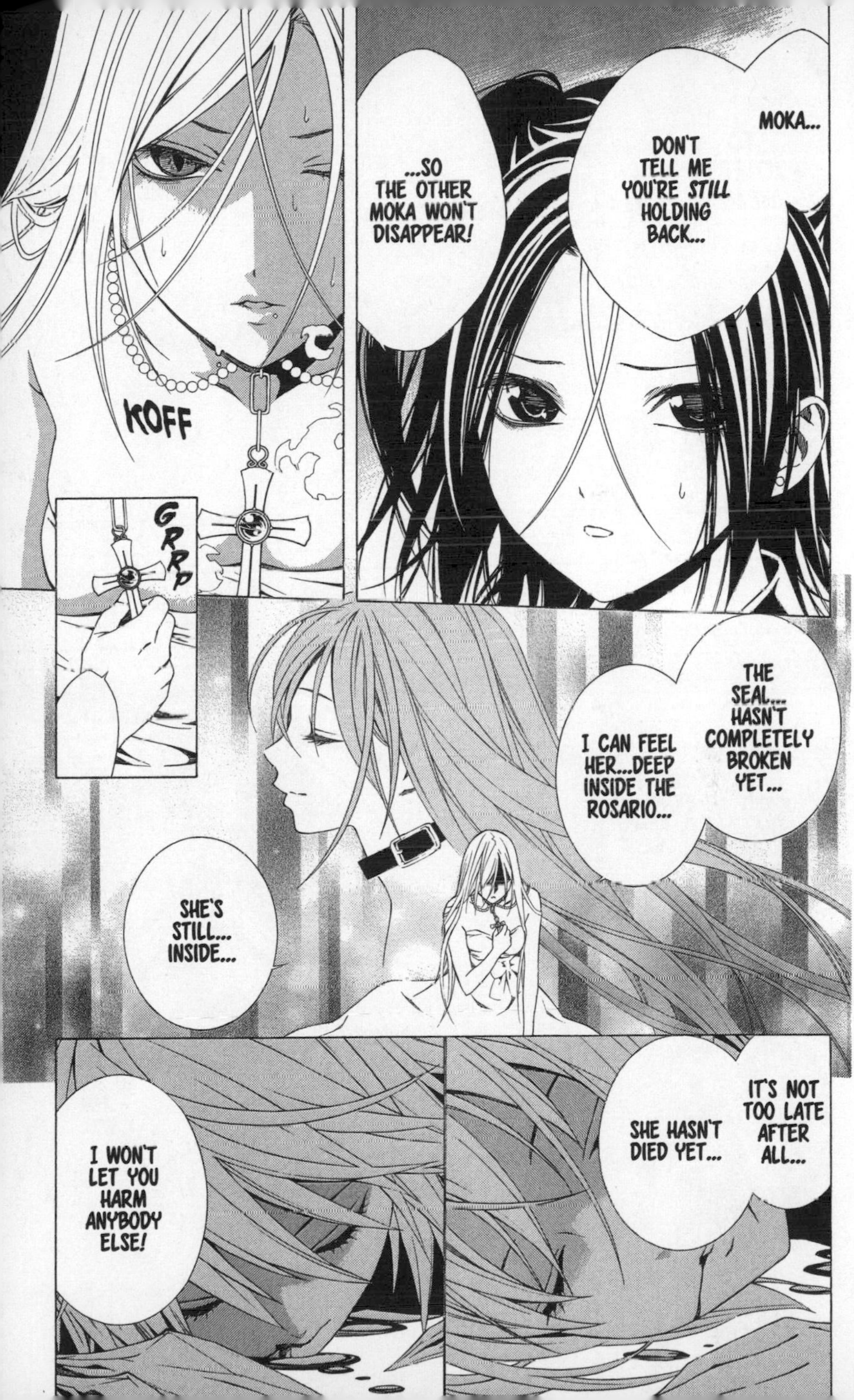
MOKA...
DON'T TELL ME YOU'RE *STILL* HOLDING BACK...
...SO THE OTHER MOKA WON'T DISAPPEAR!
KOFF
GRRP
THE SEAL... HASN'T COMPLETELY BROKEN YET...
I CAN FEEL HER...DEEP INSIDE THE ROSARIO...
SHE'S STILL... INSIDE...
IT'S NOT TOO LATE AFTER ALL...
SHE HASN'T DIED YET...
I WON'T LET YOU HARM ANYBODY ELSE!

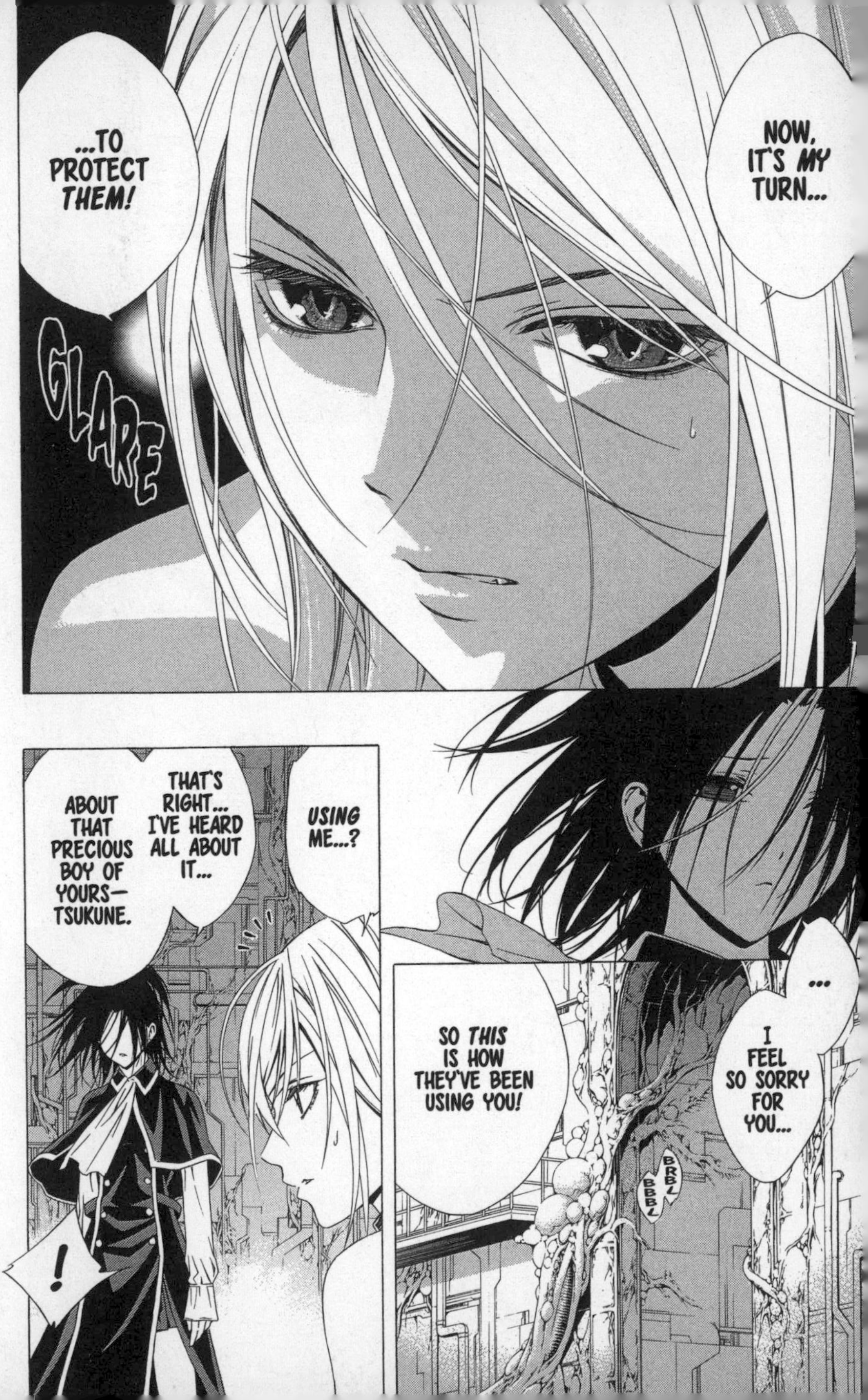
NOW, IT'S MY TURN...
...TO PROTECT THEM!
GLARE
...
I FEEL SO SORRY FOR YOU...
SO THIS IS HOW THEY'VE BEEN USING YOU!
BRBL
BBBL
USING ME...?
THAT'S RIGHT... I'VE HEARD ALL ABOUT IT...
ABOUT THAT PRECIOUS BOY OF YOURS—TSUKUNE.
!

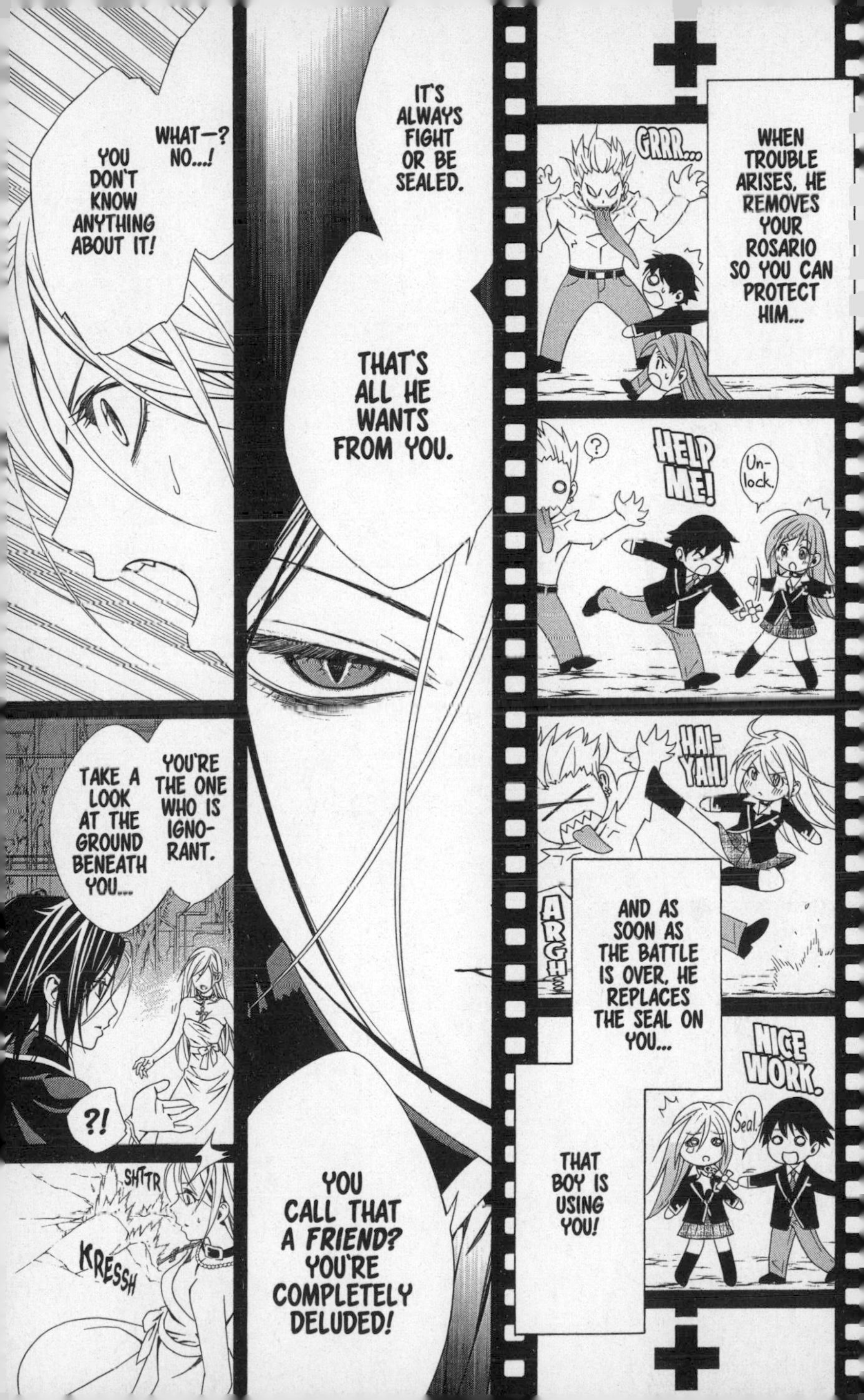
WHEN TROUBLE ARISES, HE REMOVES YOUR ROSARIO SO YOU CAN PROTECT HIM...
GRRR...
Un-lock.
HELP ME!
?
HAI-YAH!
AND AS SOON AS THE BATTLE IS OVER, HE REPLACES THE SEAL ON YOU...
ARGH...
NICE WORK.
Seal.
THAT BOY IS USING YOU!
IT'S ALWAYS FIGHT OR BE SEALED.
THAT'S ALL HE WANTS FROM YOU.
YOU CALL THAT A *FRIEND?* YOU'RE COMPLETELY DELUDED!
WHAT—? NO...!
YOU DON'T KNOW ANYTHING ABOUT IT!
YOU'RE THE ONE WHO IS IGNO-RANT.
TAKE A LOOK AT THE GROUND BENEATH YOU...
?!
SHTTR
KRESSH

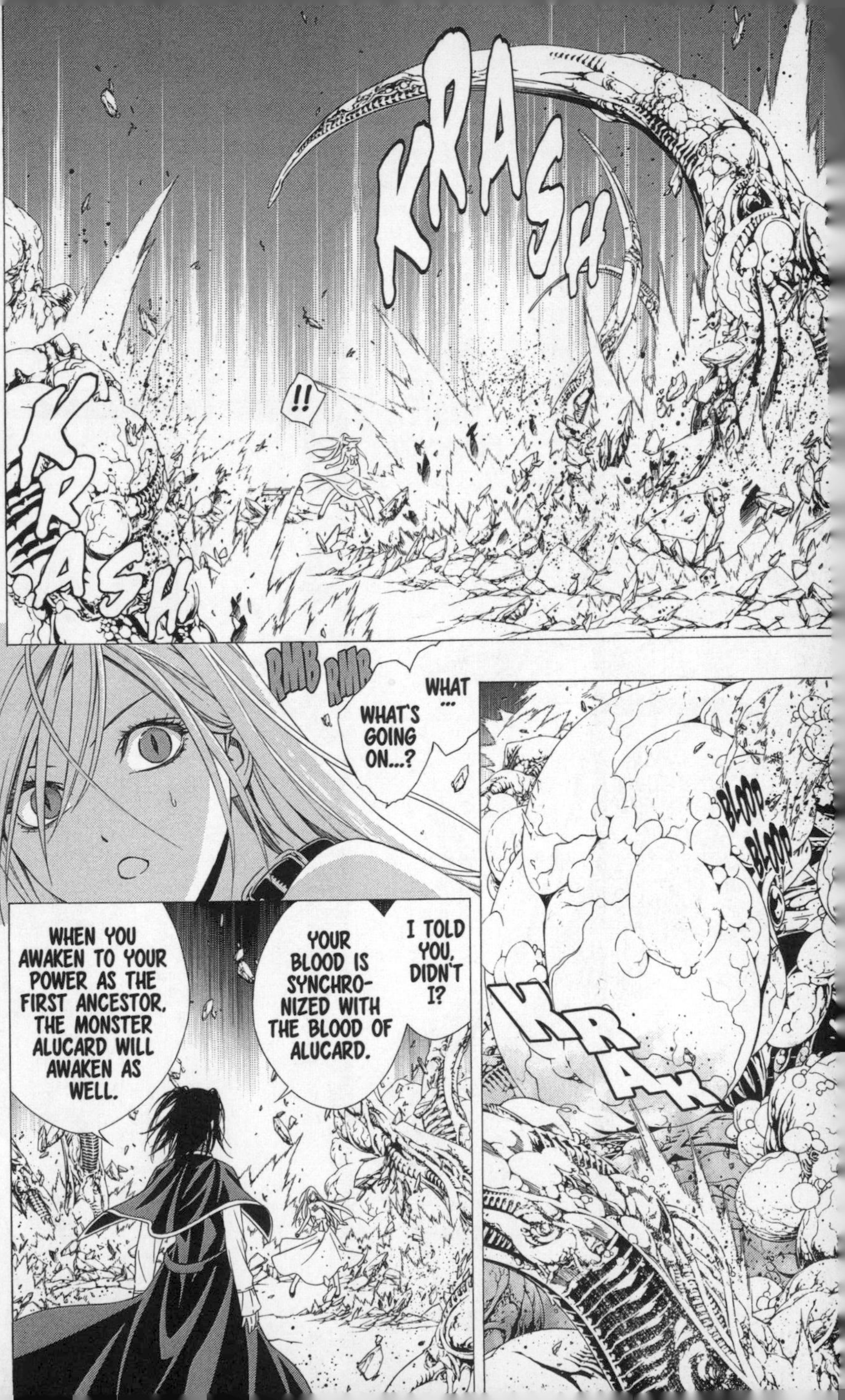
KRASH
KRASH
!!
BLOOD BLOOD
KRAK
RMB RMB
WHAT...
WHAT'S GOING ON...?
I TOLD YOU, DIDN'T I?
YOUR BLOOD IS SYNCHRO-NIZED WITH THE BLOOD OF ALUCARD.
WHEN YOU AWAKEN TO YOUR POWER AS THE FIRST ANCESTOR, THE MONSTER ALUCARD WILL AWAKEN AS WELL.

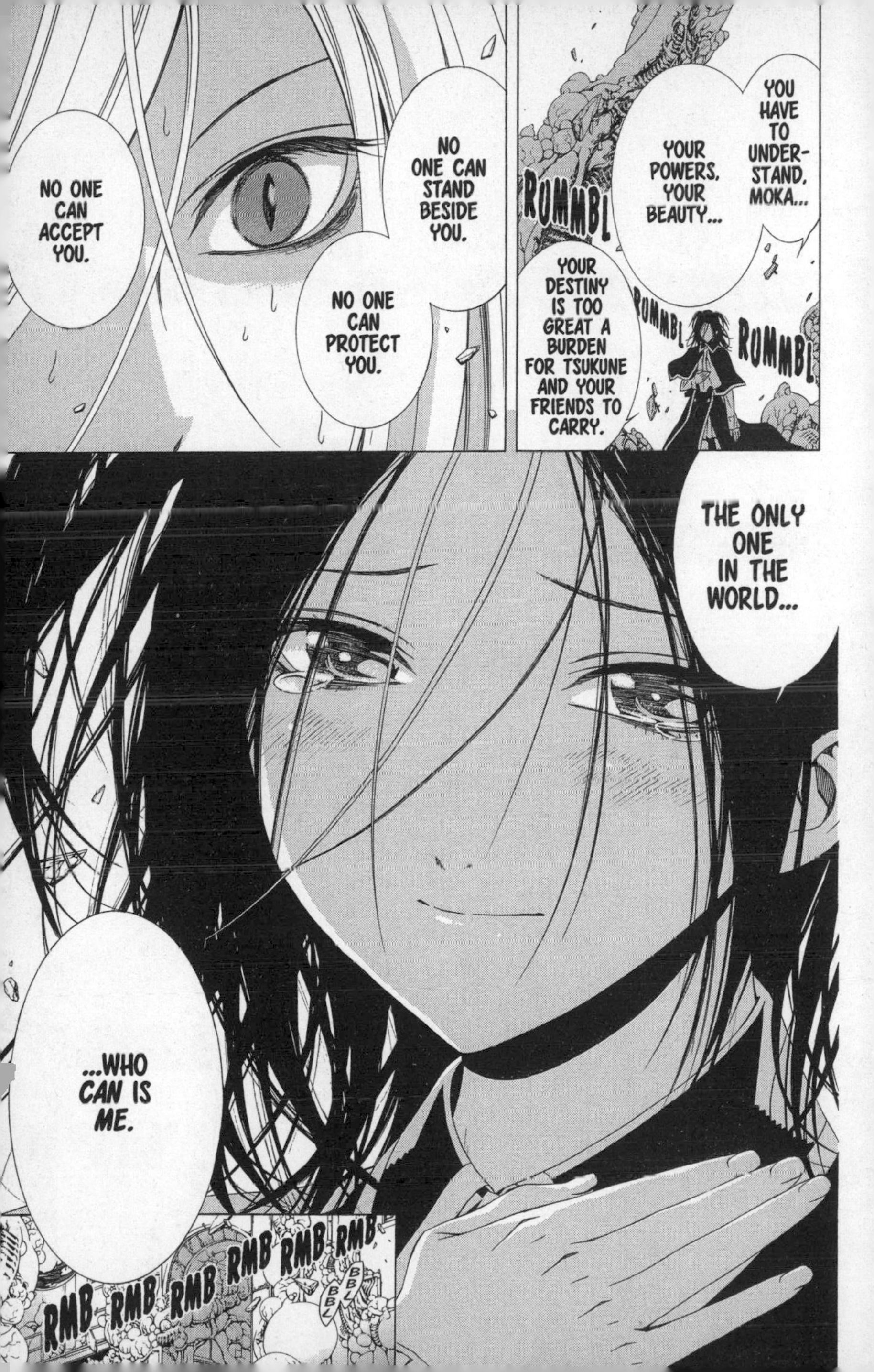
YOU HAVE TO UNDER-STAND, MOKA...
YOUR POWERS, YOUR BEAUTY...
RUMMBL
YOUR DESTINY IS TOO GREAT A BURDEN FOR TSUKUNE AND YOUR FRIENDS TO CARRY.
RUMMBL
RUMMBL
NO ONE CAN STAND BESIDE YOU.
NO ONE CAN PROTECT YOU.
NO ONE CAN ACCEPT YOU.
THE ONLY ONE IN THE WORLD...
...WHO CAN IS ME.
RMB RMB RMB RMB RMB RMB RMB RMB
BBL BBL

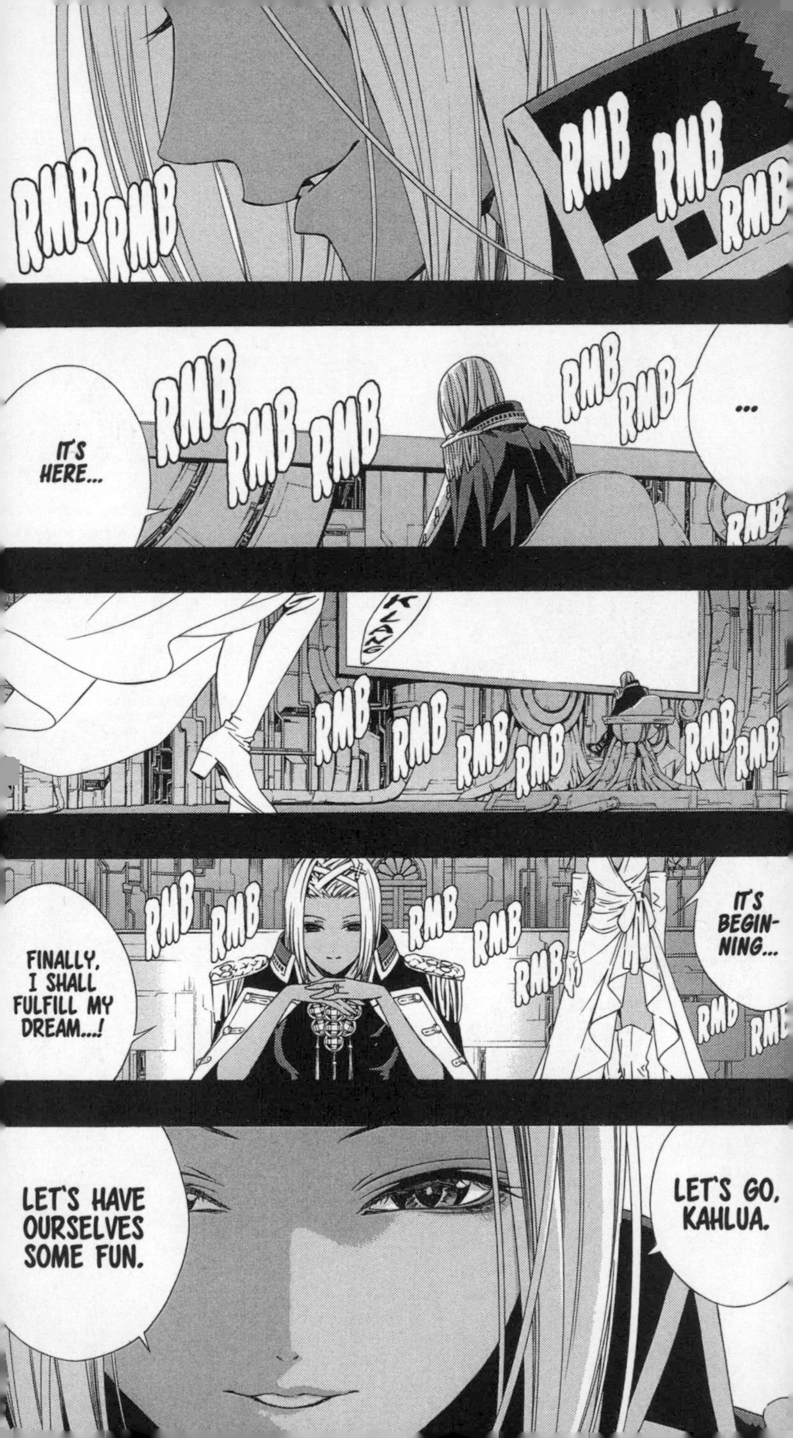
RMB RMB RMB
RMB RMB
...
RMB
RMB RMB
RMB RMB RMB
IT'S HERE...
KLANG
RMB RMB
RMB RMB
RMB RMB
IT'S BEGINNING...
RMB RMB RMB
RMB RMB
FINALLY, I SHALL FULFILL MY DREAM...!
LET'S GO, KAHLUA.
LET'S HAVE OURSELVES SOME FUN.

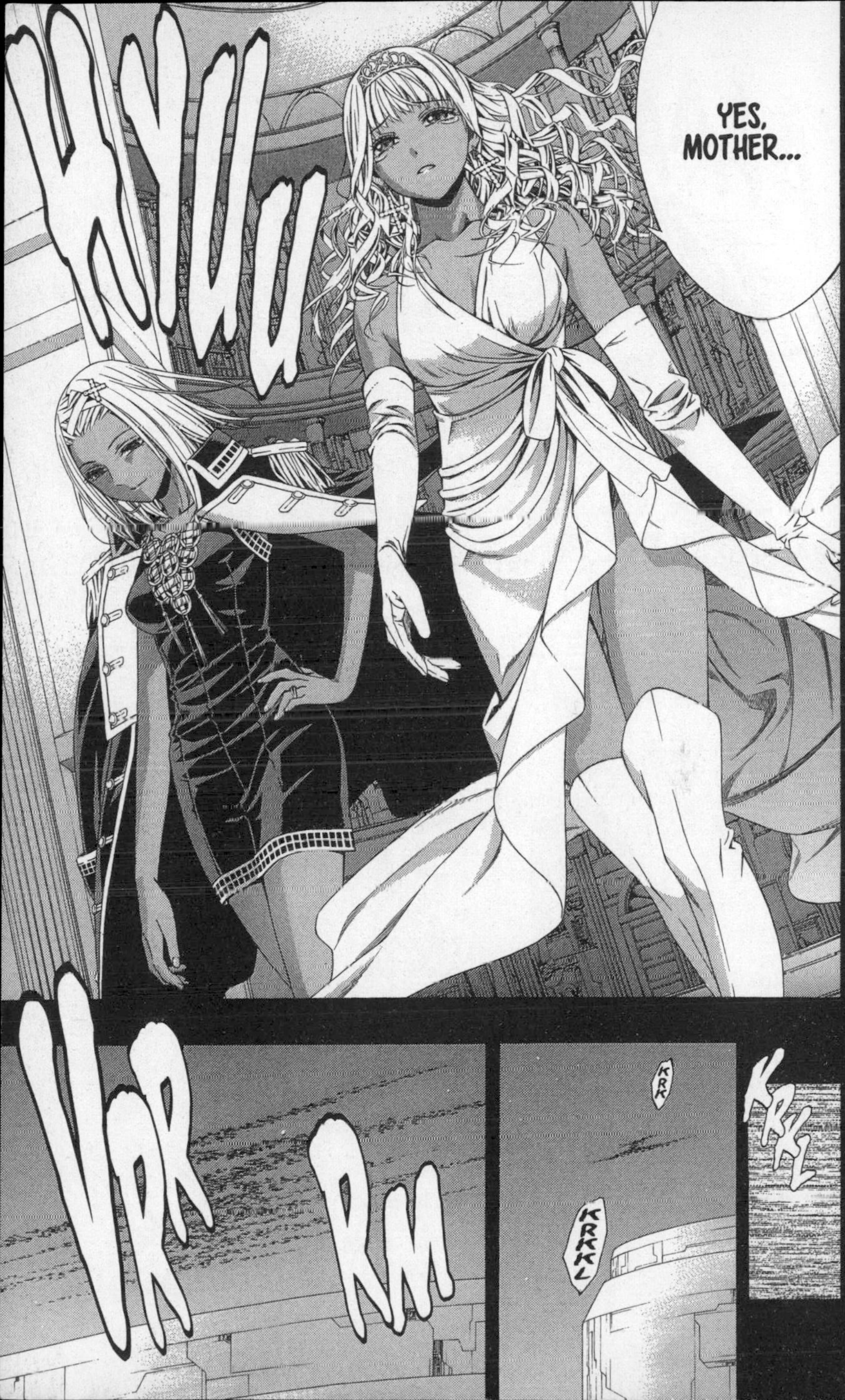
YES, MOTHER...
KRK
KRKKL
VRRRM

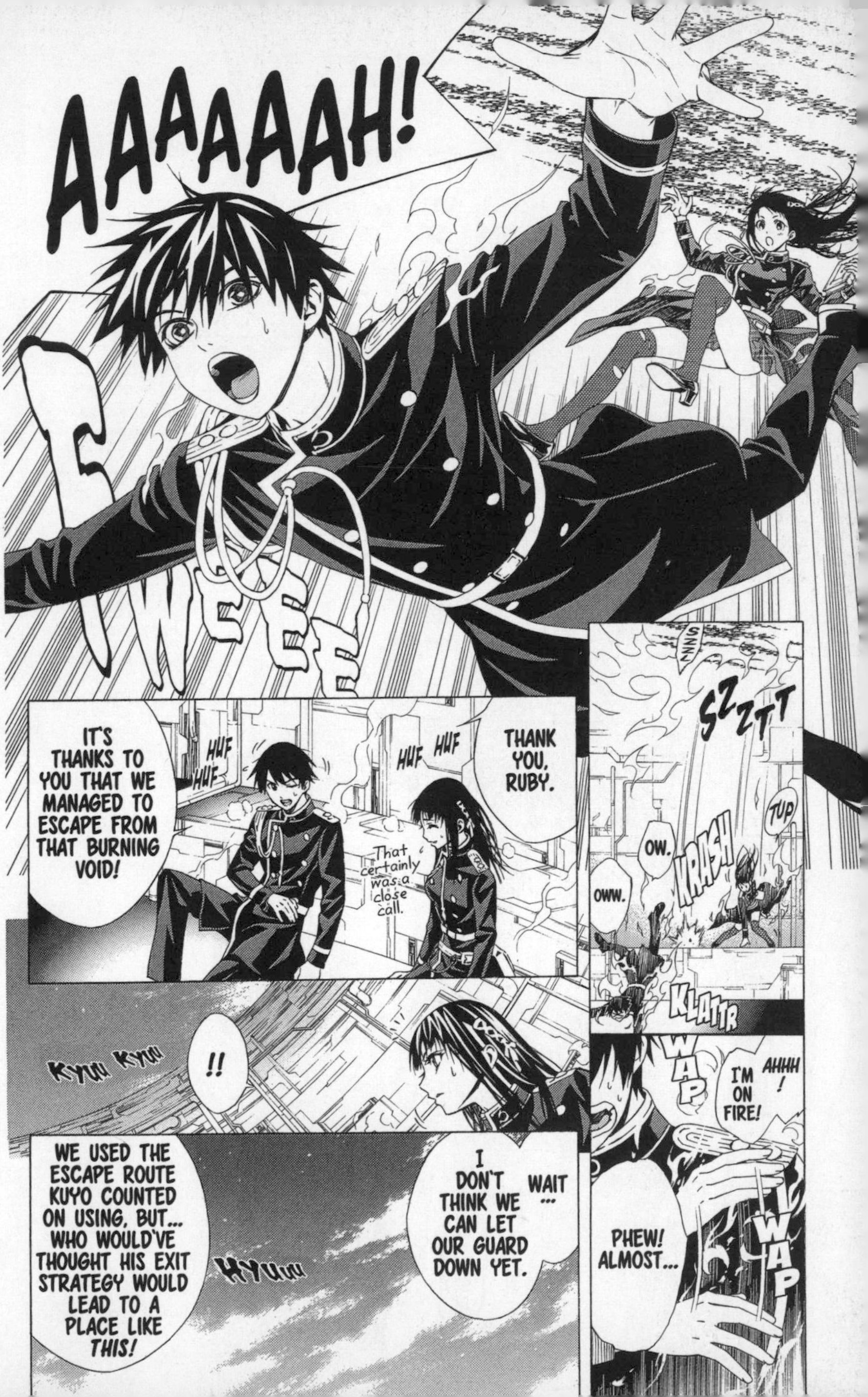
AAAAAAH!
FWEEE
SZZZ
SZZTT
TUP
OW.
KRASH
OWW.
KLATTR
AHHH!
I'M ON FIRE!
WAP
PHEW! ALMOST...
WAP
THANK YOU, RUBY.
HUF HUF
HUF HUF
That certainly was a close call.
IT'S THANKS TO YOU THAT WE MANAGED TO ESCAPE FROM THAT BURNING VOID!
!!
Kyuu Kyuu
WAIT...
I DON'T THINK WE CAN LET OUR GUARD DOWN YET.
HYUuu
WE USED THE ESCAPE ROUTE KUYO COUNTED ON USING, BUT... WHO WOULD'VE THOUGHT HIS EXIT STRATEGY WOULD LEAD TO A PLACE LIKE THIS!

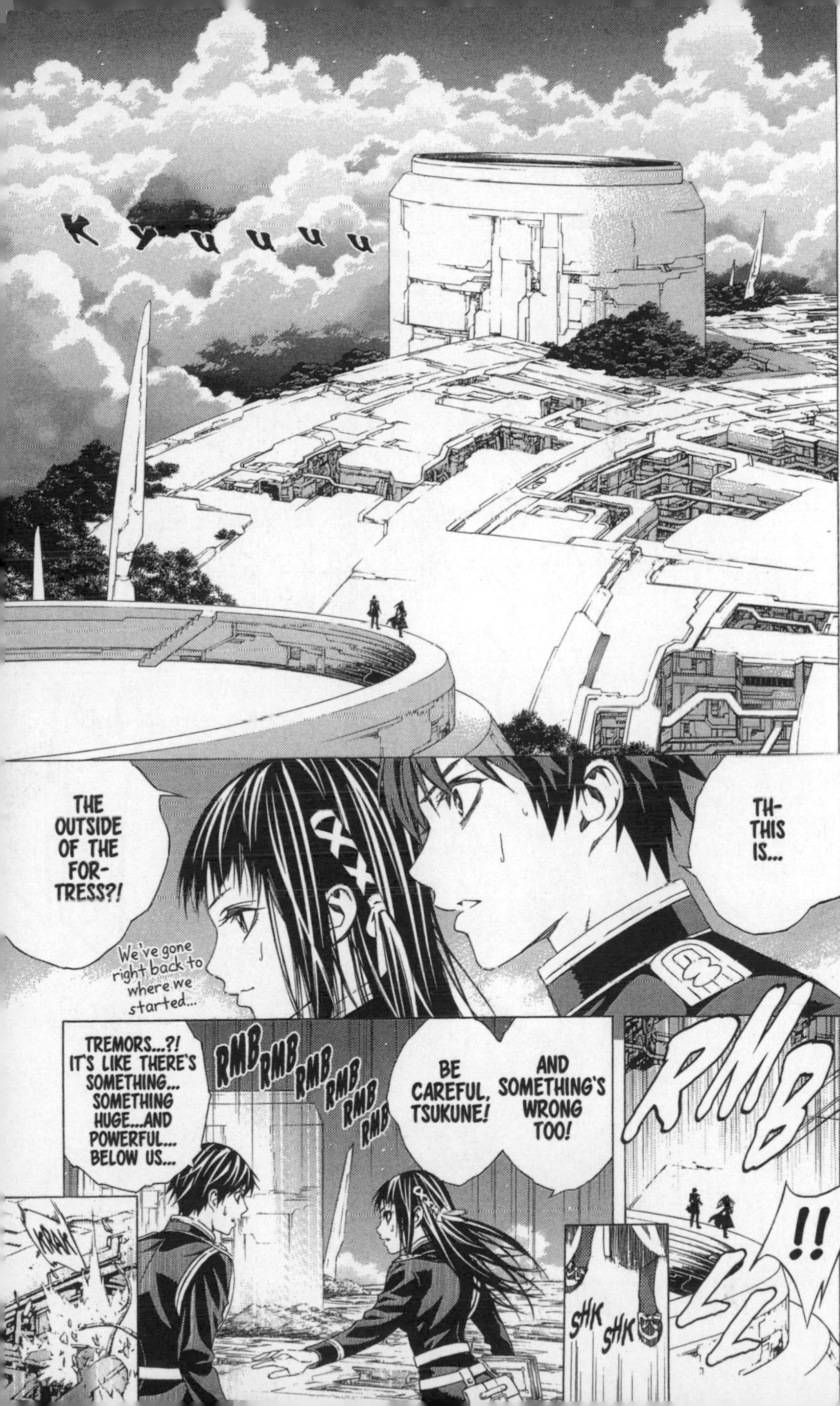
KYUUUU
TH-THIS IS...
THE OUTSIDE OF THE FORTRESS?!
We've gone right back to where we started...
RMB
!!
SHK SHK
AND SOMETHING'S WRONG TOO!
BE CAREFUL, TSUKUNE!
RMB RMB RMB RMB RMB RMB
TREMORS...?! IT'S LIKE THERE'S SOMETHING... SOMETHING HUGE...AND POWERFUL... BELOW US...
KRAK

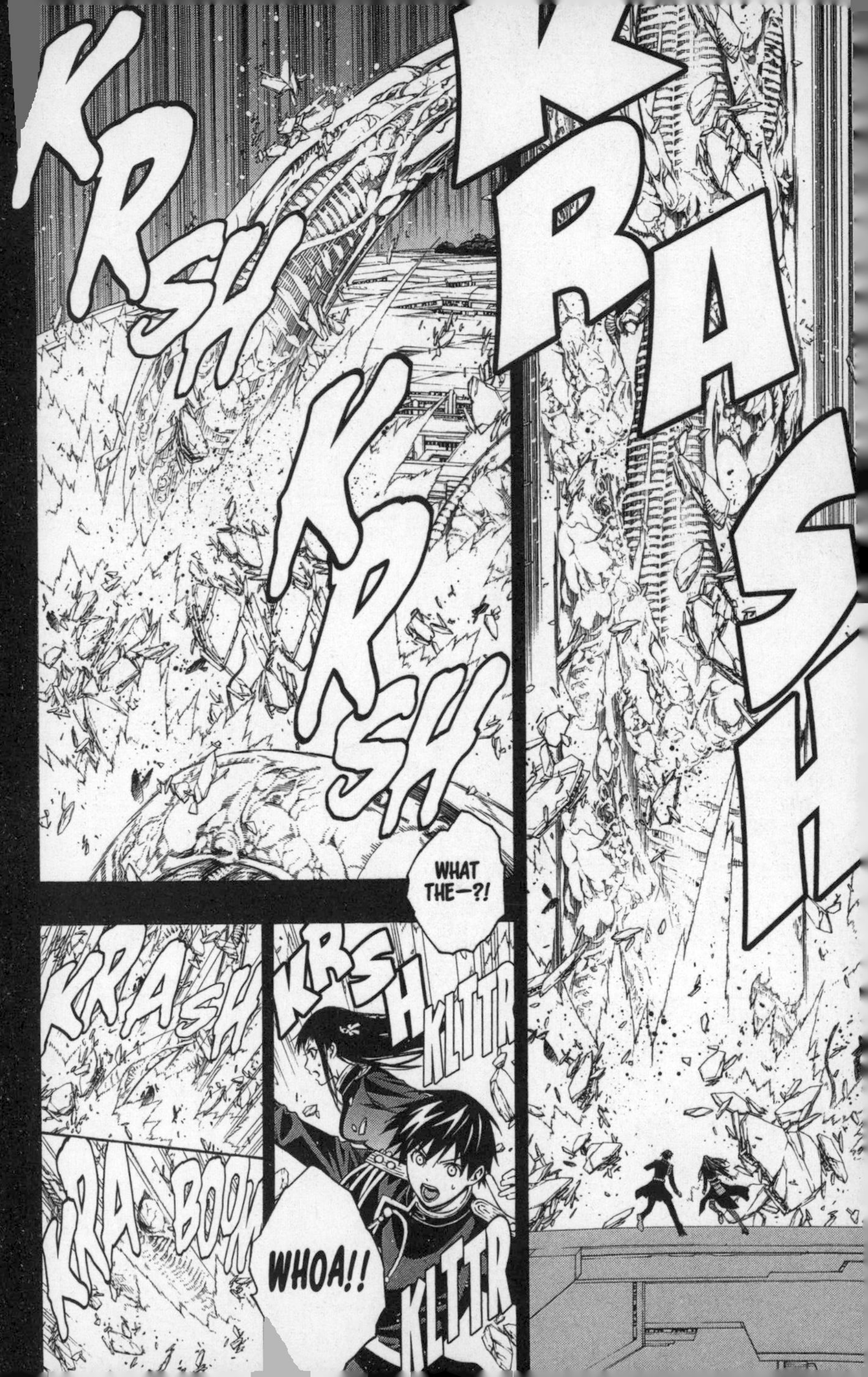
KRASH!
KRSH
KRSH
WHAT THE—?!
KRSH
KLTTR
WHOA!!
KLTTR
KRASH
KRA BOOM

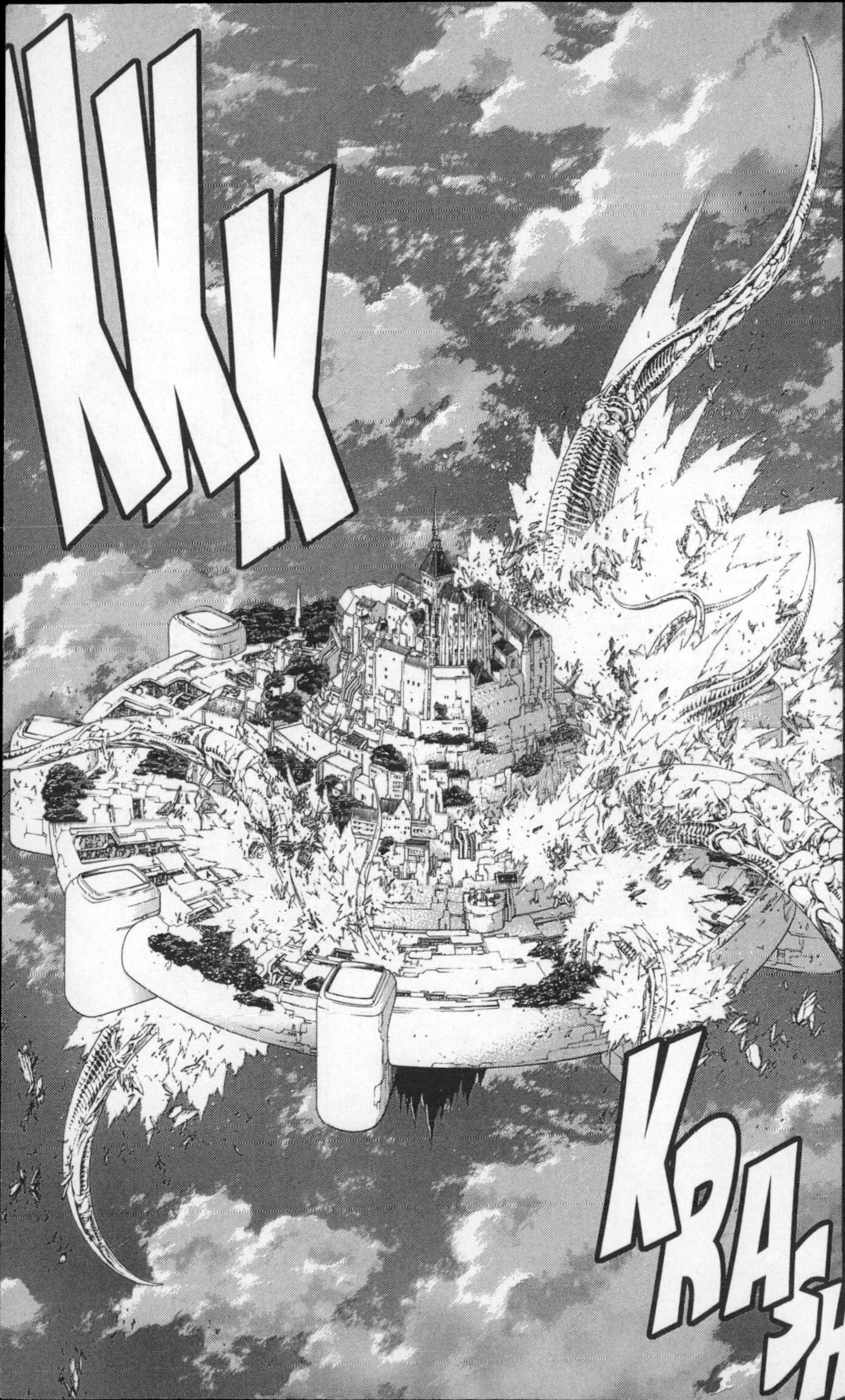
KRASH

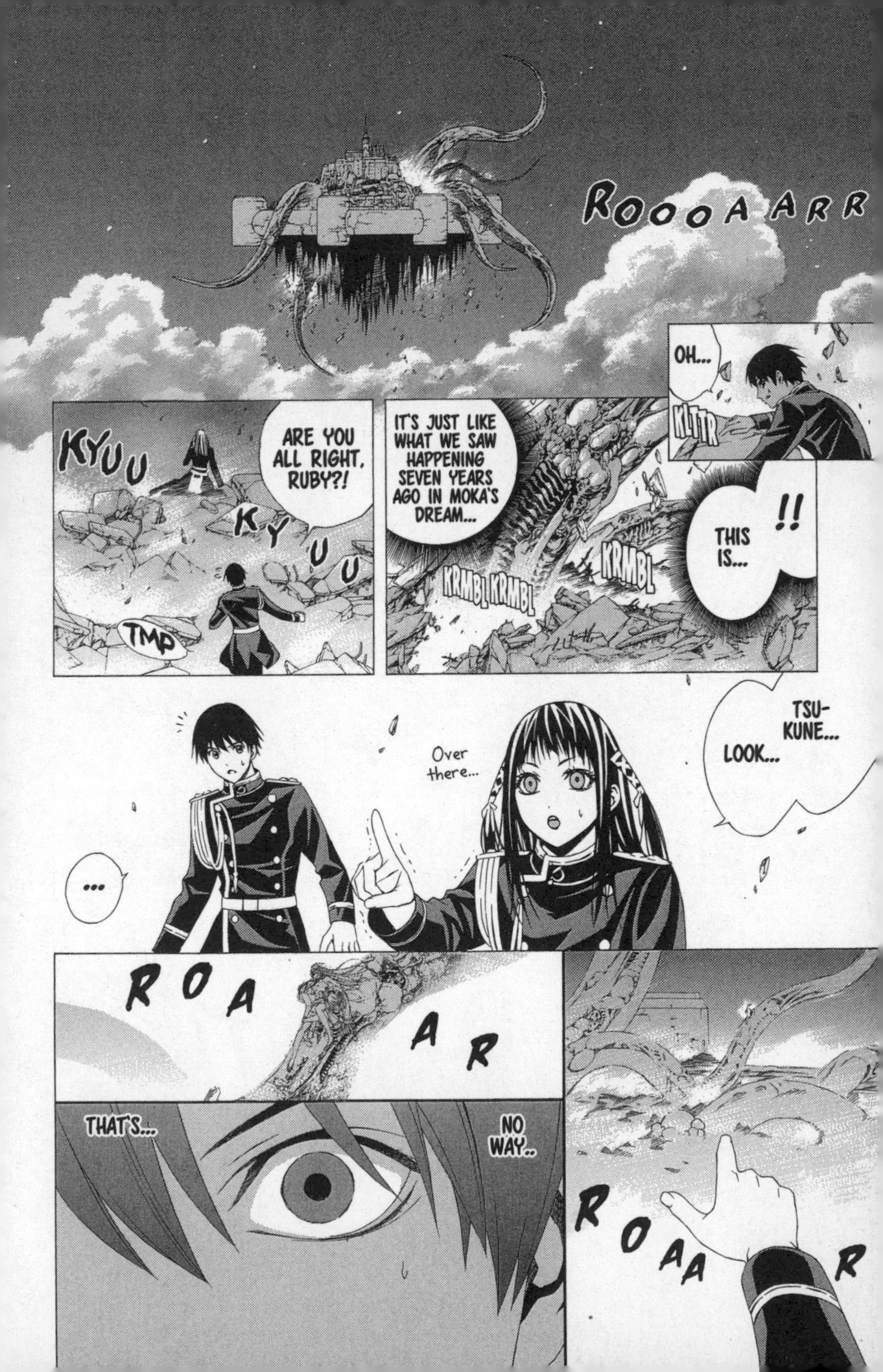
ROOOA ARR
OH...
KLTTR
!!
THIS IS...
IT'S JUST LIKE WHAT WE SAW HAPPENING SEVEN YEARS AGO IN MOKA'S DREAM...
KRMBL
KRMBL KRMBL
ARE YOU ALL RIGHT, RUBY?!
KYUU
KYUU
TMP
TSU-KUNE... LOOK...
Over there...
...
ROAAR
ROAAR
THAT'S...
NO WAY..

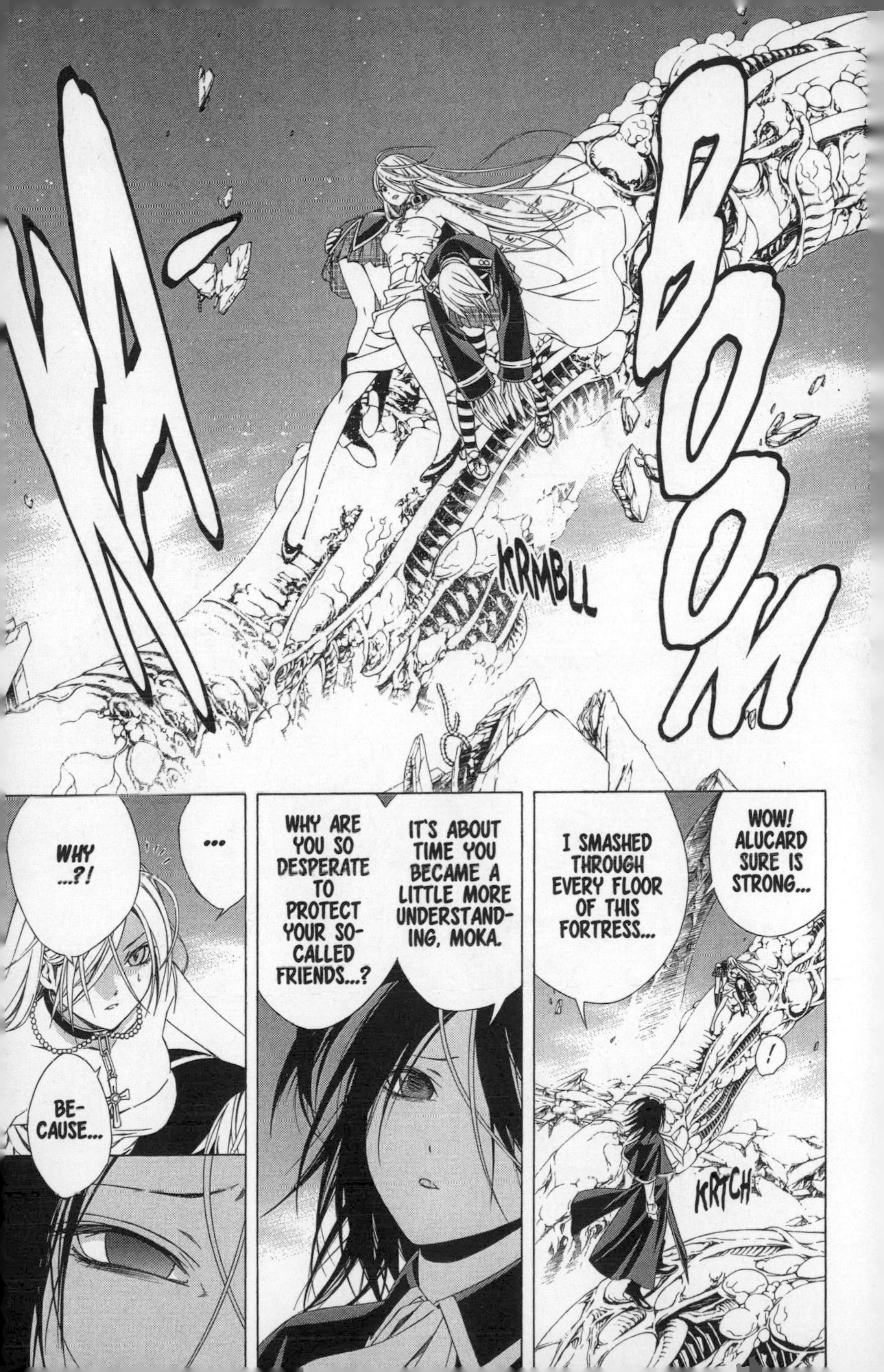
KRMBLL
WOW! ALUCARD SURE IS STRONG...
I SMASHED THROUGH EVERY FLOOR OF THIS FORTRESS...
!
KRTCH
IT'S ABOUT TIME YOU BECAME A LITTLE MORE UNDERSTANDING, MOKA.
WHY ARE YOU SO DESPERATE TO PROTECT YOUR SO-CALLED FRIENDS...?
...
WHY ...?!
BE-CAUSE...

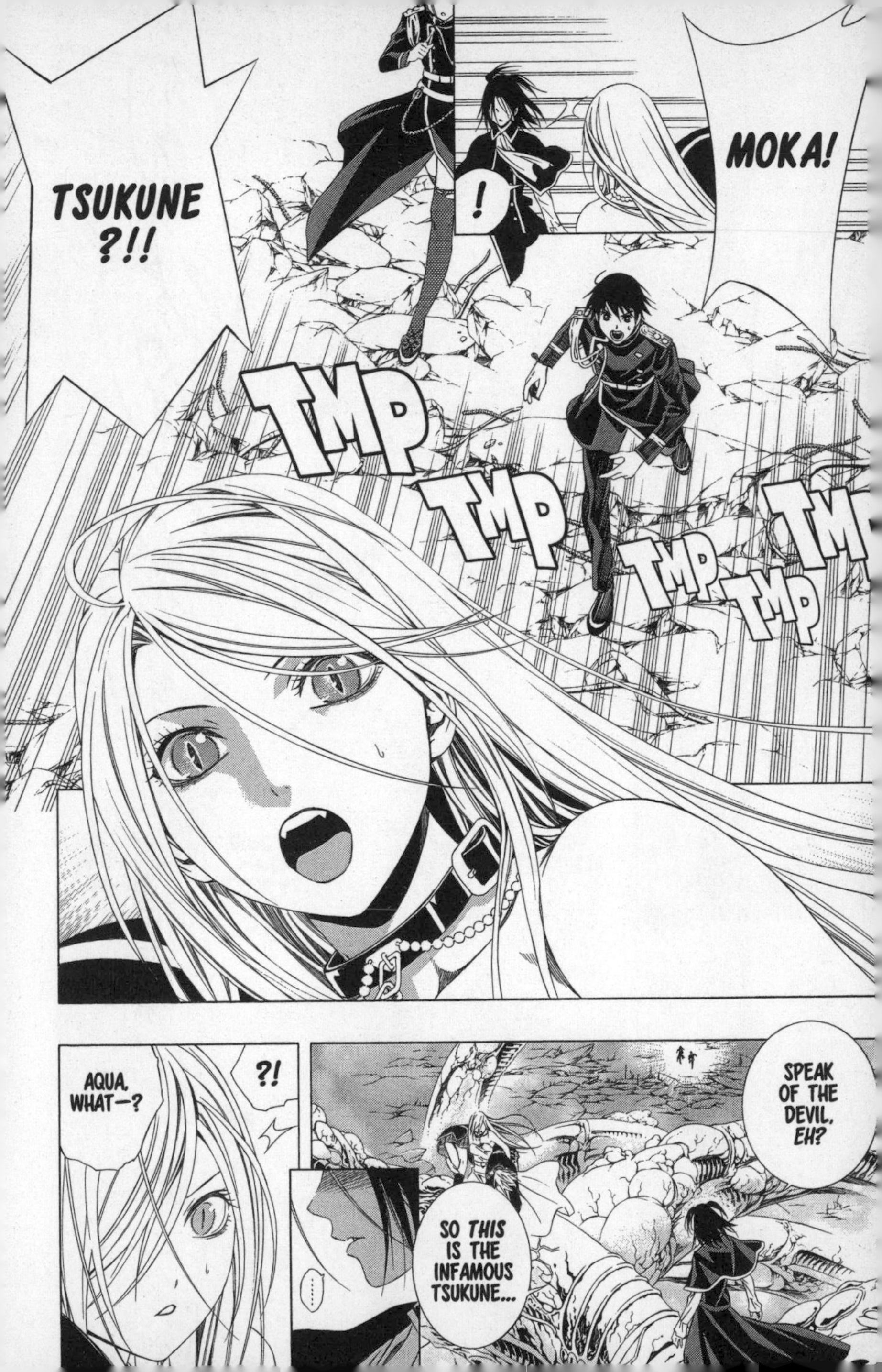
MOKA!
!
TSUKUNE ?!!
TMP
TMP
TMP
TMP
TMP
SPEAK OF THE DEVIL, EH?
SO THIS IS THE INFAMOUS TSUKUNE...
......
?!
AQUA, WHAT—?

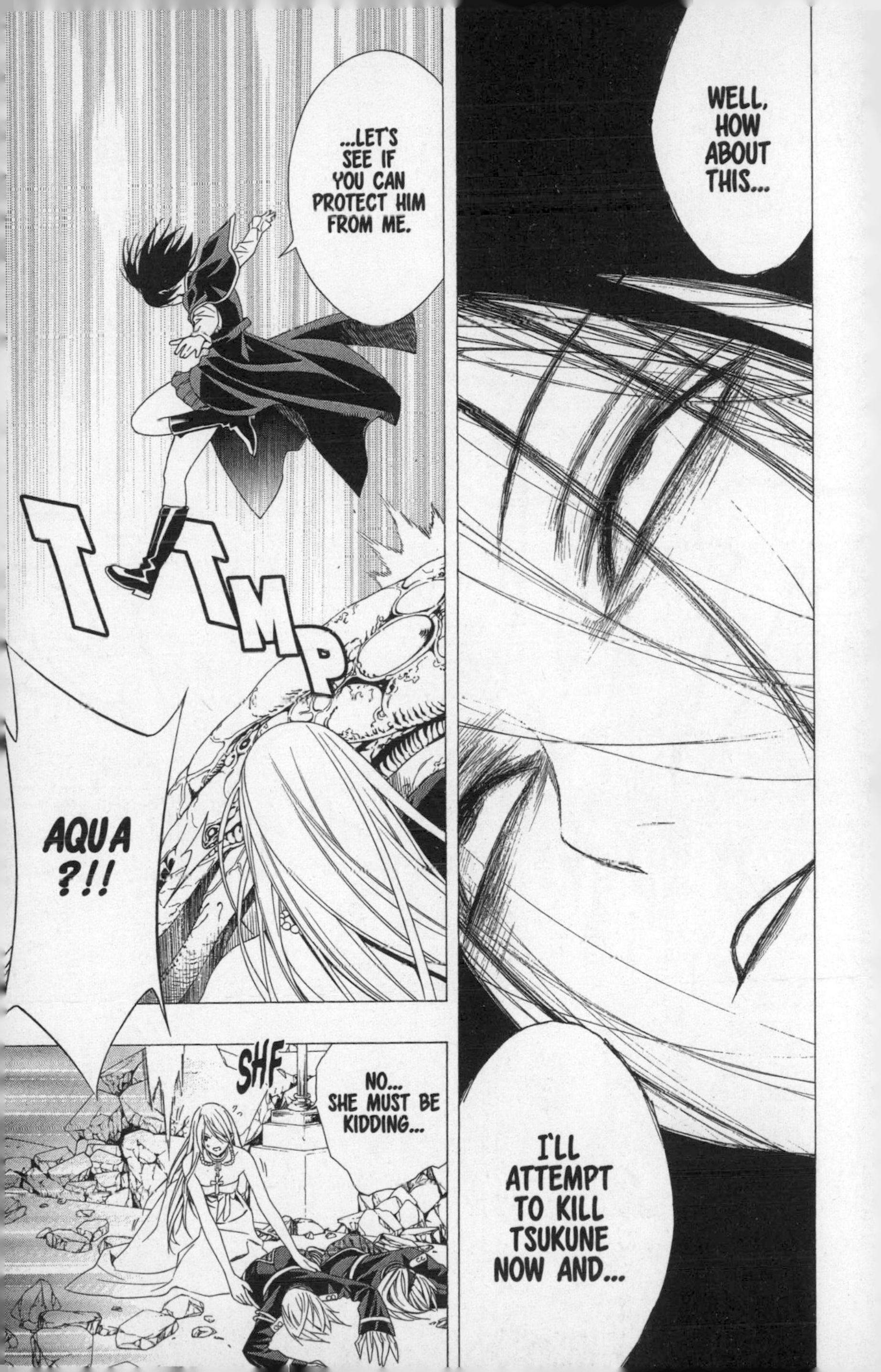
WELL, HOW ABOUT THIS...
I'LL ATTEMPT TO KILL TSUKUNE NOW AND...
...LET'S SEE IF YOU CAN PROTECT HIM FROM ME.
T TMP
AQUA ?!!
SHF
NO... SHE MUST BE KIDDING...

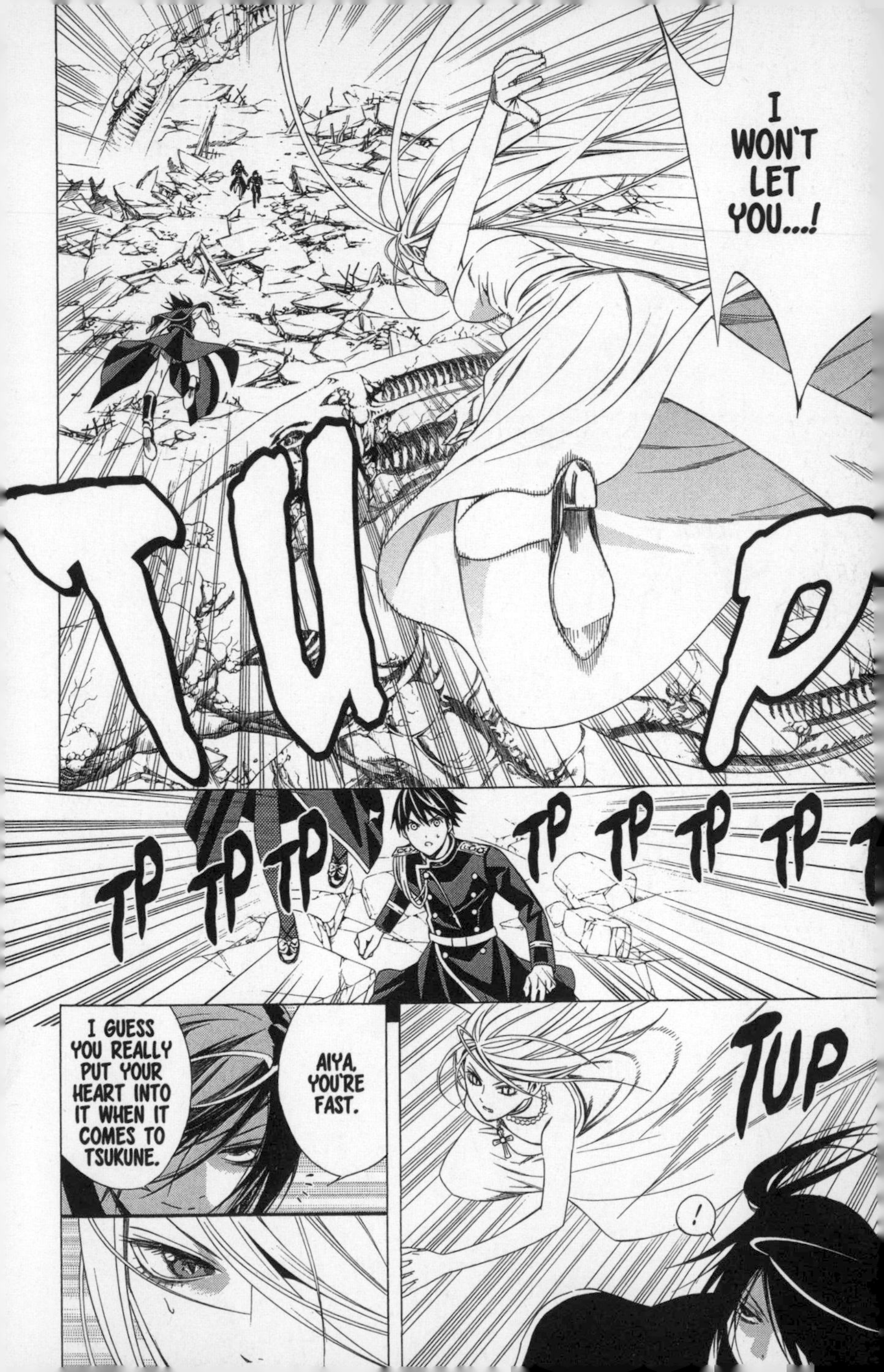
I WON'T LET YOU...!
TUP
TP TP TP TP TP TP TP
TUP
!
AIYA, YOU'RE FAST.
I GUESS YOU REALLY PUT YOUR HEART INTO IT WHEN IT COMES TO TSUKUNE.

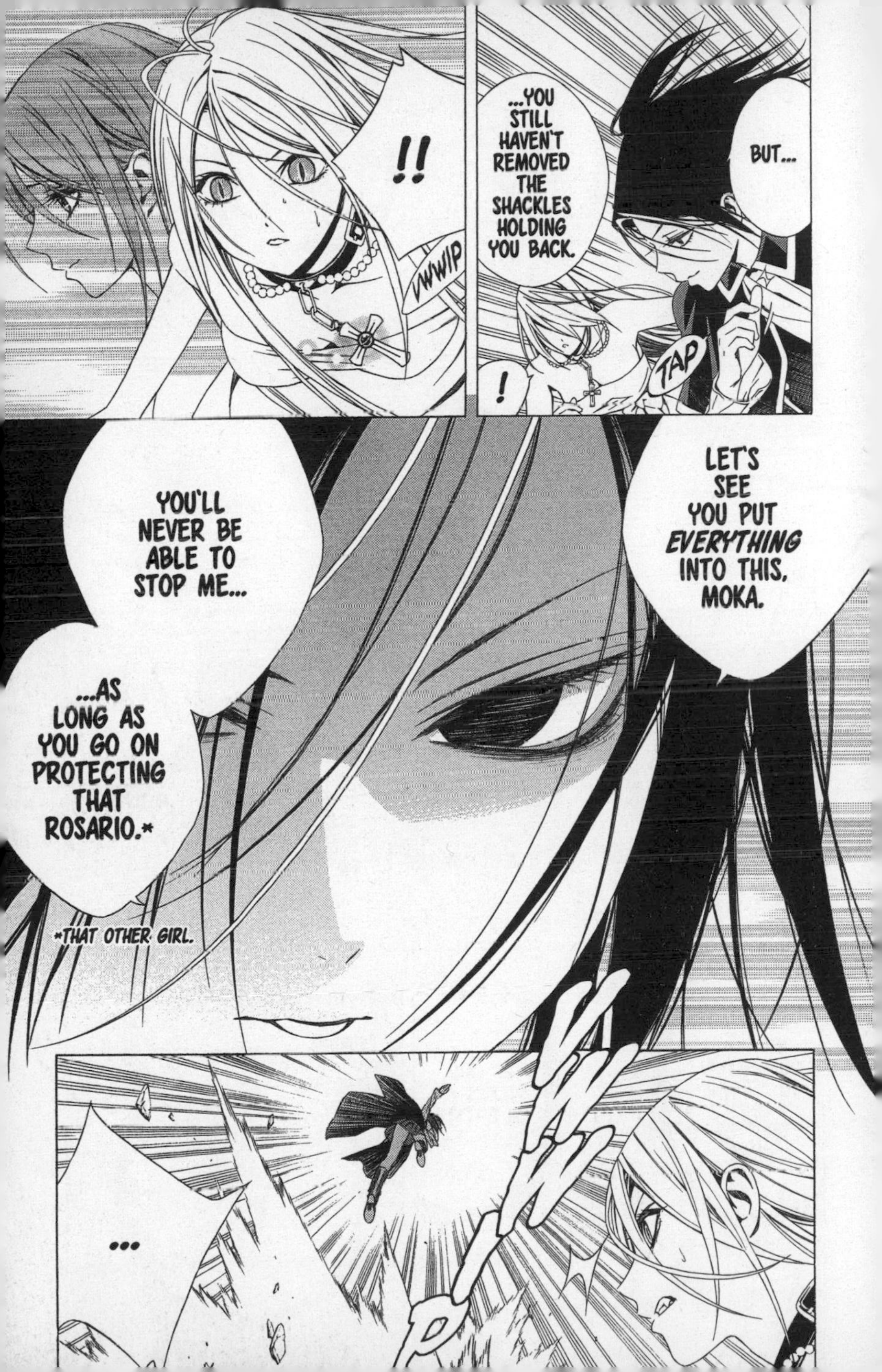
BUT...
...YOU STILL HAVEN'T REMOVED THE SHACKLES HOLDING YOU BACK.
TAP
!
!!
VWWIP
LET'S SEE YOU PUT *EVERYTHING* INTO THIS, MOKA.
YOU'LL NEVER BE ABLE TO STOP ME...
...AS LONG AS YOU GO ON PROTECTING THAT ROSARIO.*
*THAT OTHER GIRL.
...

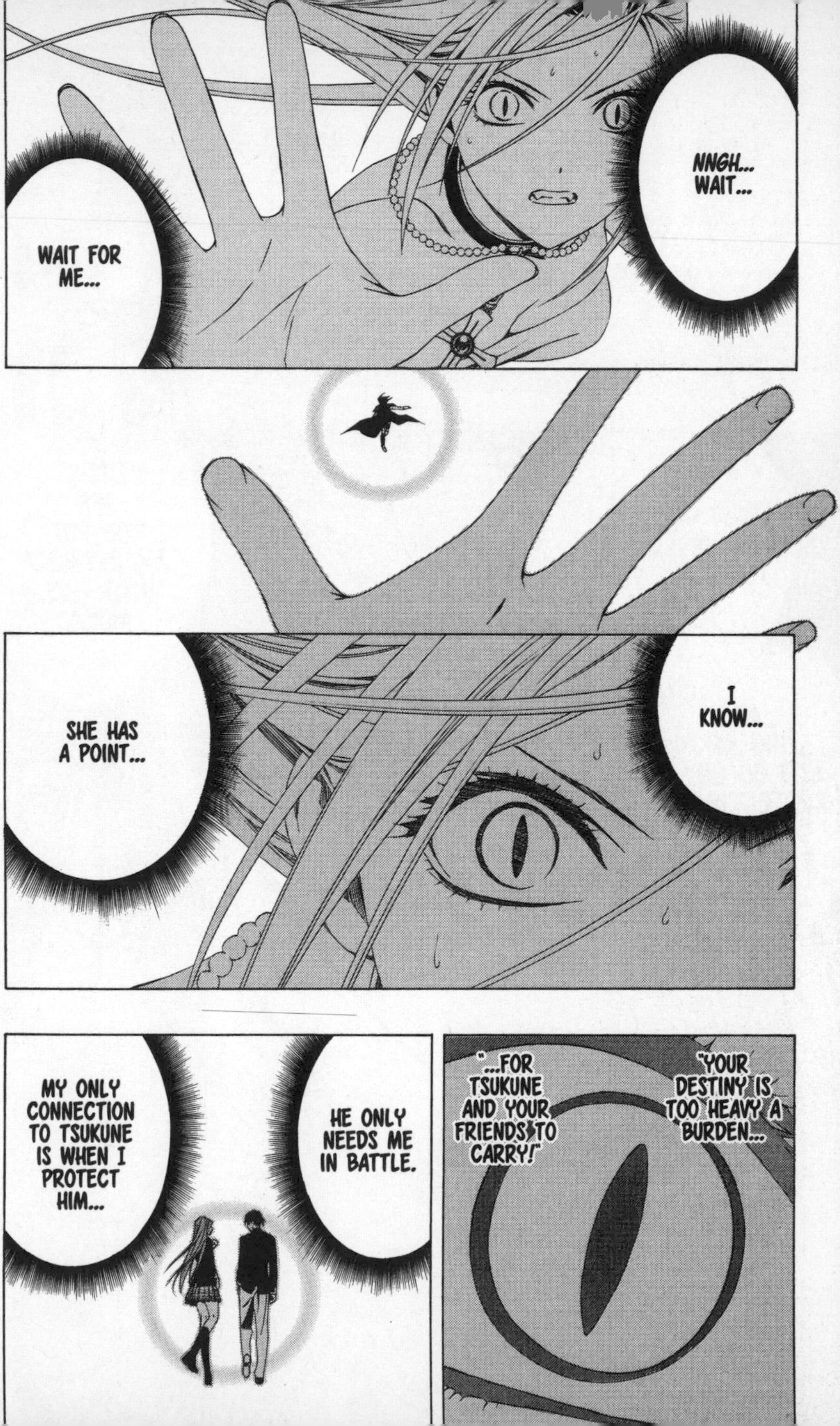
NNGH... WAIT...
WAIT FOR ME...
I KNOW...
SHE HAS A POINT...
"YOUR DESTINY IS TOO HEAVY A BURDEN...
"...FOR TSUKUNE AND YOUR FRIENDS TO CARRY!"
HE ONLY NEEDS ME IN BATTLE.
MY ONLY CONNECTION TO TSUKUNE IS WHEN I PROTECT HIM...

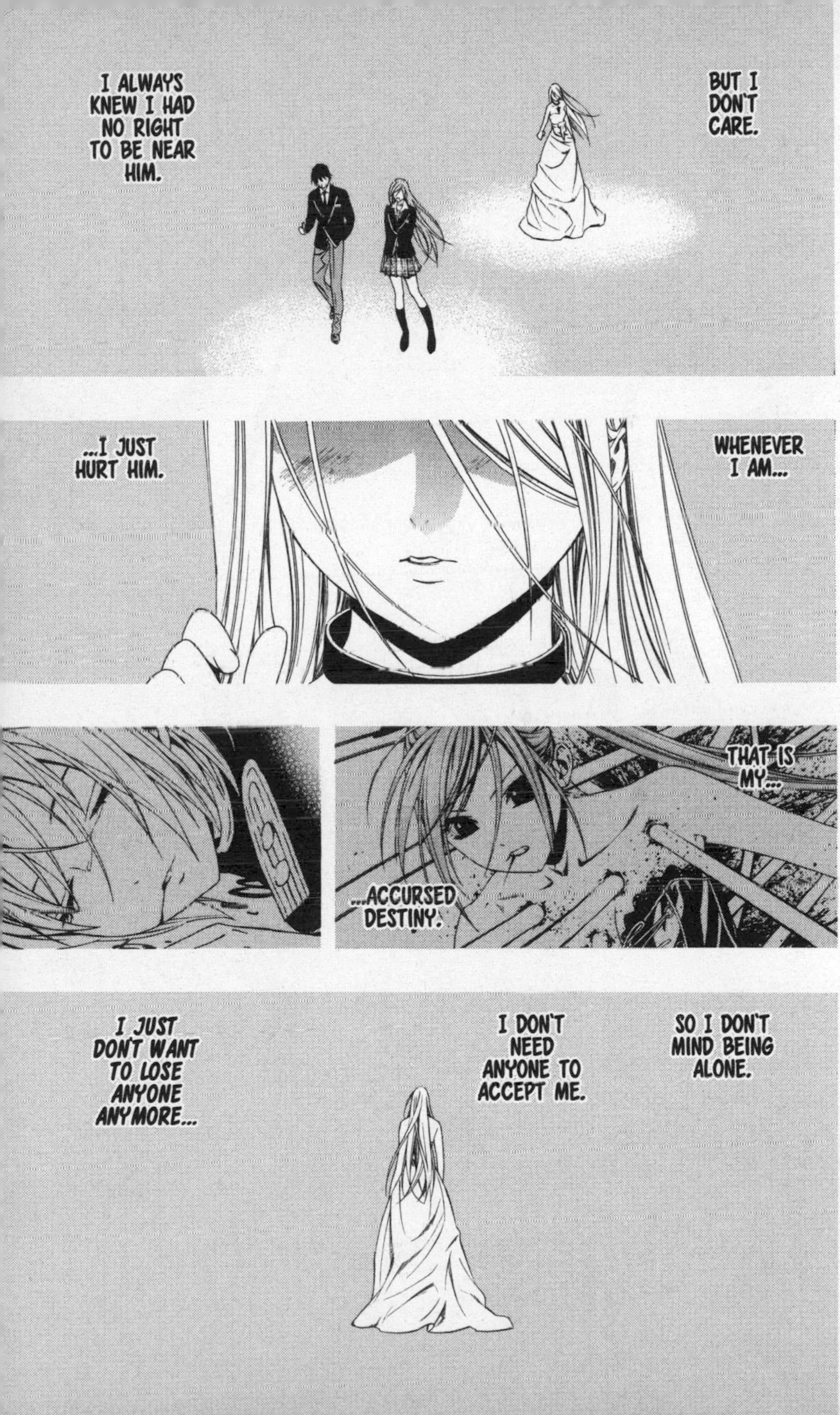
BUT I DON'T CARE.
I ALWAYS KNEW I HAD NO RIGHT TO BE NEAR HIM.
WHENEVER I AM...
...I JUST HURT HIM.
THAT IS MY...
...ACCURSED DESTINY.
SO I DON'T MIND BEING ALONE.
I DON'T NEED ANYONE TO ACCEPT ME.
I JUST DON'T WANT TO LOSE ANYONE ANYMORE...

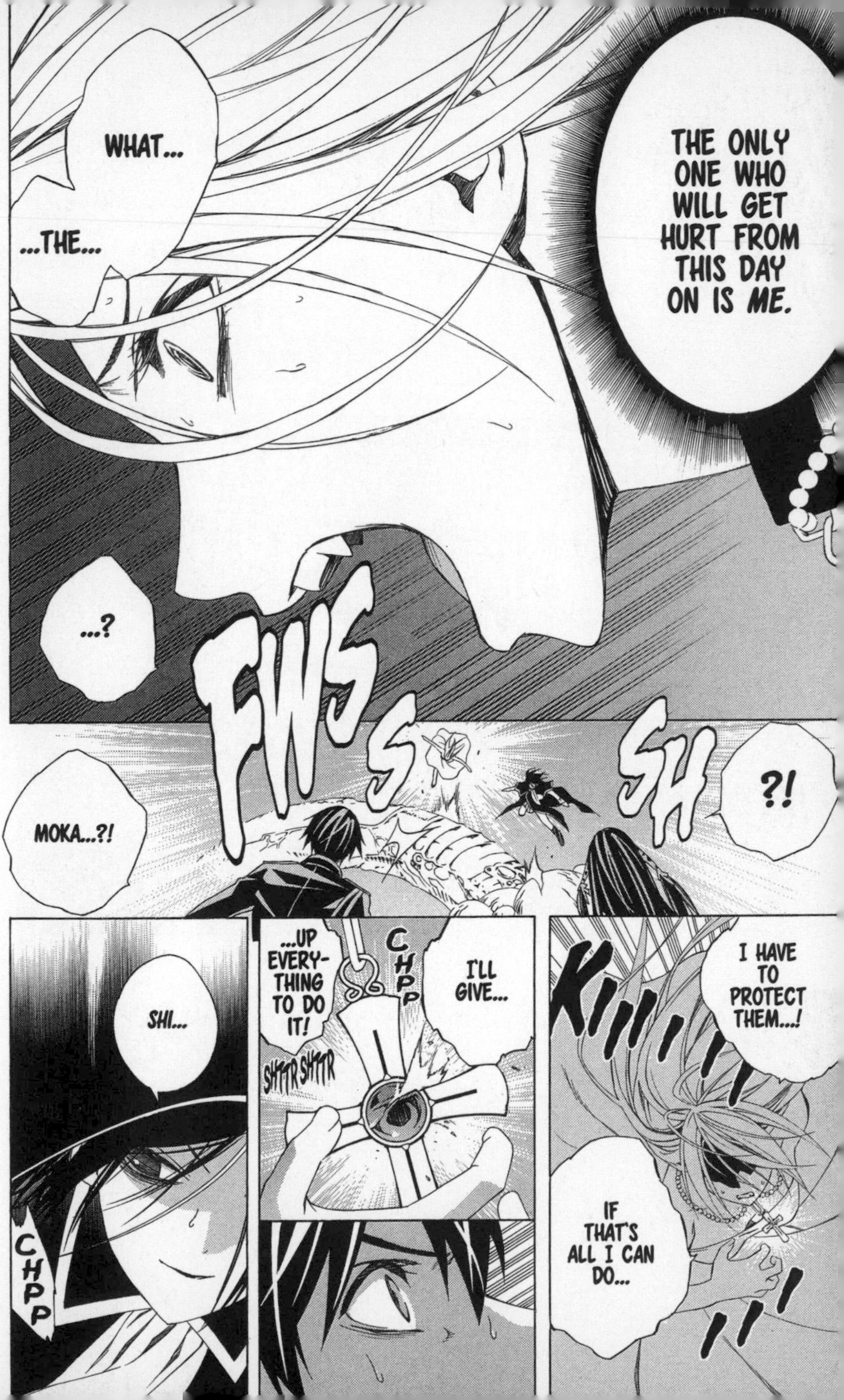
THE ONLY ONE WHO WILL GET HURT FROM THIS DAY ON IS ME.
WHAT...
...THE...
...?
FWSSSH
?!
MOKA...?!
I HAVE TO PROTECT THEM...!
KIIIIII
IF THAT'S ALL I CAN DO...
I'LL GIVE...
...UP EVERYTHING TO DO IT!
CHPP
SHTTR SHTTR
SHI...
CHPP

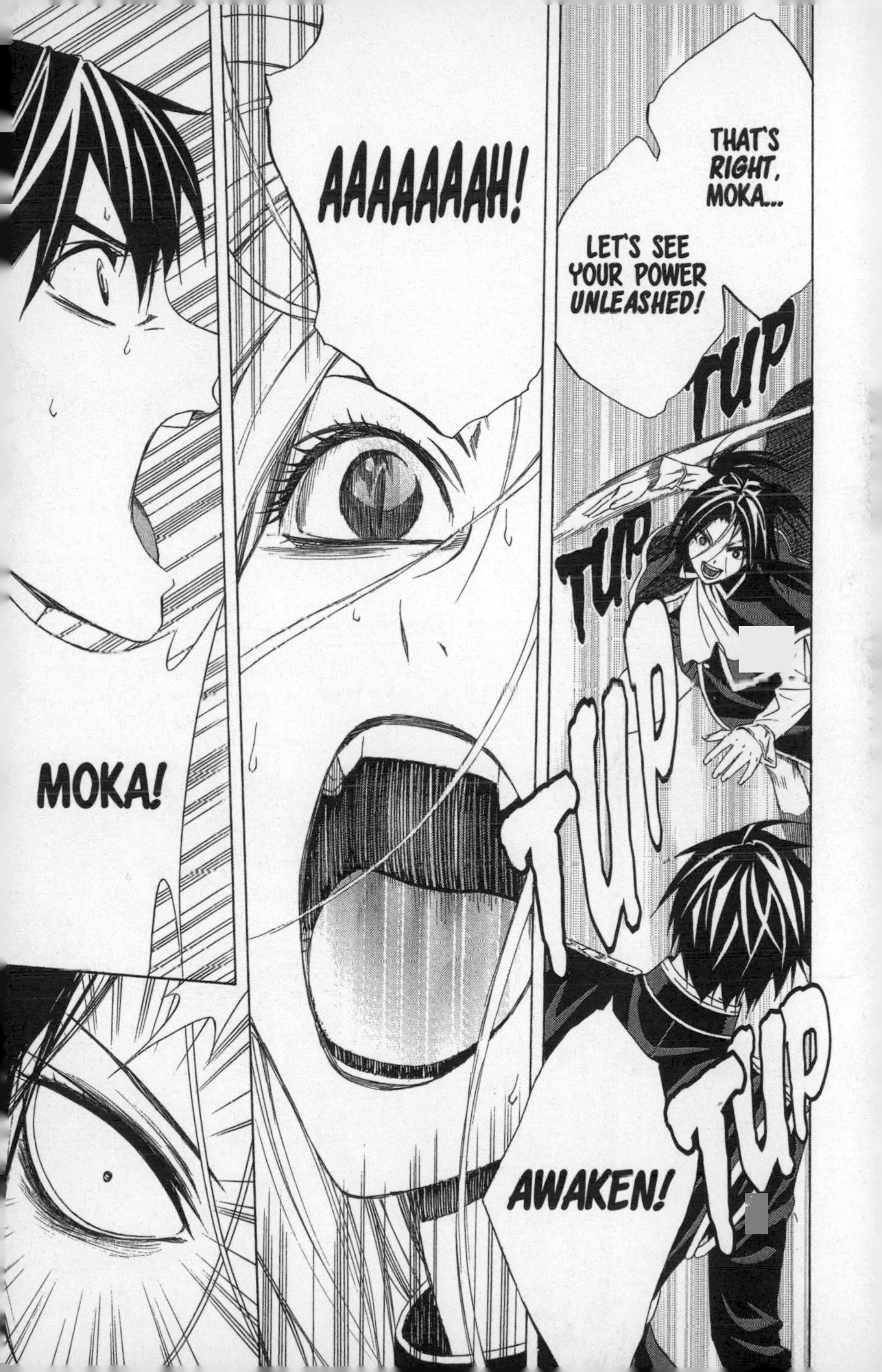
THAT'S RIGHT, MOKA...
LET'S SEE YOUR POWER UNLEASHED!
TUP
TUP
TUP
TUP
TUP
AWAKEN!
AAAAAAAH!
MOKA!

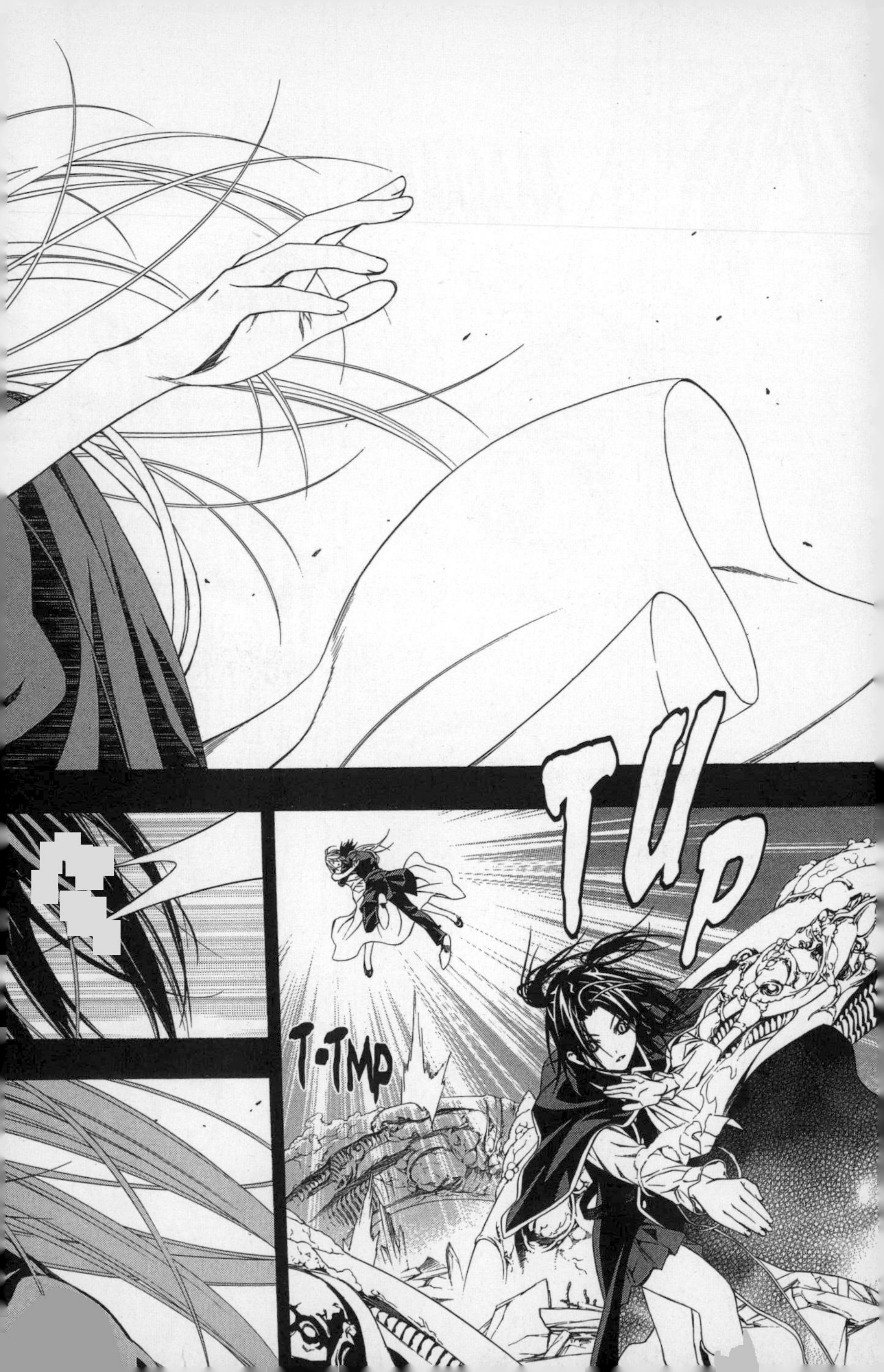
TUP
T-TMP

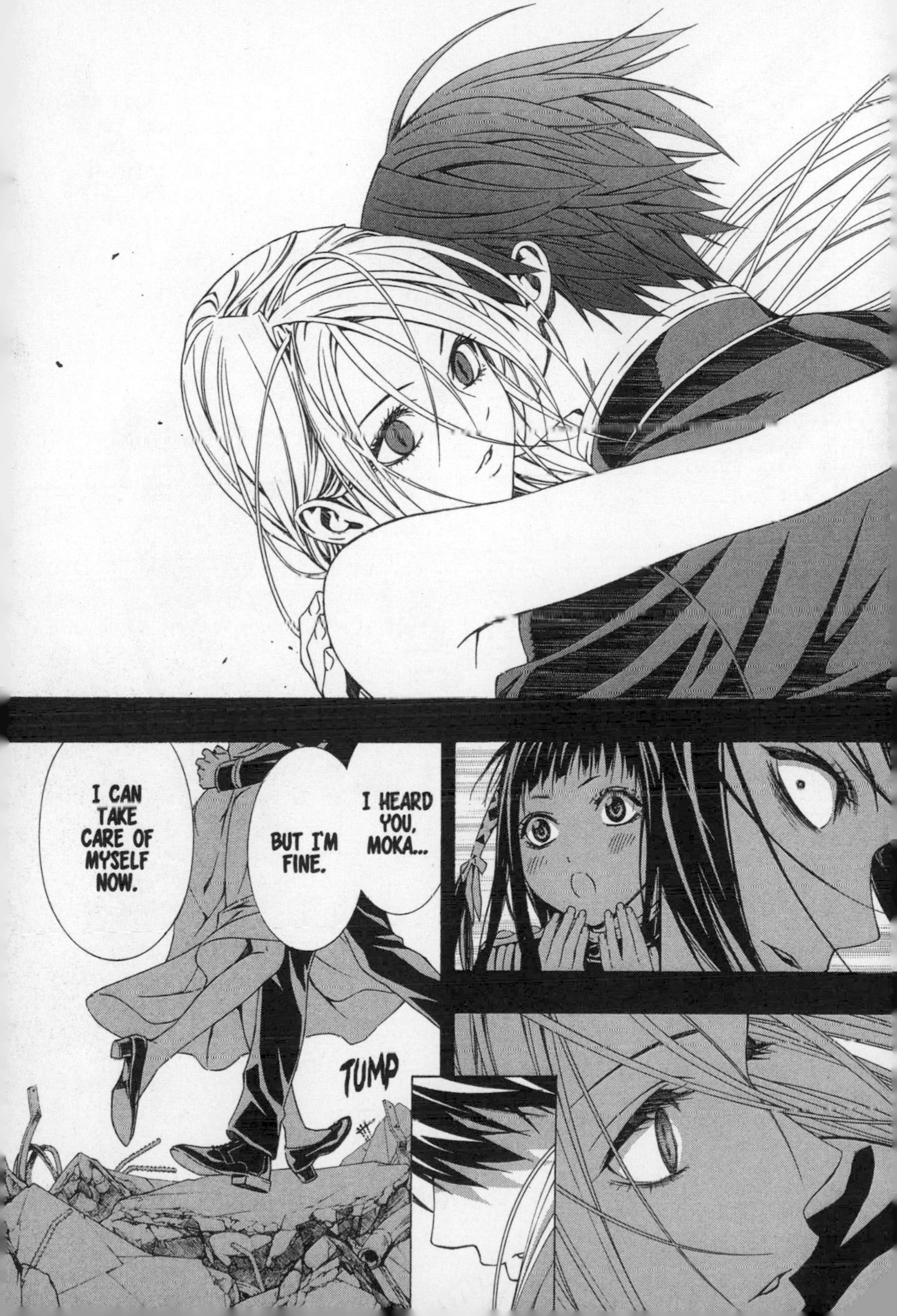
I HEARD YOU, MOKA...
BUT I'M FINE.
I CAN TAKE CARE OF MYSELF NOW.
TUMP

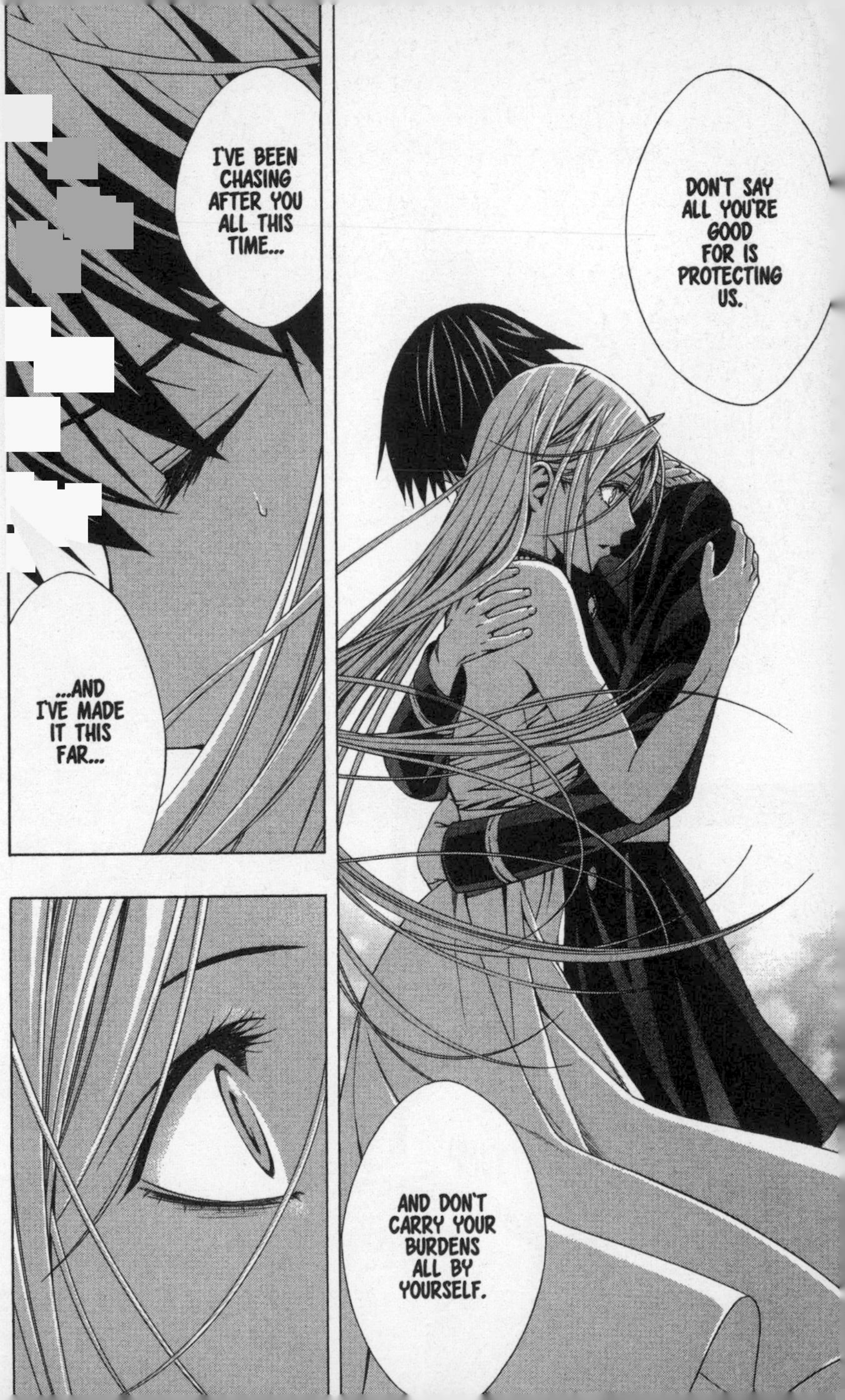
DON'T SAY ALL YOU'RE GOOD FOR IS PROTECTING US.
AND DON'T CARRY YOUR BURDENS ALL BY YOURSELF.
I'VE BEEN CHASING AFTER YOU ALL THIS TIME...
...AND I'VE MADE IT THIS FAR...

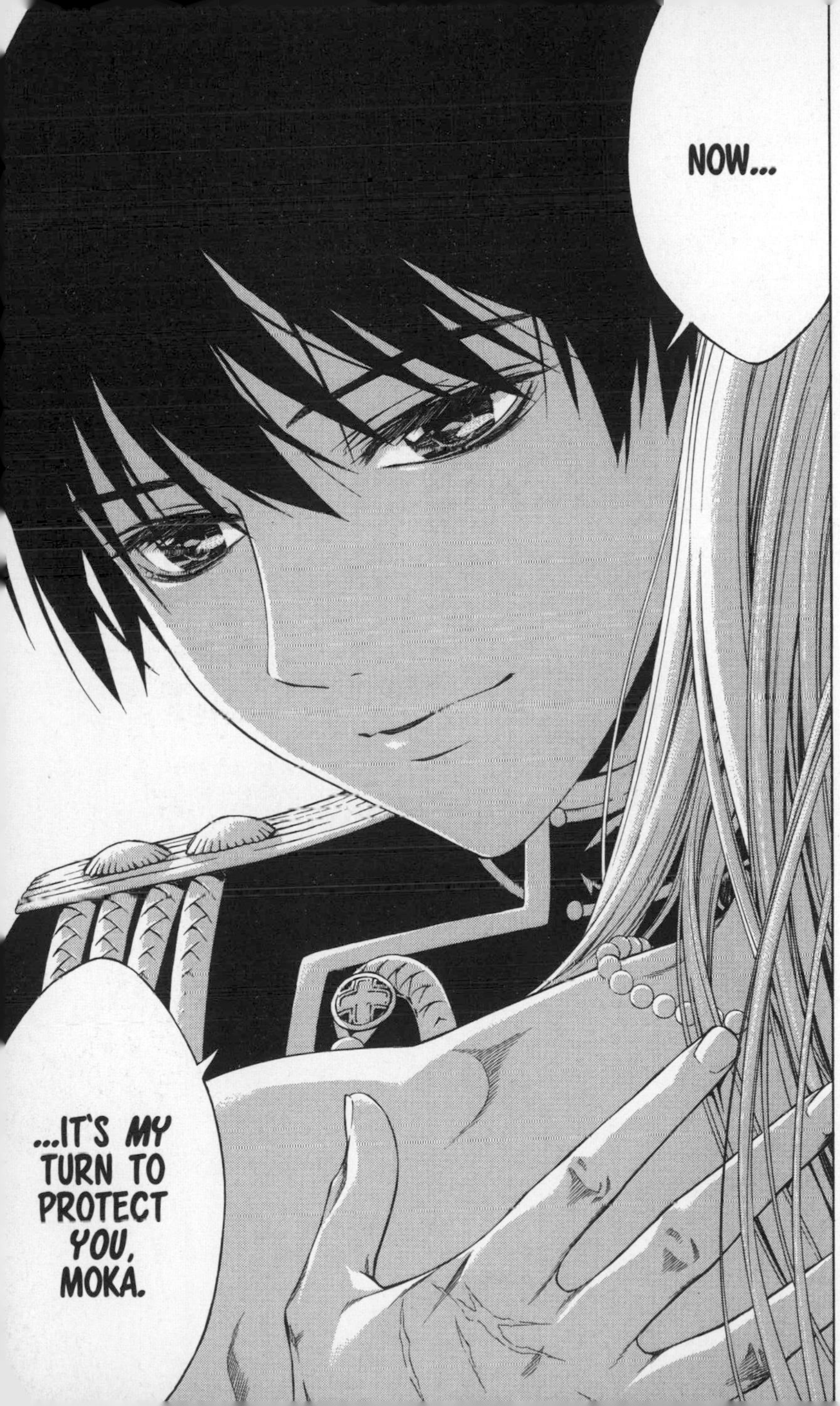
NOW...
...IT'S MY TURN TO PROTECT YOU, MOKA.

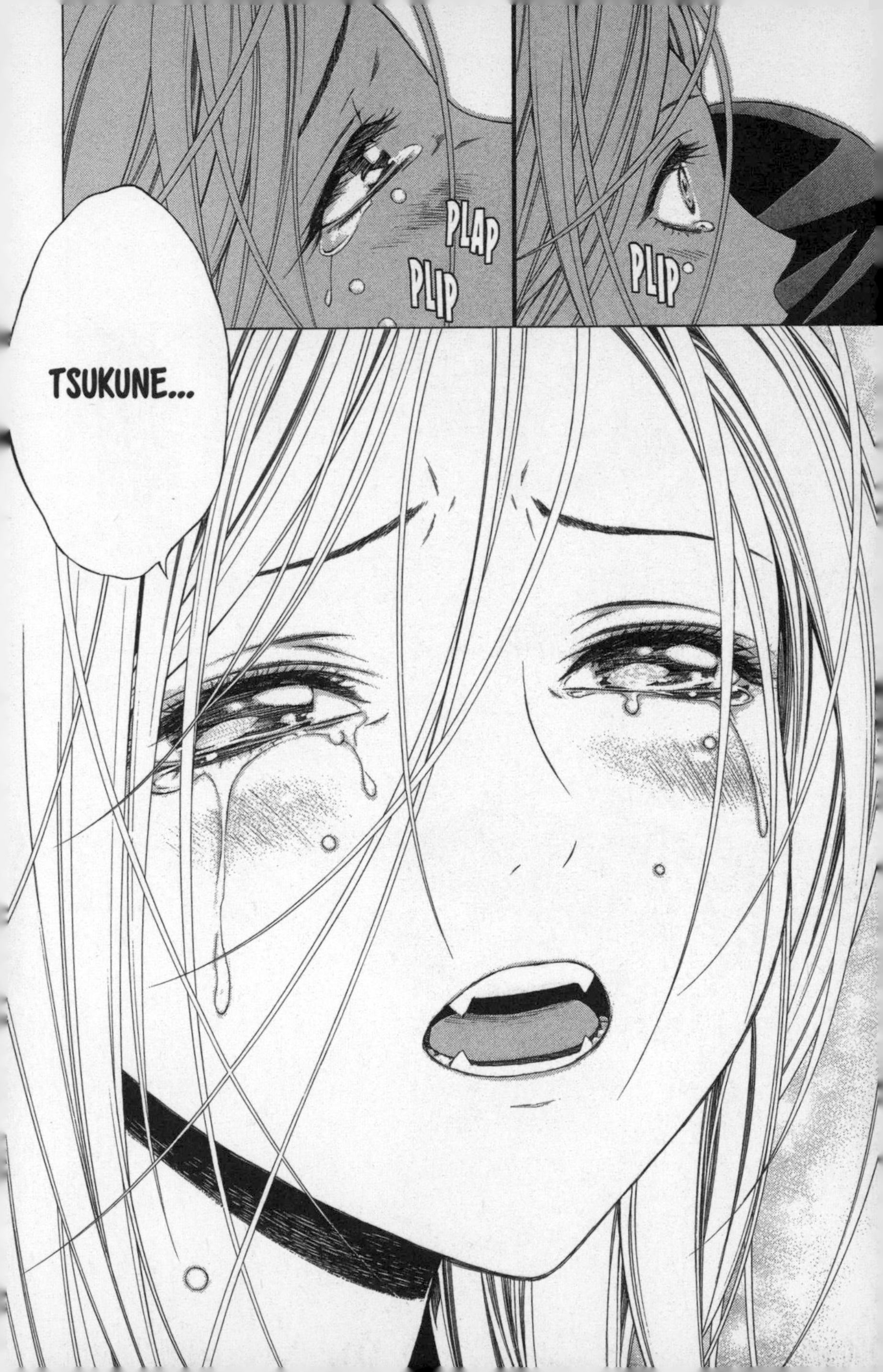
PLIP
PLAP
PLIP
TSUKUNE...

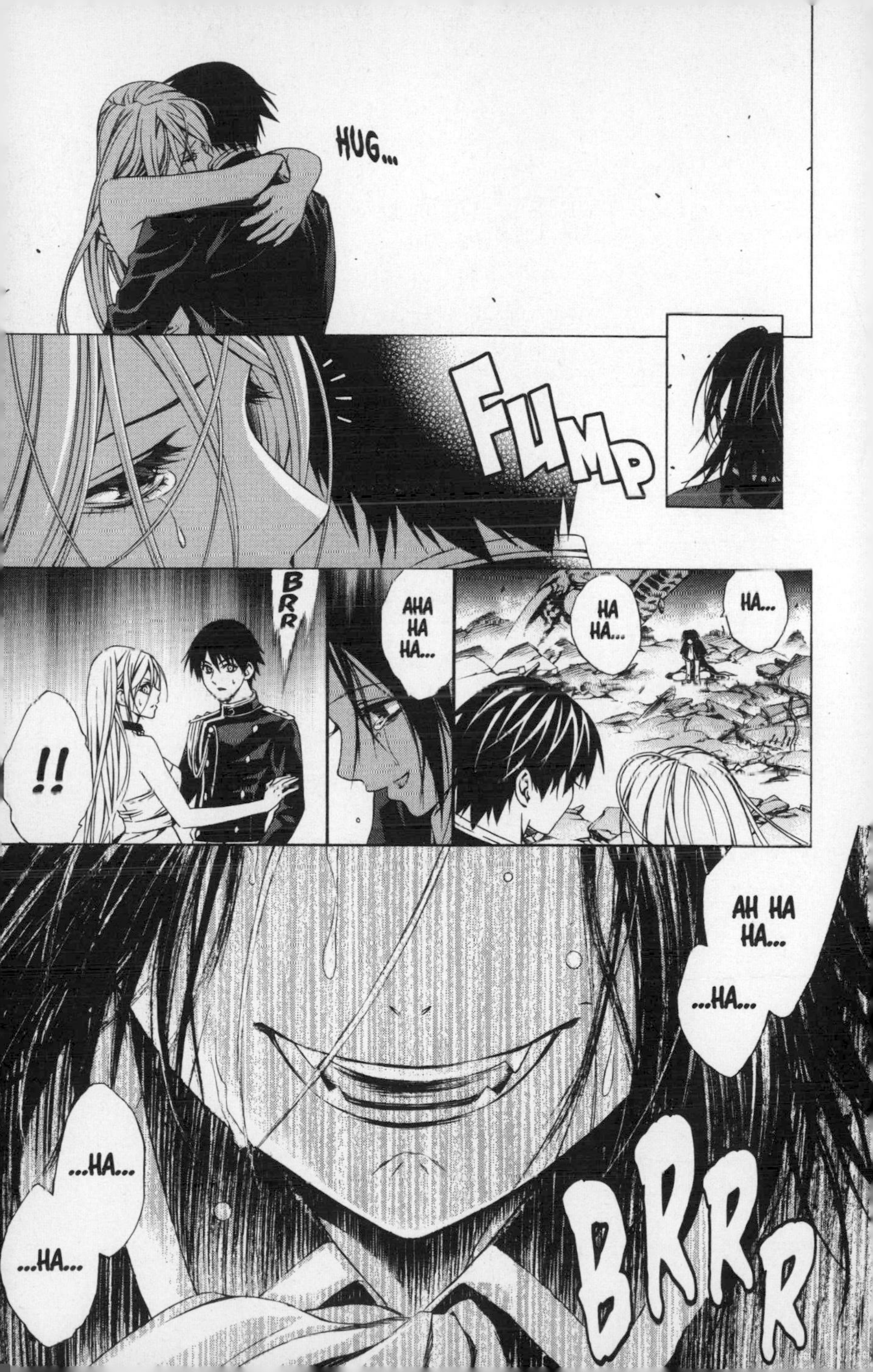
HUG...
FUMP
HA...
HA HA...
AHA HA HA...
BRR
!!
AH HA HA...
...HA...
...HA...
...HA...
BRRR

55: Battling the Dimension Sword

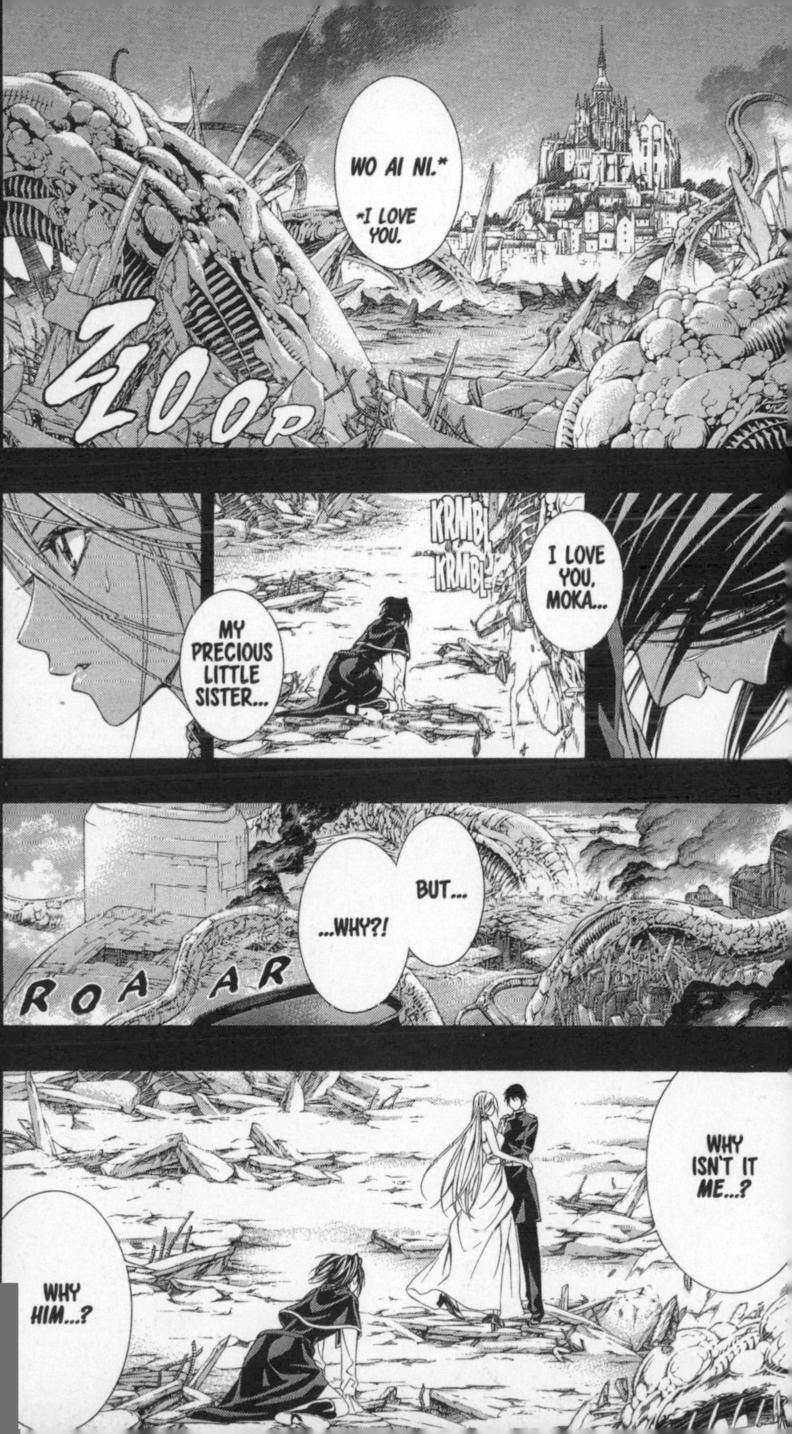
WO AI NI.*
*I LOVE YOU.
ZZOOP
I LOVE YOU, MOKA...
KRMBL KRMBL
MY PRECIOUS LITTLE SISTER...
BUT...
...WHY?!
ROAAR
WHY ISN'T IT ME...?
WHY HIM...?

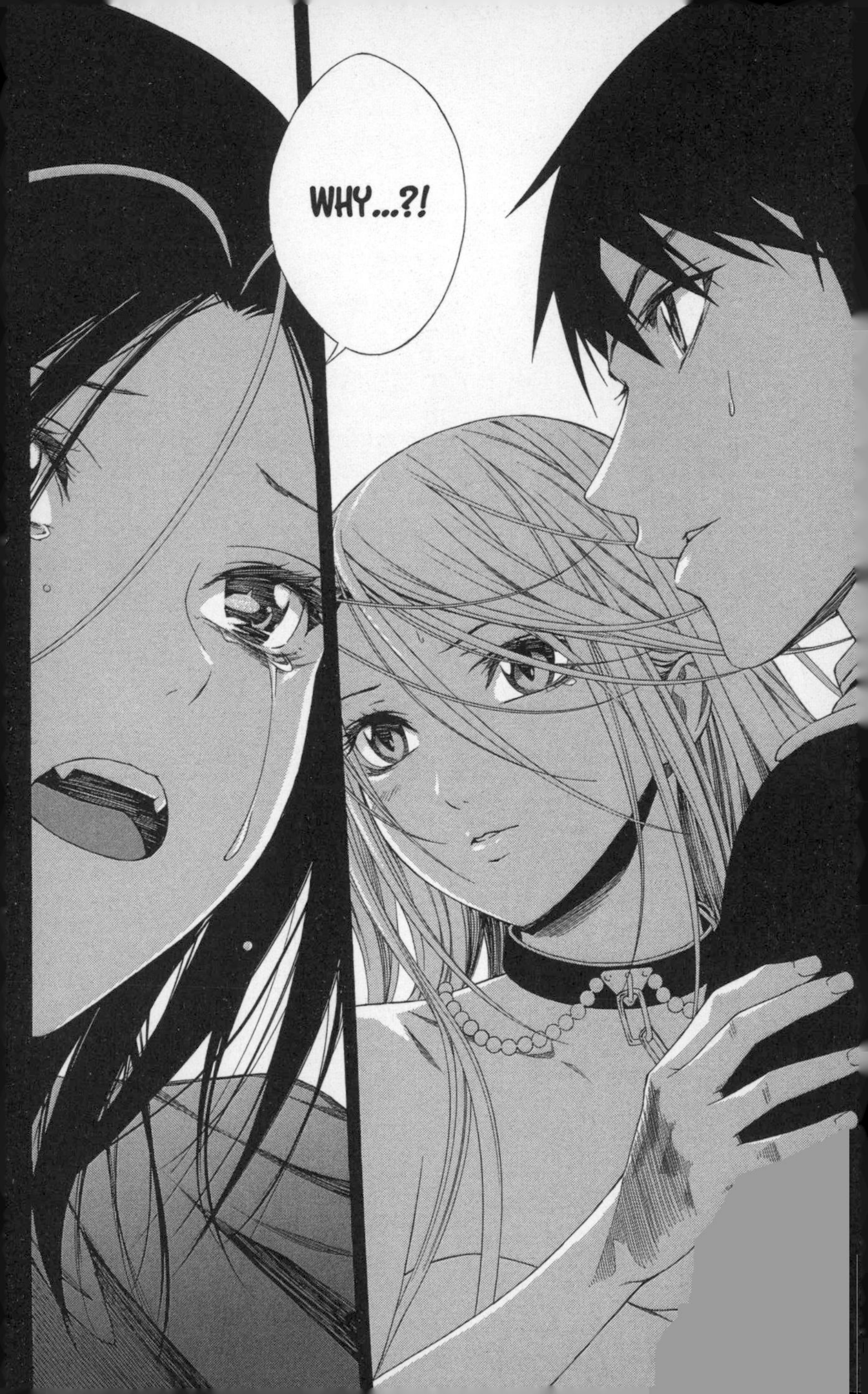
WHY...?!

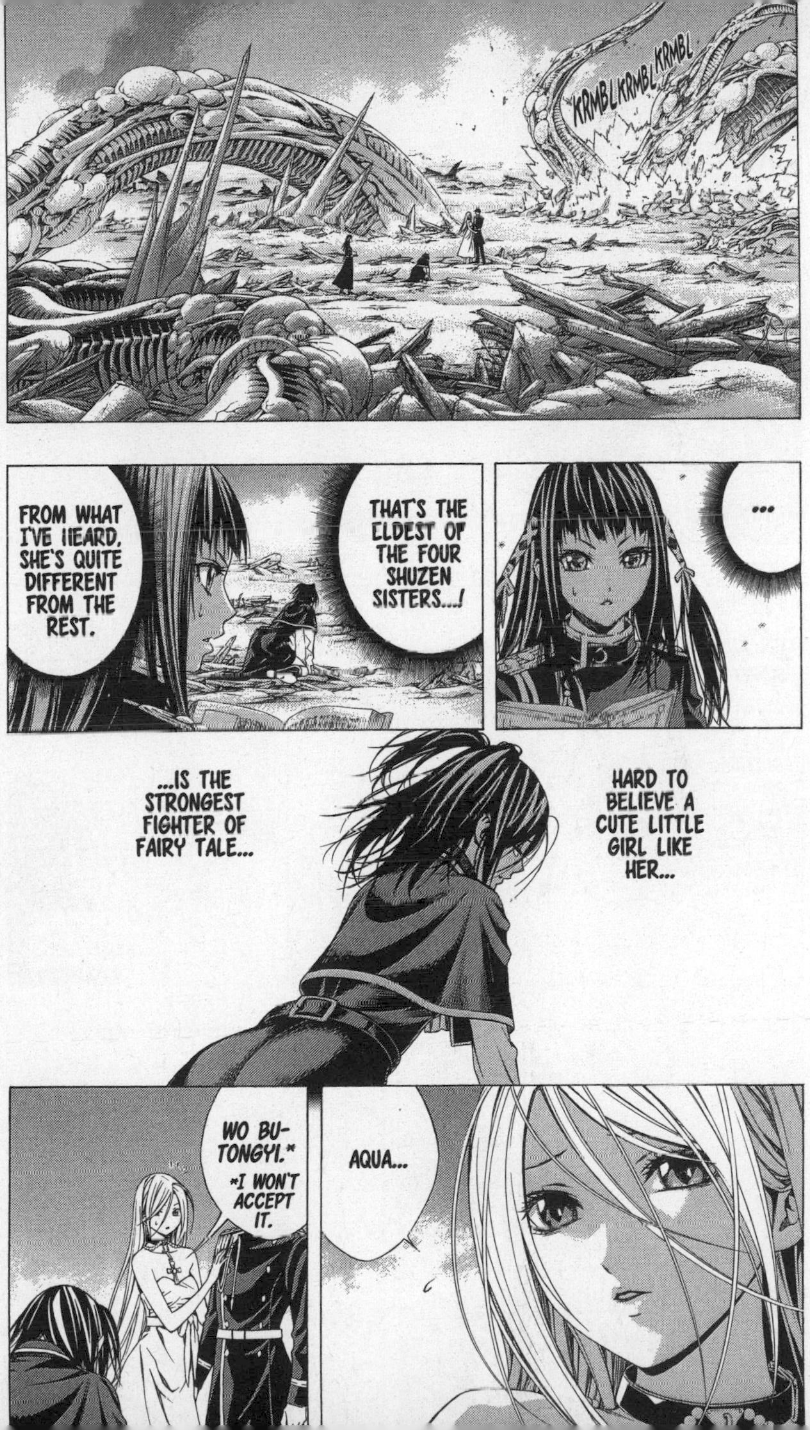
KRMBL KRMBL KRMBL
...
THAT'S THE ELDEST OF THE FOUR SHUZEN SISTERS...!
FROM WHAT I'VE HEARD, SHE'S QUITE DIFFERENT FROM THE REST.
HARD TO BELIEVE A CUTE LITTLE GIRL LIKE HER...
...IS THE STRONGEST FIGHTER OF FAIRY TALE...
AQUA...
WO BU-TONGYI.*
*I WON'T ACCEPT IT.

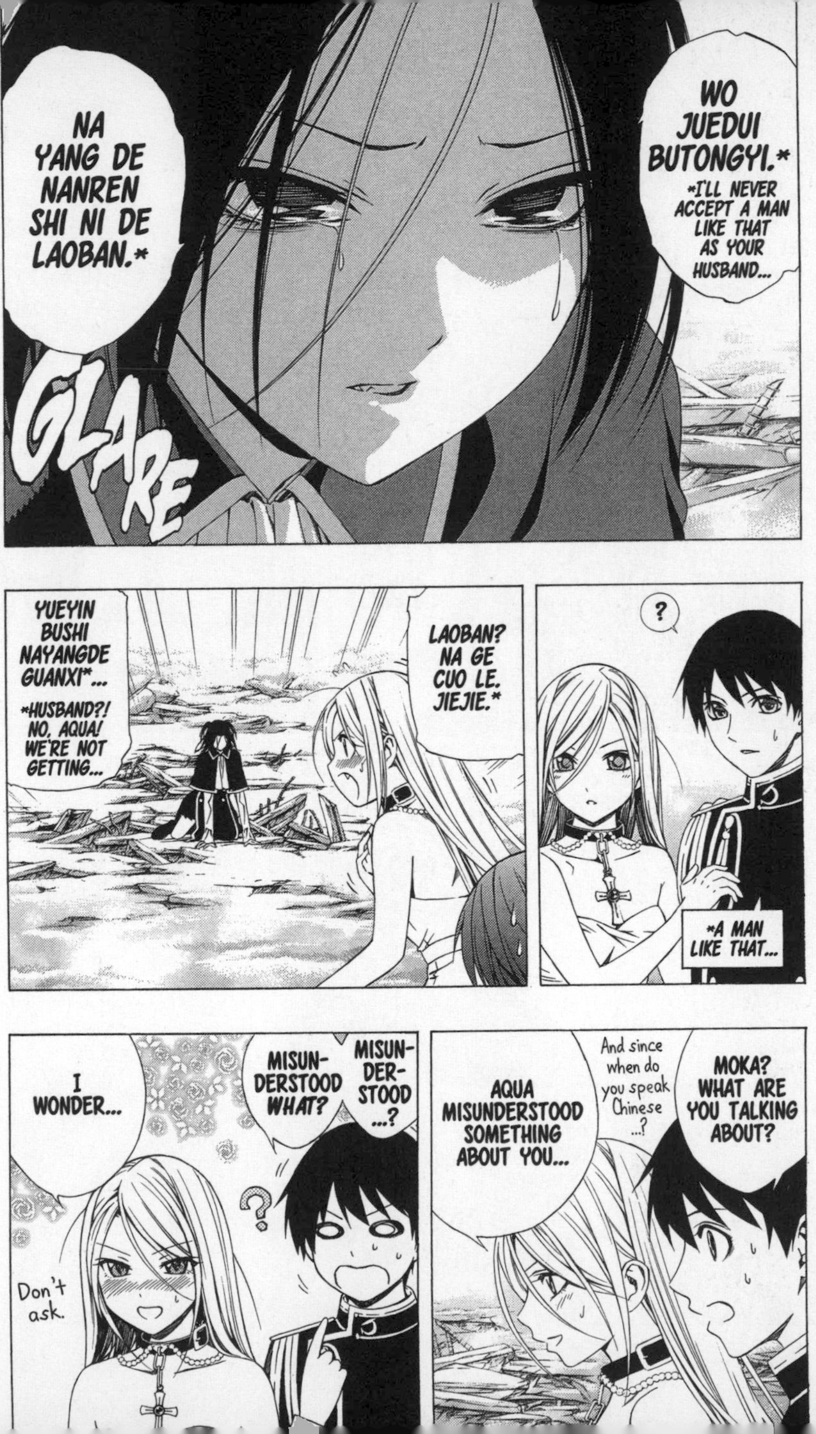
WO JUEDUI BUTONGYI.*
*I'LL NEVER ACCEPT A MAN LIKE THAT AS YOUR HUSBAND...
NA YANG DE NANREN SHI NI DE LAOBAN.*
GLARE
?
*A MAN LIKE THAT...
LAOBAN? NA GE CUO LE. JIEJIE.*
YUEYIN BUSHI NAYANGDE GUANXI*...
*HUSBAND?! NO, AQUA! WE'RE NOT GETTING...
MOKA? WHAT ARE YOU TALKING ABOUT?
And since when do you speak Chinese ...?
AQUA MISUNDERSTOOD SOMETHING ABOUT YOU...
MISUN-DER-STOOD ...?
MISUN-DERSTOOD WHAT?
I WONDER...
Don't ask.

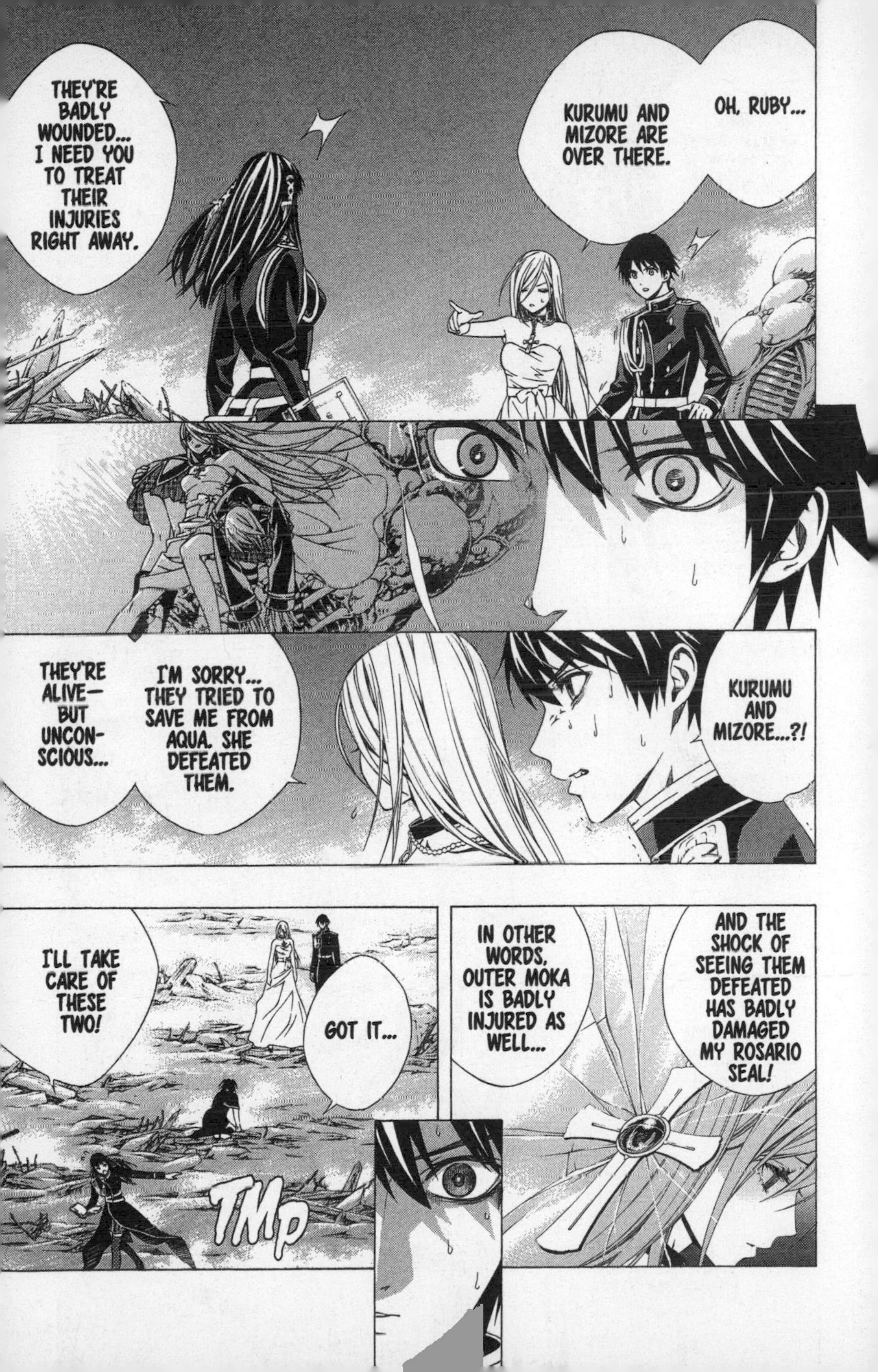
OH, RUBY...
KURUMU AND MIZORE ARE OVER THERE.
THEY'RE BADLY WOUNDED... I NEED YOU TO TREAT THEIR INJURIES RIGHT AWAY.
KURUMU AND MIZORE...?!
I'M SORRY... THEY TRIED TO SAVE ME FROM AQUA. SHE DEFEATED THEM.
THEY'RE ALIVE—BUT UNCONSCIOUS...
AND THE SHOCK OF SEEING THEM DEFEATED HAS BADLY DAMAGED MY ROSARIO SEAL!
IN OTHER WORDS, OUTER MOKA IS BADLY INJURED AS WELL...
I'LL TAKE CARE OF THESE TWO!
GOT IT...
TMP

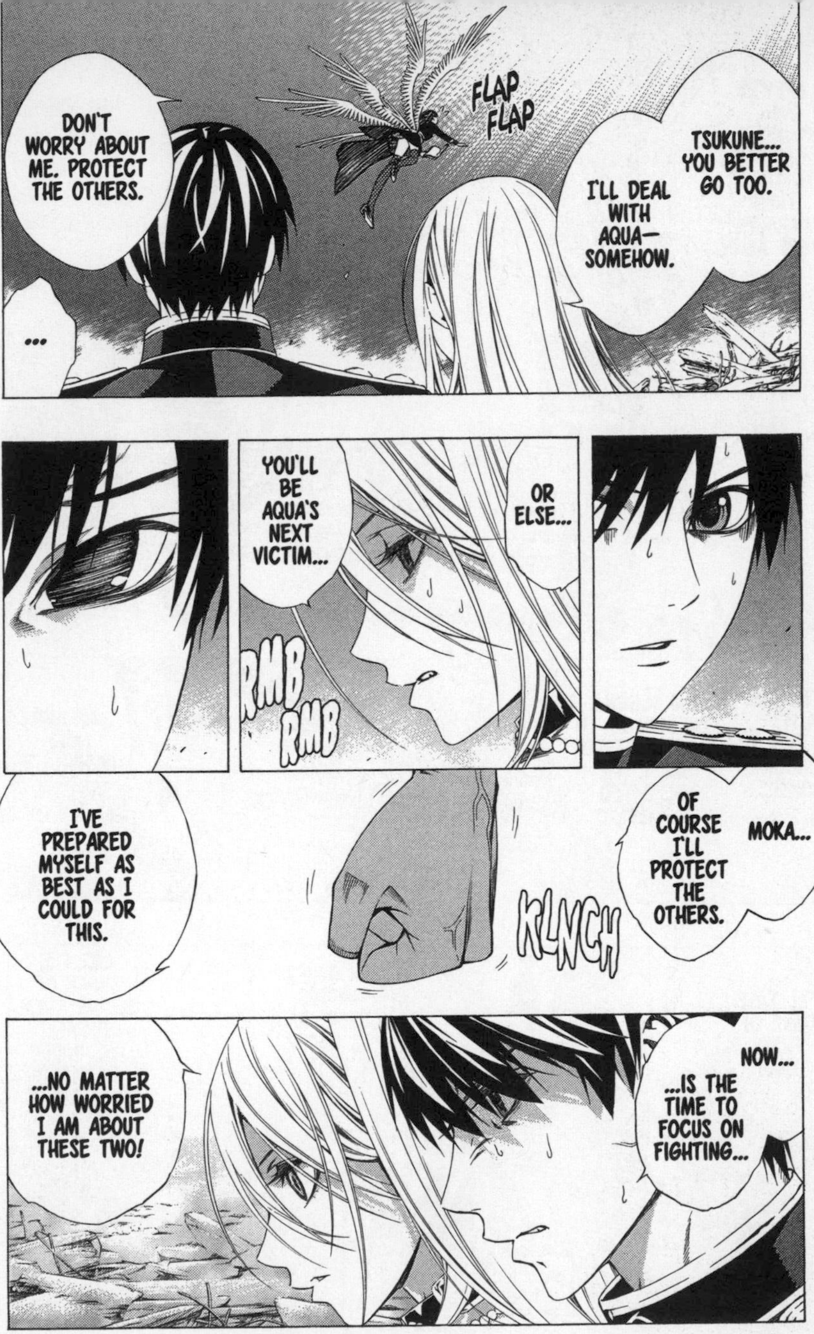
TSUKUNE... YOU BETTER GO TOO.
I'LL DEAL WITH AQUA—SOMEHOW.
FLAP FLAP
DON'T WORRY ABOUT ME. PROTECT THE OTHERS.
...
OR ELSE...
YOU'LL BE AQUA'S NEXT VICTIM...
RMB RMB
MOKA...
OF COURSE I'LL PROTECT THE OTHERS.
KLNCH
I'VE PREPARED MYSELF AS BEST AS I COULD FOR THIS.
NOW...
...IS THE TIME TO FOCUS ON FIGHTING...
...NO MATTER HOW WORRIED I AM ABOUT THESE TWO!

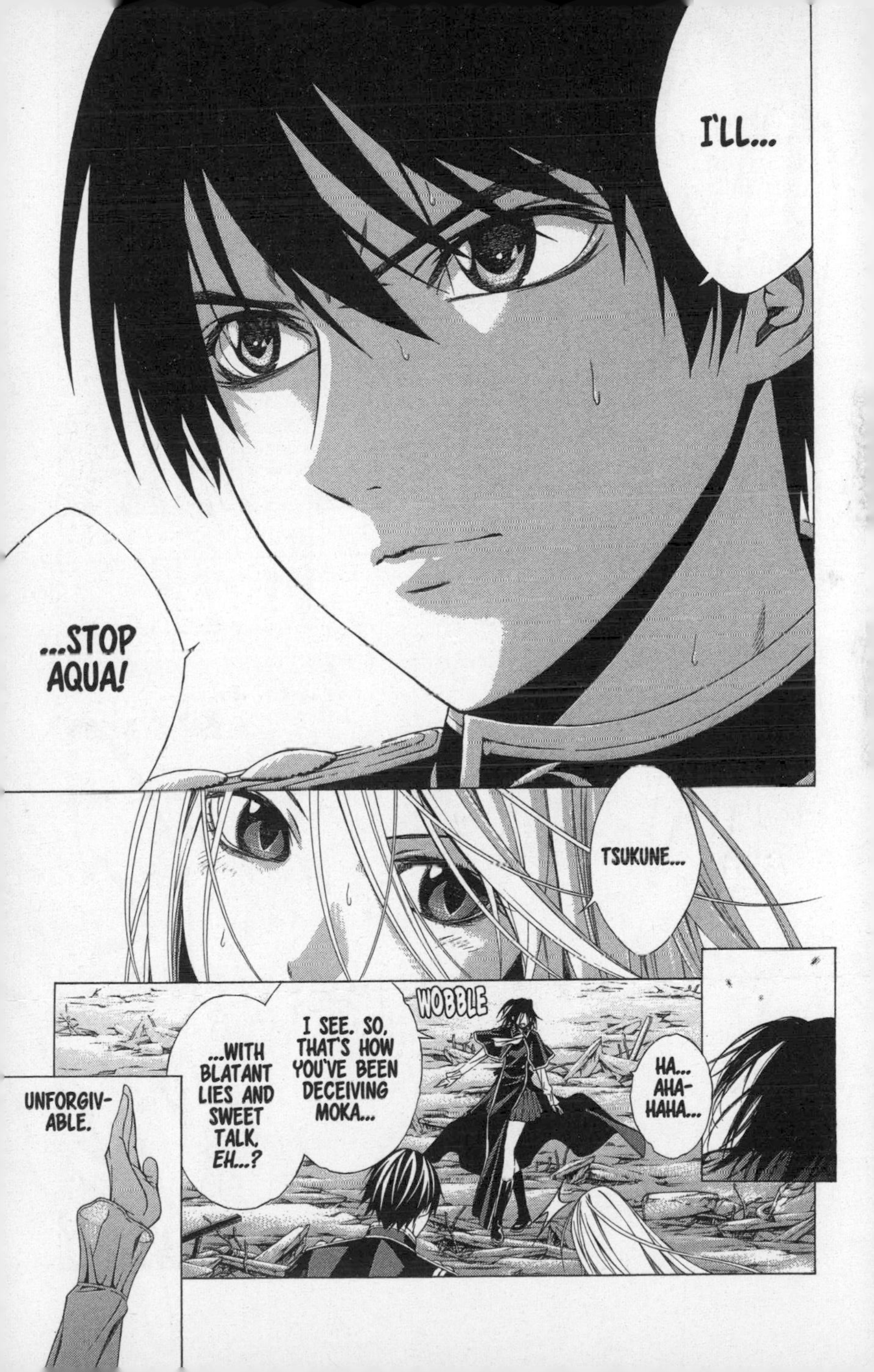
I'LL...
...STOP AQUA!
TSUKUNE...
HA... AHA-HAHA...
WOBBLE
I SEE. SO, THAT'S HOW YOU'VE BEEN DECEIVING MOKA...
...WITH BLATANT LIES AND SWEET TALK, EH...?
UNFORGIV-ABLE.

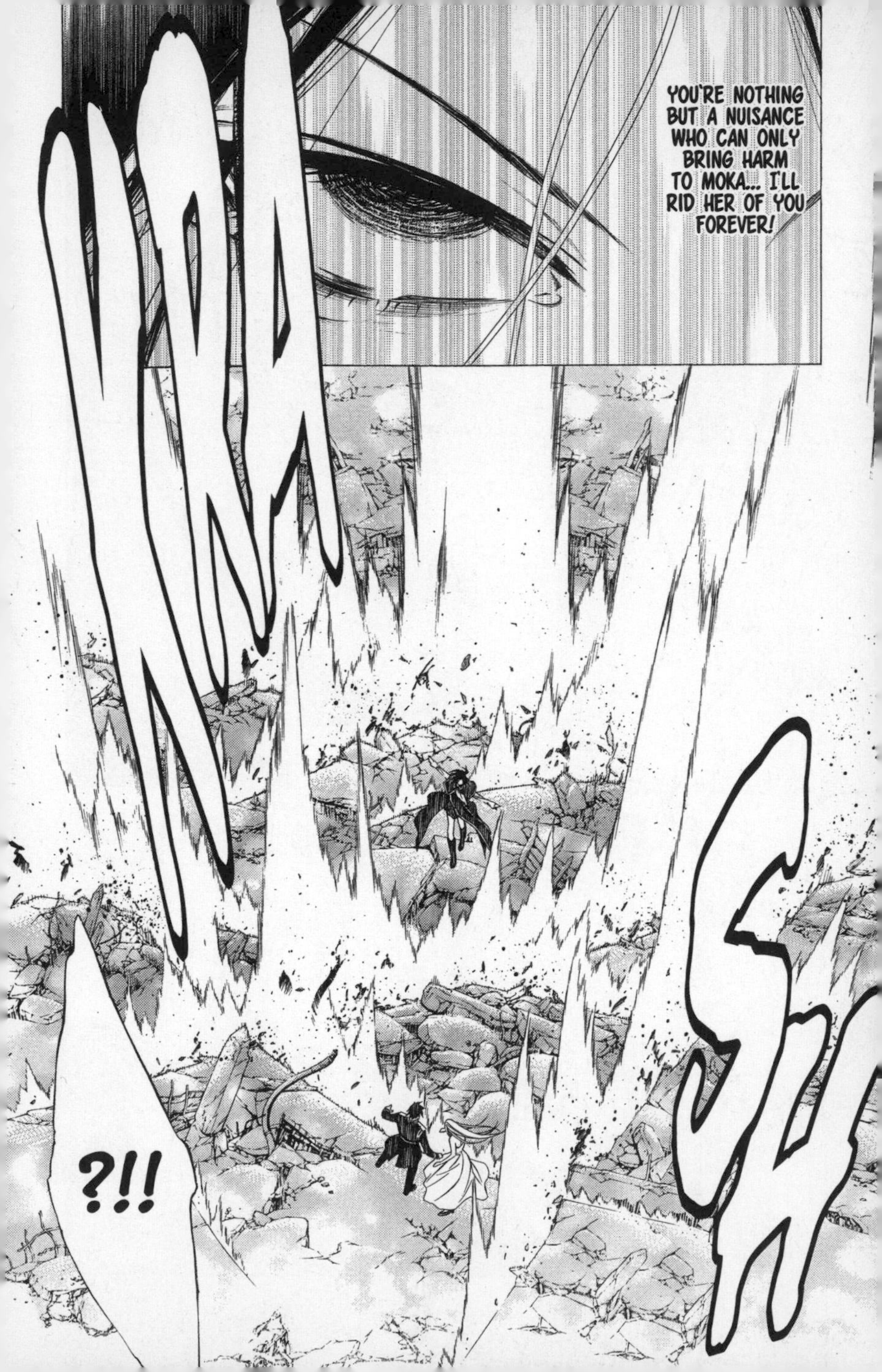
YOU'RE NOTHING BUT A NUISANCE WHO CAN ONLY BRING HARM TO MOKA... I'LL RID HER OF YOU FOREVER!
?!!

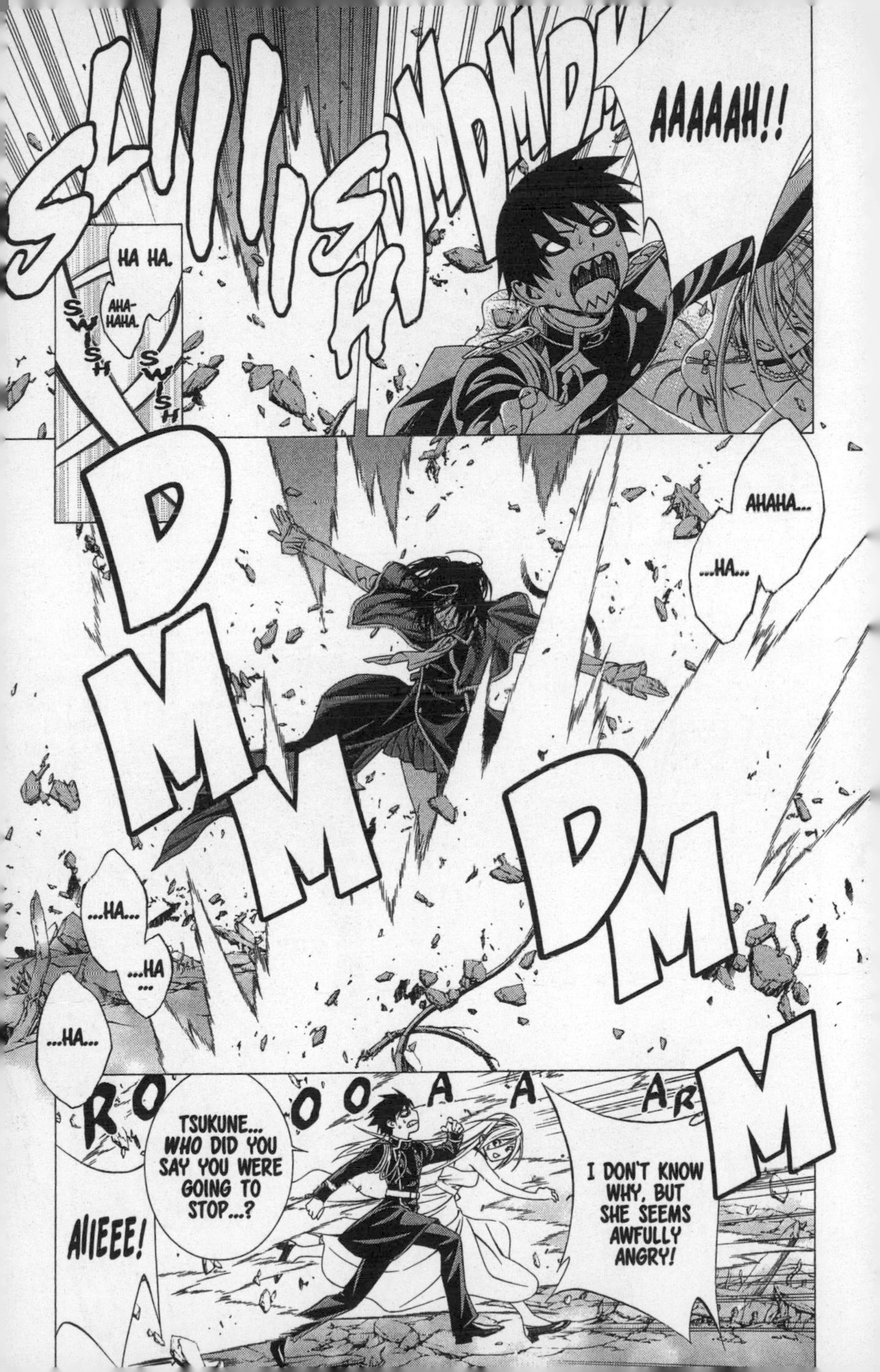
AAAAAH!!
HA HA.
AHA-HAHA.
SWISH
SWISH
AHAHA...
...HA...
...HA...
...HA
...
...HA...
ROOOAAARM
I DON'T KNOW WHY, BUT SHE SEEMS AWFULLY ANGRY!
TSUKUNE... WHO DID YOU SAY YOU WERE GOING TO STOP...?
AIIEEE!

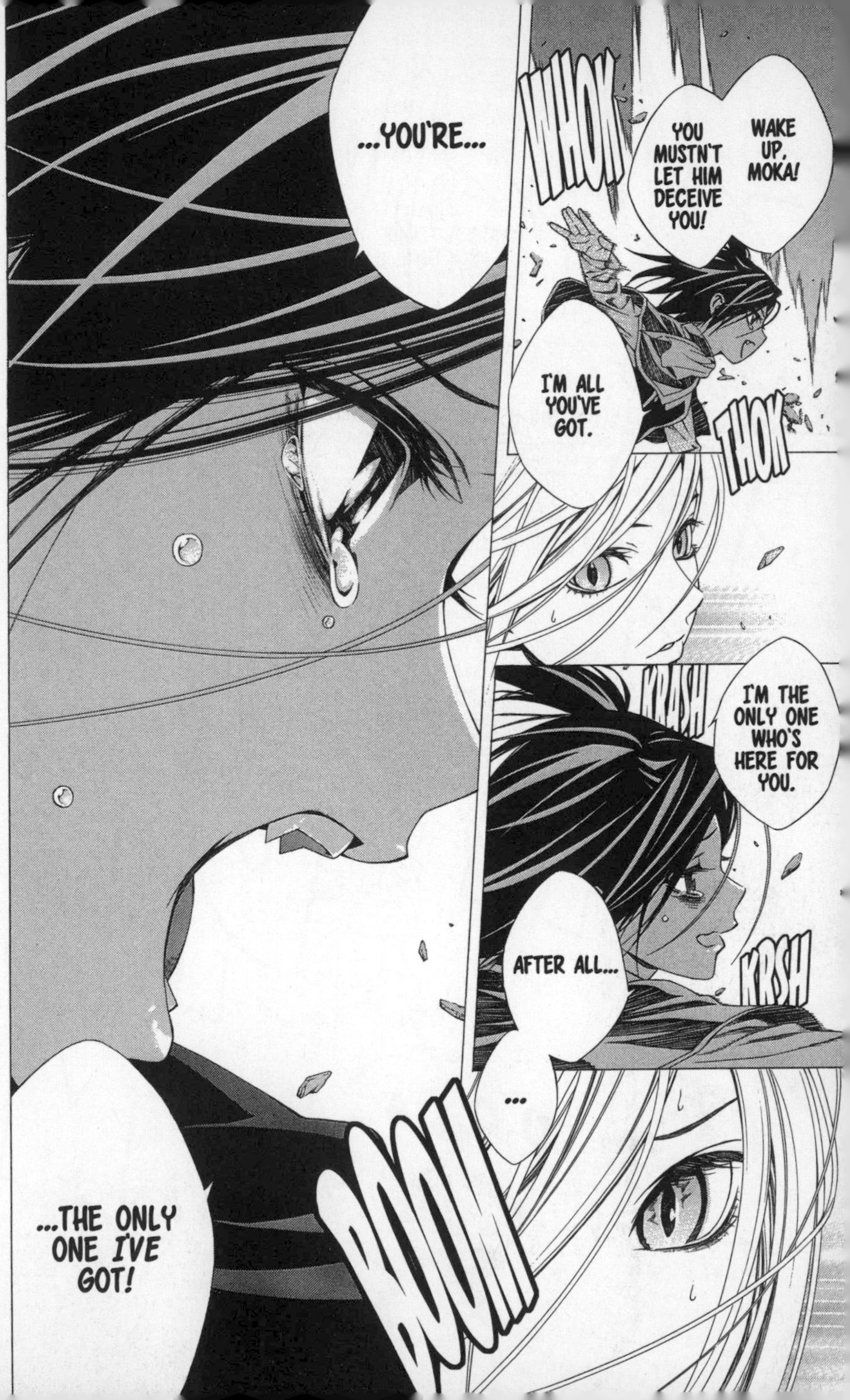
WHOK
WAKE UP, MOKA!
YOU MUSTN'T LET HIM DECEIVE YOU!
THOK
I'M ALL YOU'VE GOT.
KRASH
I'M THE ONLY ONE WHO'S HERE FOR YOU.
KRSH
AFTER ALL...
...
BOOM
...YOU'RE...
...THE ONLY ONE *I'VE* GOT!

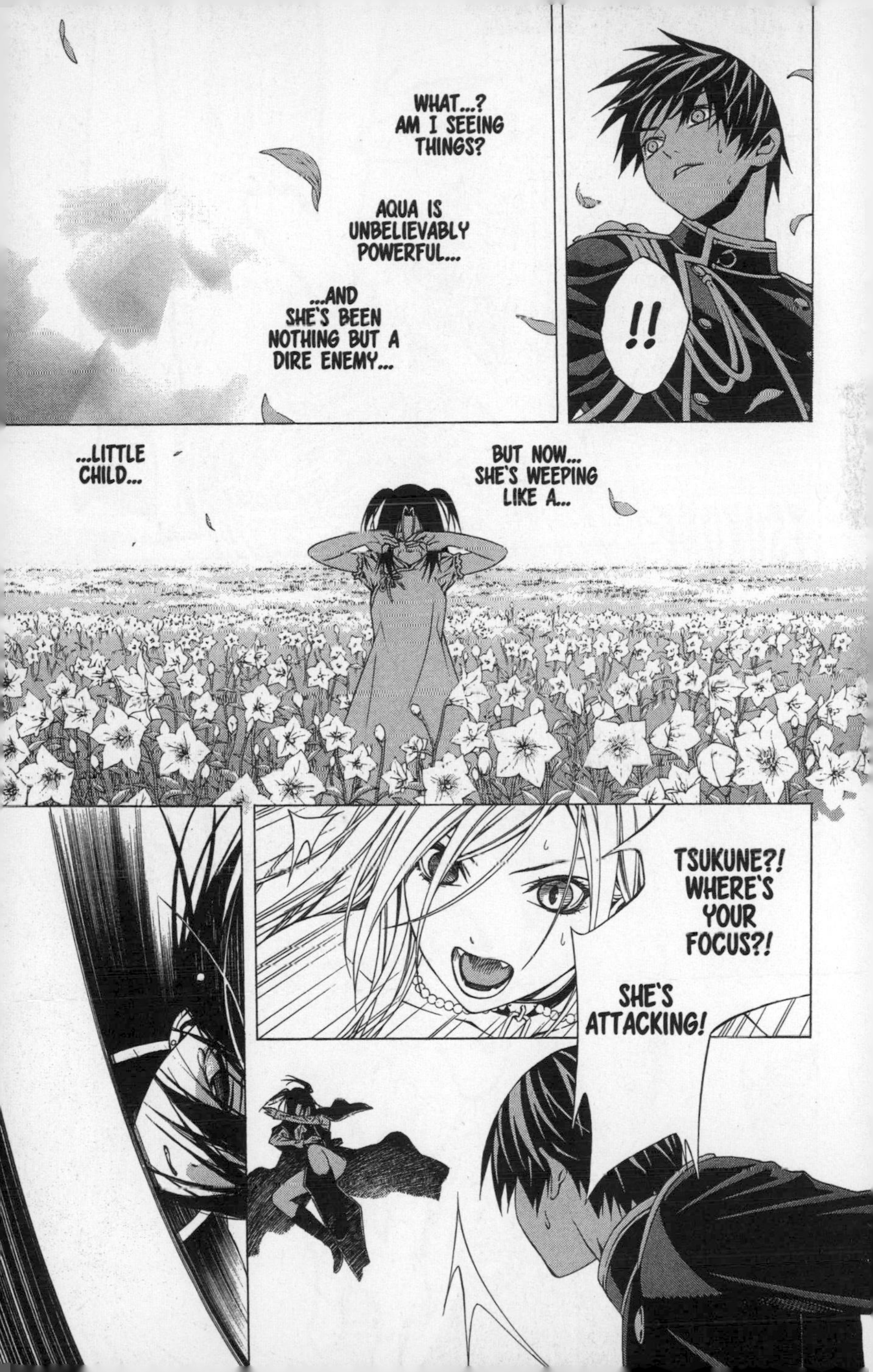
!!
WHAT...? AM I SEEING THINGS?
AQUA IS UNBELIEVABLY POWERFUL...
...AND SHE'S BEEN NOTHING BUT A DIRE ENEMY...
BUT NOW... SHE'S WEEPING LIKE A...
...LITTLE CHILD...
TSUKUNE?! WHERE'S YOUR FOCUS?!
SHE'S ATTACKING!

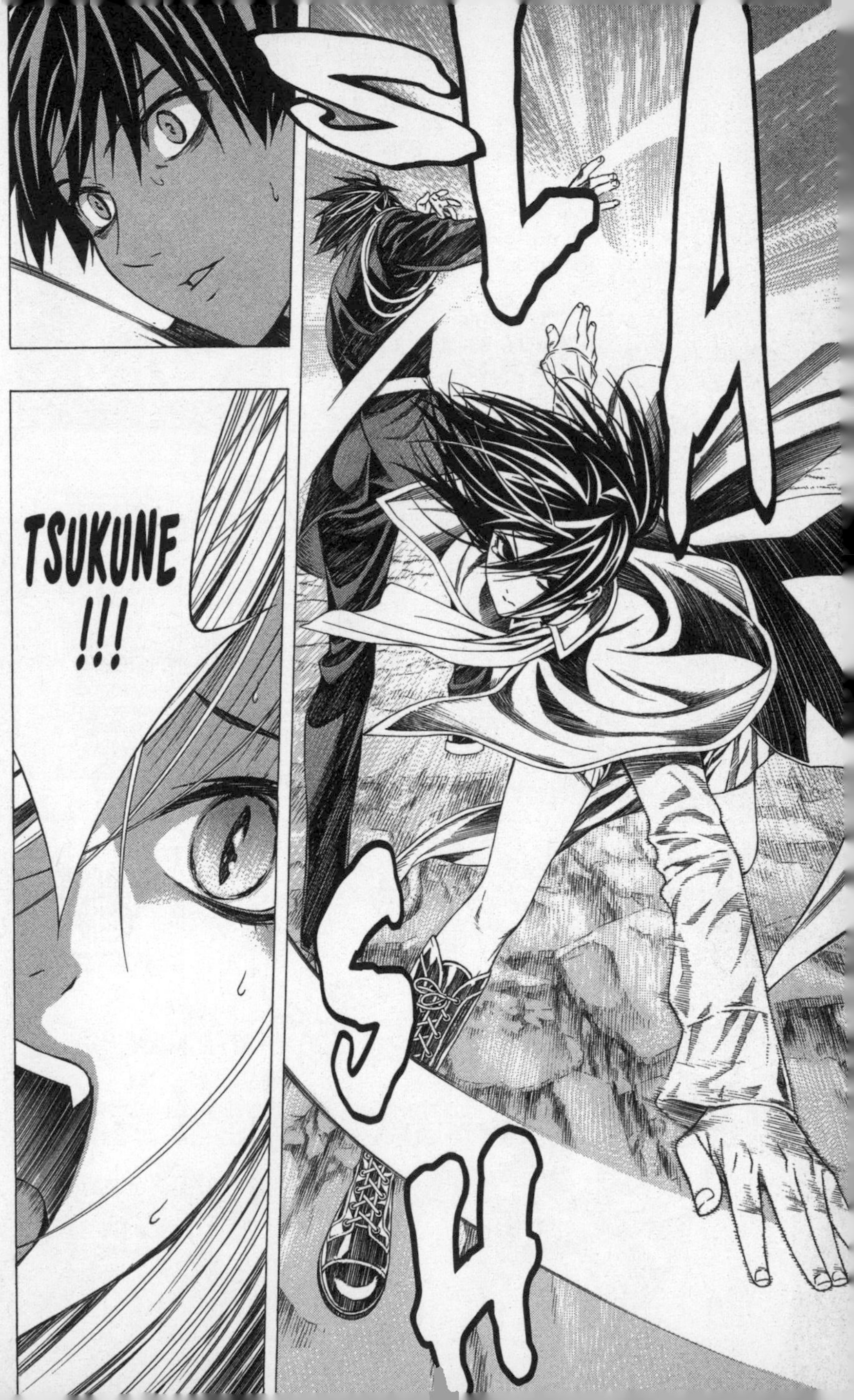
SLASH
TSUKUNE !!!

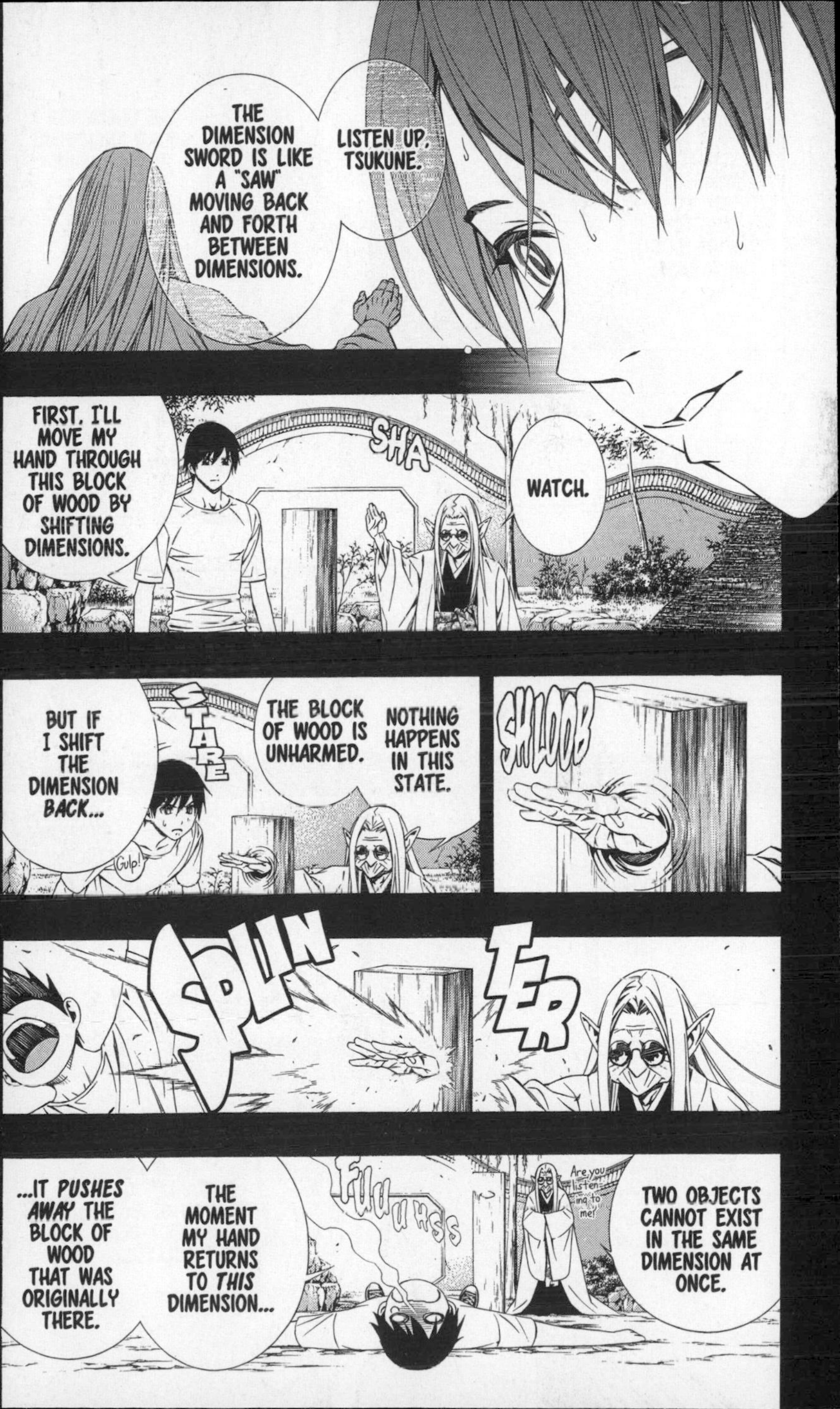
LISTEN UP, TSUKUNE.
THE DIMENSION SWORD IS LIKE A "SAW" MOVING BACK AND FORTH BETWEEN DIMENSIONS.
WATCH.
SHA
FIRST, I'LL MOVE MY HAND THROUGH THIS BLOCK OF WOOD BY SHIFTING DIMENSIONS.
SHLOOB
NOTHING HAPPENS IN THIS STATE.
THE BLOCK OF WOOD IS UNHARMED.
STARE
BUT IF I SHIFT THE DIMENSION *BACK*...
Gulp!
SPLIN
TER
TWO OBJECTS CANNOT EXIST IN THE SAME DIMENSION AT ONCE.
Are you listening to me!
FUUUUHSS
THE MOMENT MY HAND RETURNS TO *THIS* DIMENSION...
...IT *PUSHES AWAY* THE BLOCK OF WOOD THAT WAS ORIGINALLY THERE.

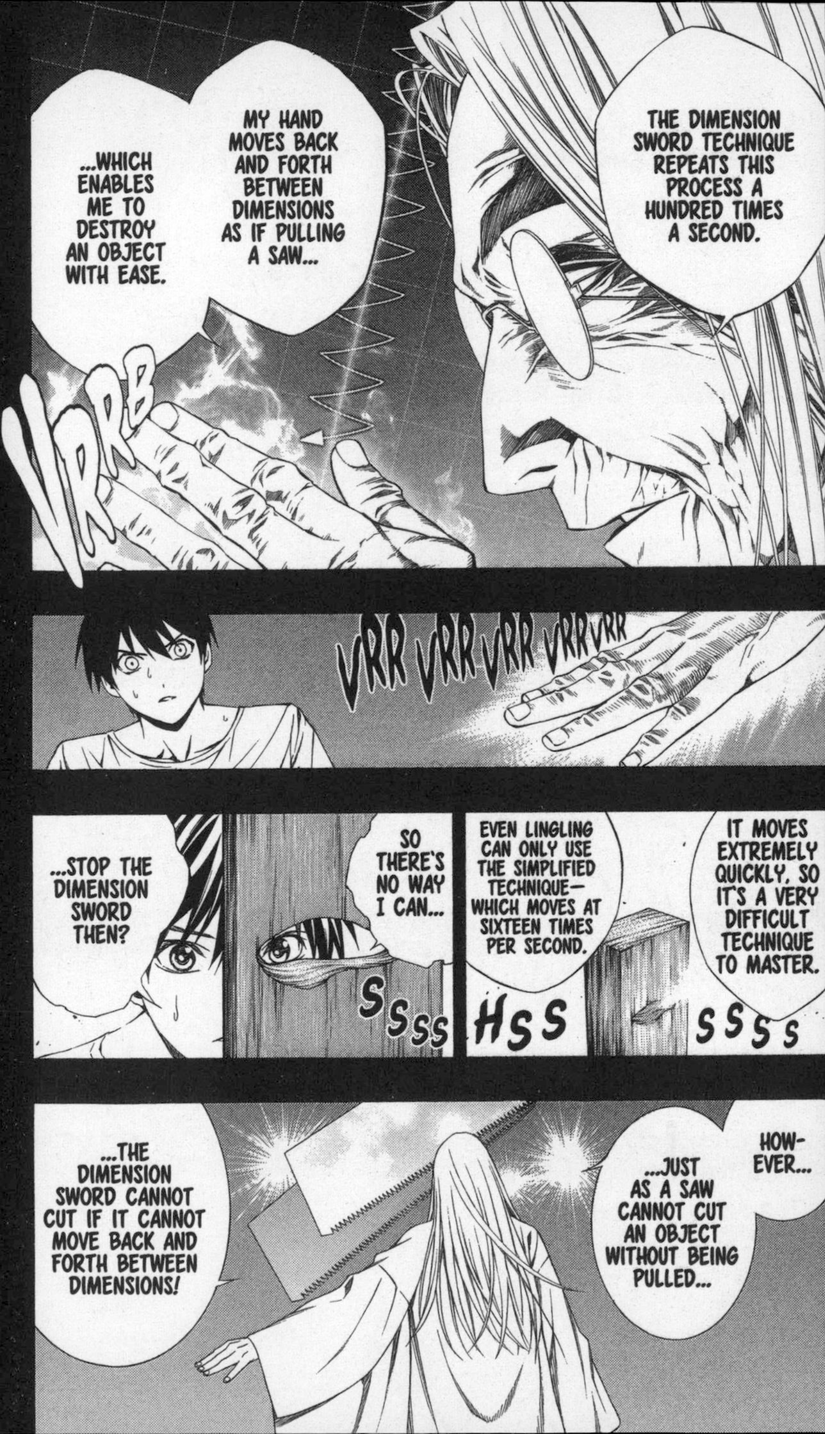
THE DIMENSION SWORD TECHNIQUE REPEATS THIS PROCESS A HUNDRED TIMES A SECOND.
MY HAND MOVES BACK AND FORTH BETWEEN DIMENSIONS AS IF PULLING A SAW...
...WHICH ENABLES ME TO DESTROY AN OBJECT WITH EASE.
VRRB
VRR VRR VRR VRR VRR
IT MOVES EXTREMELY QUICKLY, SO IT'S A VERY DIFFICULT TECHNIQUE TO MASTER.
EVEN LINGLING CAN ONLY USE THE SIMPLIFIED TECHNIQUE— WHICH MOVES AT SIXTEEN TIMES PER SECOND.
SSSS
HSS
SO THERE'S NO WAY I CAN...
SSSS
...STOP THE DIMENSION SWORD THEN?
HOW-EVER...
...JUST AS A SAW CANNOT CUT AN OBJECT WITHOUT BEING PULLED...
...THE DIMENSION SWORD CANNOT CUT IF IT CANNOT MOVE BACK AND FORTH BETWEEN DIMENSIONS!

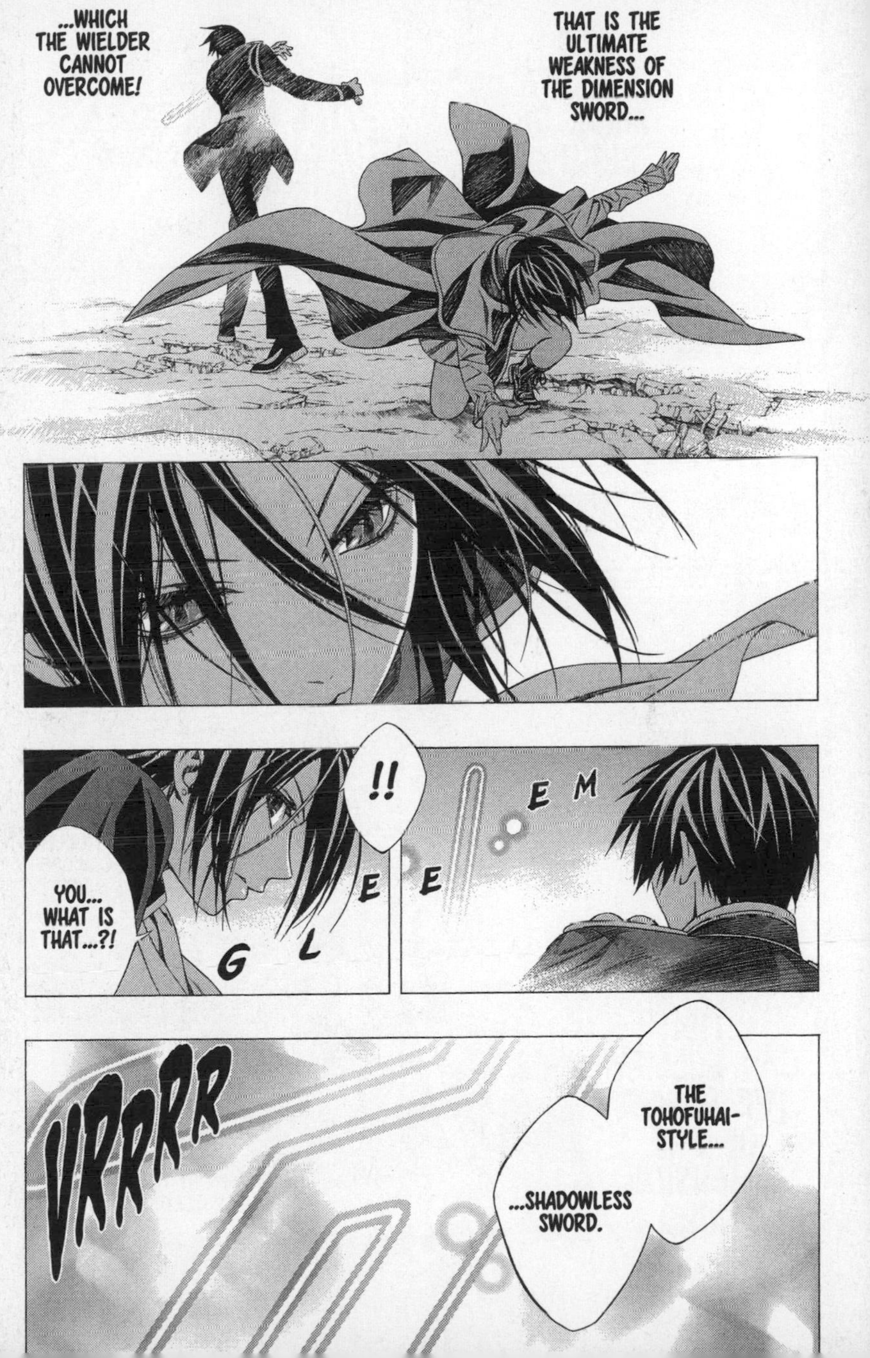
THAT IS THE ULTIMATE WEAKNESS OF THE DIMENSION SWORD...
...WHICH THE WIELDER CANNOT OVERCOME!
GLEEEM
!!
YOU... WHAT IS THAT...?!
THE TOHOFUHAI-STYLE...
...SHADOWLESS SWORD.
VRRRR

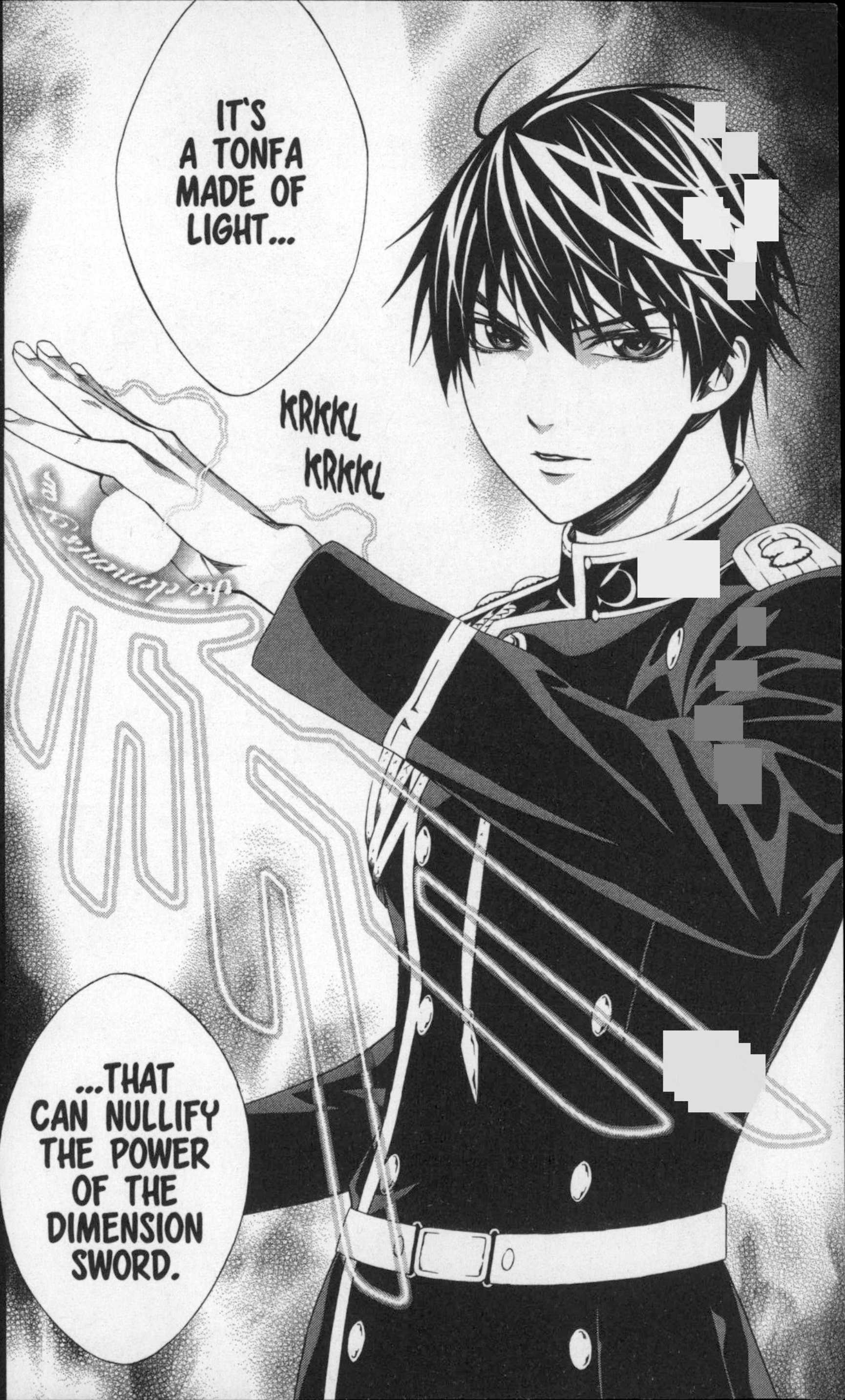
IT'S A TONFA MADE OF LIGHT...
KRKKL KRKKL
...THAT CAN NULLIFY THE POWER OF THE DIMENSION SWORD.

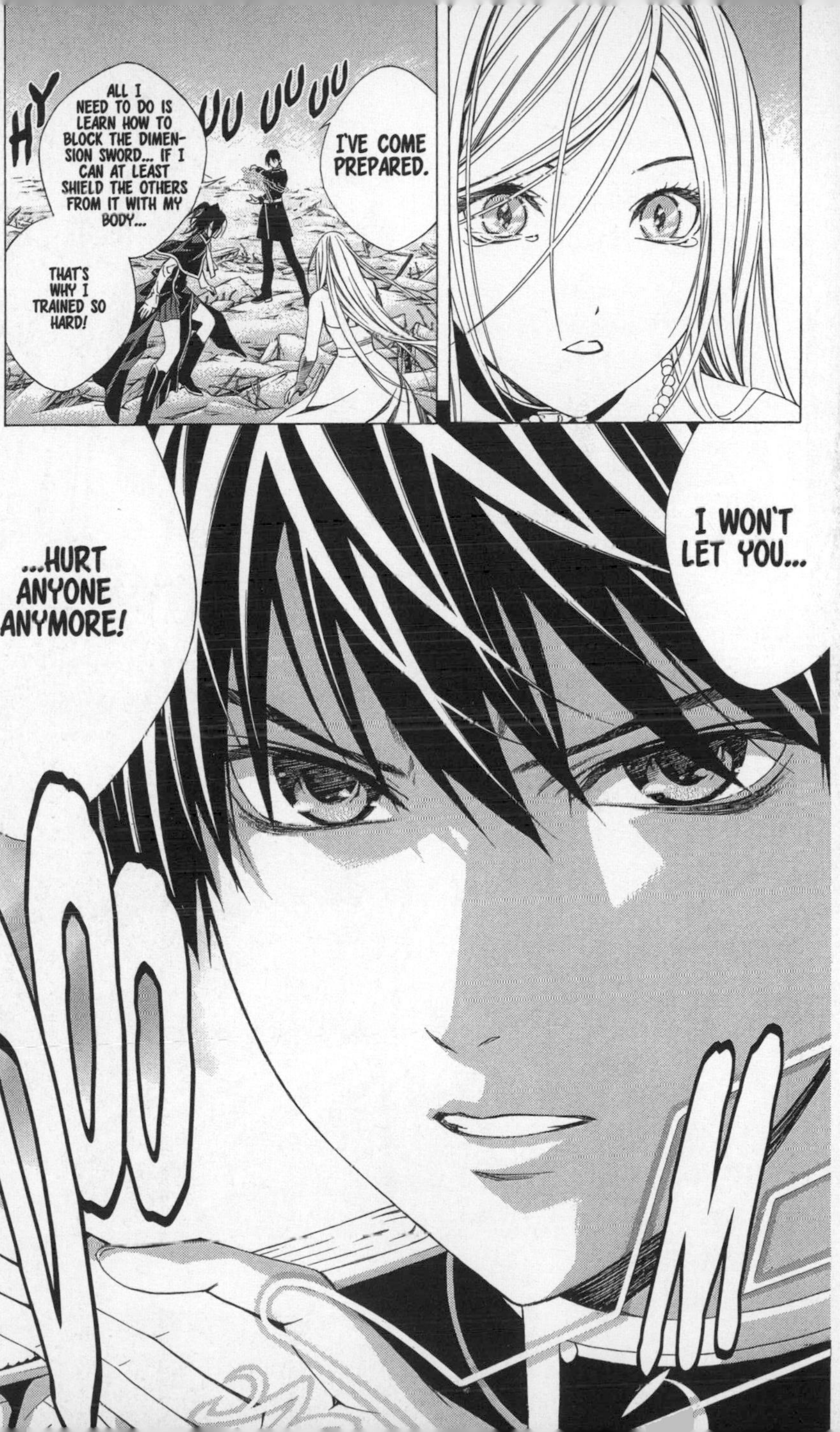
HYUU UUUU
I'VE COME PREPARED.
ALL I NEED TO DO IS LEARN HOW TO BLOCK THE DIMENSION SWORD... IF I CAN AT LEAST SHIELD THE OTHERS FROM IT WITH MY BODY...
THAT'S WHY I TRAINED SO HARD!
I WON'T LET YOU...
...HURT ANYONE ANYMORE!

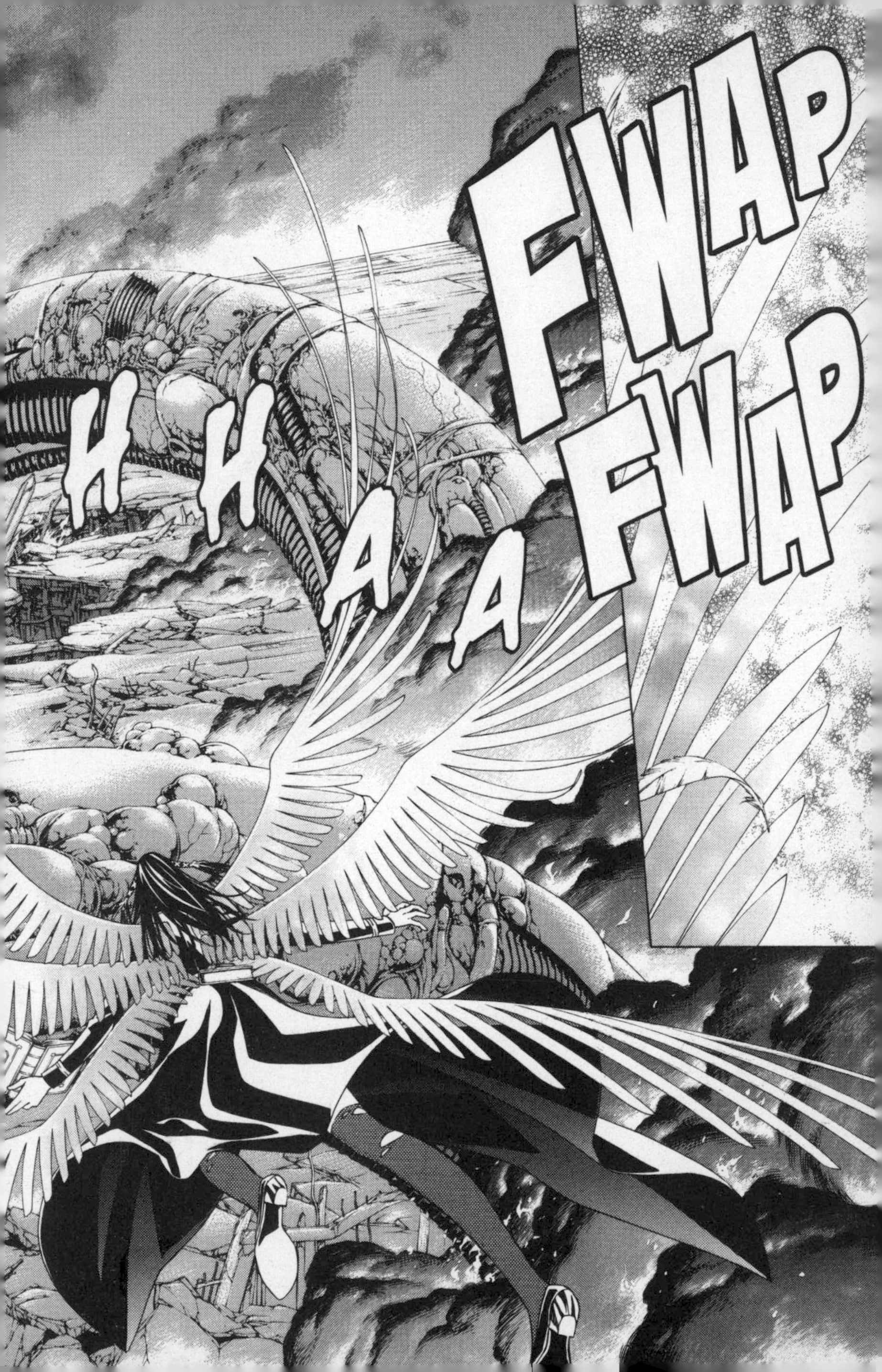
FWAP
FWAP
HHAA

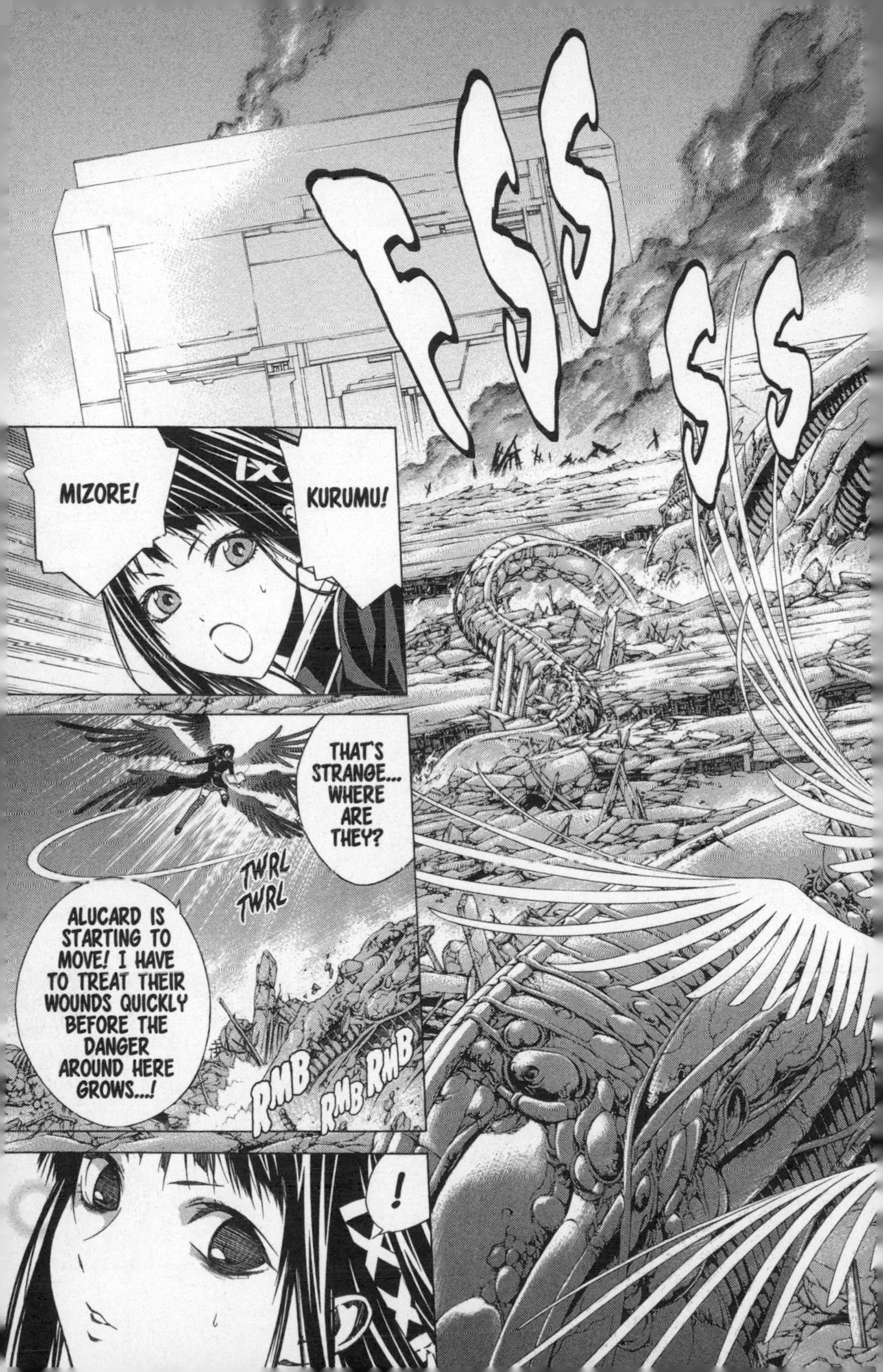
FSSSSS
KURUMU!
MIZORE!
THAT'S STRANGE... WHERE ARE THEY?
TWRL TWRL
ALUCARD IS STARTING TO MOVE! I HAVE TO TREAT THEIR WOUNDS QUICKLY BEFORE THE DANGER AROUND HERE GROWS...!
RMB RMB RMB
!

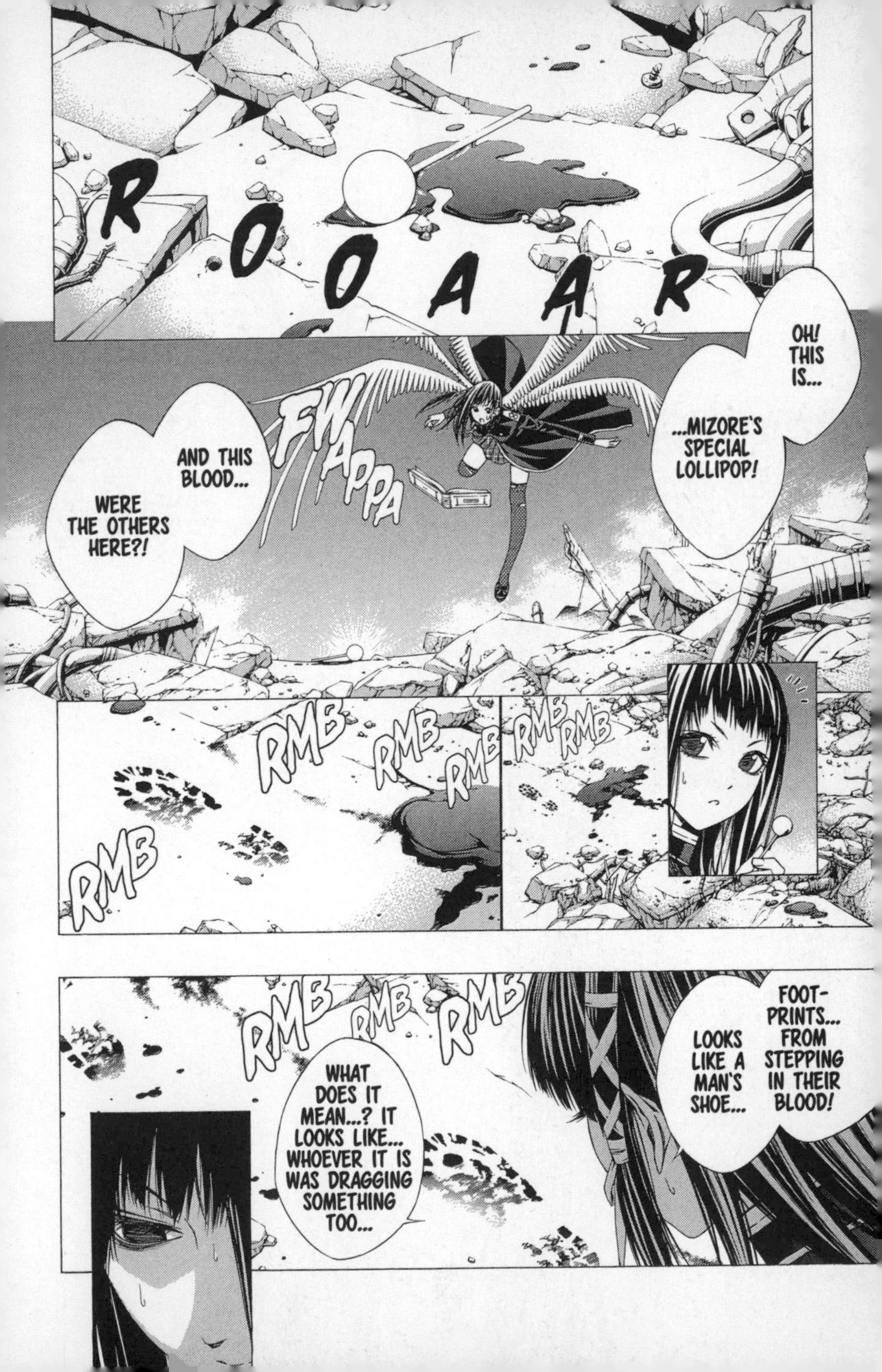
ROOOAAR
OH! THIS IS... ...MIZORE'S SPECIAL LOLLIPOP!
FWAPPA
AND THIS BLOOD... WERE THE OTHERS HERE?!
RMB RMB
RMB RMB RMB
RMB
FOOT-PRINTS... FROM STEPPING IN THEIR BLOOD!
LOOKS LIKE A MAN'S SHOE...
RMB RMB RMB
WHAT DOES IT MEAN...? IT LOOKS LIKE... WHOEVER IT IS WAS DRAGGING SOMETHING TOO...

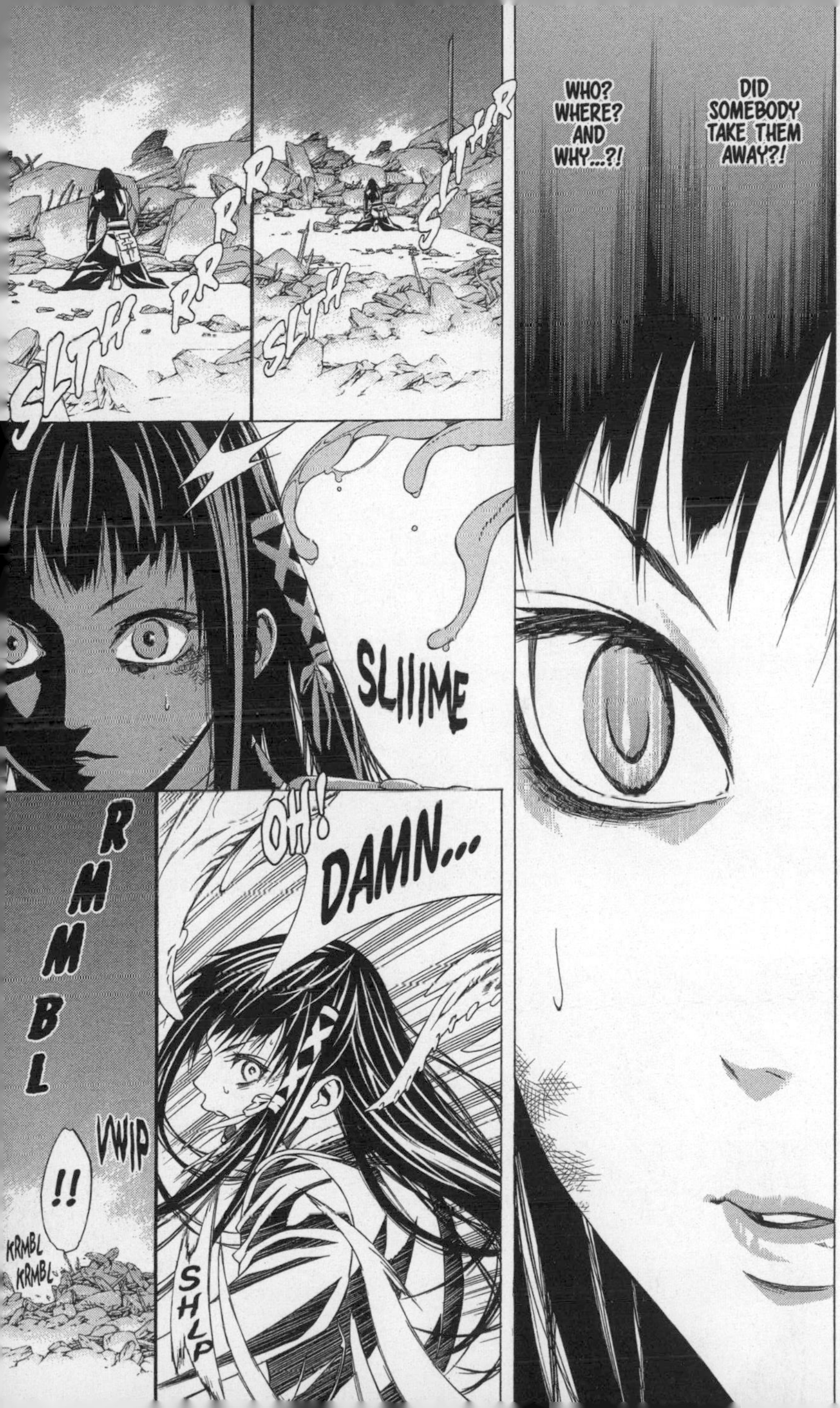
DID SOMEBODY TAKE THEM AWAY?!
WHO? WHERE? AND WHY...?!
SLTH SLTHR
SLTH RRRRR
SLIIIME
OH!
DAMN...
SHLP
VWIP
RMMBL
!!
KRMBL KRMBL

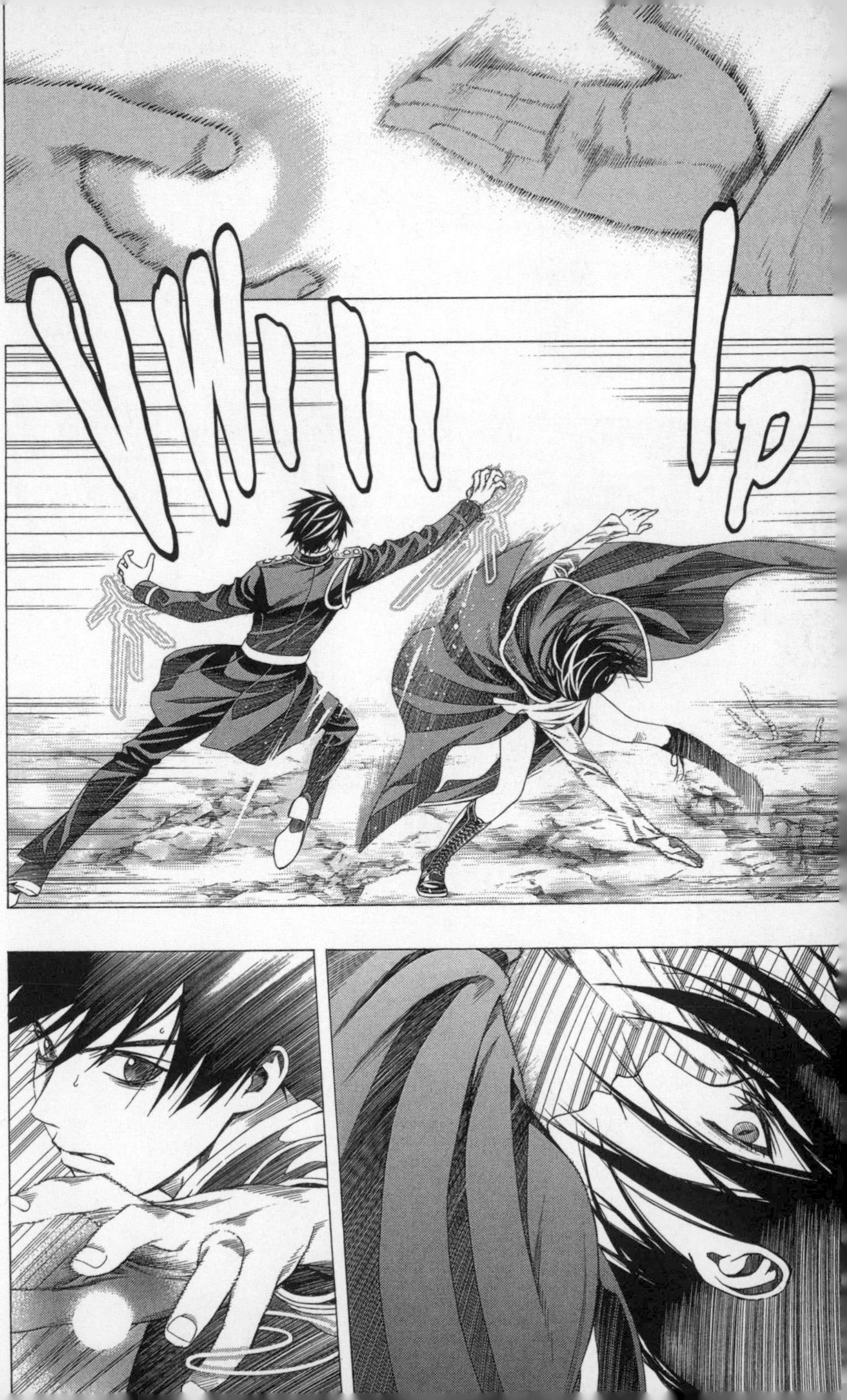
VWIIIIP

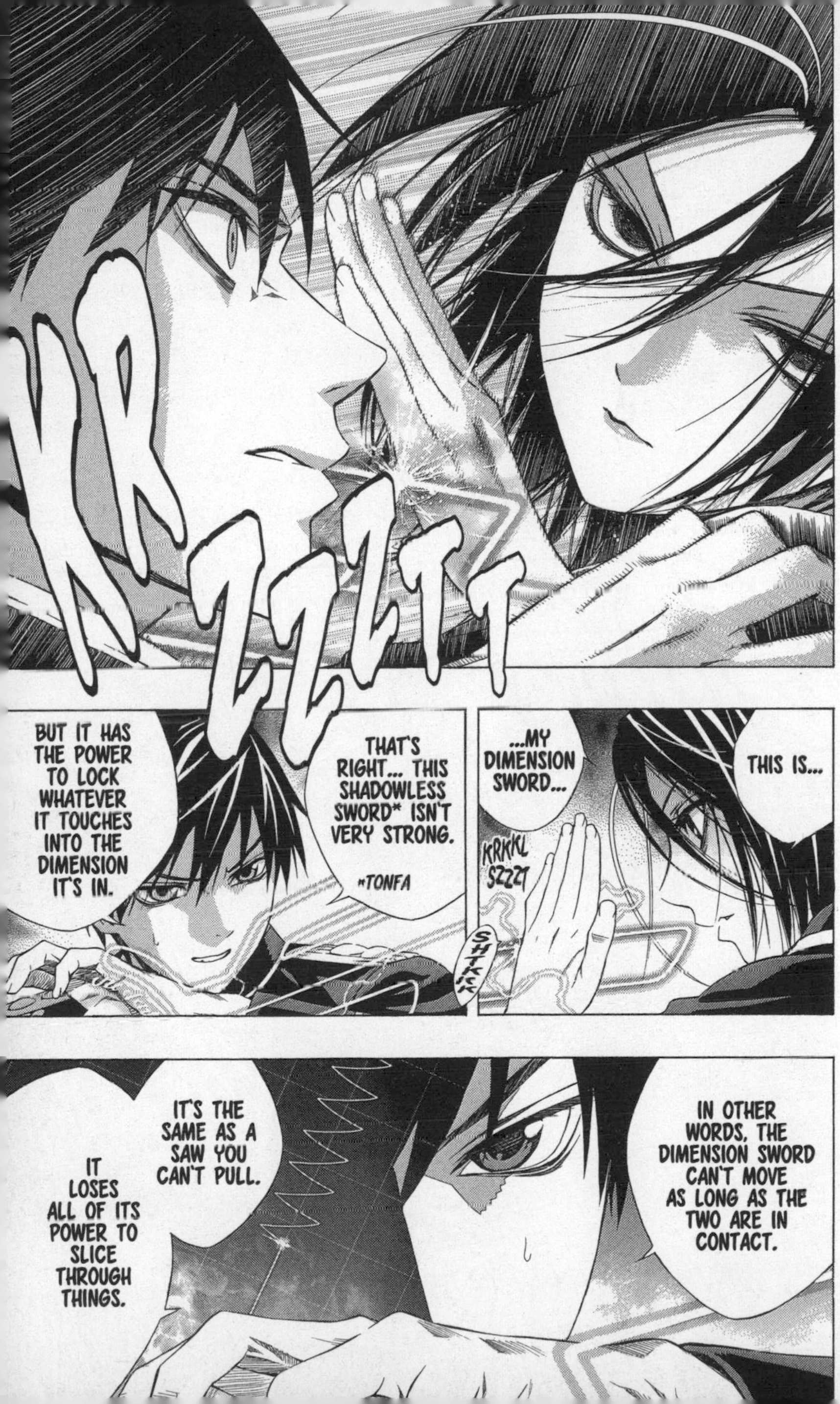
VRZZZTT
THIS IS...
...MY DIMENSION SWORD...
KRKKL SZZZT
SHTKKK
THAT'S RIGHT... THIS SHADOWLESS SWORD* ISN'T VERY STRONG.
*TONFA
BUT IT HAS THE POWER TO LOCK WHATEVER IT TOUCHES INTO THE DIMENSION IT'S IN.
IN OTHER WORDS, THE DIMENSION SWORD CAN'T MOVE AS LONG AS THE TWO ARE IN CONTACT.
IT'S THE SAME AS A SAW YOU CAN'T PULL.
IT LOSES ALL OF ITS POWER TO SLICE THROUGH THINGS.

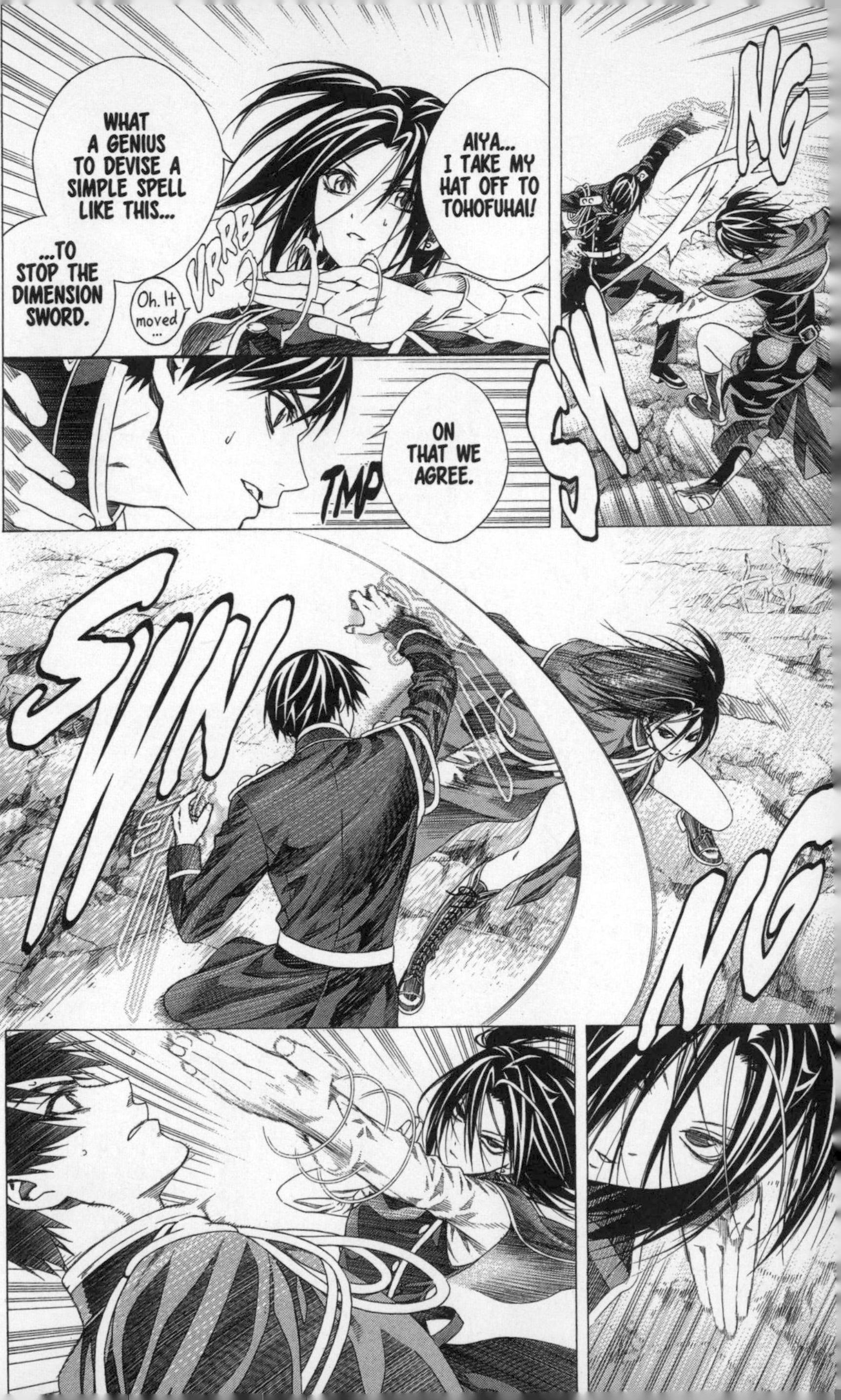
NG
SW
AIYA... I TAKE MY HAT OFF TO TOHOFUHAI!
WHAT A GENIUS TO DEVISE A SIMPLE SPELL LIKE THIS...
...TO STOP THE DIMENSION SWORD.
VRRB
Oh. It moved...
ON THAT WE AGREE.
TMP
SWI
NG

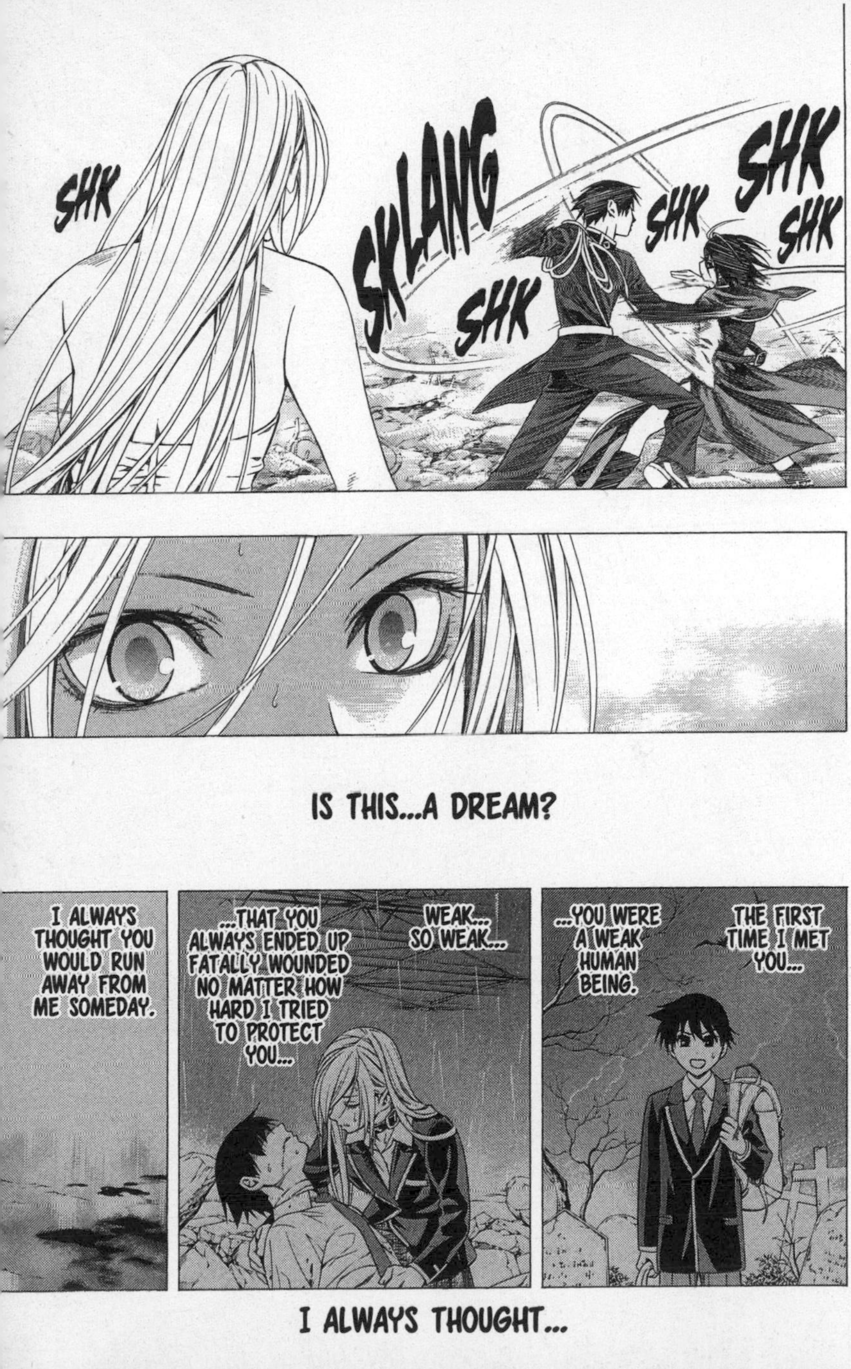
SHK
SHK
SHK
SHK
SKLANG
SHK
SHK
IS THIS...A DREAM?
THE FIRST TIME I MET YOU...
...YOU WERE A WEAK HUMAN BEING.
WEAK... SO WEAK...
...THAT YOU ALWAYS ENDED UP FATALLY WOUNDED NO MATTER HOW HARD I TRIED TO PROTECT YOU...
I ALWAYS THOUGHT YOU WOULD RUN AWAY FROM ME SOMEDAY.
I ALWAYS THOUGHT...

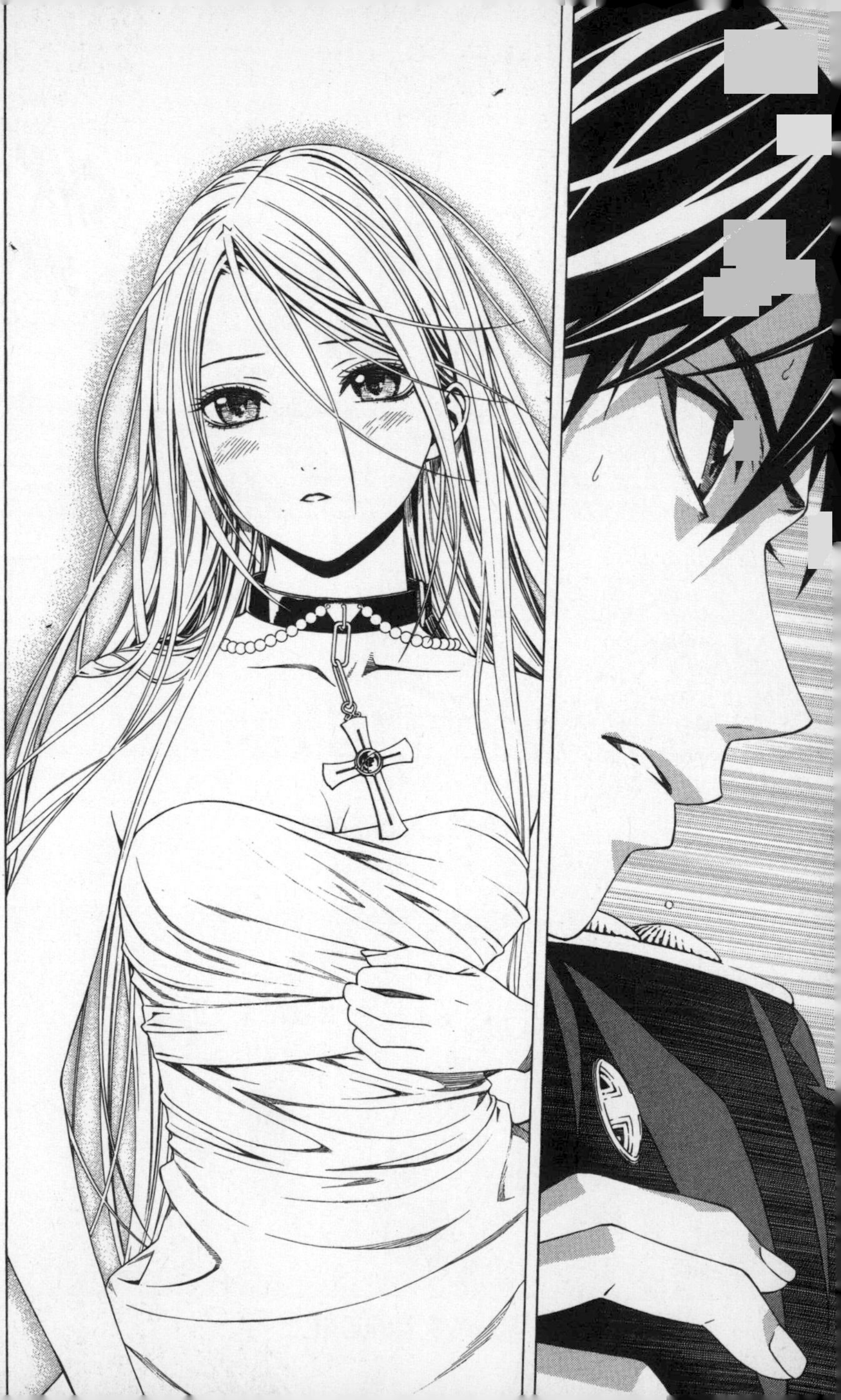

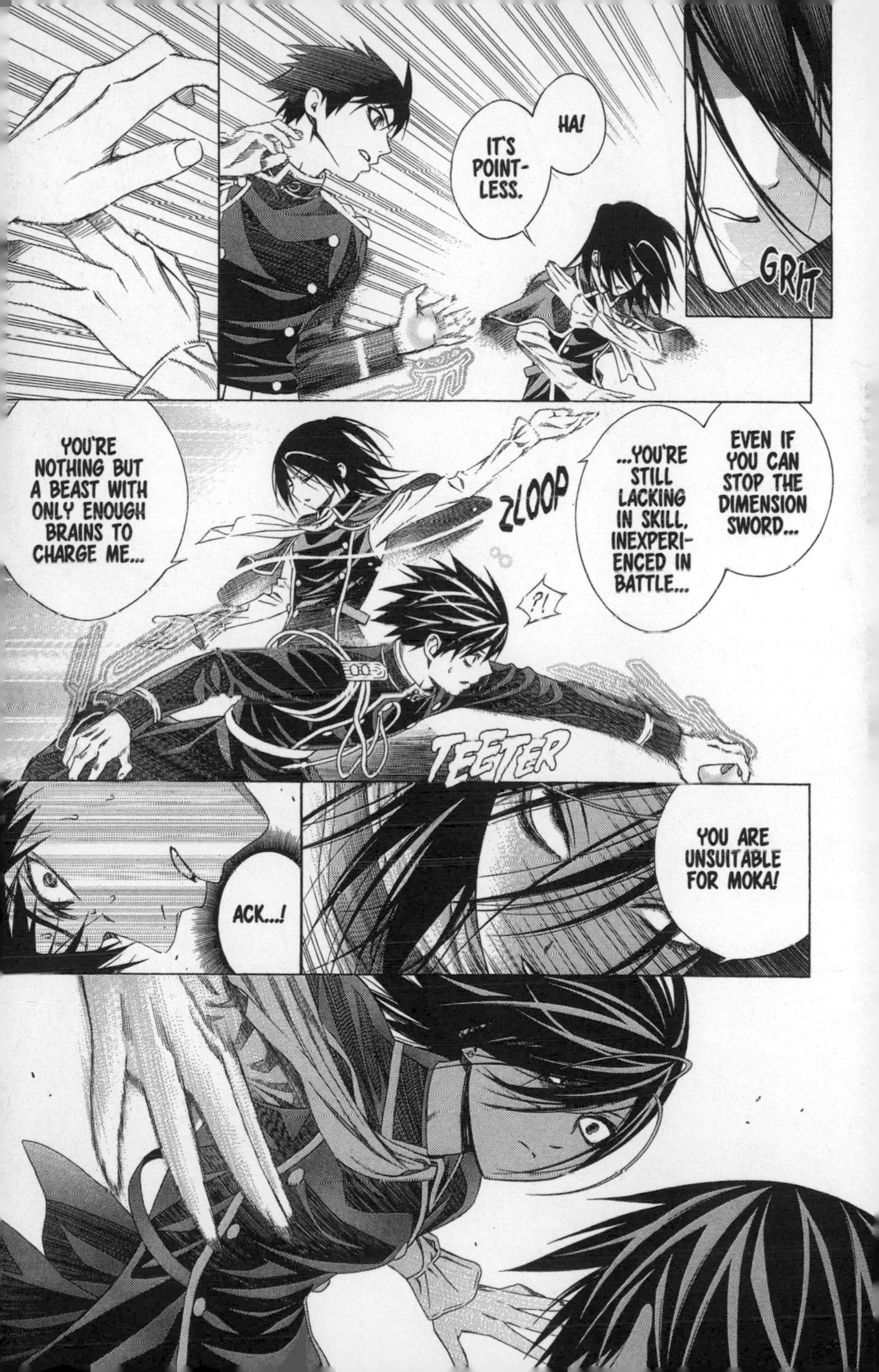
GRIT
HA!
IT'S POINT-LESS.
EVEN IF YOU CAN STOP THE DIMENSION SWORD...
...YOU'RE STILL LACKING IN SKILL, INEXPERI-ENCED IN BATTLE...
ZLOOP
?!
YOU'RE NOTHING BUT A BEAST WITH ONLY ENOUGH BRAINS TO CHARGE ME...
TEETER
YOU ARE UNSUITABLE FOR MOKA!
ACK...!

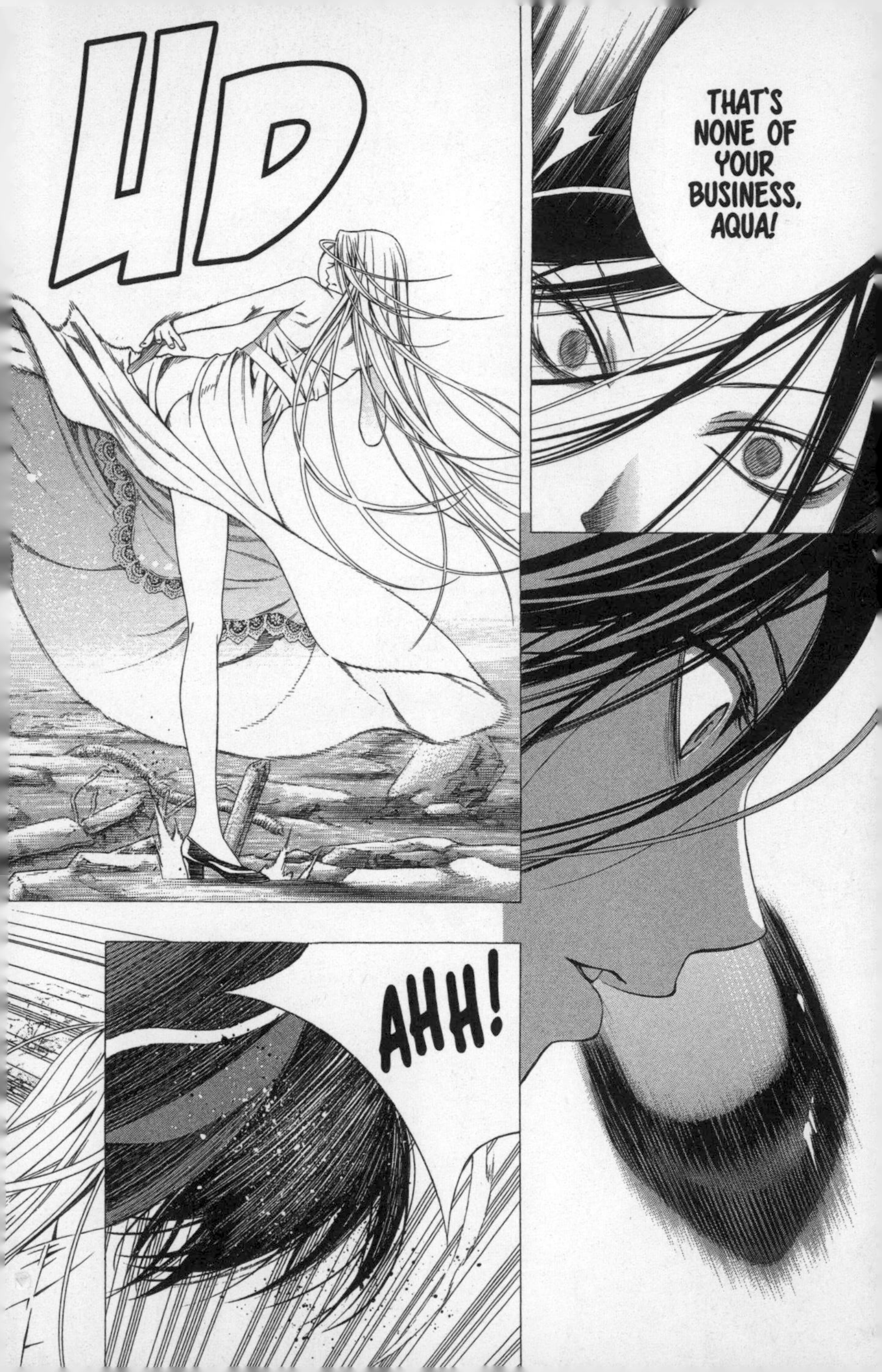
THAT'S NONE OF YOUR BUSINESS, AQUA!
UD
AHH!

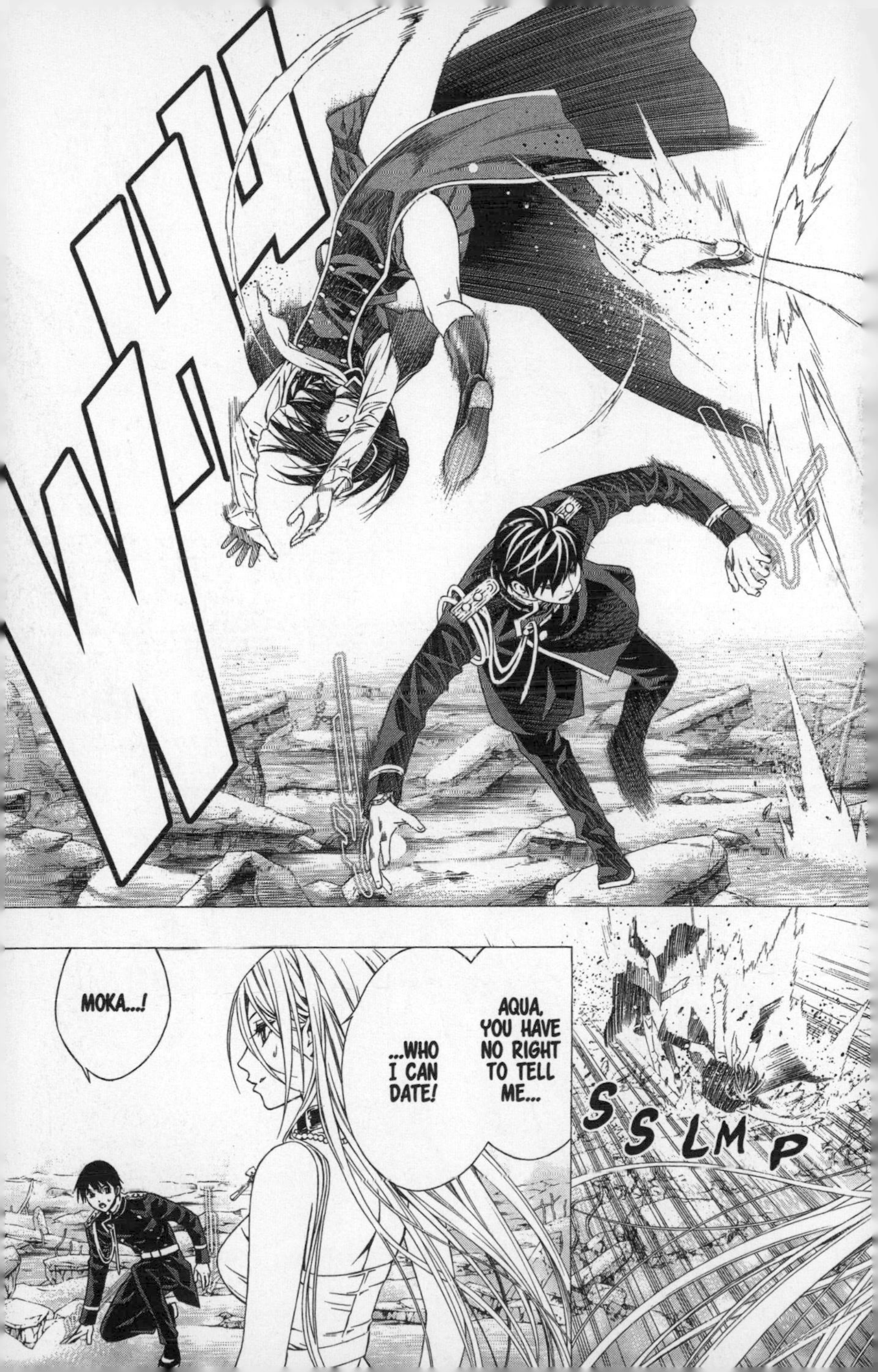

SSLMP
AQUA, YOU HAVE NO RIGHT TO TELL ME...
...WHO I CAN DATE!
MOKA...!

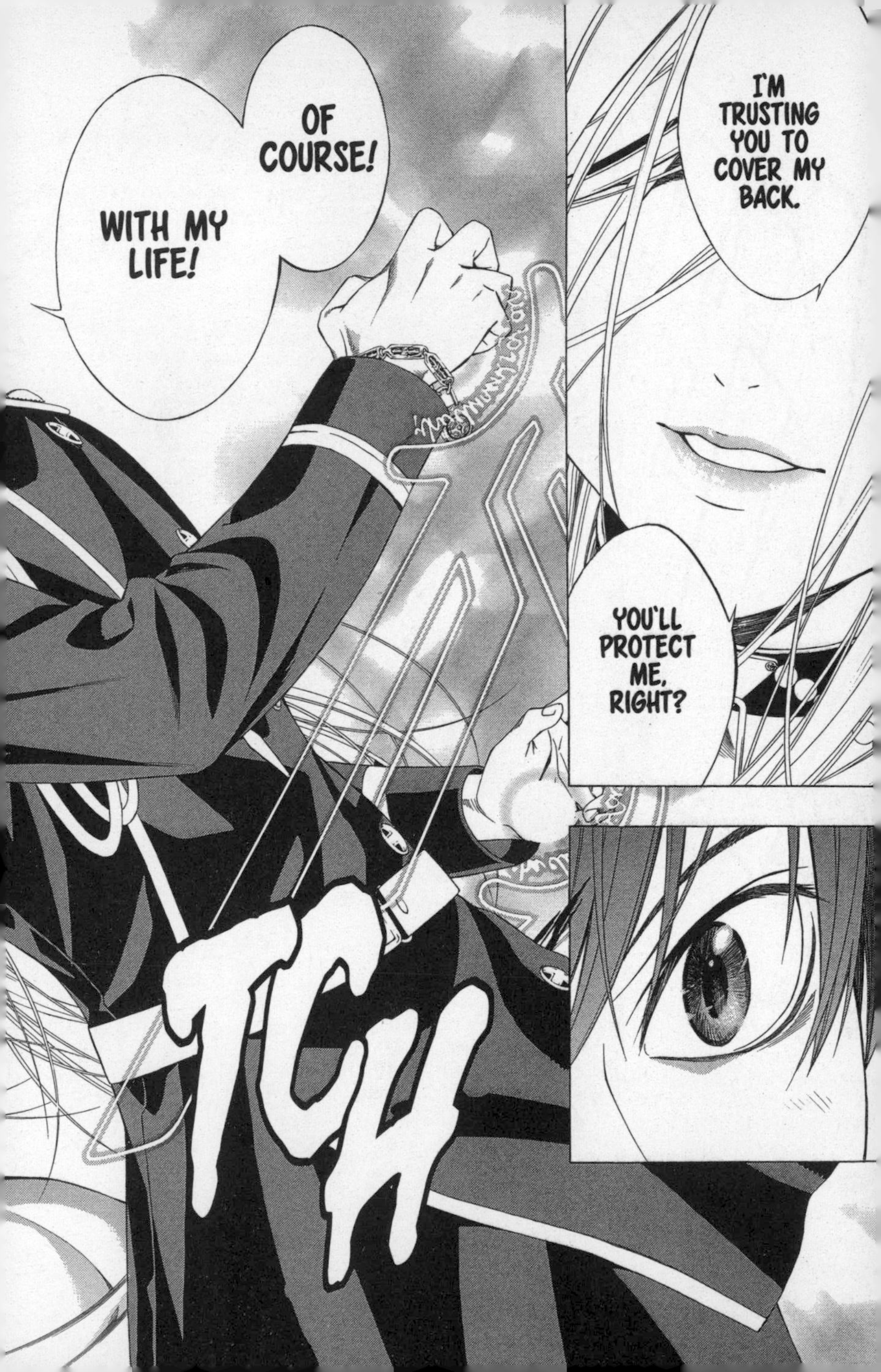
I'M TRUSTING YOU TO COVER MY BACK.
YOU'LL PROTECT ME, RIGHT?
OF COURSE!
WITH MY LIFE!
TCH

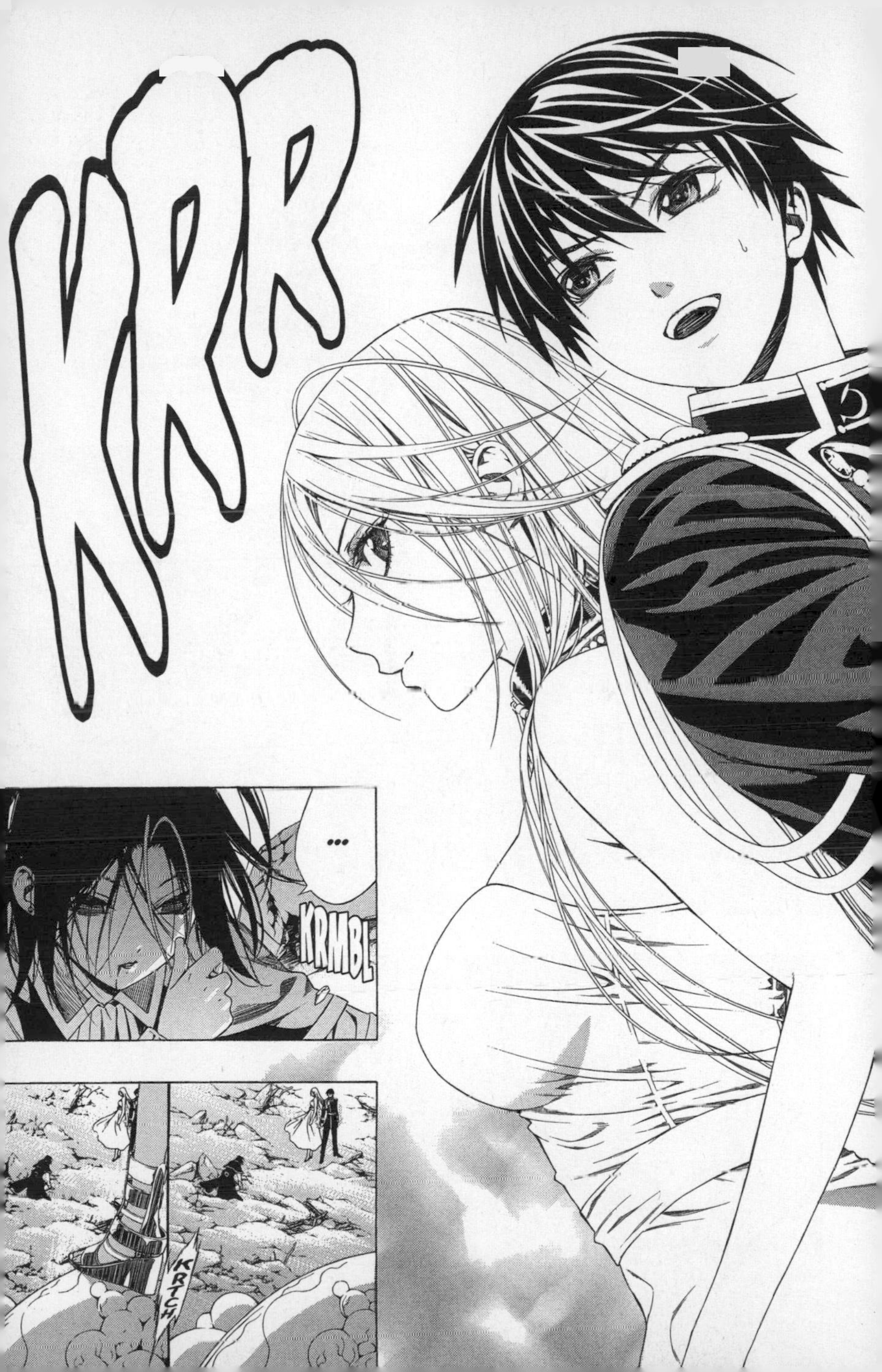
KRR
...
KRMBL
KRTCH

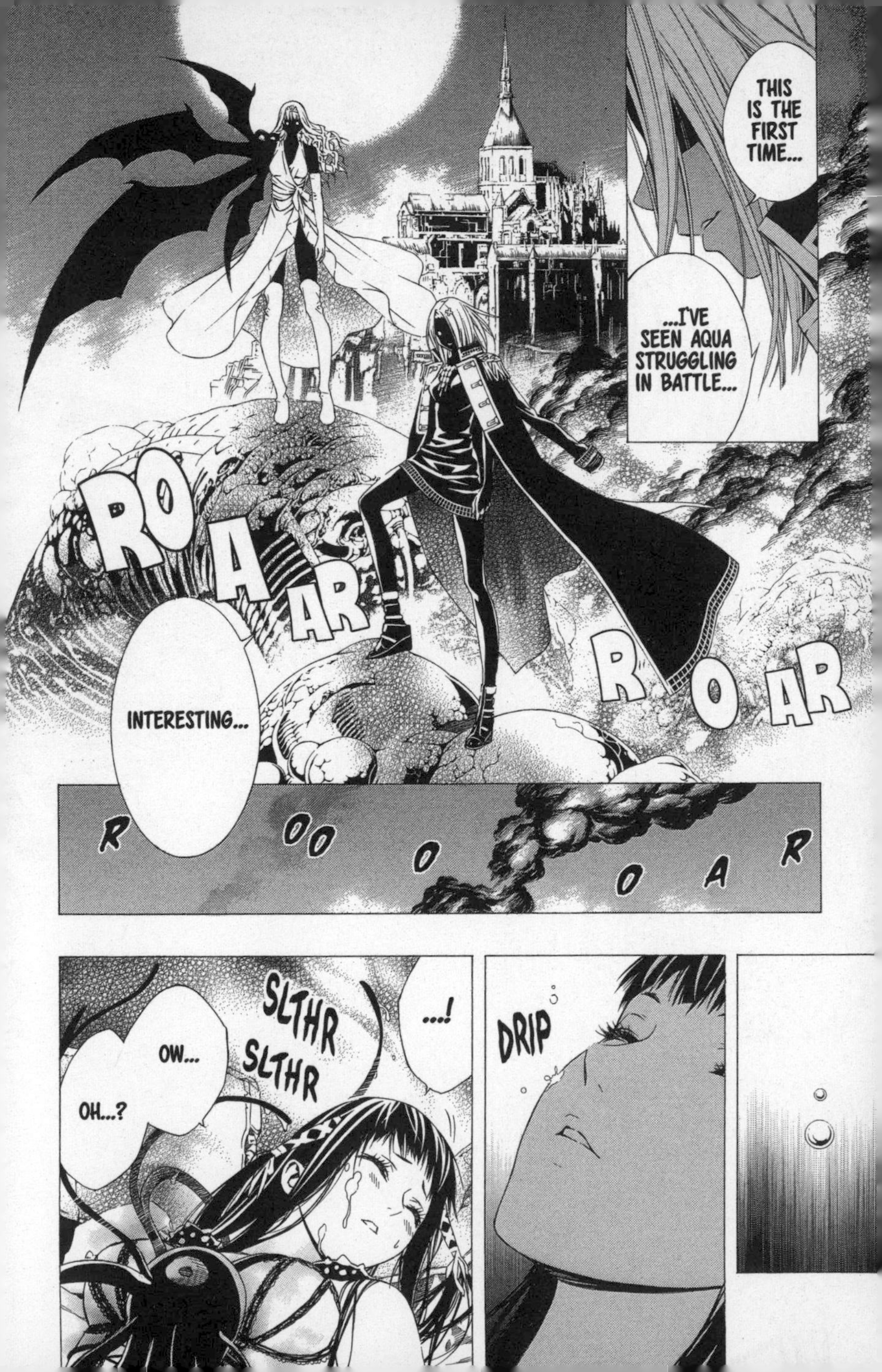
THIS IS THE FIRST TIME...
...I'VE SEEN AQUA STRUGGLING IN BATTLE...
ROAR
ROAR
INTERESTING...
ROOOOOAR
DRIP
...!
SLTHR SLTHR
OW...
OH...?

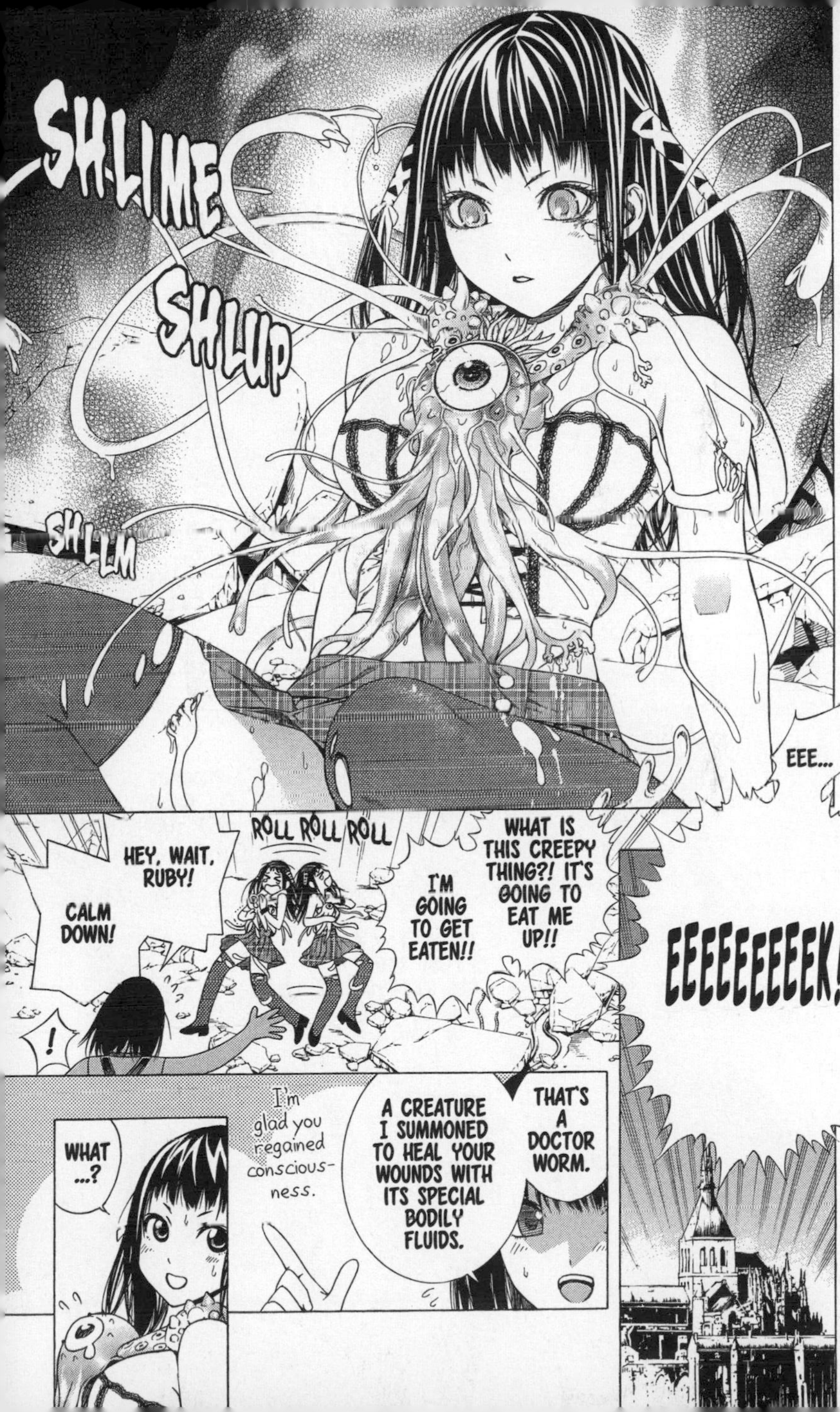
SHLIME
SHLUP
SHLLM
EEE...
EEEEEEEEEK!!
WHAT IS THIS CREEPY THING?! IT'S GOING TO EAT ME UP!!
I'M GOING TO GET EATEN!!
ROLL ROLL ROLL
HEY, WAIT, RUBY!
CALM DOWN!
!
THAT'S A DOCTOR WORM.
A CREATURE I SUMMONED TO HEAL YOUR WOUNDS WITH ITS SPECIAL BODILY FLUIDS.
I'm glad you regained conscious-ness.
WHAT ...?

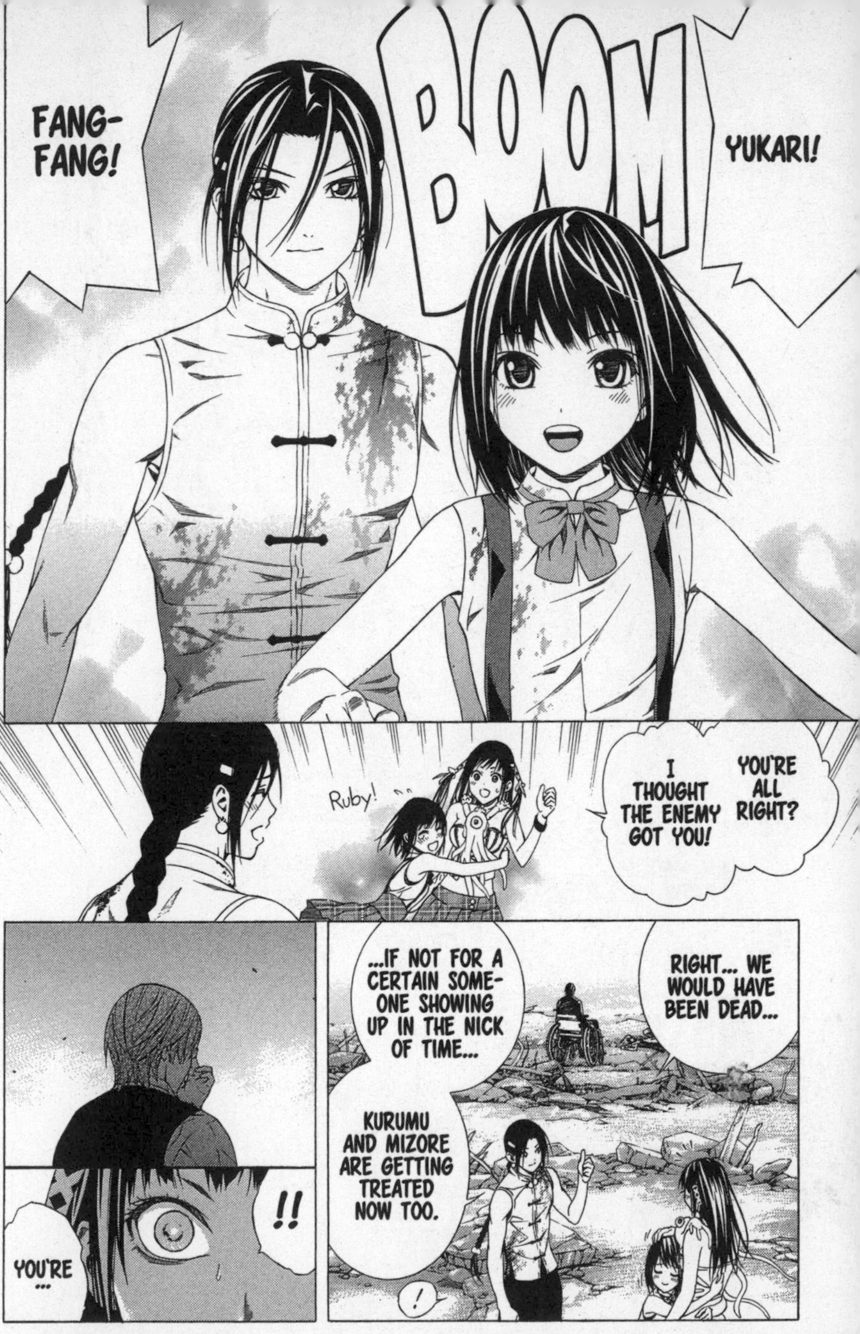
YUKARI!
BOOM
FANG-FANG!
YOU'RE ALL RIGHT?
I THOUGHT THE ENEMY GOT YOU!
Ruby!
RIGHT... WE WOULD HAVE BEEN DEAD...
...IF NOT FOR A CERTAIN SOME-ONE SHOWING UP IN THE NICK OF TIME...
KURUMU AND MIZORE ARE GETTING TREATED NOW TOO.
!
!!
YOU'RE ...

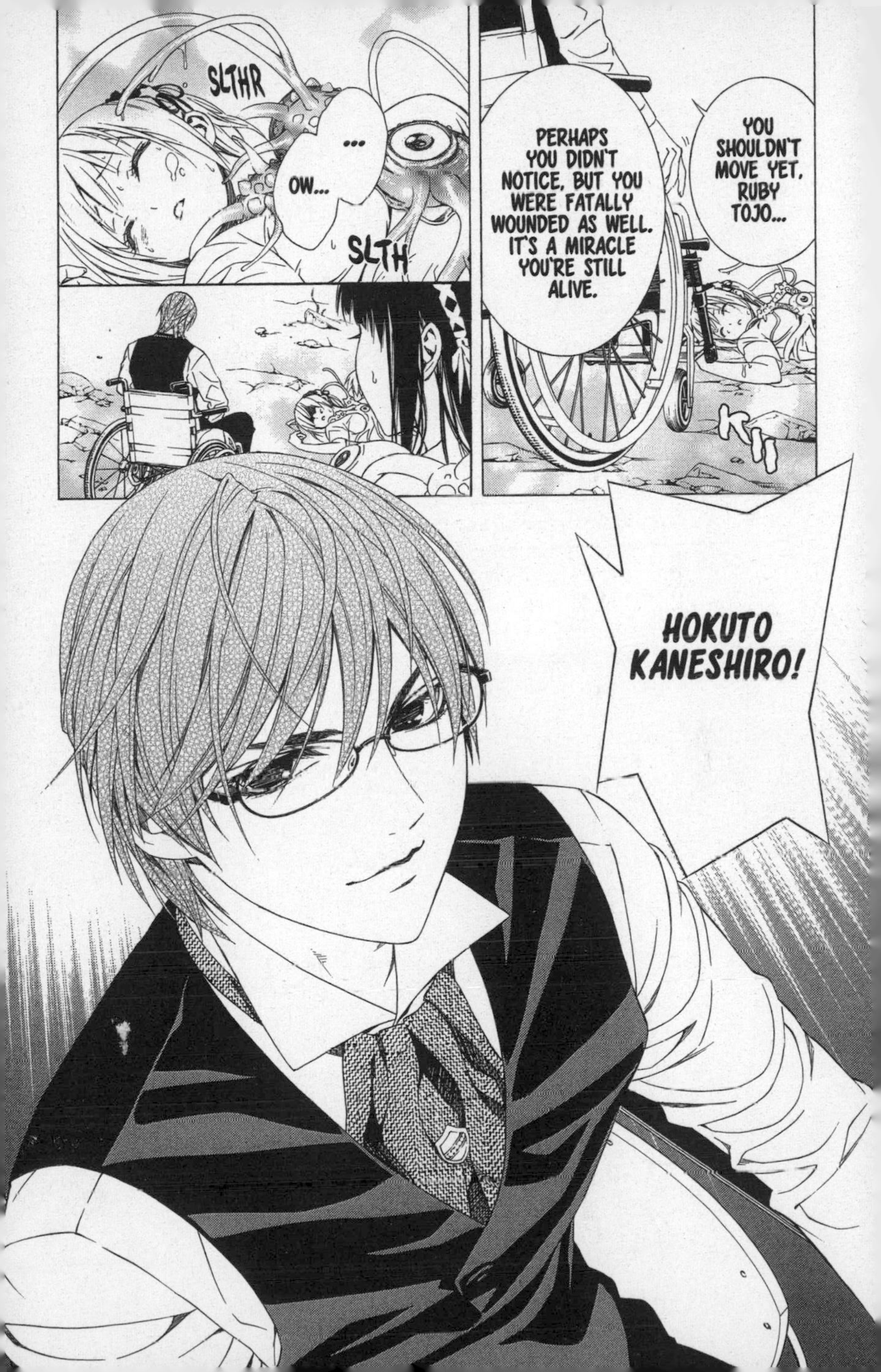
YOU SHOULDN'T MOVE YET, RUBY TOJO...
PERHAPS YOU DIDN'T NOTICE, BUT YOU WERE FATALLY WOUNDED AS WELL. IT'S A MIRACLE YOU'RE STILL ALIVE.
KII
SLTHR
...
OW...
SLTH
HOKUTO KANESHIRO!

56: Lost

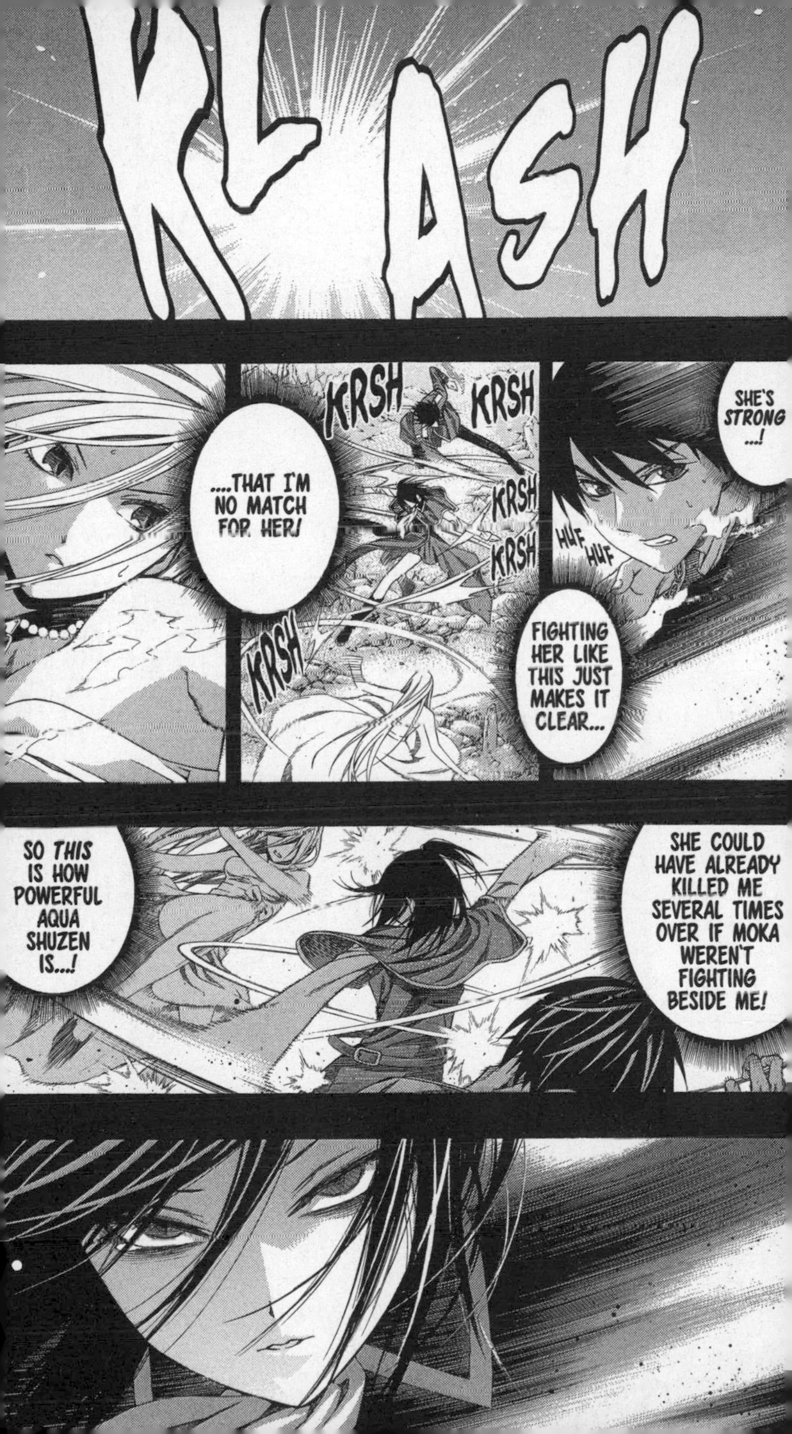
KLASH
SHE'S STRONG ...!
HUF HUF
FIGHTING HER LIKE THIS JUST MAKES IT CLEAR...
KRSH KRSH
KRSH
KRSH
KRSH
....THAT I'M NO MATCH FOR HER!
SHE COULD HAVE ALREADY KILLED ME SEVERAL TIMES OVER IF MOKA WEREN'T FIGHTING BESIDE ME!
SO THIS IS HOW POWERFUL AQUA SHUZEN IS...!

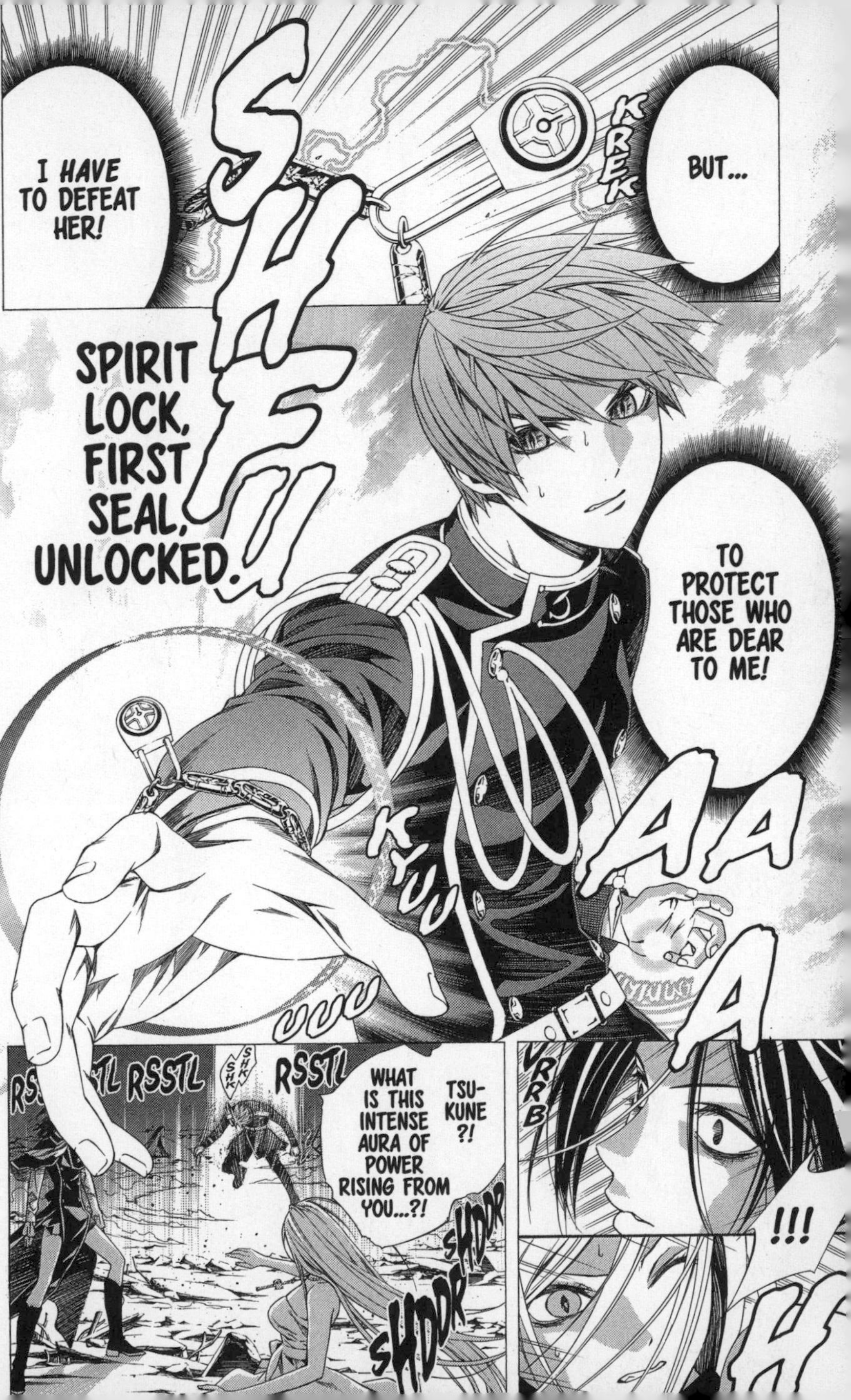
KREK
BUT...
I HAVE TO DEFEAT HER!
SPIRIT LOCK, FIRST SEAL, UNLOCKED.
TO PROTECT THOSE WHO ARE DEAR TO ME!
AA
A
KYUUU
VRRB
!!!
RSSTL
RSSTL
SHK SHK
TSU-KUNE?!
WHAT IS THIS INTENSE AURA OF POWER RISING FROM YOU...?!
SHDDR
SHDDR

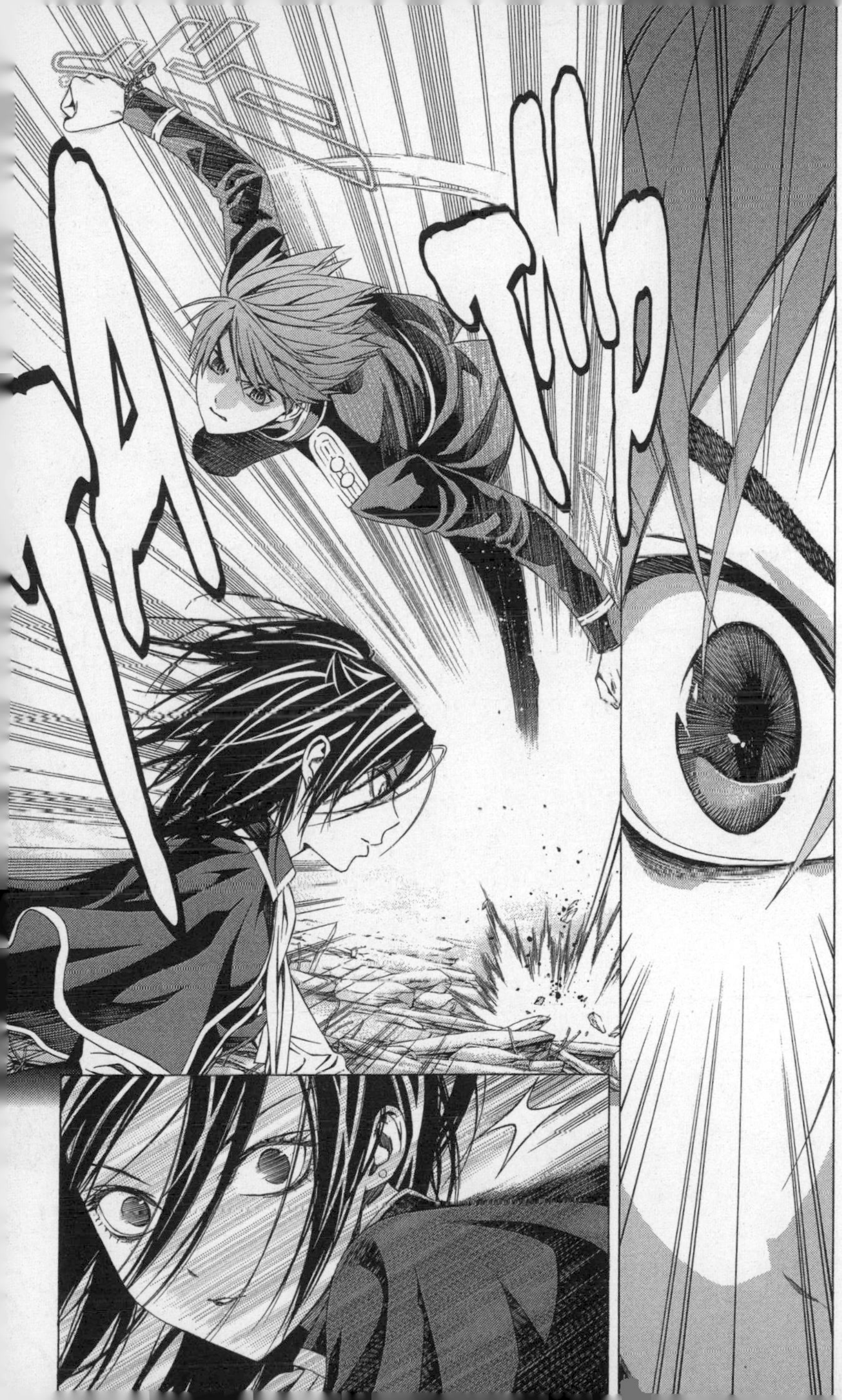
TMP

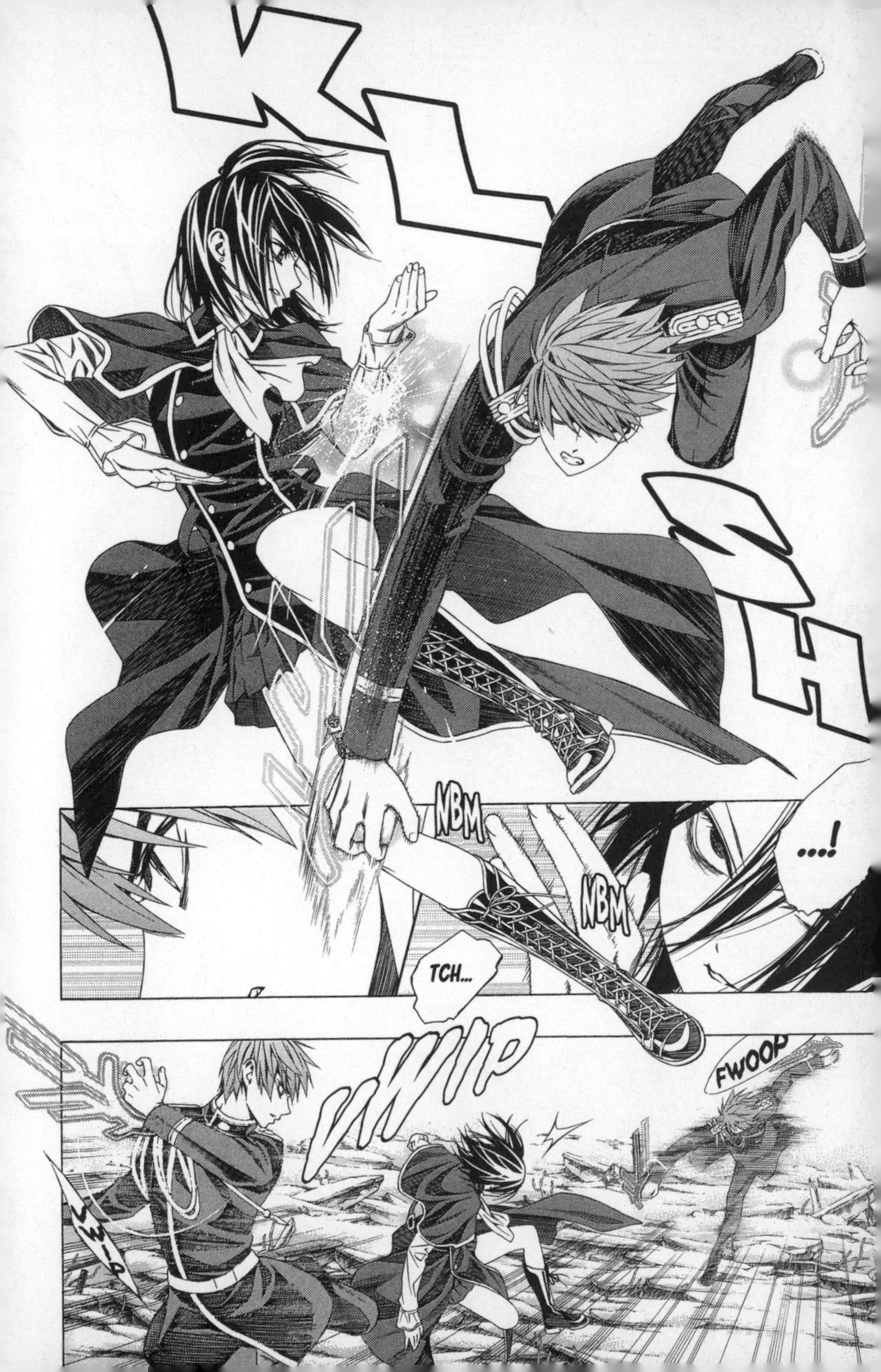
SH
...!
NBM
NBM
TCH...
FWOOP
WIP
VWIP

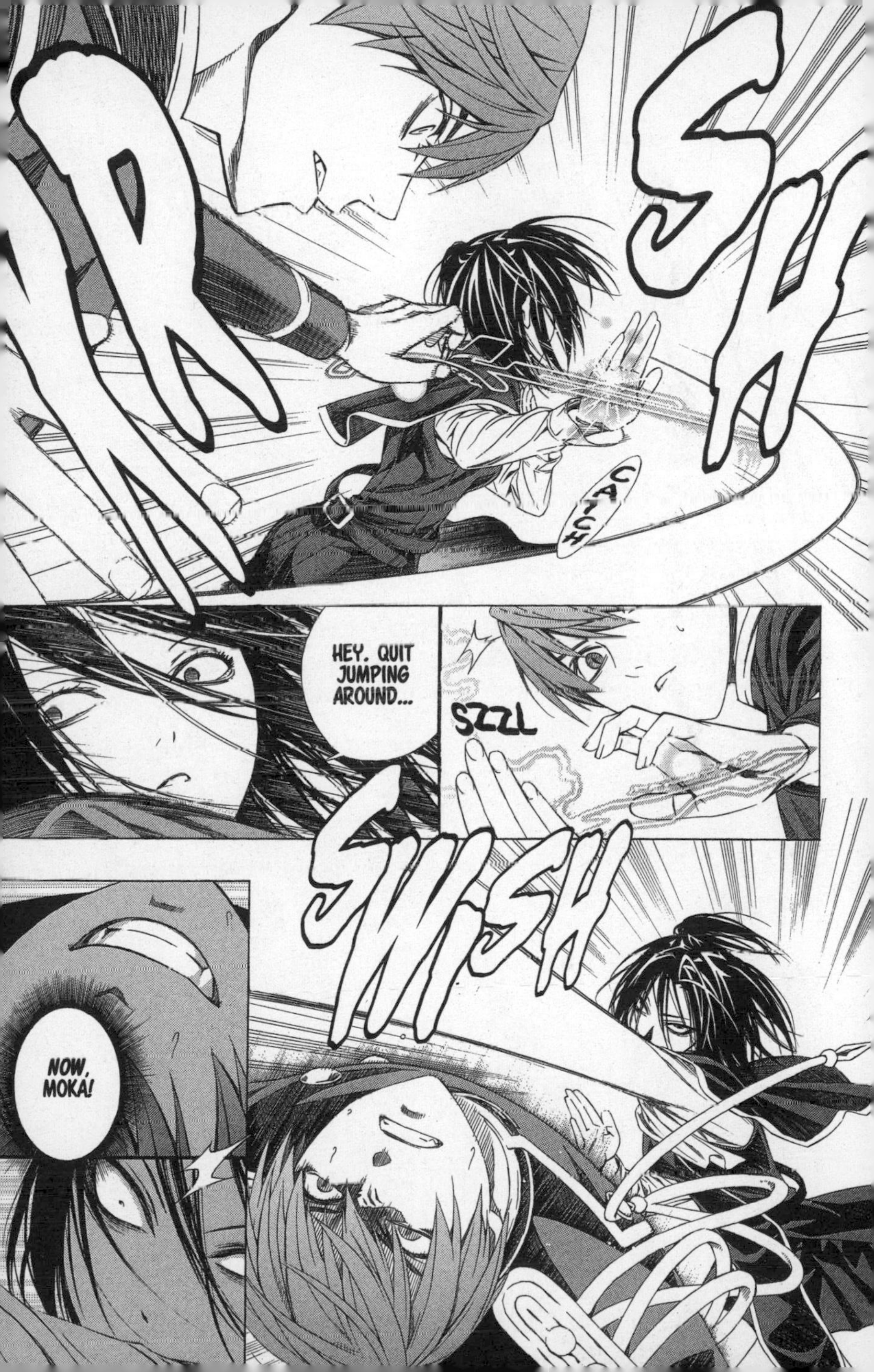
SHA
CATCH
SZZL
HEY. QUIT JUMPING AROUND...
SWISH
NOW, MOKA!

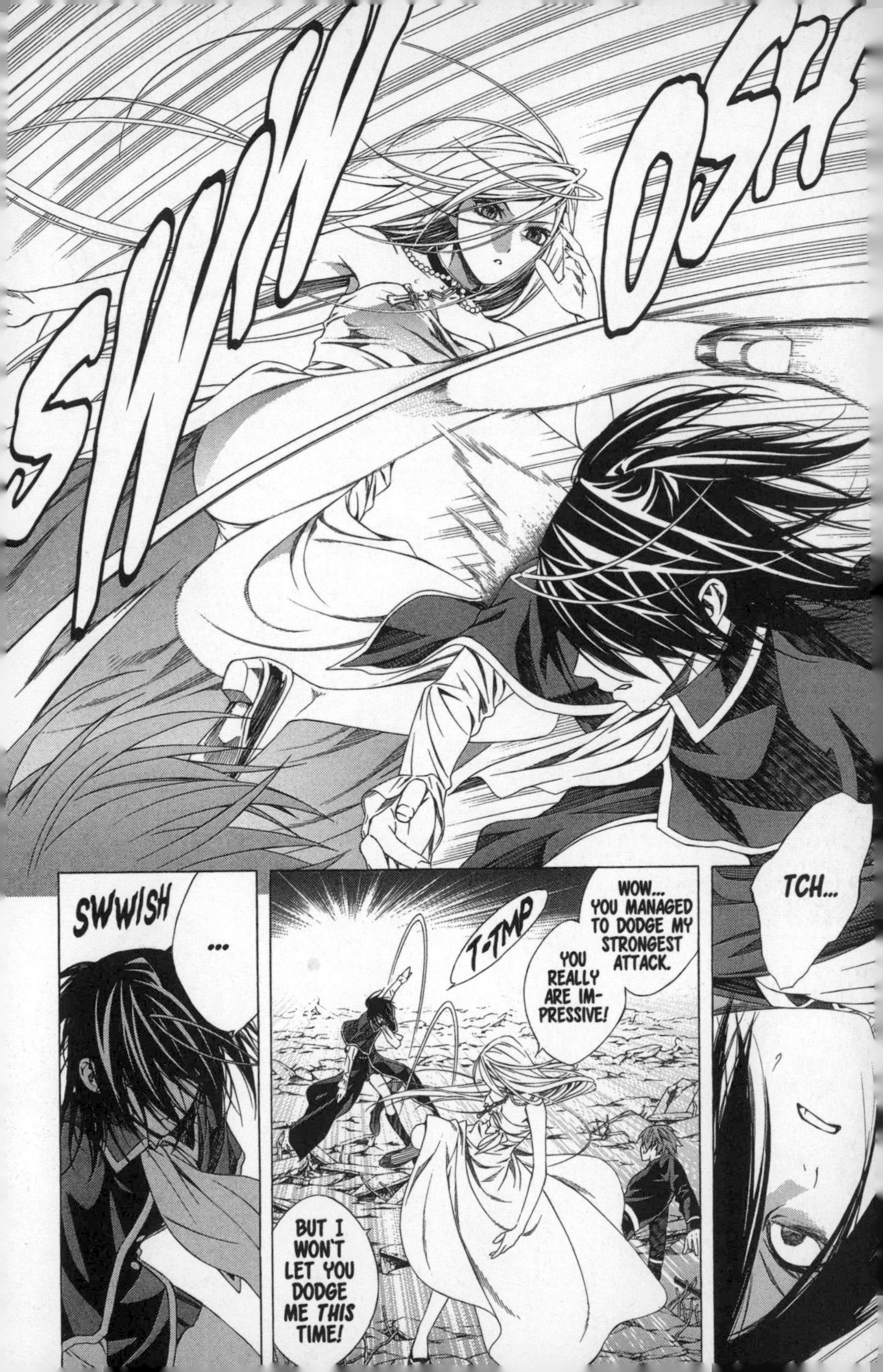
SWOOSH
TCH...
WOW... YOU MANAGED TO DODGE MY STRONGEST ATTACK.
YOU REALLY ARE IM-PRESSIVE!
T-TMP
BUT I WON'T LET YOU DODGE ME *THIS* TIME!
SWWISH
...

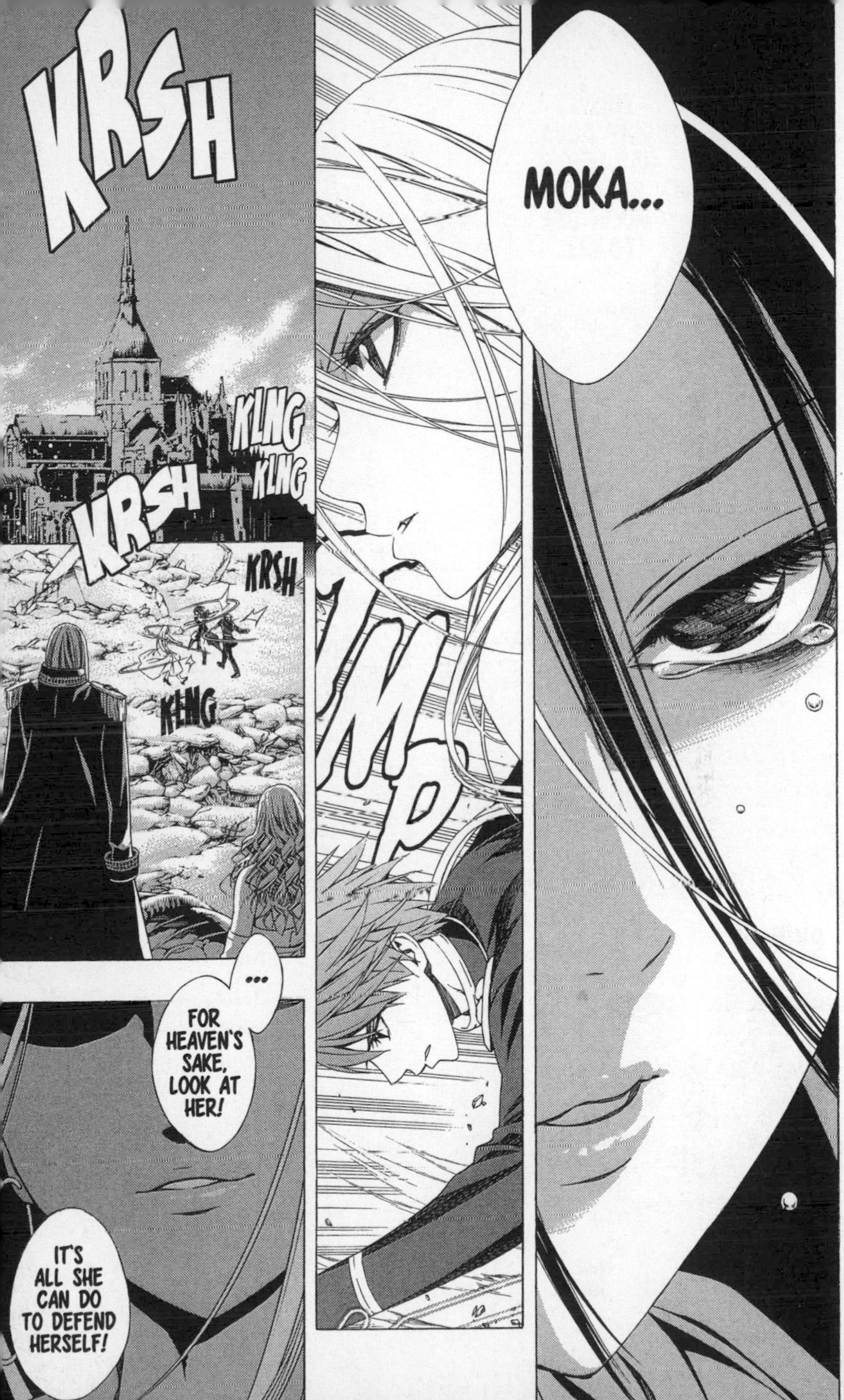
MOKA...
KRSH
KLNG
KLNG
KRSH
KRSH
KLNG
...
FOR HEAVEN'S SAKE, LOOK AT HER!
IT'S ALL SHE CAN DO TO DEFEND HERSELF!

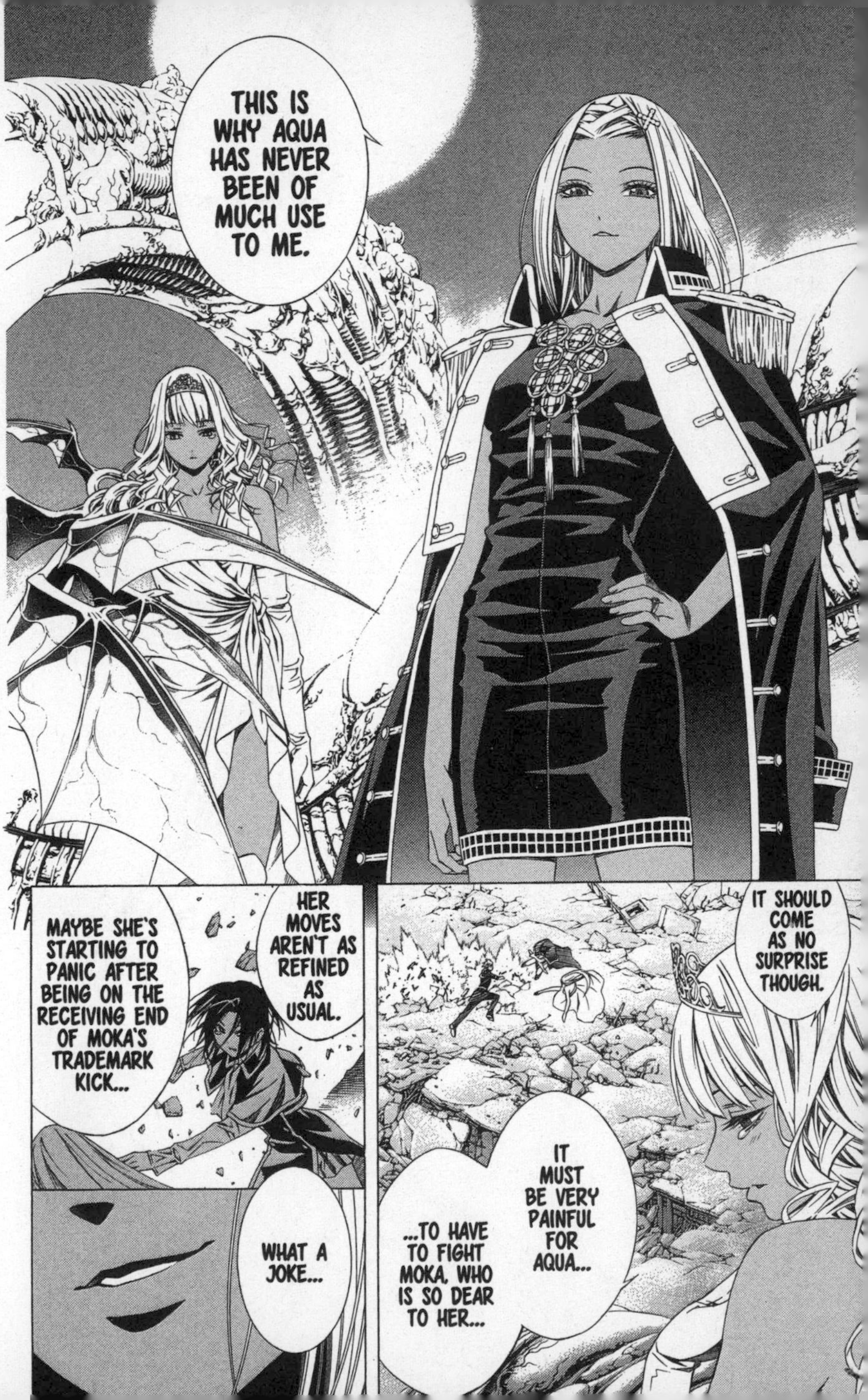
THIS IS WHY AQUA HAS NEVER BEEN OF MUCH USE TO ME.
IT SHOULD COME AS NO SURPRISE THOUGH.
IT MUST BE VERY PAINFUL FOR AQUA...
...TO HAVE TO FIGHT MOKA, WHO IS SO DEAR TO HER...
HER MOVES AREN'T AS REFINED AS USUAL.
MAYBE SHE'S STARTING TO PANIC AFTER BEING ON THE RECEIVING END OF MOKA'S TRADEMARK KICK...
WHAT A JOKE...

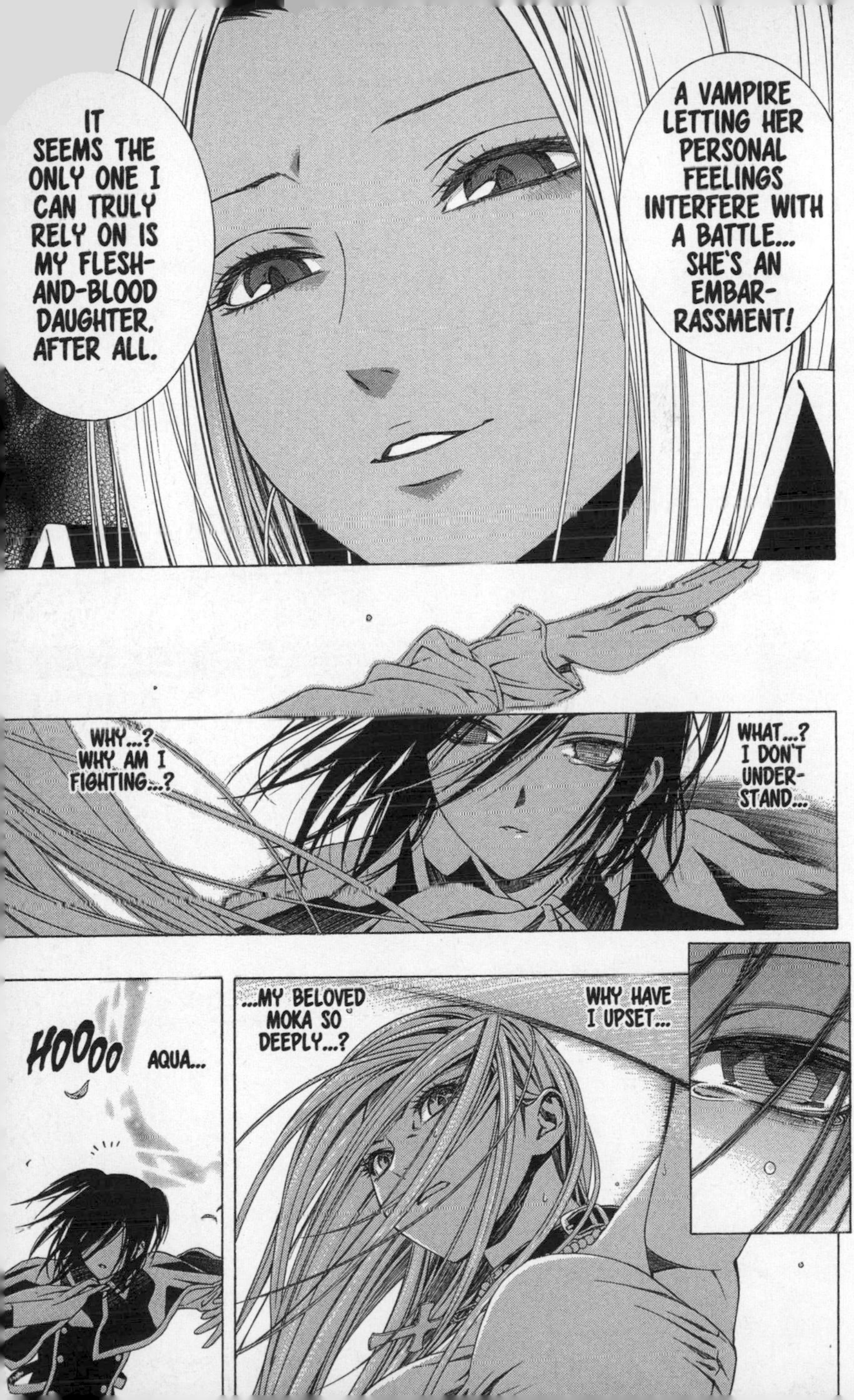
A VAMPIRE LETTING HER PERSONAL FEELINGS INTERFERE WITH A BATTLE... SHE'S AN EMBAR-RASSMENT!
IT SEEMS THE ONLY ONE I CAN TRULY RELY ON IS MY FLESH-AND-BLOOD DAUGHTER, AFTER ALL.
WHAT...? I DON'T UNDER-STAND...
WHY...? WHY AM I FIGHTING...?
WHY HAVE I UPSET...
...MY BELOVED MOKA SO DEEPLY...?
AQUA...
HOOoo

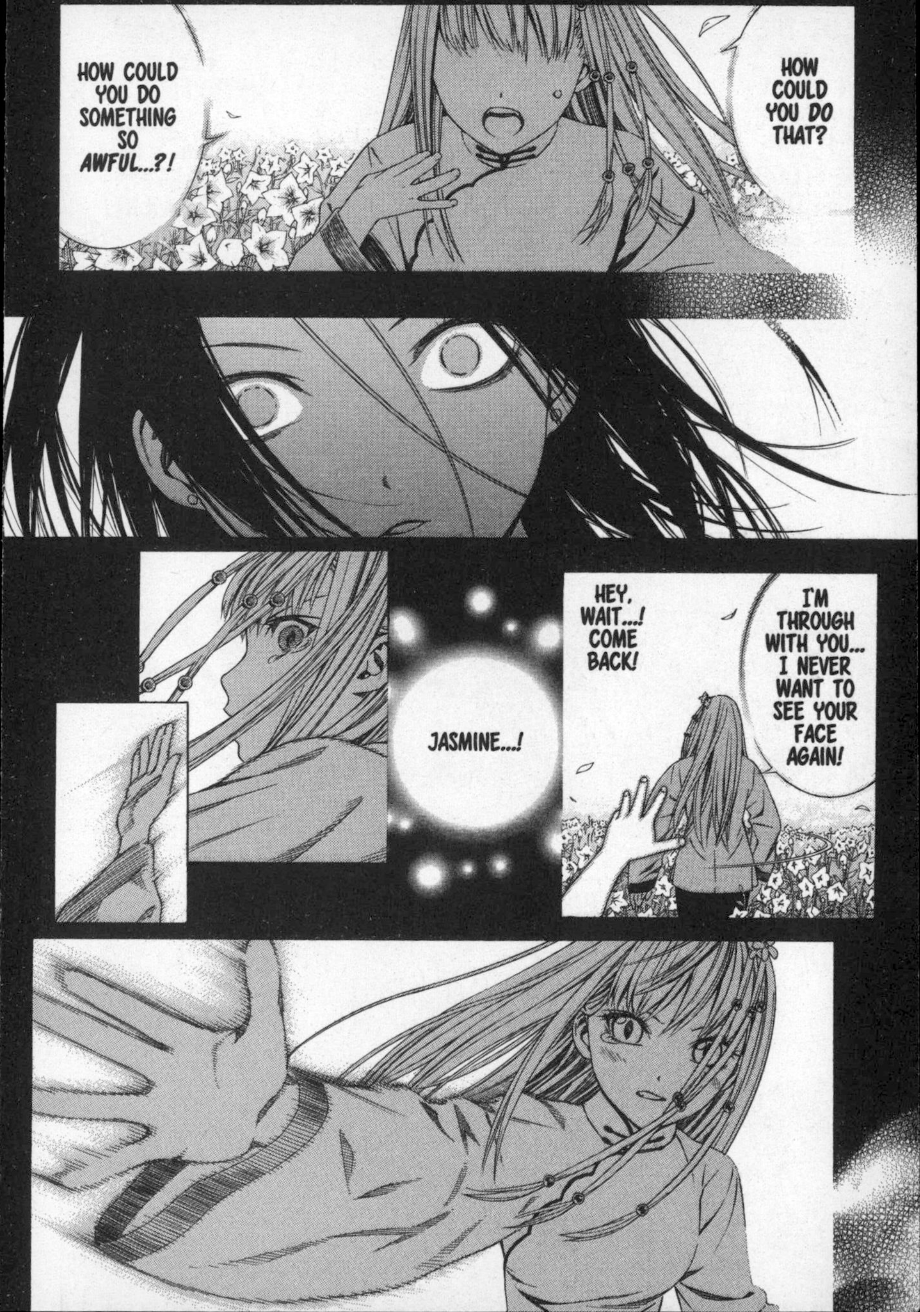
HOW COULD YOU DO THAT?
HOW COULD YOU DO SOMETHING SO AWFUL...?!
I'M THROUGH WITH YOU... I NEVER WANT TO SEE YOUR FACE AGAIN!
HEY, WAIT...! COME BACK!
JASMINE...!

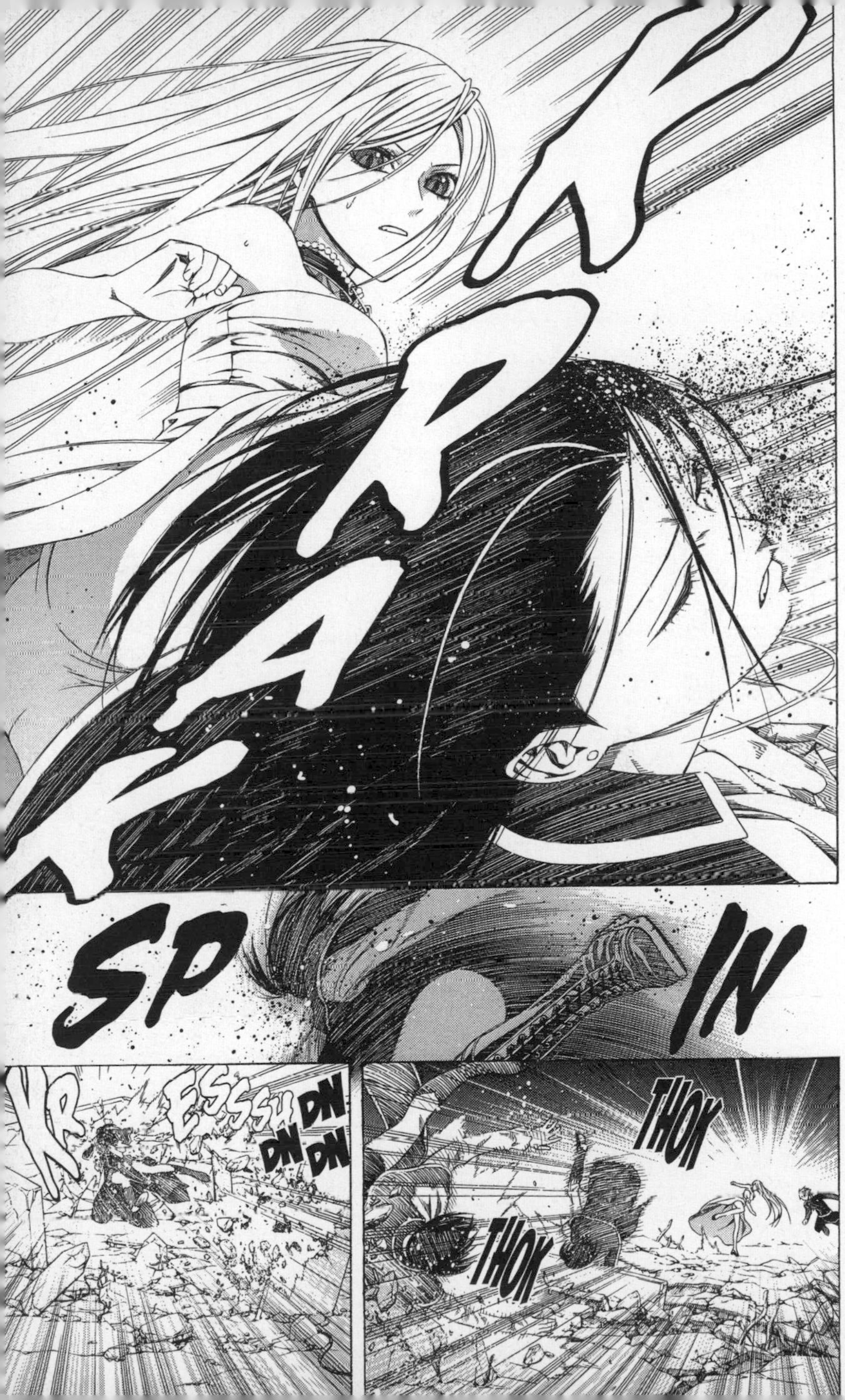

KRAK
SPIN
THOK
THOK
DN DN DN DN

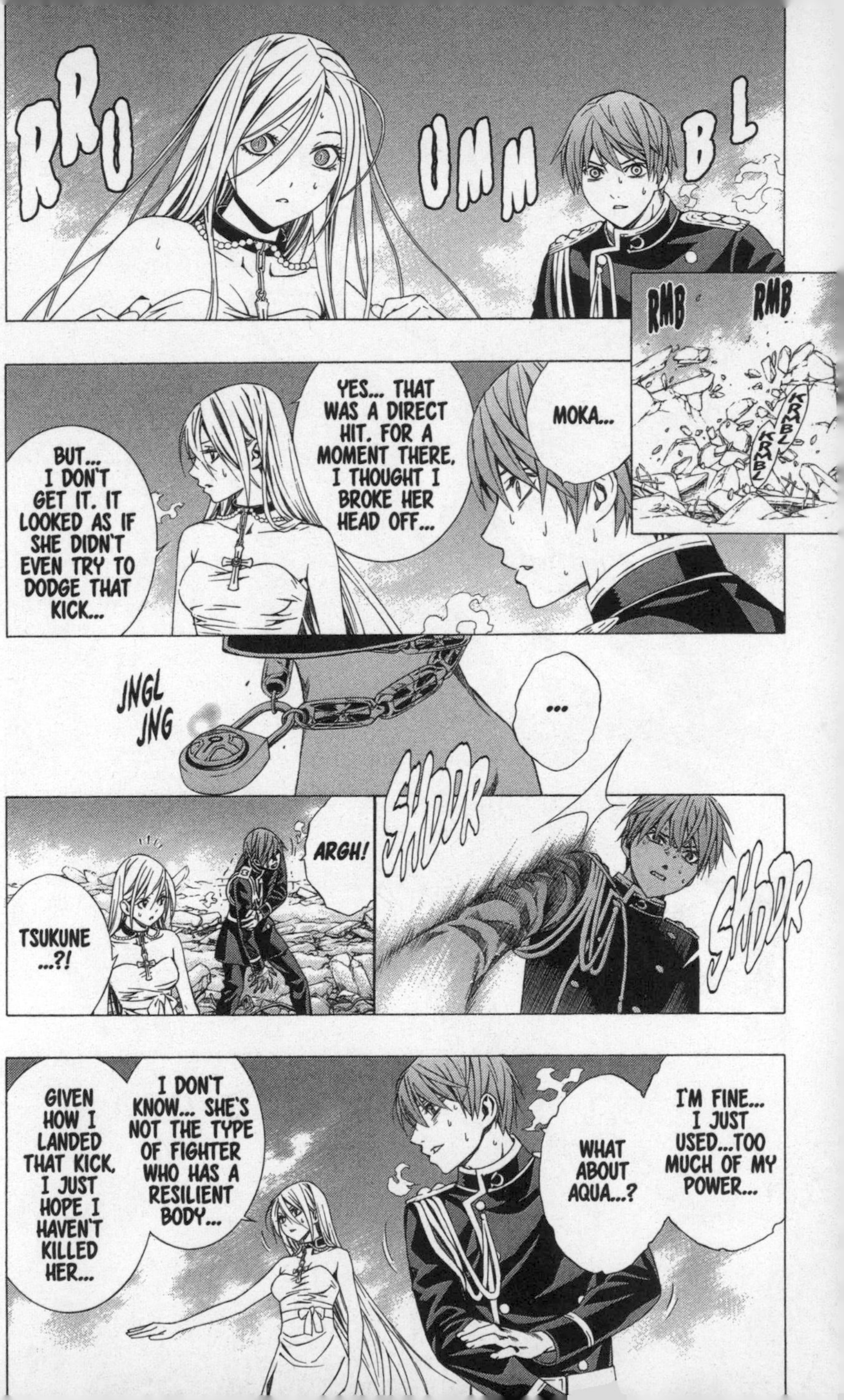
RRUMMBL
RMB RMB
KRMBL KRMBL
MOKA...
YES... THAT WAS A DIRECT HIT. FOR A MOMENT THERE, I THOUGHT I BROKE HER HEAD OFF...
BUT... I DON'T GET IT. IT LOOKED AS IF SHE DIDN'T EVEN TRY TO DODGE THAT KICK...
JNGL JNG
...
SHDDR
SHDDR
ARGH!
TSUKUNE ...?!
I'M FINE... I JUST USED...TOO MUCH OF MY POWER...
WHAT ABOUT AQUA...?
I DON'T KNOW... SHE'S NOT THE TYPE OF FIGHTER WHO HAS A RESILIENT BODY...
GIVEN HOW I LANDED THAT KICK, I JUST HOPE I HAVEN'T KILLED HER...

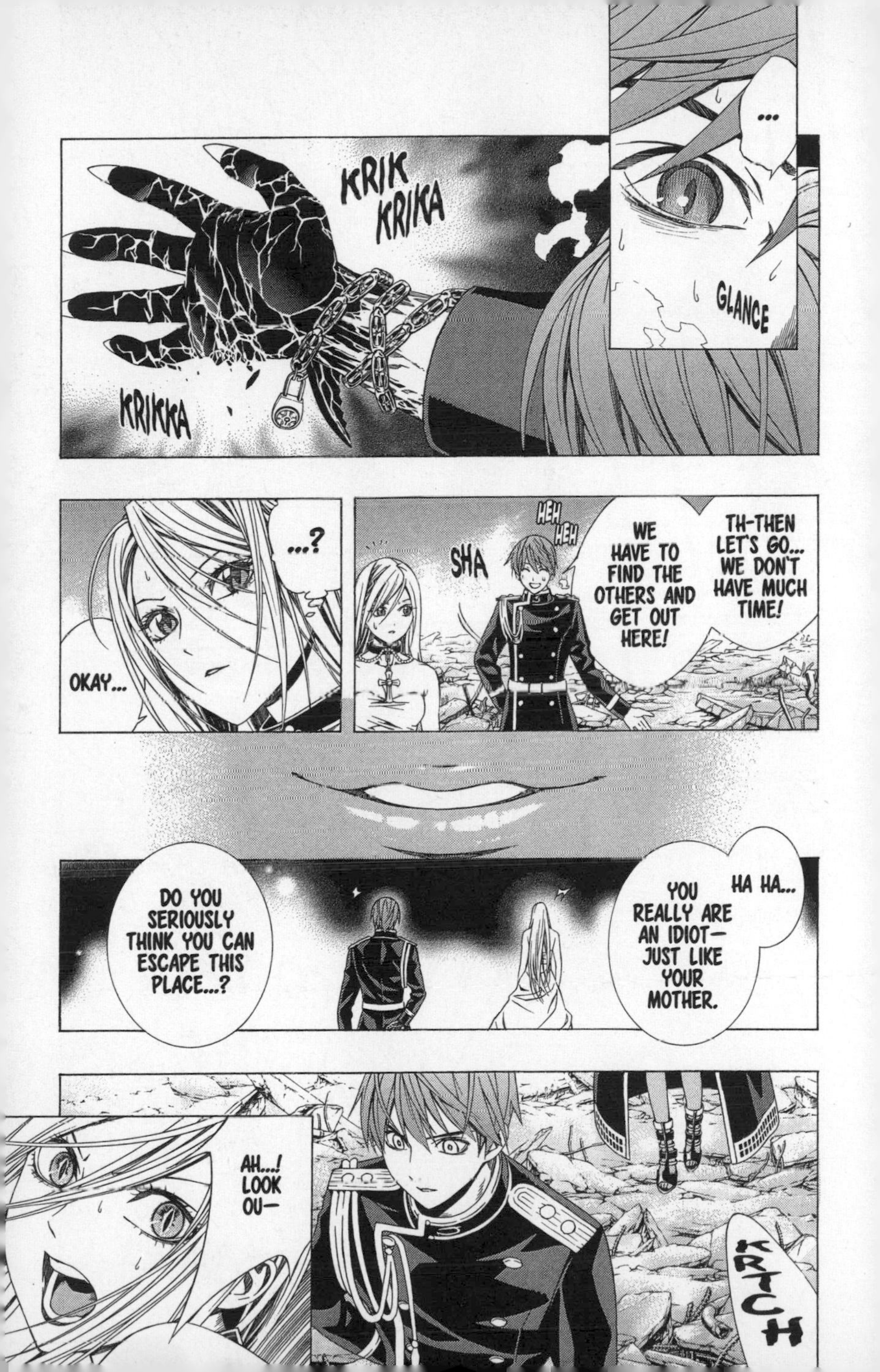
...
GLANCE
KRIK KRIKA
KRIKKA
HEH HEH
SHA
TH-THEN LET'S GO... WE DON'T HAVE MUCH TIME!
WE HAVE TO FIND THE OTHERS AND GET OUT HERE!
...?
OKAY...
HA HA...
YOU REALLY ARE AN IDIOT— JUST LIKE YOUR MOTHER.
DO YOU SERIOUSLY THINK YOU CAN ESCAPE THIS PLACE...?
KRTCH
AH...! LOOK OU—

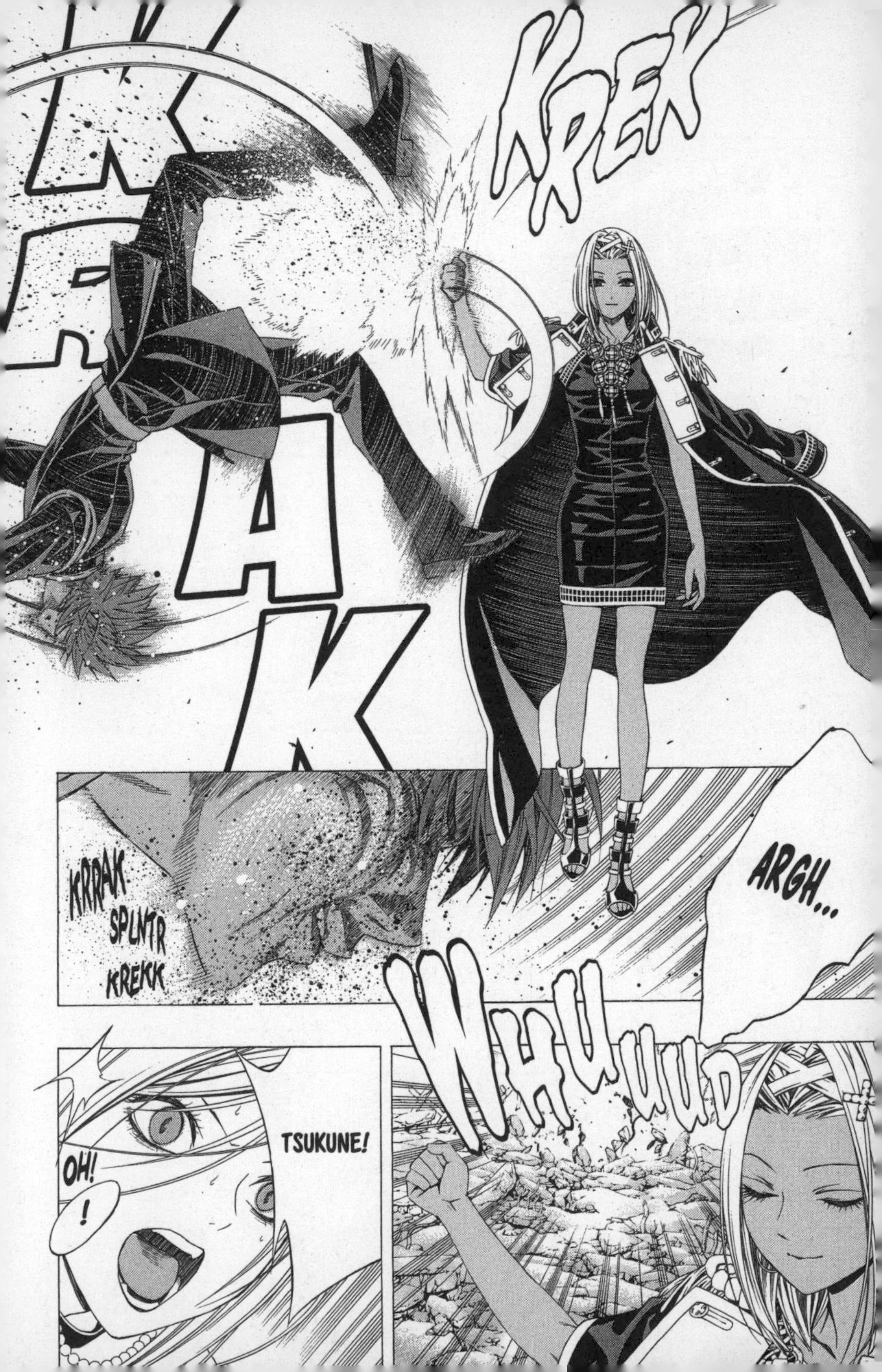
KREK
ARGH...
KRRAK
SPLNTR
KREKK
WHUUUD
TSUKUNE!
OH!
!

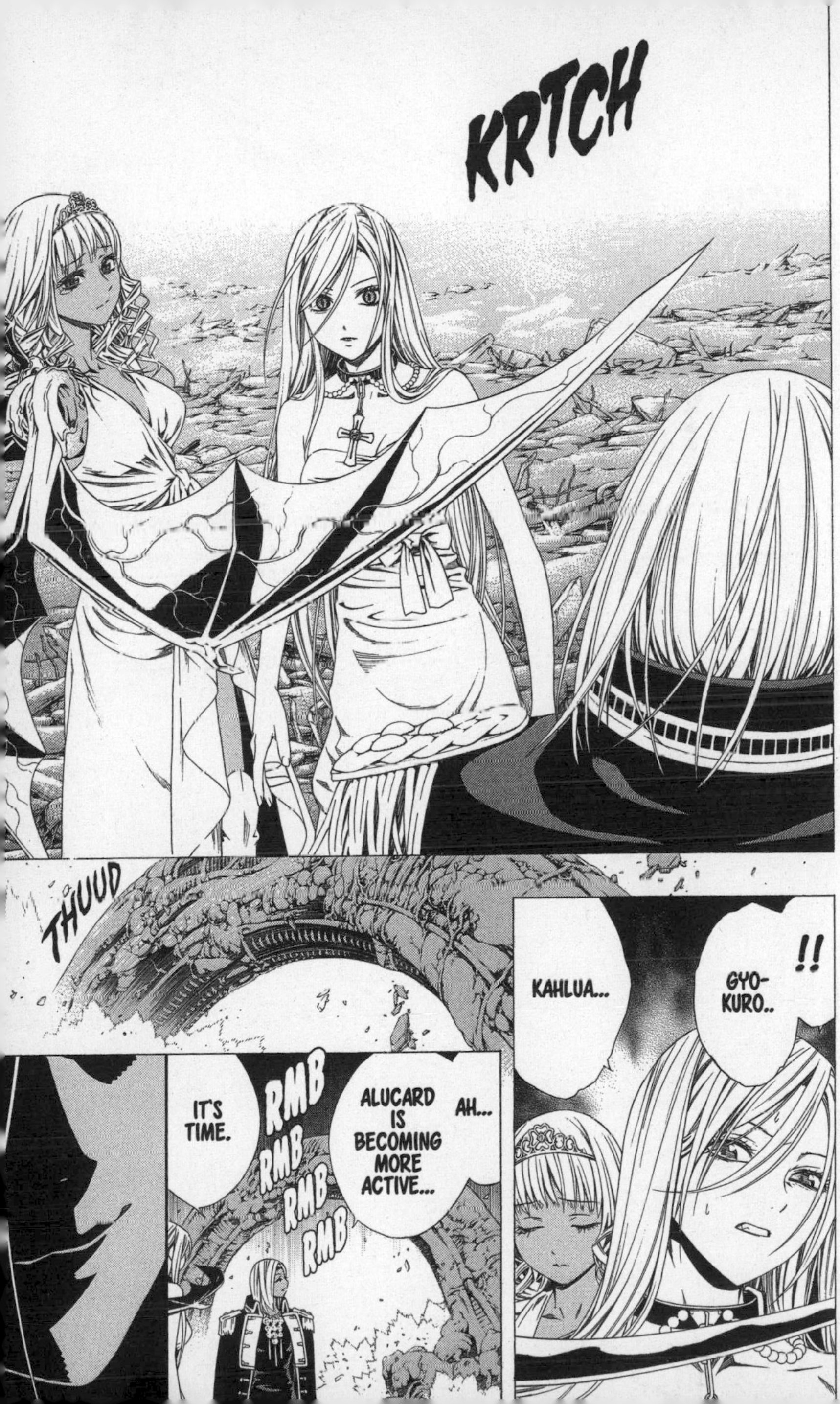
KRTCH
THUUD
!!
GYO-KURO..
KAHLUA...
AH...
ALUCARD IS BECOMING MORE ACTIVE...
RMB RMB RMB RMB RMB
IT'S TIME.

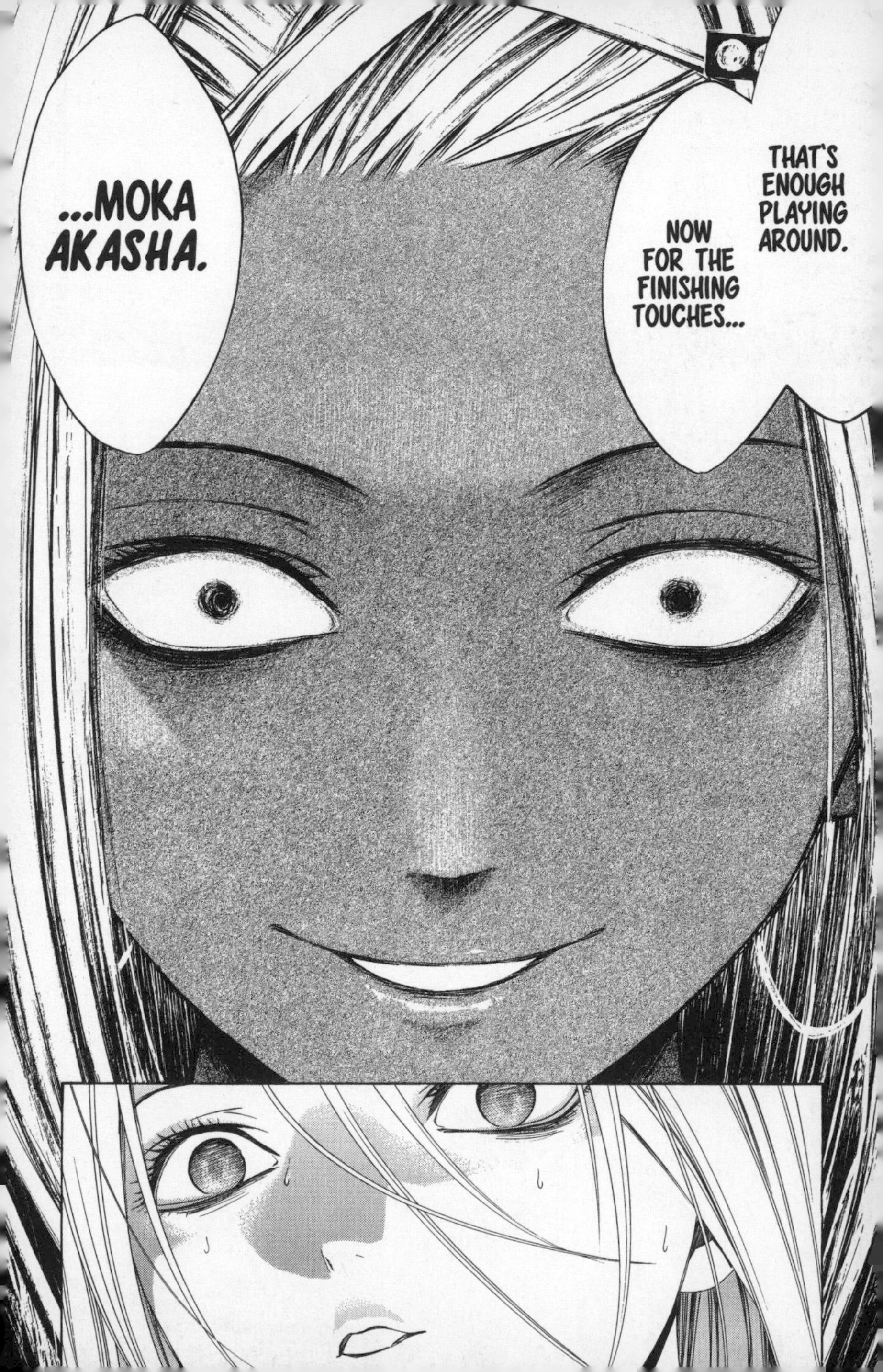
THAT'S ENOUGH PLAYING AROUND.
NOW FOR THE FINISHING TOUCHES...
...MOKA AKASHA.

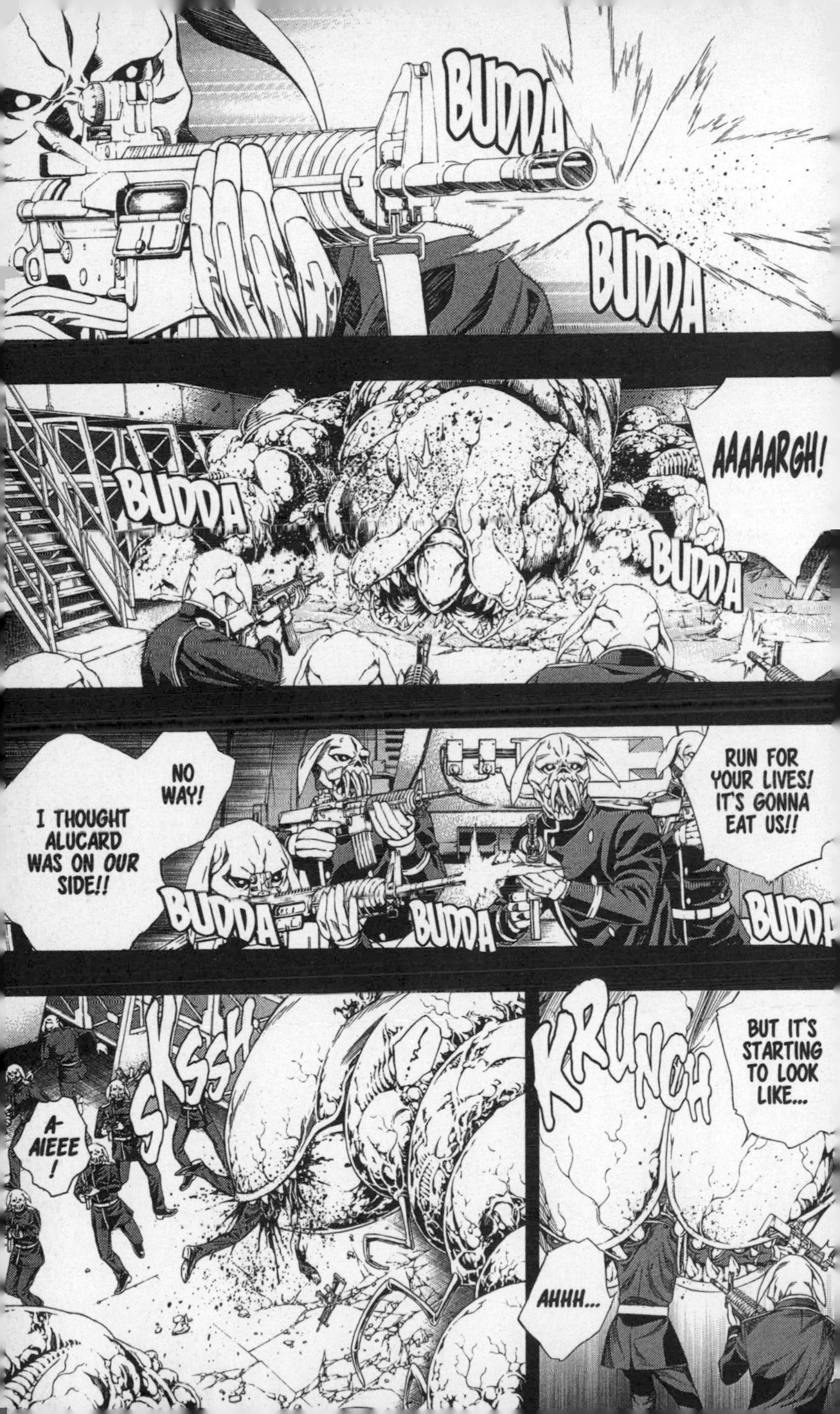
BUDDA
BUDDA
AAAAARGH!
BUDDA
BUDDA
RUN FOR YOUR LIVES! IT'S GONNA EAT US!!
BUDD
NO WAY!
I THOUGHT ALUCARD WAS ON OUR SIDE!!
BUDDA
BUDDA
BUT IT'S STARTING TO LOOK LIKE...
KRUNCH
AHHH...
SKSSH
A-AIEEE!

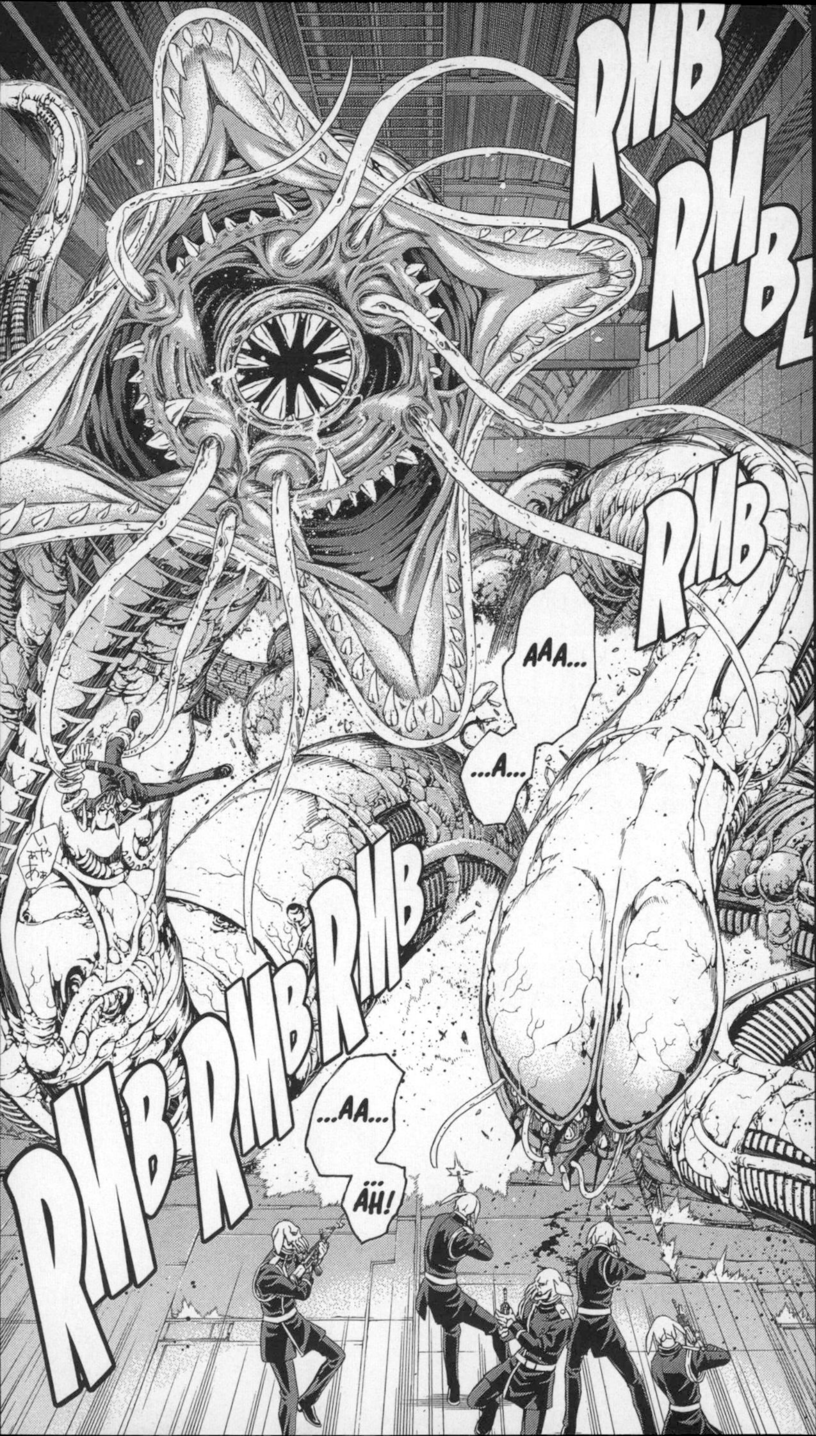
RMB
RMBL
RMB
AAA...
...A...
...AA...
ÄH!
RMB RMB RMB

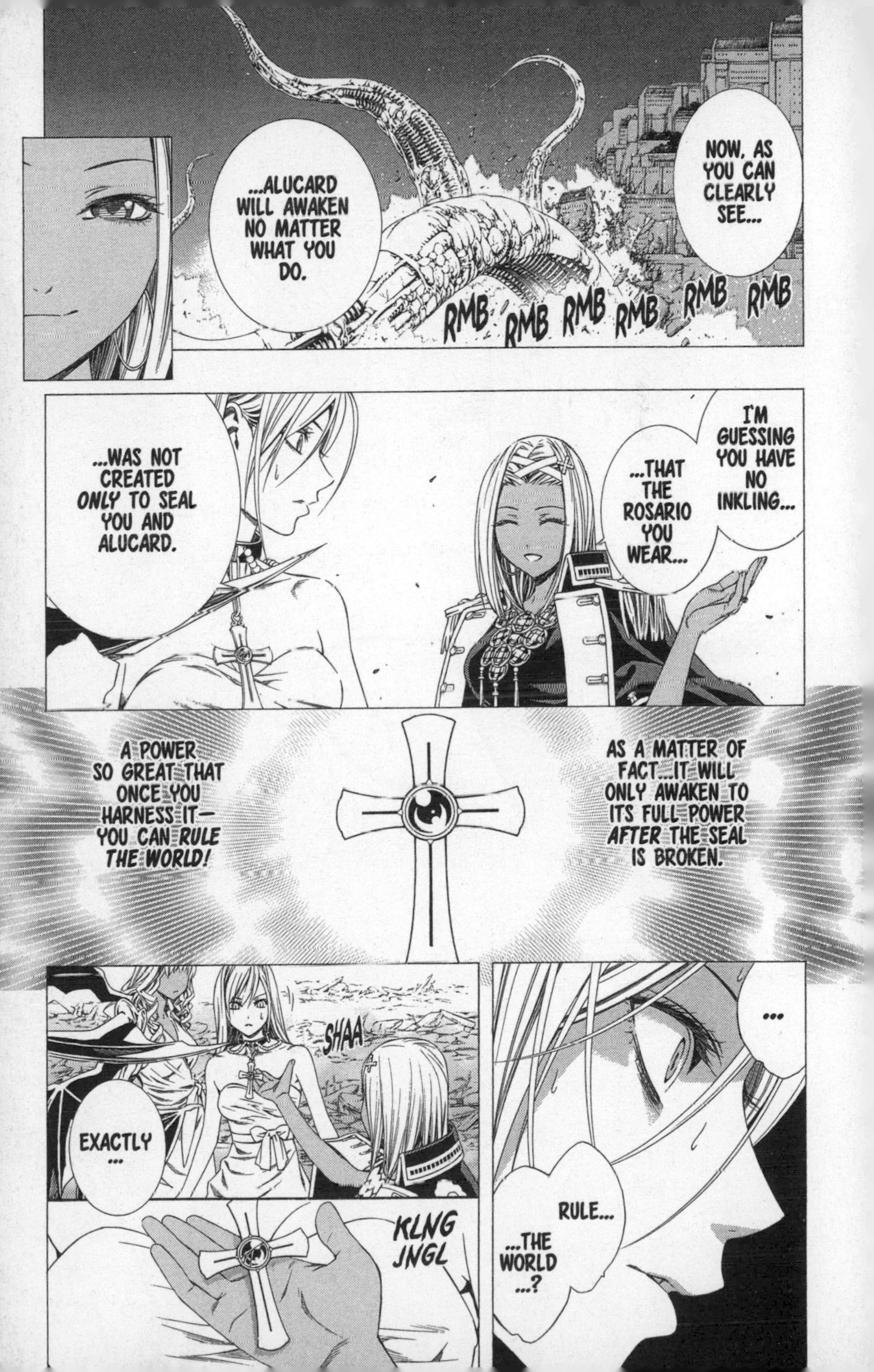
NOW, AS YOU CAN CLEARLY SEE...
RMB RMB RMB RMB RMB RMB
...ALUCARD WILL AWAKEN NO MATTER WHAT YOU DO.
I'M GUESSING YOU HAVE NO INKLING...
...THAT THE ROSARIO YOU WEAR...
...WAS NOT CREATED ONLY TO SEAL YOU AND ALUCARD.
AS A MATTER OF FACT...IT WILL ONLY AWAKEN TO ITS FULL POWER AFTER THE SEAL IS BROKEN.
A POWER SO GREAT THAT ONCE YOU HARNESS IT—YOU CAN RULE THE WORLD!
...
RULE...
...THE WORLD ...?
SHAA
EXACTLY ...
KLNG JNGL

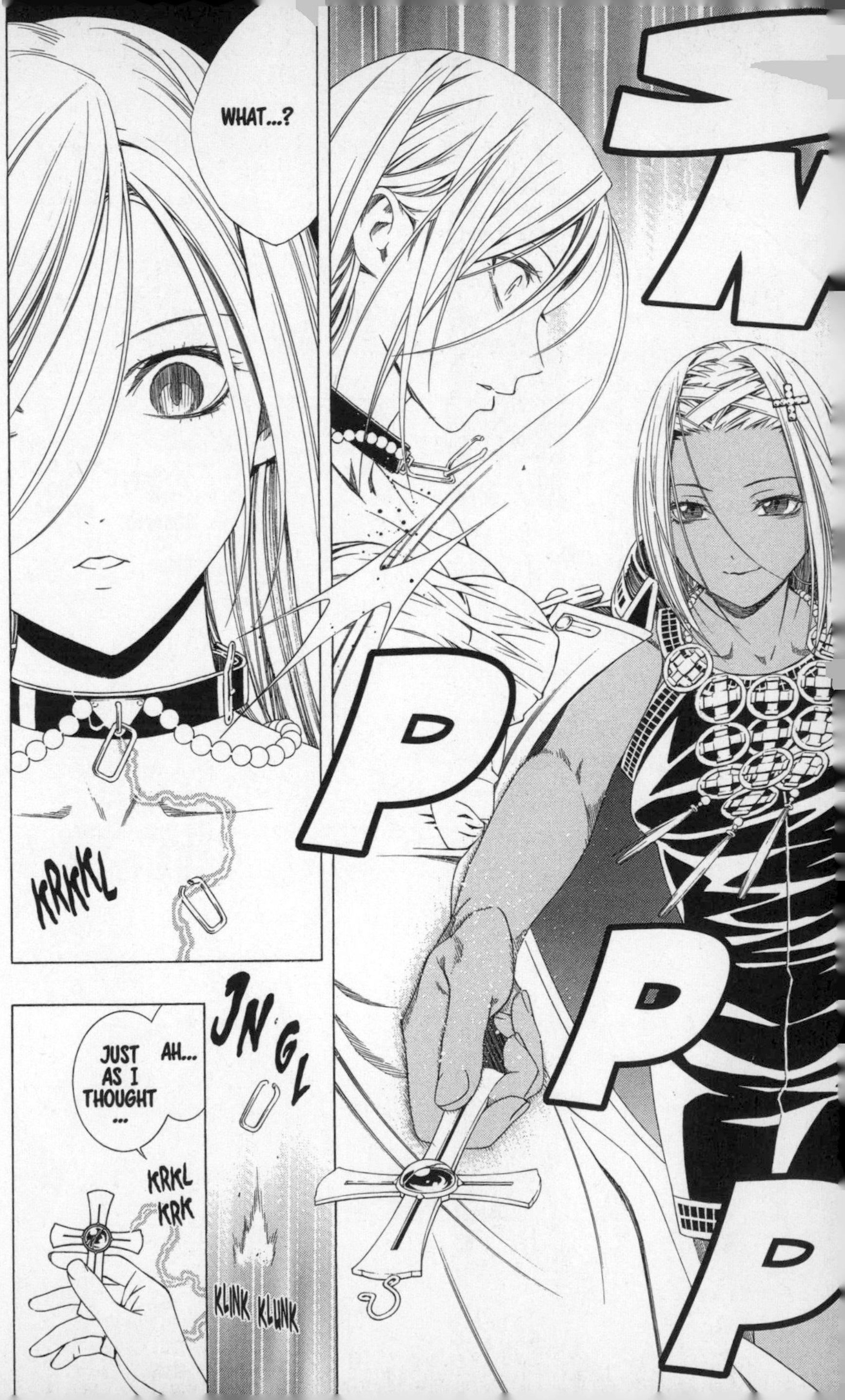
PPPP
JNGL
KLINK KLUNK
WHAT...?
KRKKL
AH...
JUST AS I THOUGHT ...
KRKL KRK

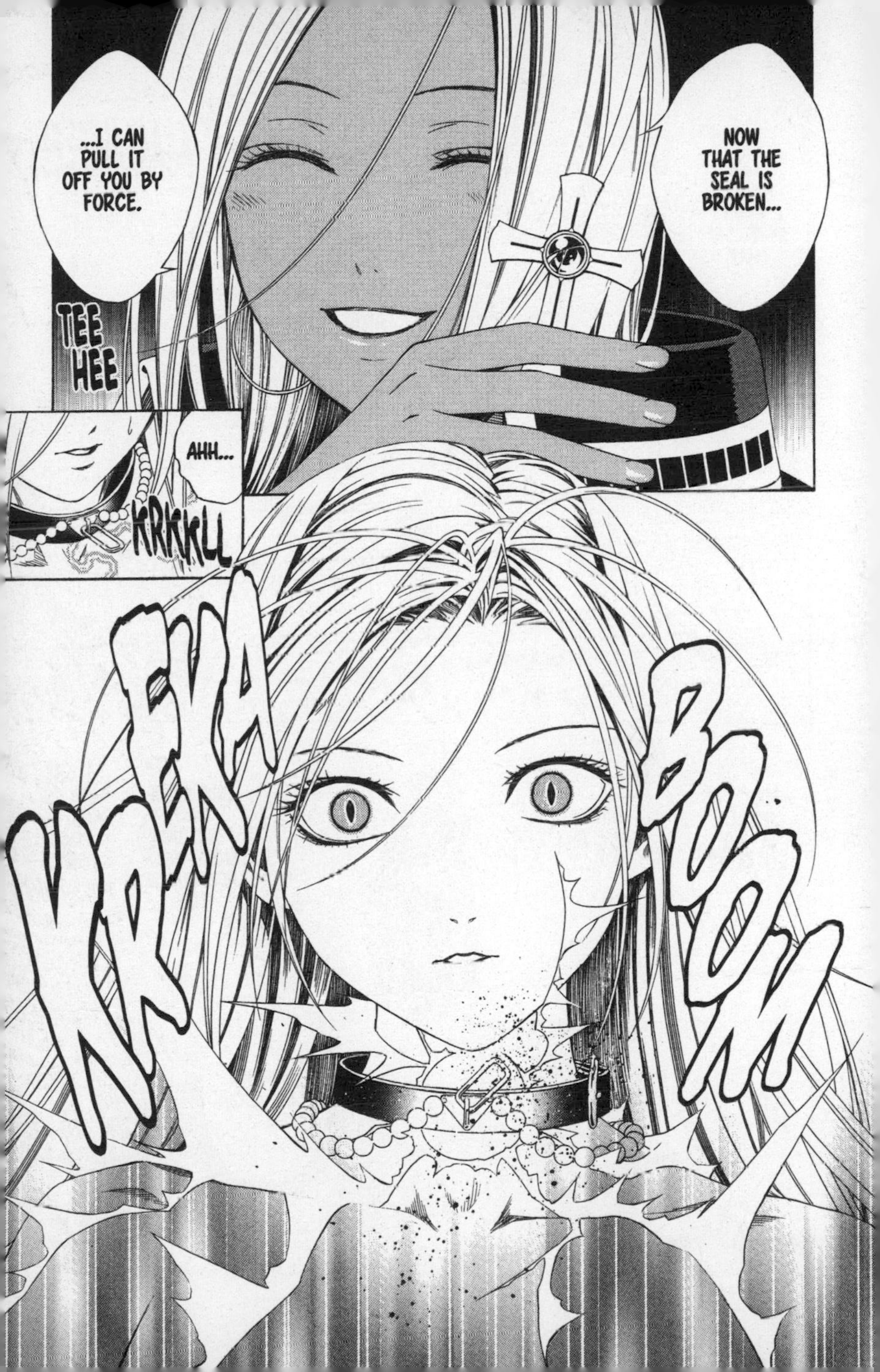
NOW THAT THE SEAL IS BROKEN...
...I CAN PULL IT OFF YOU BY FORCE.
TEE HEE
AHH...
KRKKLL
KREKA BOOM

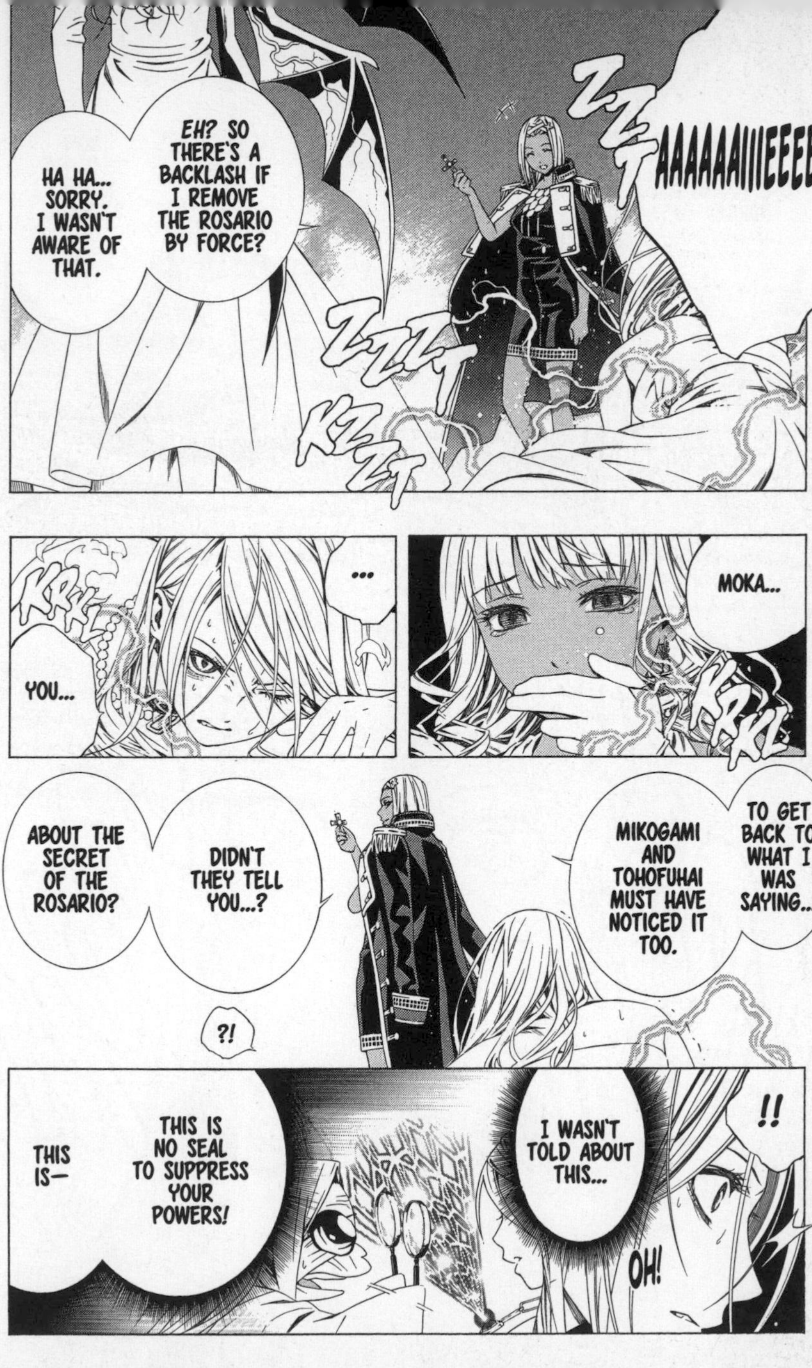
ZZZT
AAAAAIIIEEEE!
EH? SO THERE'S A BACKLASH IF I REMOVE THE ROSARIO BY FORCE?
HA HA... SORRY. I WASN'T AWARE OF THAT.
ZZZT
KZZZT
MOKA...
KRKL
...
KRKL
YOU...
TO GET BACK TO WHAT I WAS SAYING...
MIKOGAMI AND TOHOFUHAI MUST HAVE NOTICED IT TOO.
DIDN'T THEY TELL YOU...?
ABOUT THE SECRET OF THE ROSARIO?
?!
!!
I WASN'T TOLD ABOUT THIS...
OH!
THIS IS NO SEAL TO SUPPRESS YOUR POWERS!
THIS IS—

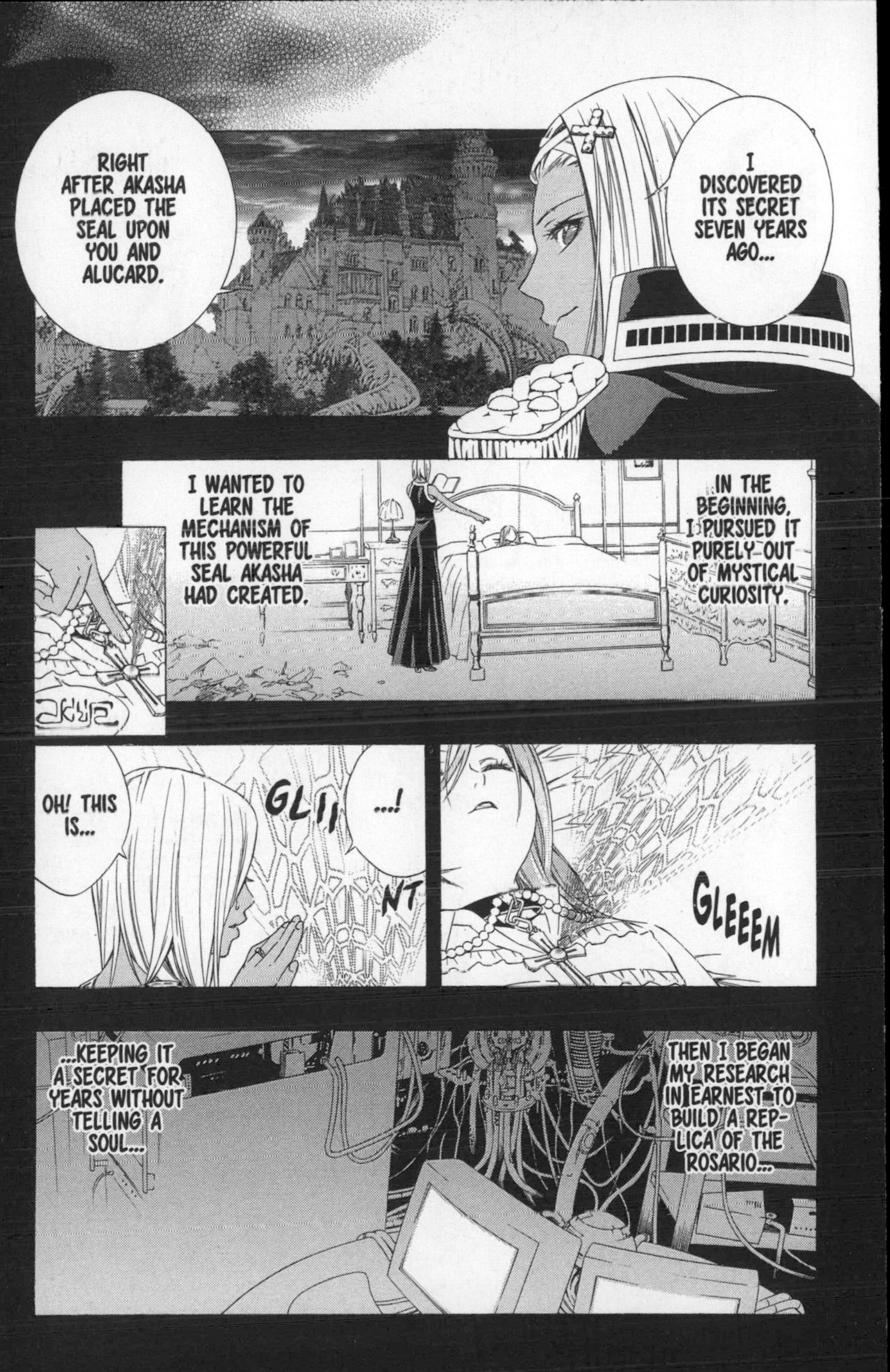
I DISCOVERED ITS SECRET SEVEN YEARS AGO...
RIGHT AFTER AKASHA PLACED THE SEAL UPON YOU AND ALUCARD.
IN THE BEGINNING, I PURSUED IT PURELY OUT OF MYSTICAL CURIOSITY.
I WANTED TO LEARN THE MECHANISM OF THIS POWERFUL SEAL AKASHA HAD CREATED.
GLEEEM
...!
GLIINT
OH! THIS IS...
THEN I BEGAN MY RESEARCH IN EARNEST TO BUILD A REPLICA OF THE ROSARIO...
...KEEPING IT A SECRET FOR YEARS WITHOUT TELLING A SOUL...

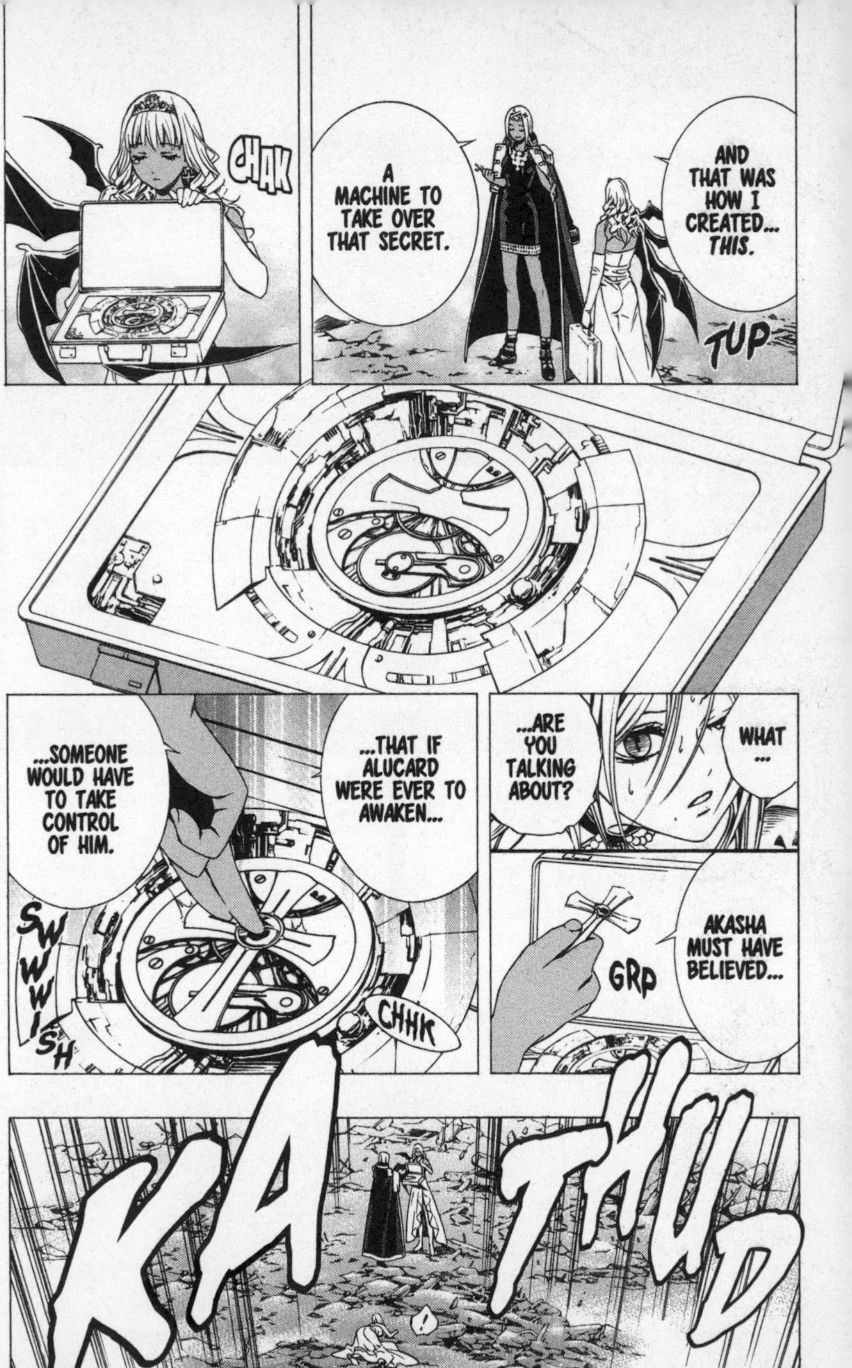
AND THAT WAS HOW I CREATED... THIS.
A MACHINE TO TAKE OVER THAT SECRET.
TUP
CHAK
WHAT ...
...ARE YOU TALKING ABOUT?
AKASHA MUST HAVE BELIEVED...
GRP
...THAT IF ALUCARD WERE EVER TO AWAKEN...
...SOMEONE WOULD HAVE TO TAKE CONTROL OF HIM.
SWWWISH
CHHK
KA THUD
!

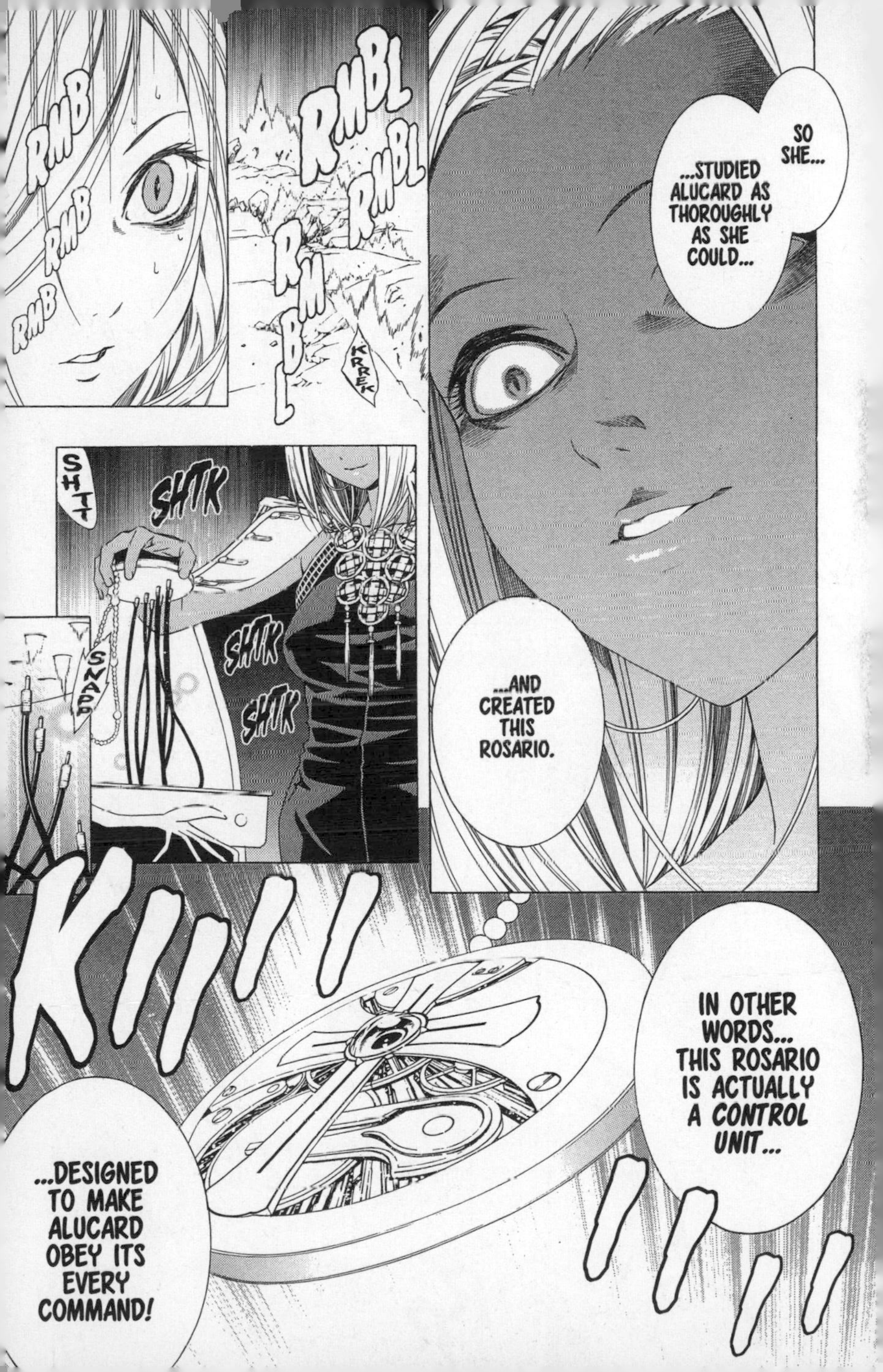
SO SHE...
...STUDIED ALUCARD AS THOROUGHLY AS SHE COULD...
...AND CREATED THIS ROSARIO.
RMBL
RMBL
RMBL
KRREK
RMB
RMB
RMB
RMB
SHTT
SHTK
SHTK
SHTK
SNAP
KIIIIIIII
IN OTHER WORDS... THIS ROSARIO IS ACTUALLY A CONTROL UNIT...
...DESIGNED TO MAKE ALUCARD OBEY ITS EVERY COMMAND!

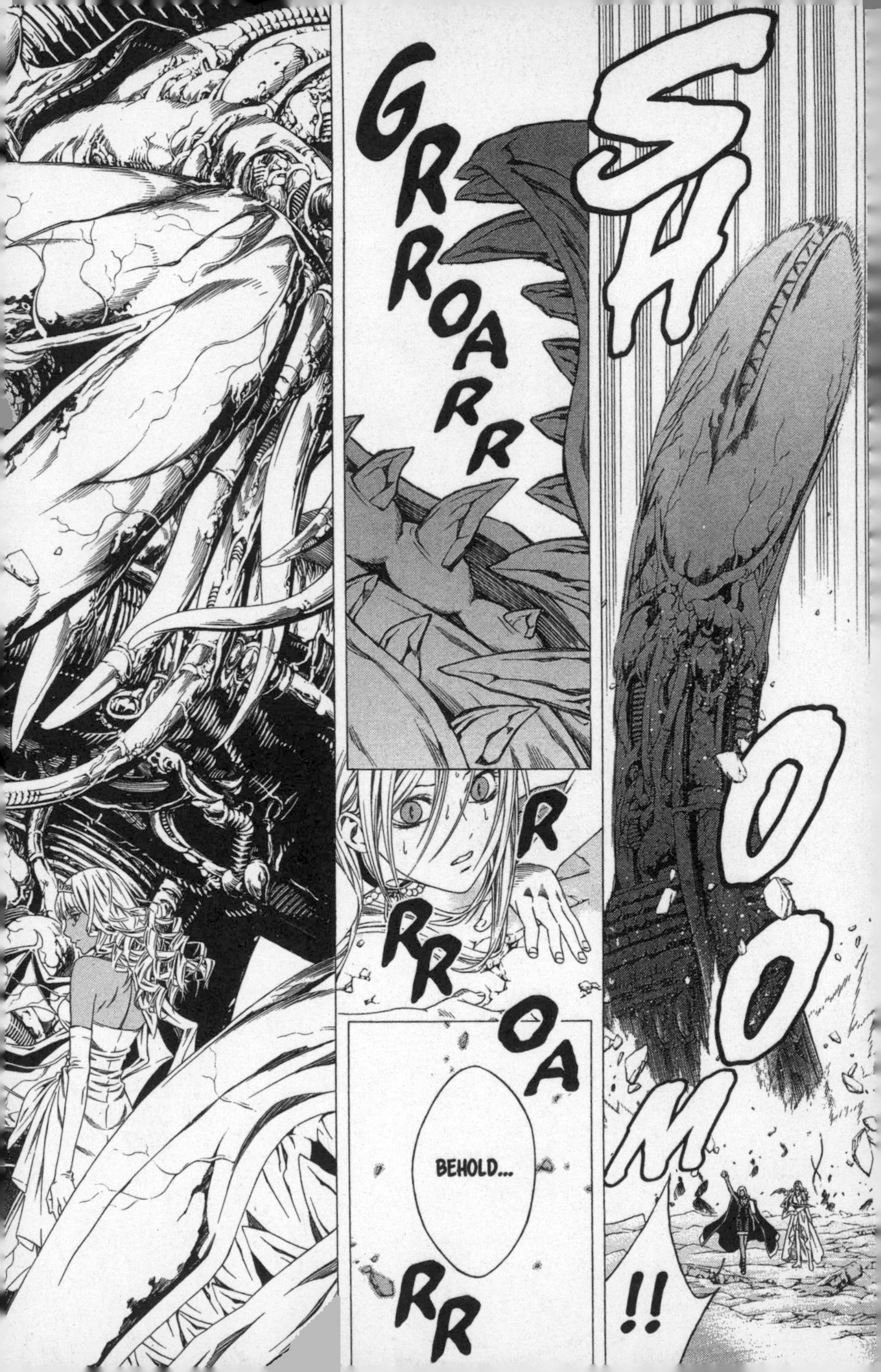
SHOOM!!
GRROARR
RRROARR
BEHOLD...

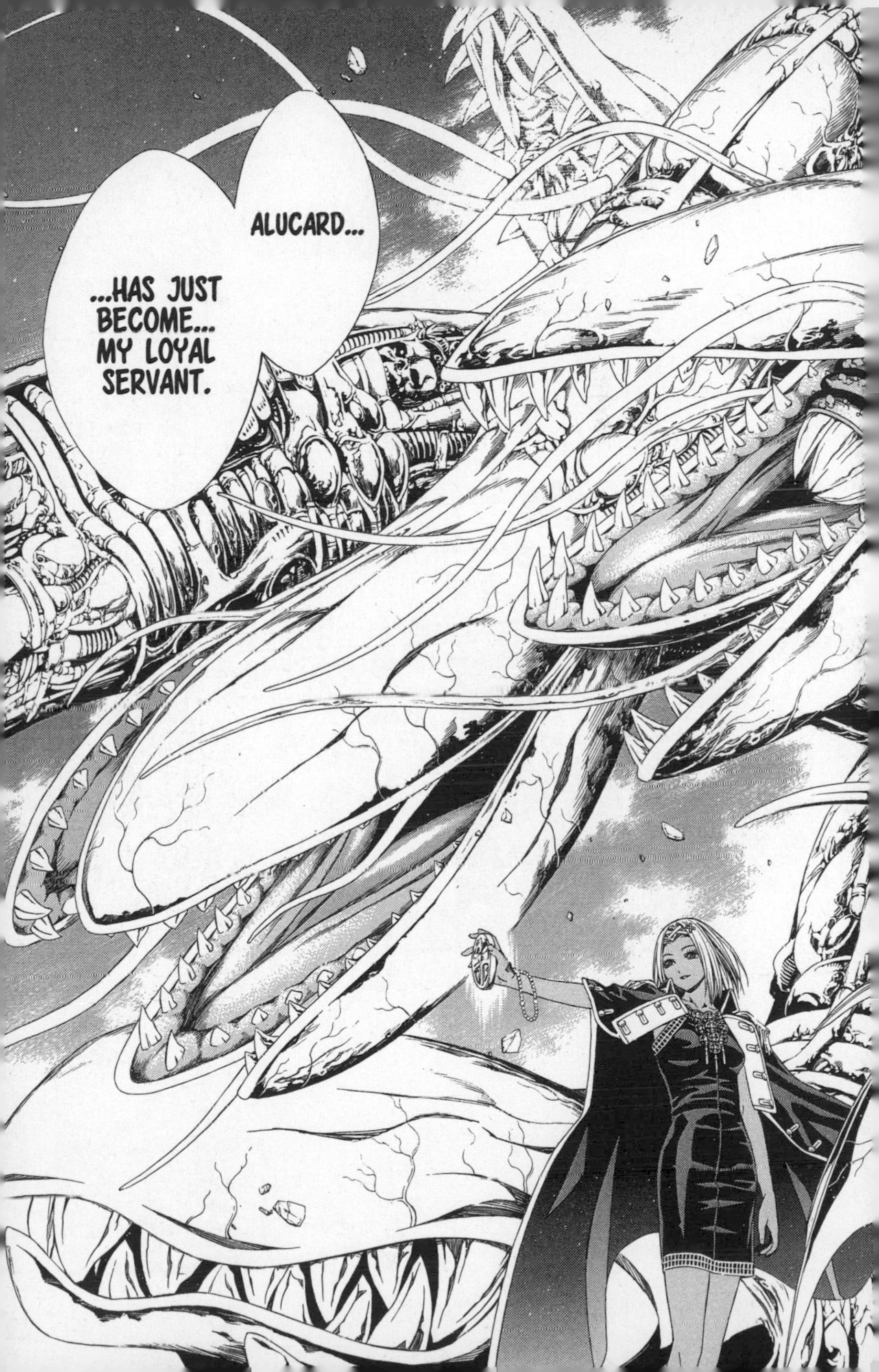
ALUCARD...
...HAS JUST BECOME... MY LOYAL SERVANT.

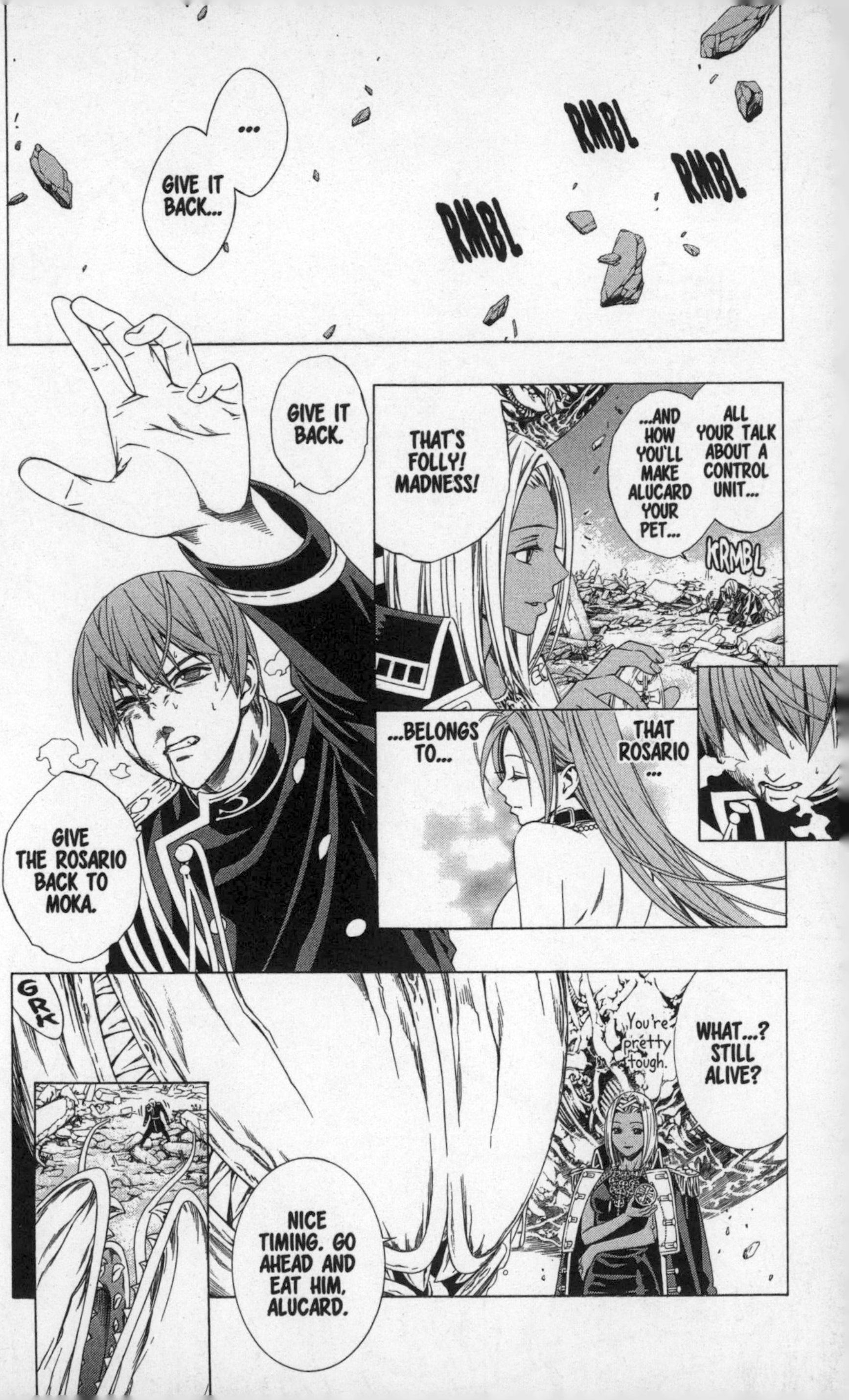
RMBL
RMBL
RMBL
...
GIVE IT BACK...
ALL YOUR TALK ABOUT A CONTROL UNIT...
...AND HOW YOU'LL MAKE ALUCARD YOUR PET...
THAT'S FOLLY! MADNESS!
KRMBL
THAT ROSARIO ...
...BELONGS TO...
GIVE IT BACK.
GIVE THE ROSARIO BACK TO MOKA.
WHAT...? STILL ALIVE?
You're pretty tough.
NICE TIMING. GO AHEAD AND EAT HIM, ALUCARD.
GRK

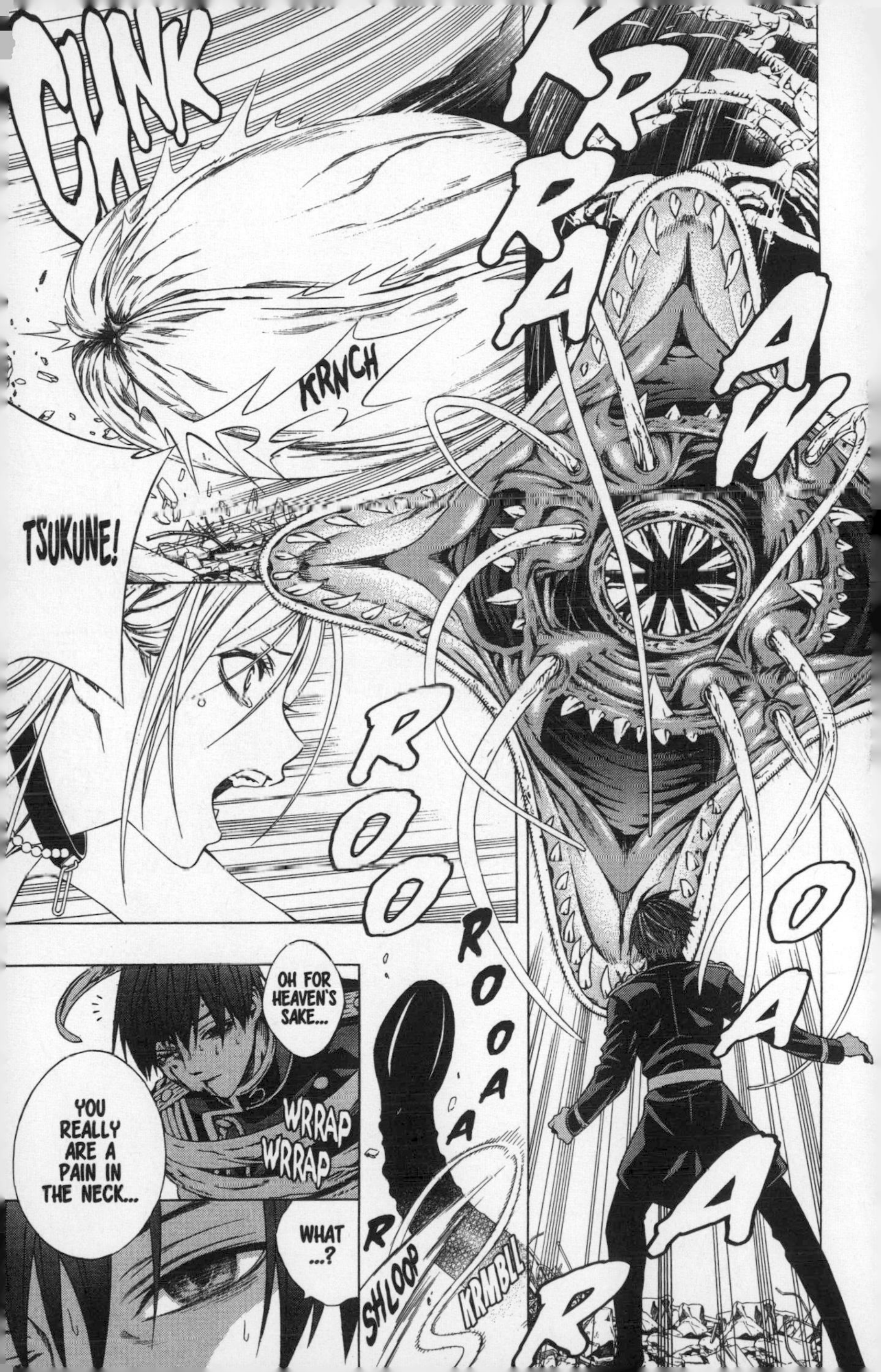
KRRAAW
ROOO
OAAR
ROOOAAR
SHLOOP
KRMBLL
CHINK
KRNCH
TSUKUNE!
OH FOR HEAVEN'S SAKE...
YOU REALLY ARE A PAIN IN THE NECK...
WRRAP WRRAP
WHAT ...?

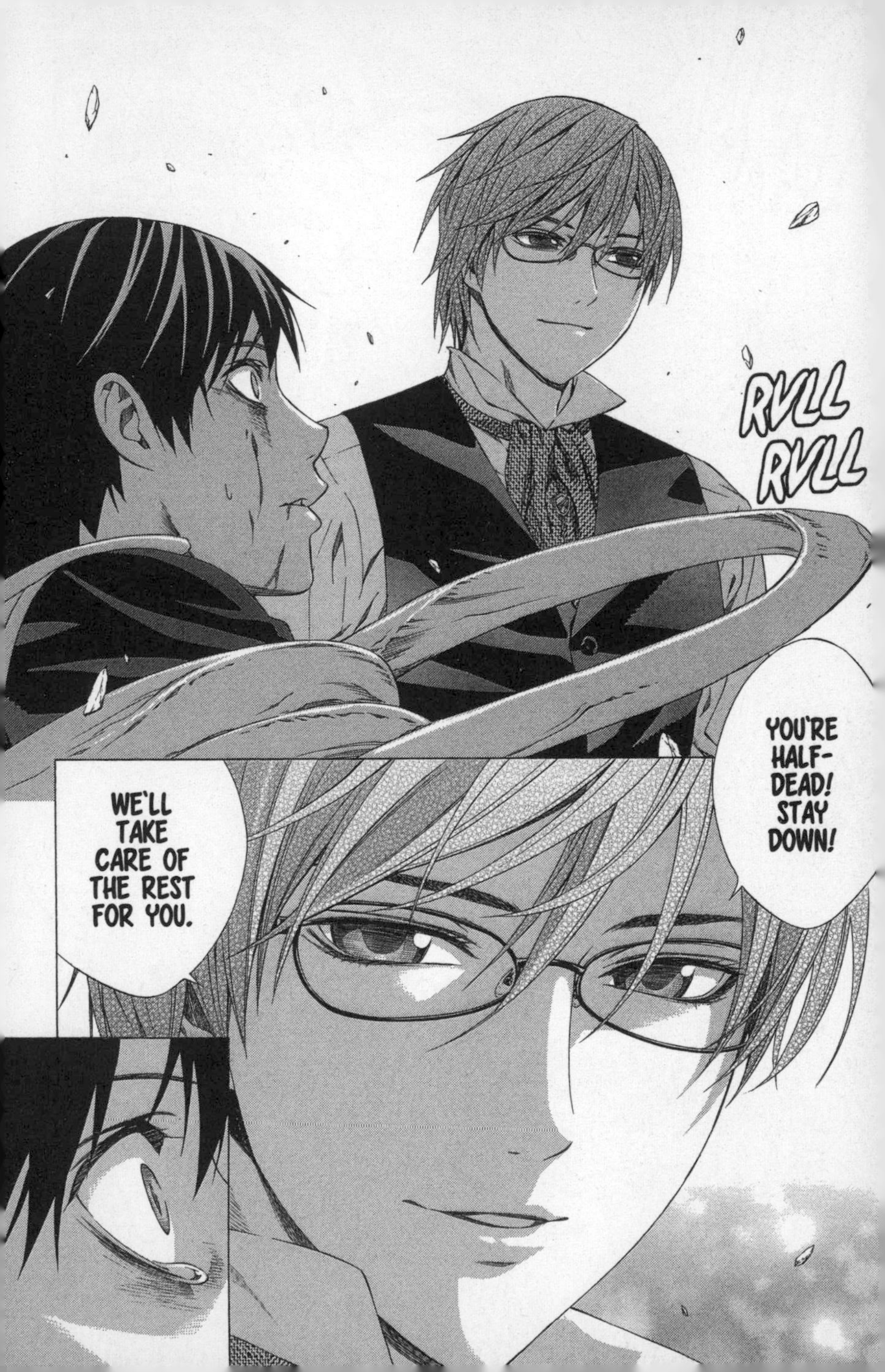
RVLL RVLL
YOU'RE HALF-DEAD! STAY DOWN!
WE'LL TAKE CARE OF THE REST FOR YOU.

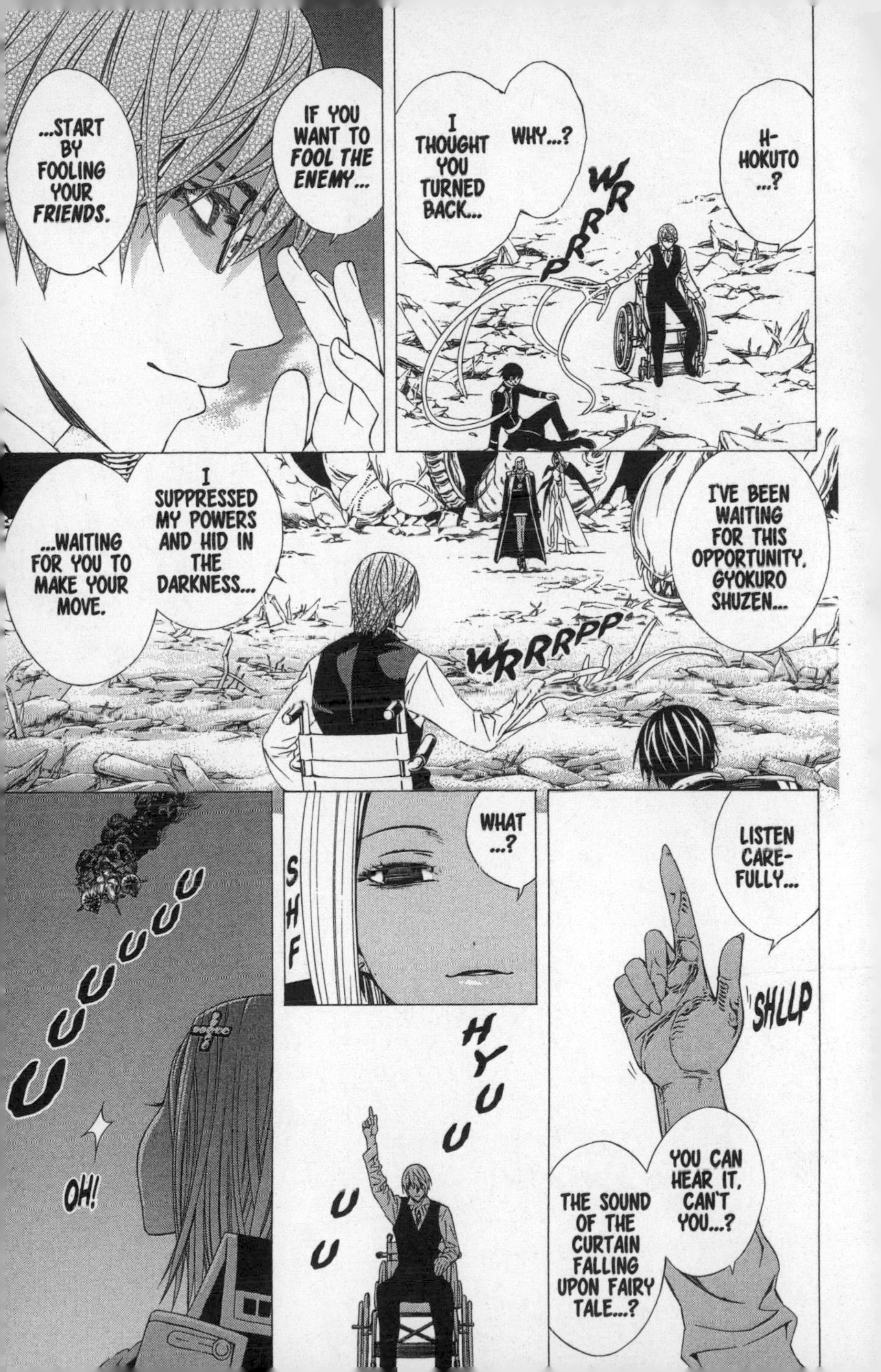
H-HOKUTO...?
WHY...?
I THOUGHT YOU TURNED BACK...
WRRRRP
IF YOU WANT TO FOOL THE ENEMY...
...START BY FOOLING YOUR FRIENDS.
I'VE BEEN WAITING FOR THIS OPPORTUNITY, GYOKURO SHUZEN...
WRRRPP
I SUPPRESSED MY POWERS AND HID IN THE DARKNESS...
...WAITING FOR YOU TO MAKE YOUR MOVE.
LISTEN CARE-FULLY...
SHLLP
YOU CAN HEAR IT, CAN'T YOU...?
THE SOUND OF THE CURTAIN FALLING UPON FAIRY TALE...?
WHAT...?
SHF
HYUUUUU
UUUUUUUU
OH!

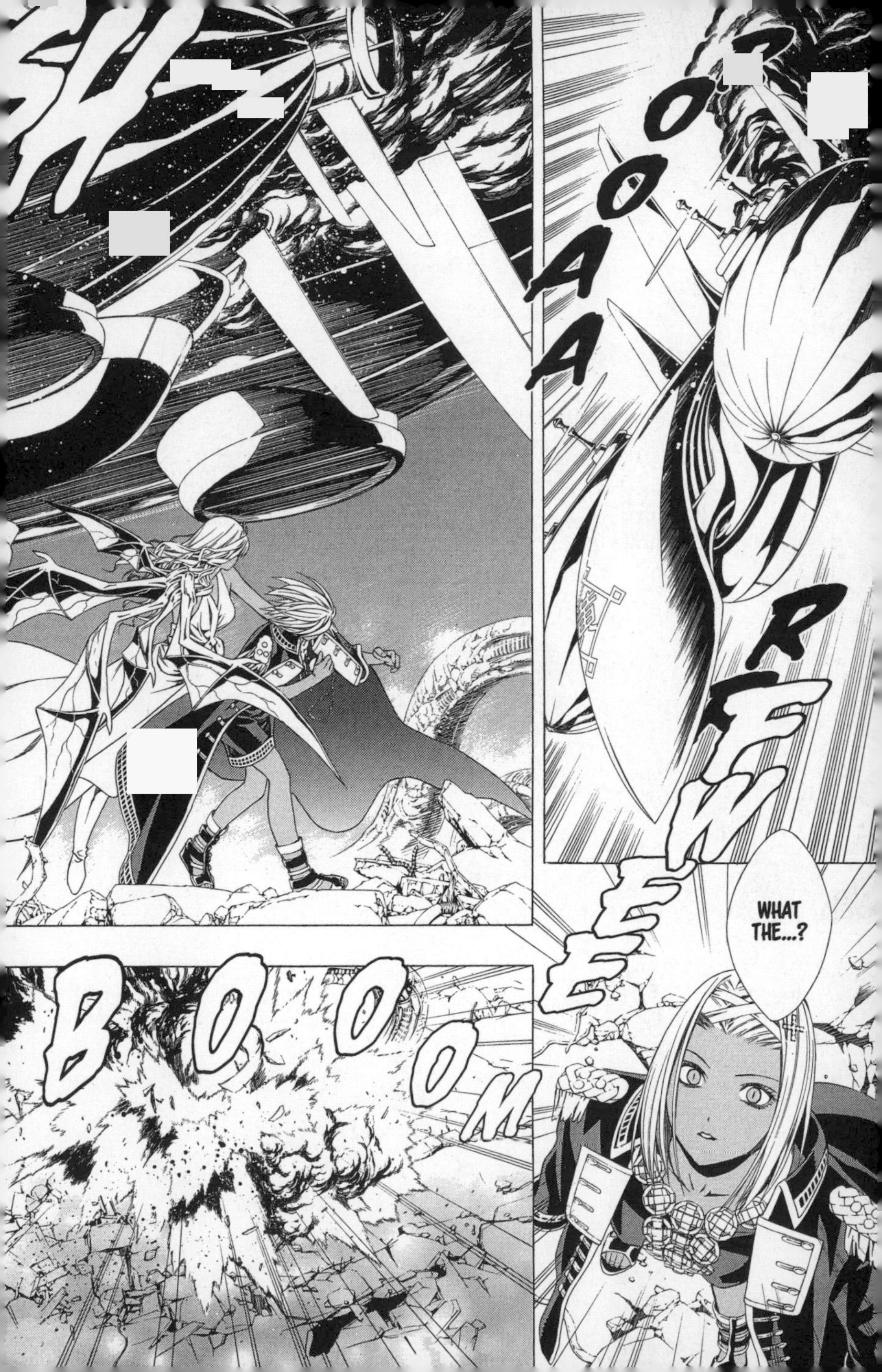
WHAT THE...?
BOOOOM

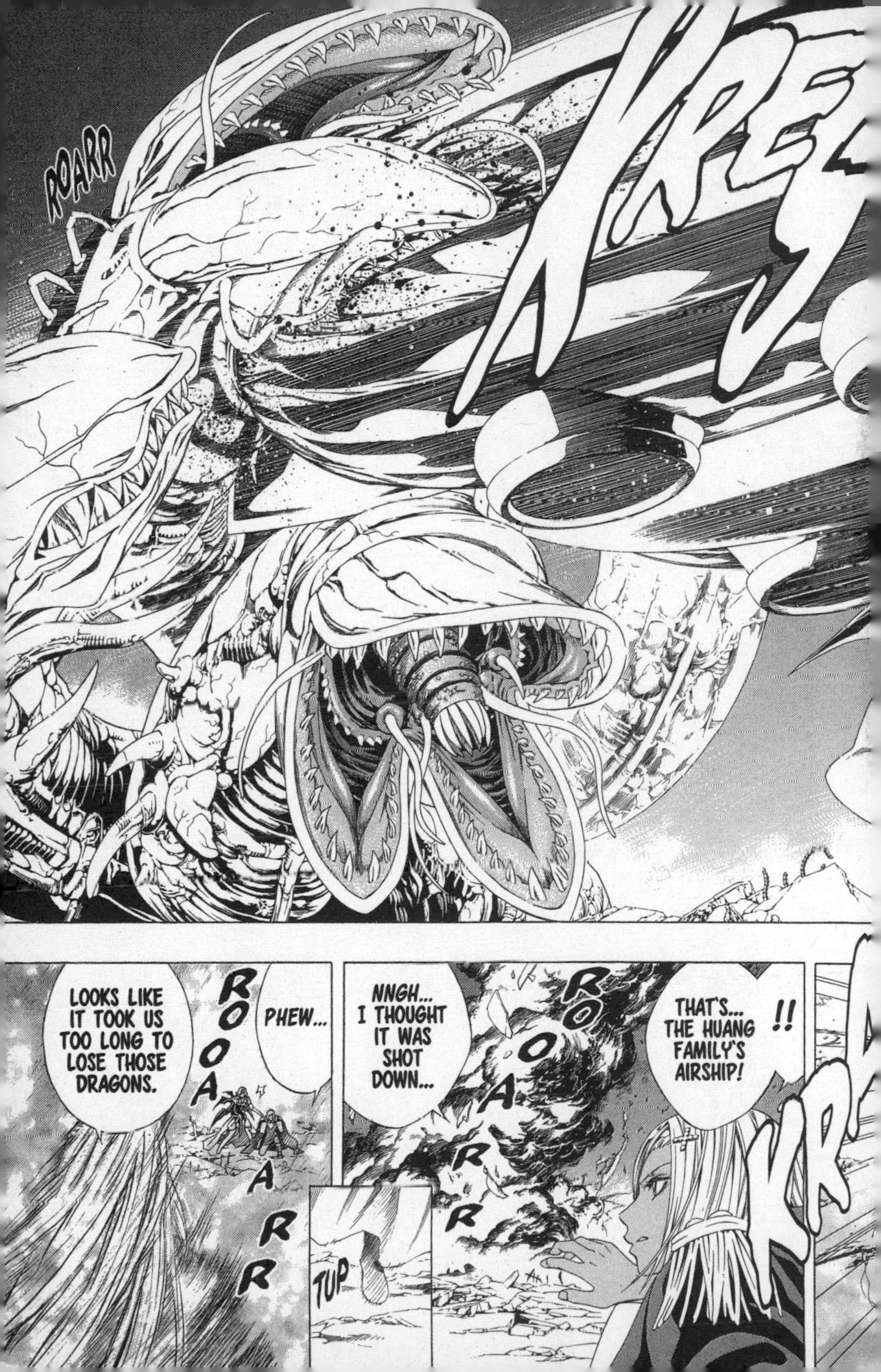
ROARR
!!
THAT'S... THE HUANG FAMILY'S AIRSHIP!
ROOARRR
NNGH... I THOUGHT IT WAS SHOT DOWN...
TUP
PHEW...
ROOAARRR
LOOKS LIKE IT TOOK US TOO LONG TO LOSE THOSE DRAGONS.

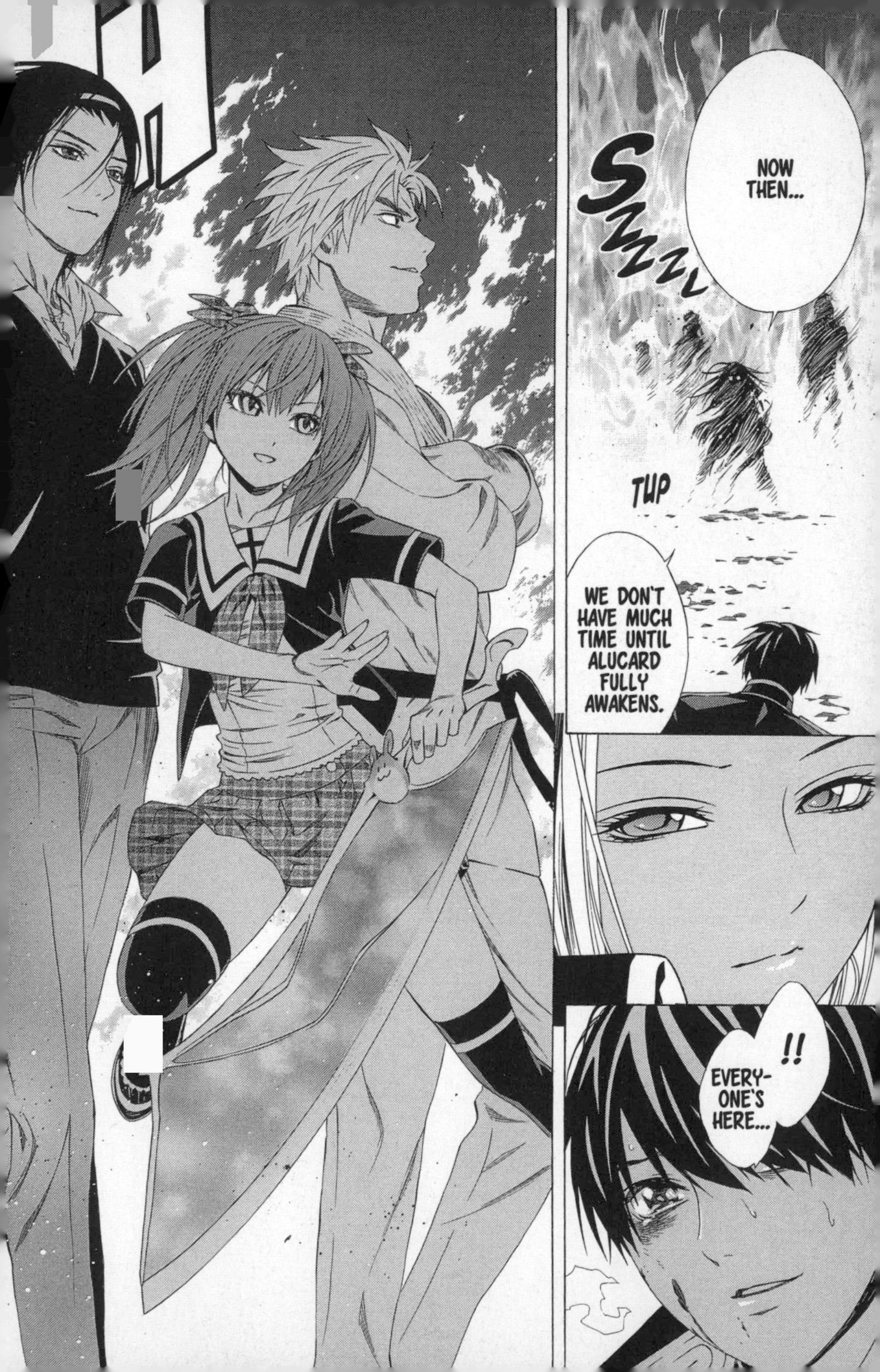
NOW THEN...
SZZZZL
TUP
WE DON'T HAVE MUCH TIME UNTIL ALUCARD FULLY AWAKENS.
!!
EVERY-ONE'S HERE...

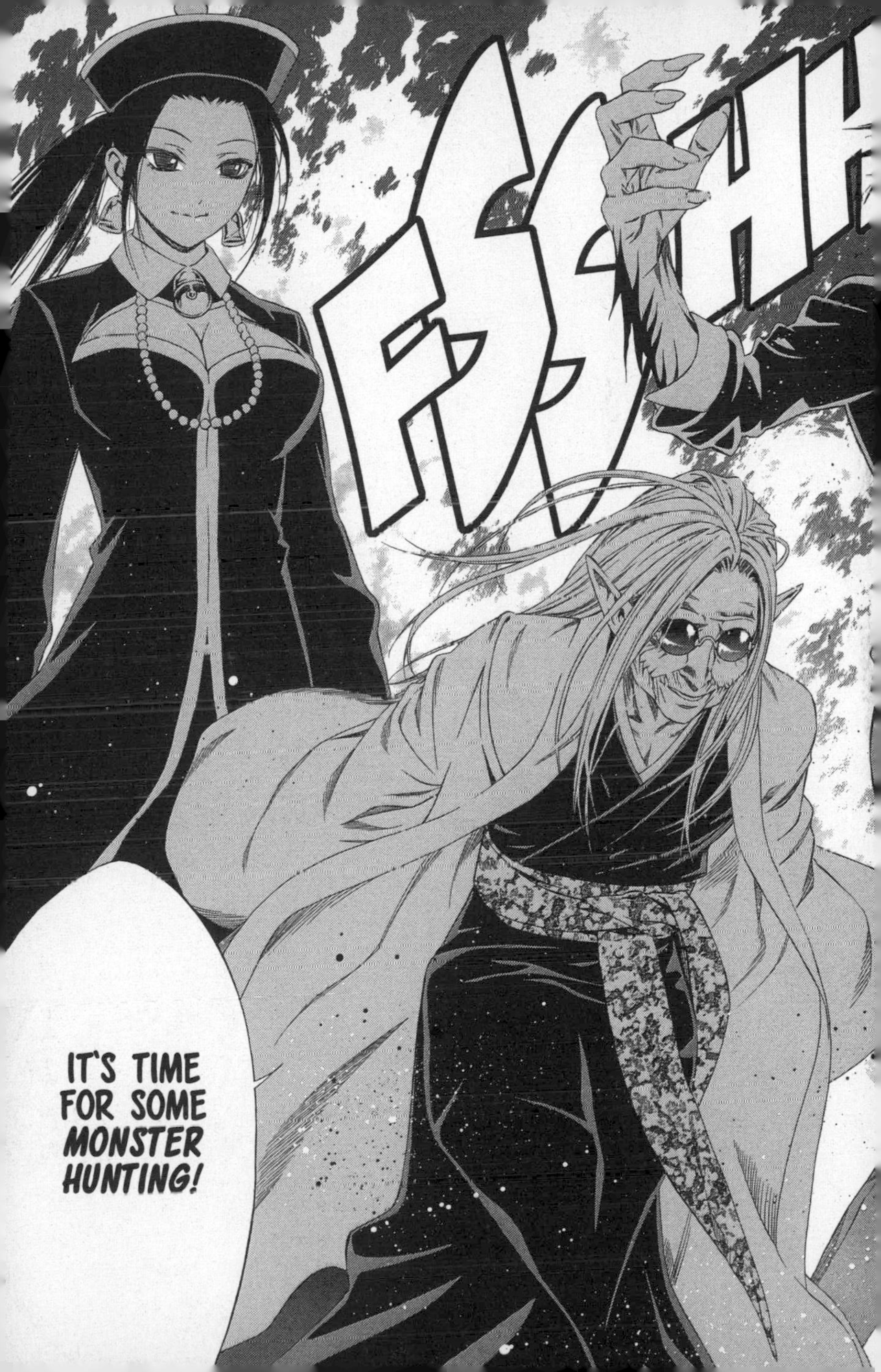
FSSHH
IT'S TIME FOR SOME MONSTER HUNTING!

57: Rock 'n' Roll #1

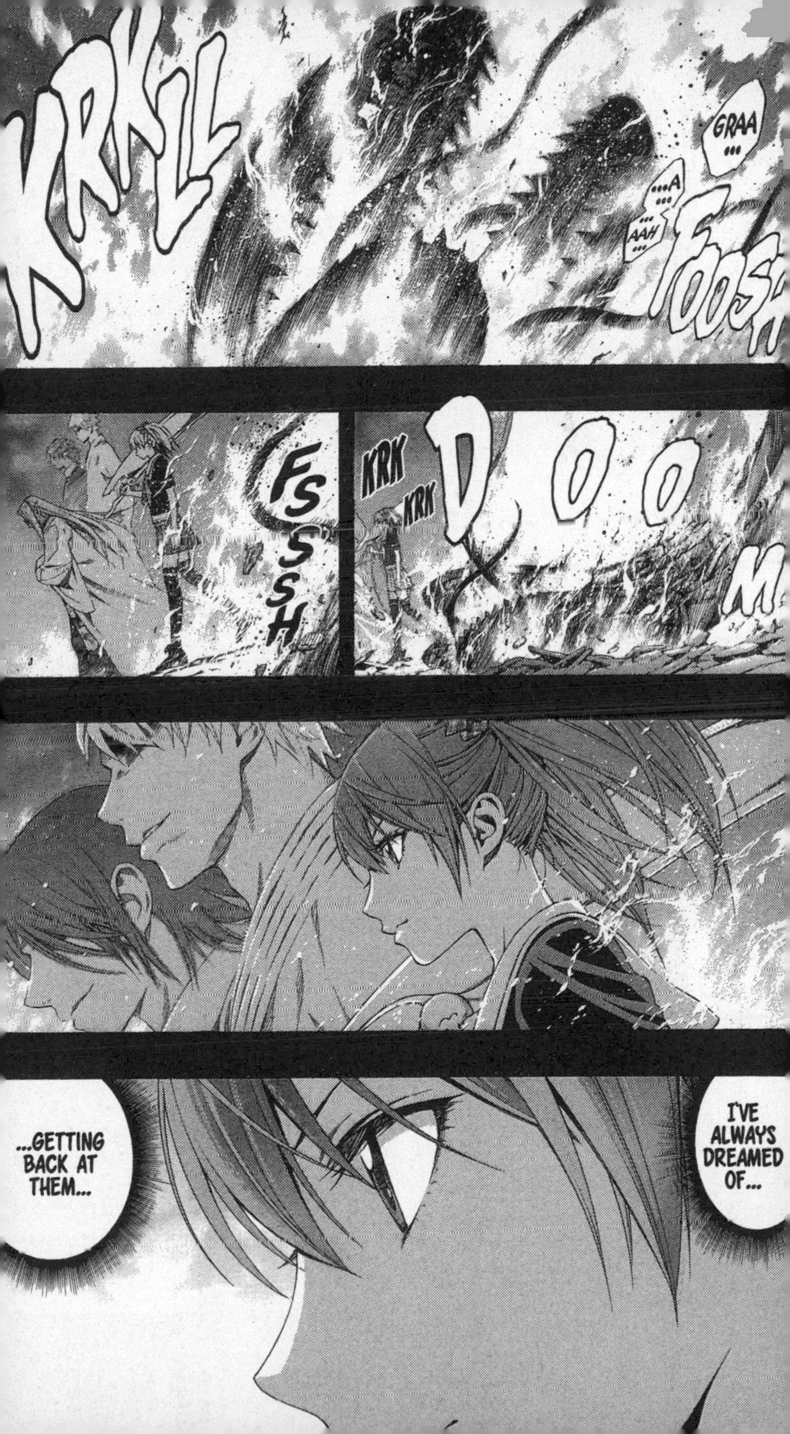
GRAA...
...A... AAH...
FOOSH
KRKLL
KRK KRK
DOOOM
FSSSH
I'VE ALWAYS DREAMED OF...
...GETTING BACK AT THEM...

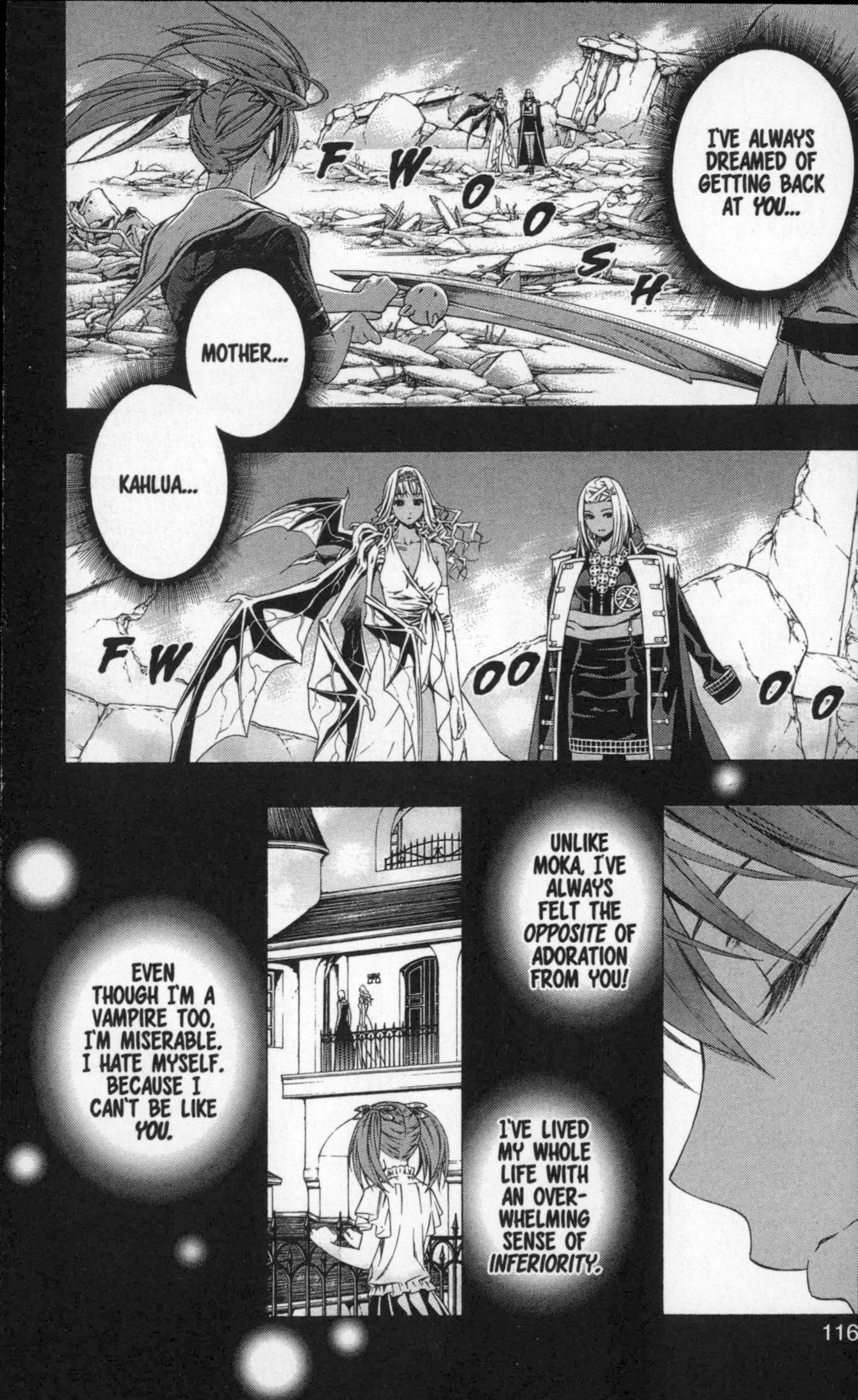
I'VE ALWAYS DREAMED OF GETTING BACK AT YOU...
FWOOSH
MOTHER...
KAHLUA...
FWOOOO
UNLIKE MOKA, I'VE ALWAYS FELT THE OPPOSITE OF ADORATION FROM YOU!
I'VE LIVED MY WHOLE LIFE WITH AN OVER-WHELMING SENSE OF INFERIORITY.
EVEN THOUGH I'M A VAMPIRE TOO, I'M MISERABLE. I HATE MYSELF. BECAUSE I CAN'T BE LIKE YOU.

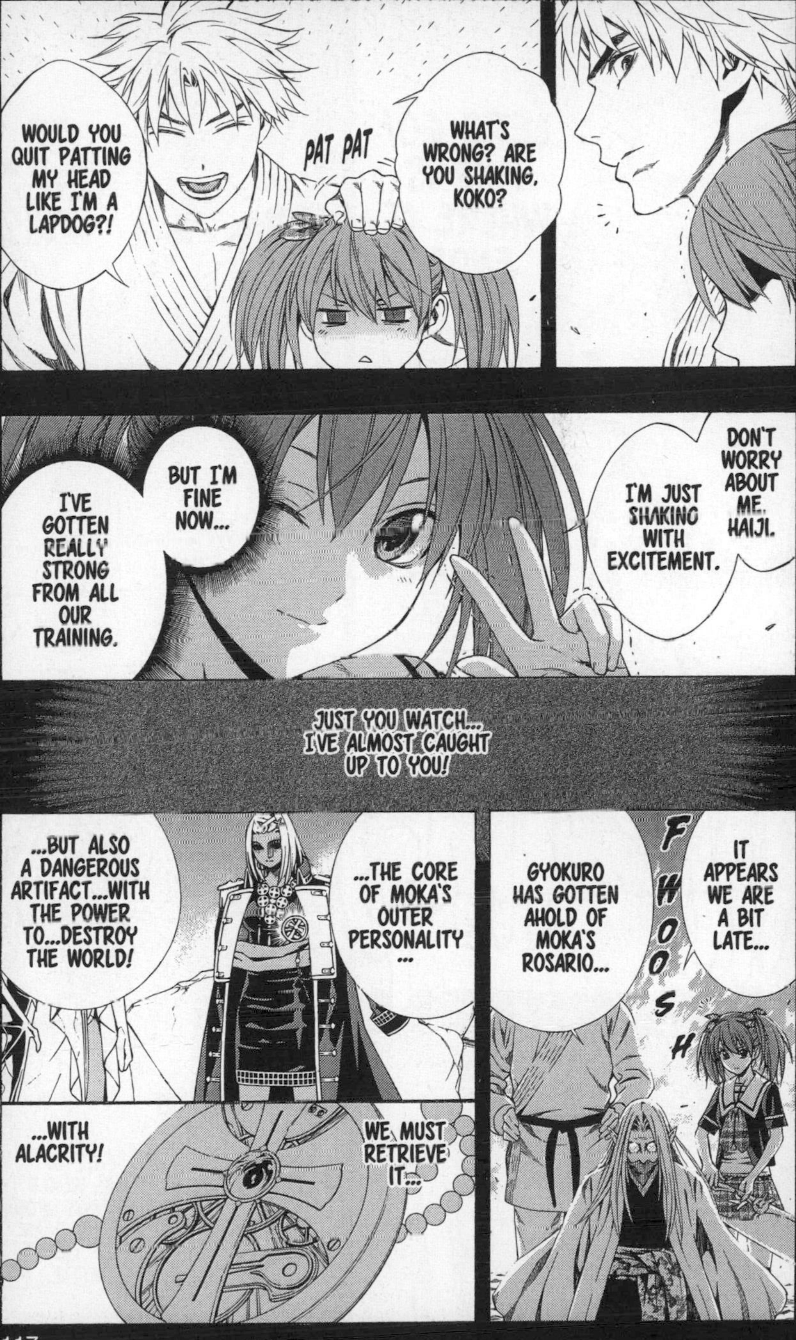
WHAT'S WRONG? ARE YOU SHAKING, KOKO?
PAT PAT
WOULD YOU QUIT PATTING MY HEAD LIKE I'M A LAPDOG?!
DON'T WORRY ABOUT ME. HAIJI.
I'M JUST SHAKING WITH EXCITEMENT.
BUT I'M FINE NOW...
I'VE GOTTEN REALLY STRONG FROM ALL OUR TRAINING.
JUST YOU WATCH... I'VE ALMOST CAUGHT UP TO YOU!
IT APPEARS WE ARE A BIT LATE...
FWOOSH
GYOKURO HAS GOTTEN AHOLD OF MOKA'S ROSARIO...
...THE CORE OF MOKA'S OUTER PERSONALITY...
...BUT ALSO A DANGEROUS ARTIFACT...WITH THE POWER TO...DESTROY THE WORLD!
WE MUST RETRIEVE IT...
...WITH ALACRITY!

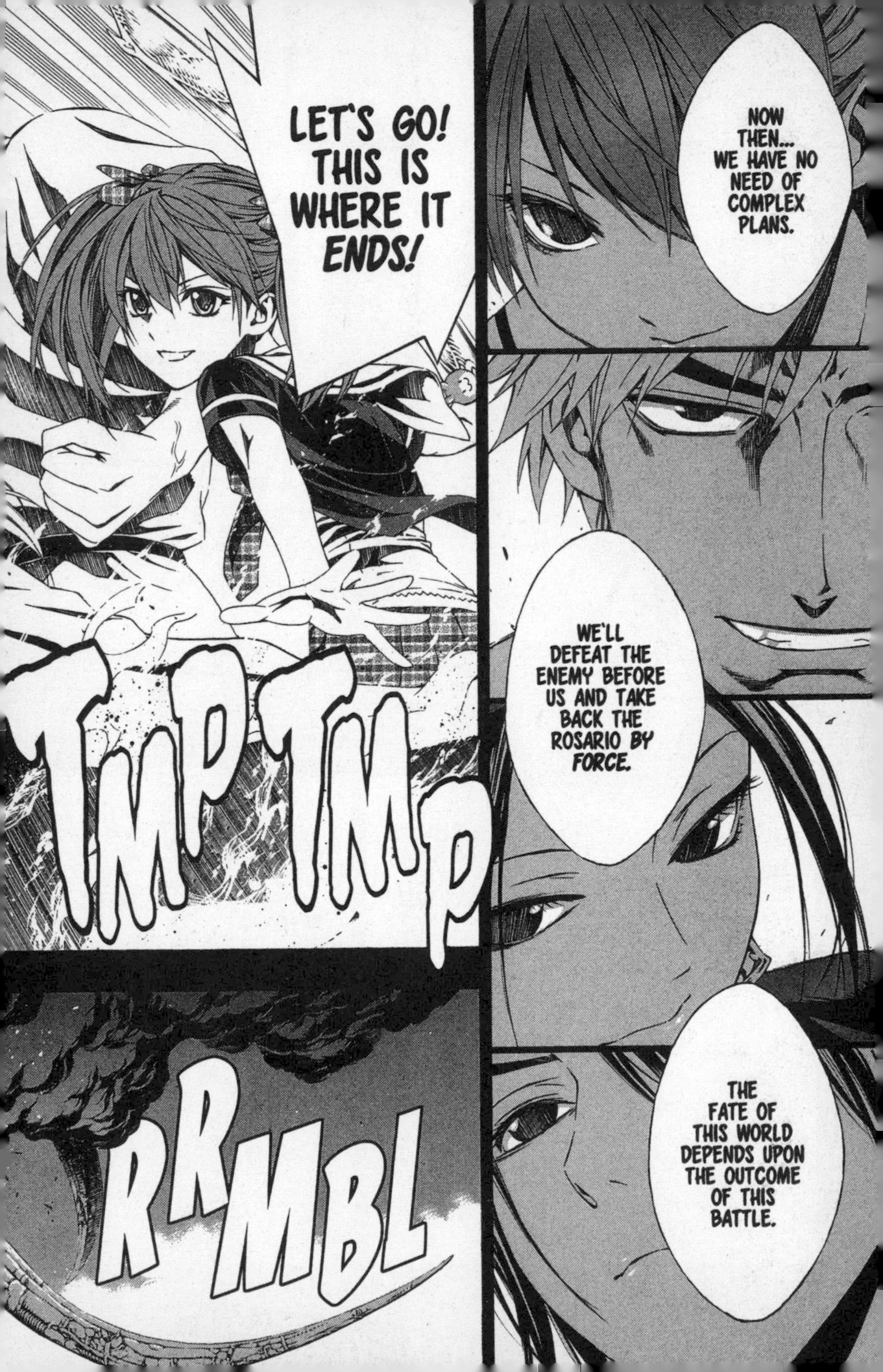
NOW THEN... WE HAVE NO NEED OF COMPLEX PLANS.
WE'LL DEFEAT THE ENEMY BEFORE US AND TAKE BACK THE ROSARIO BY FORCE.
THE FATE OF THIS WORLD DEPENDS UPON THE OUTCOME OF THIS BATTLE.
LET'S GO! THIS IS WHERE IT ENDS!
TMP TMP
RRMBL

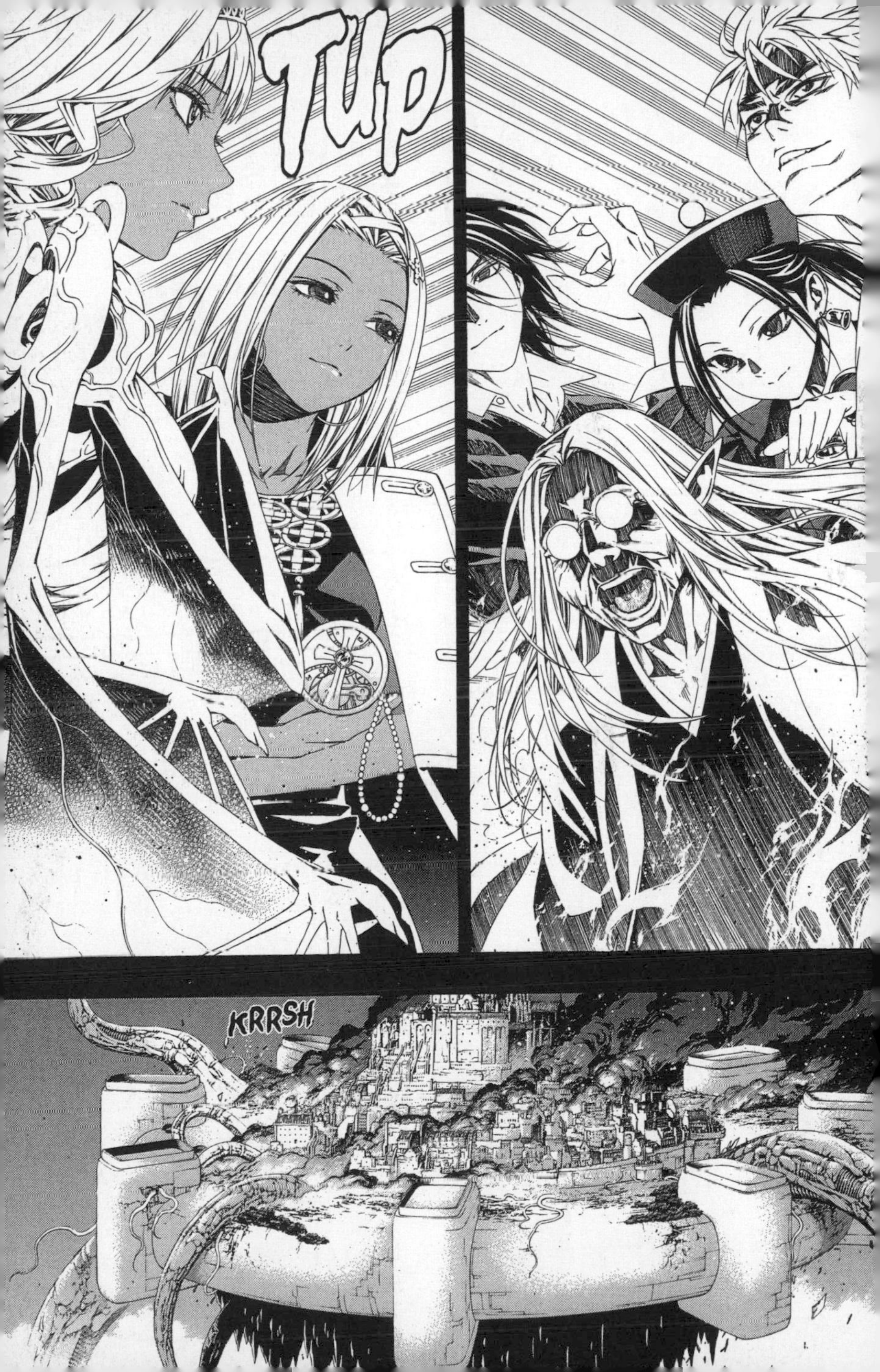
TUP
KRRSH

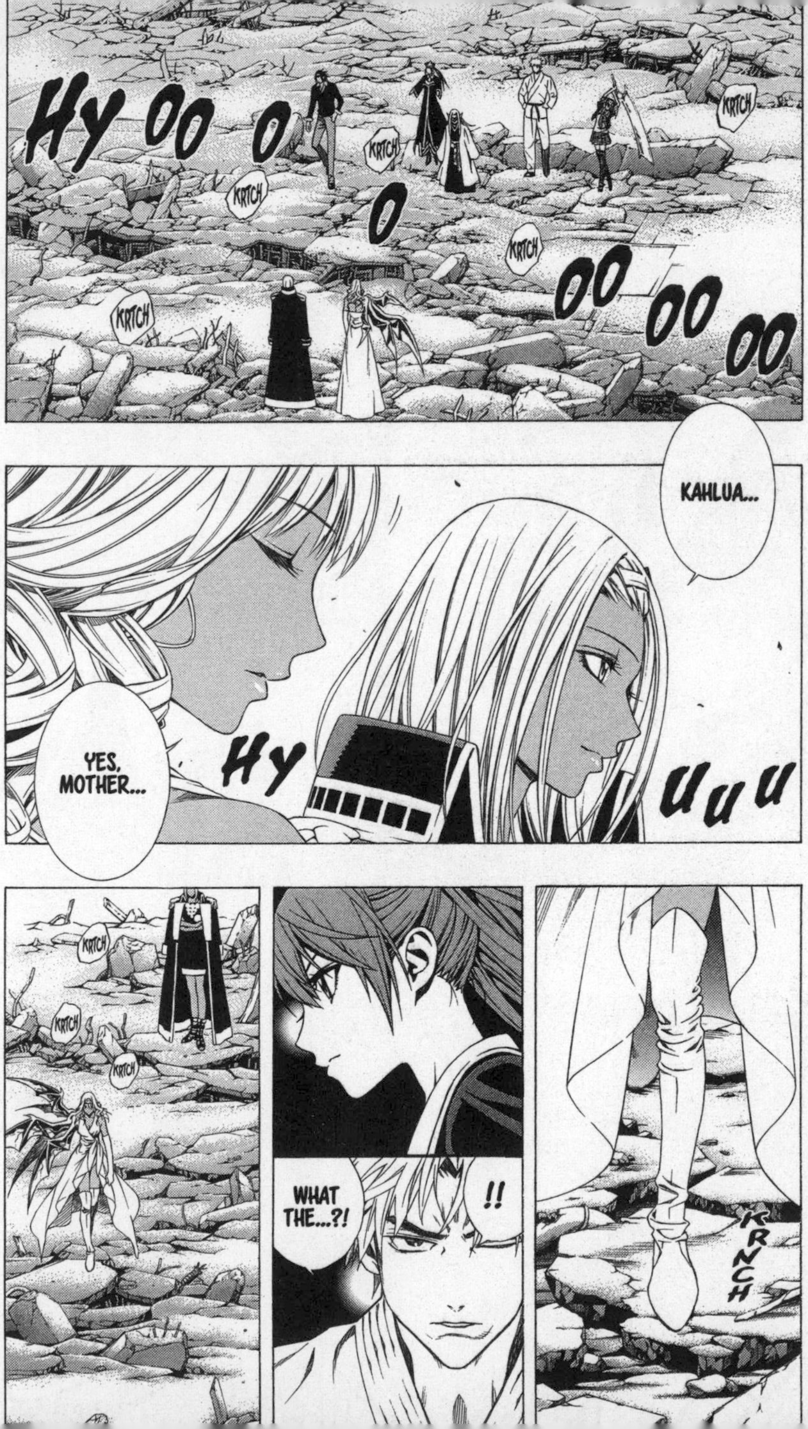

KRTCH
HYOOOOOOOOOOOOOO
KRTCH
KRTCH
KRTCH
KRTCH
KAHLUA...
HYUUU
YES, MOTHER...
KRNCH
!!
WHAT THE...?!
KRTCH
KRTCH
KRTCH

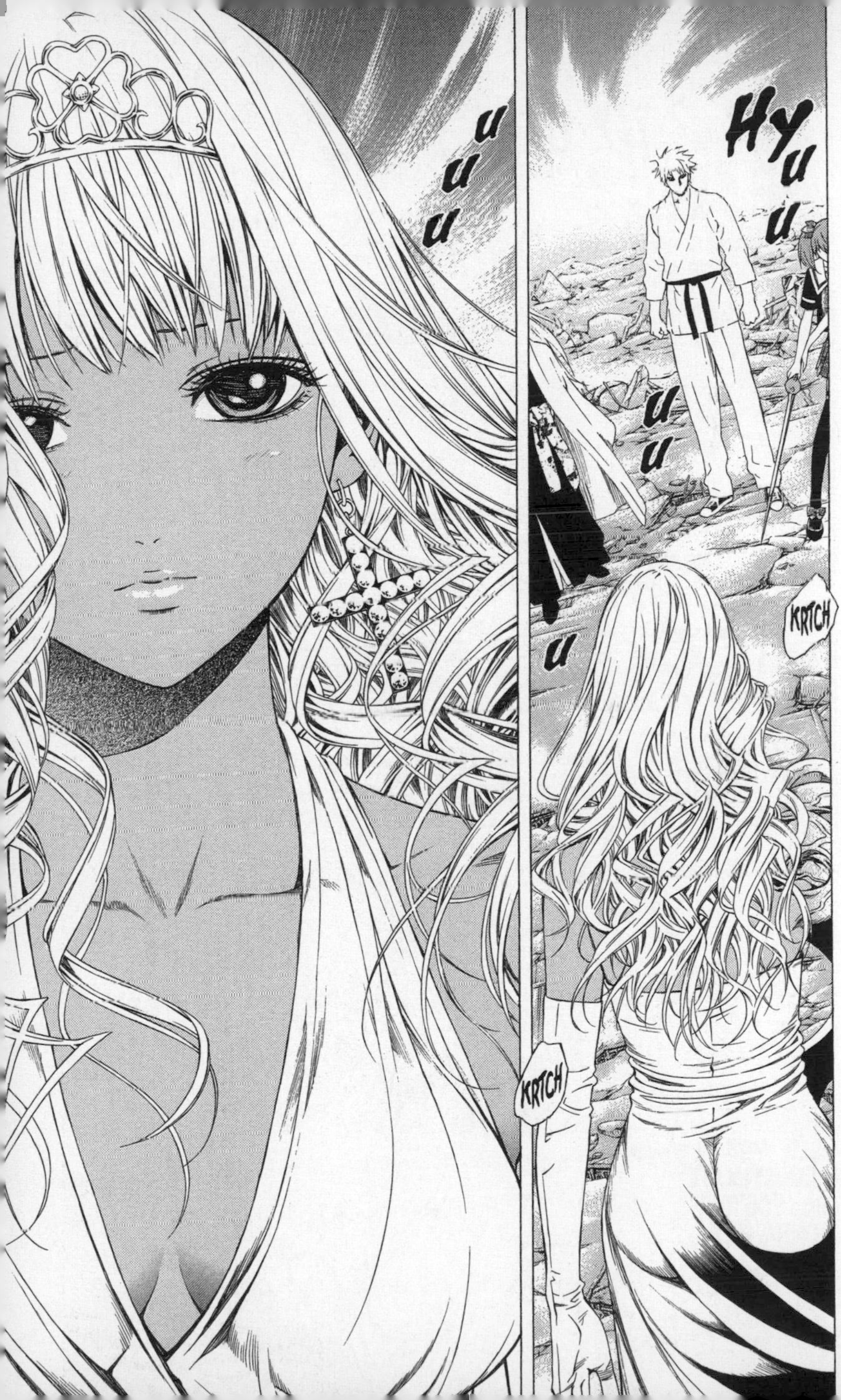
HYuuu
uuu
u
KRTCH
KRTCH
uuuu

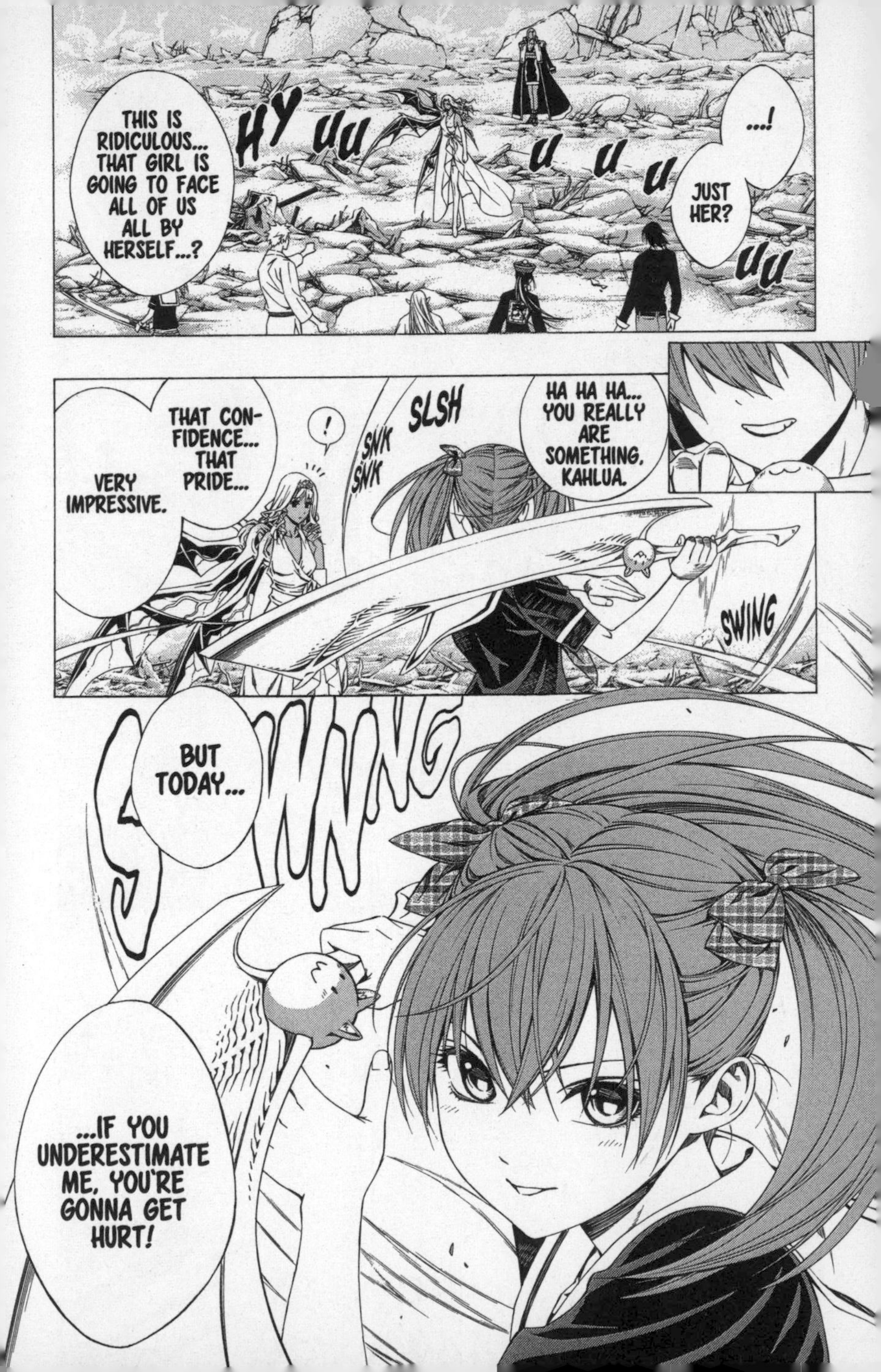
...!
JUST HER?
HYUUUUUUUU
THIS IS RIDICULOUS... THAT GIRL IS GOING TO FACE ALL OF US ALL BY HERSELF...?
HA HA HA... YOU REALLY ARE SOMETHING, KAHLUA.
SLSH
SNK SNK
!
THAT CON-FIDENCE... THAT PRIDE...
VERY IMPRESSIVE.
SWING
BUT TODAY...
...IF YOU UNDERESTIMATE ME, YOU'RE GONNA GET HURT!

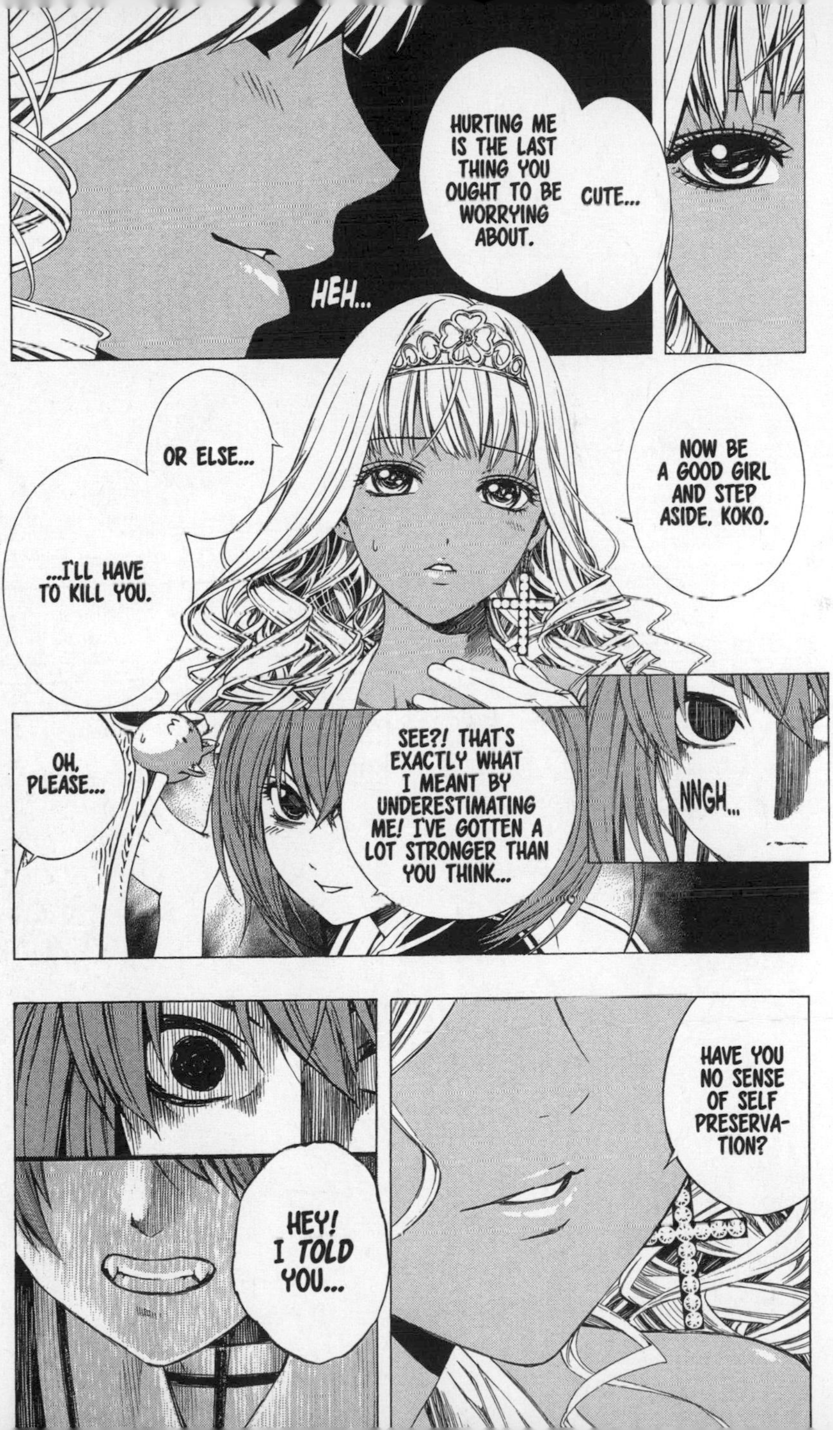
CUTE...
HURTING ME IS THE LAST THING YOU OUGHT TO BE WORRYING ABOUT.
HEH...
NOW BE A GOOD GIRL AND STEP ASIDE, KOKO.
OR ELSE...
...I'LL HAVE TO KILL YOU.
NNGH...
SEE?! THAT'S EXACTLY WHAT I MEANT BY UNDERESTIMATING ME! I'VE GOTTEN A LOT STRONGER THAN YOU THINK...
OH, PLEASE...
HAVE YOU NO SENSE OF SELF PRESERVATION?
HEY! I *TOLD* YOU...

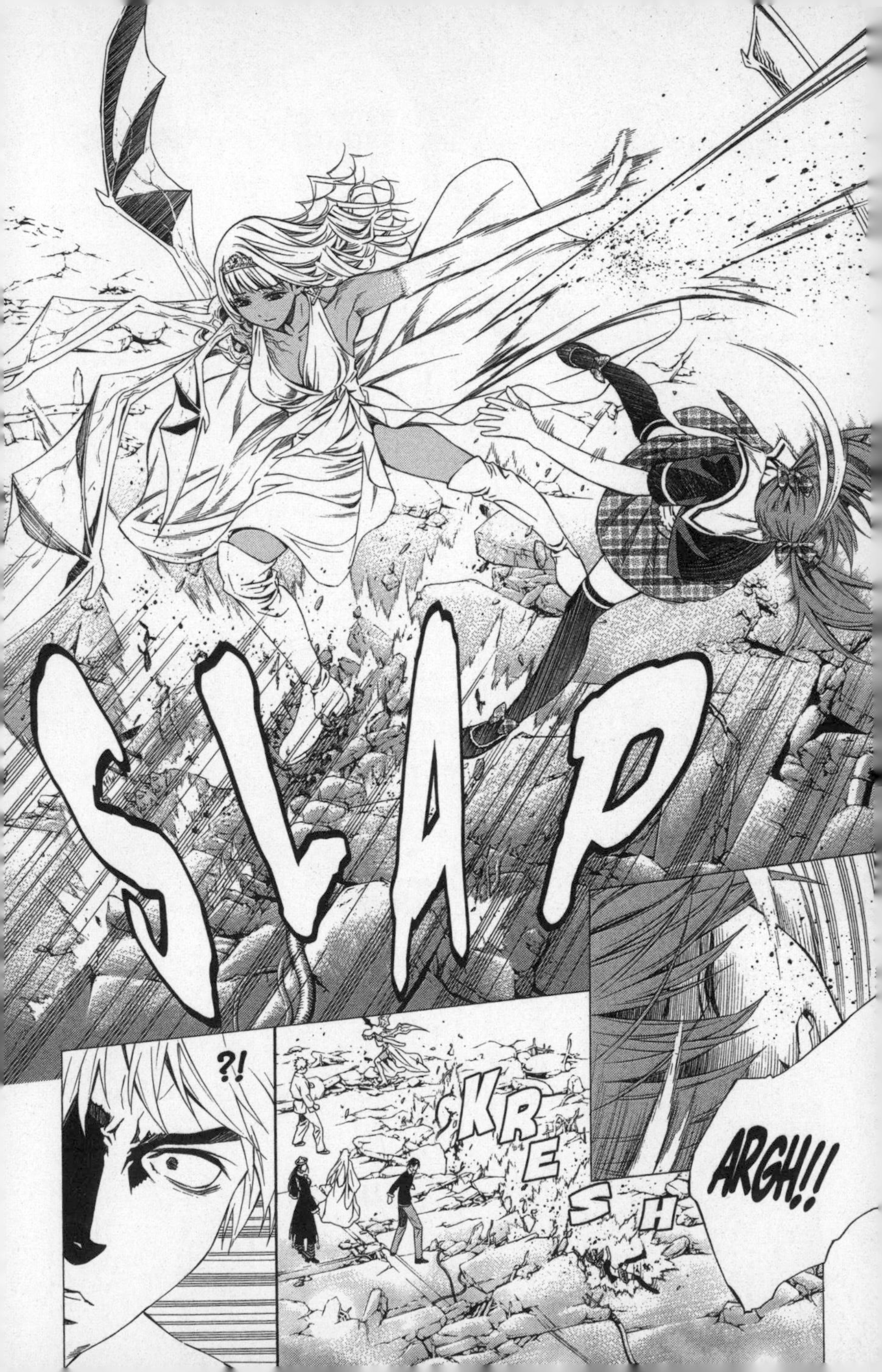
SLAP
ARGH!!
KRESH
?!

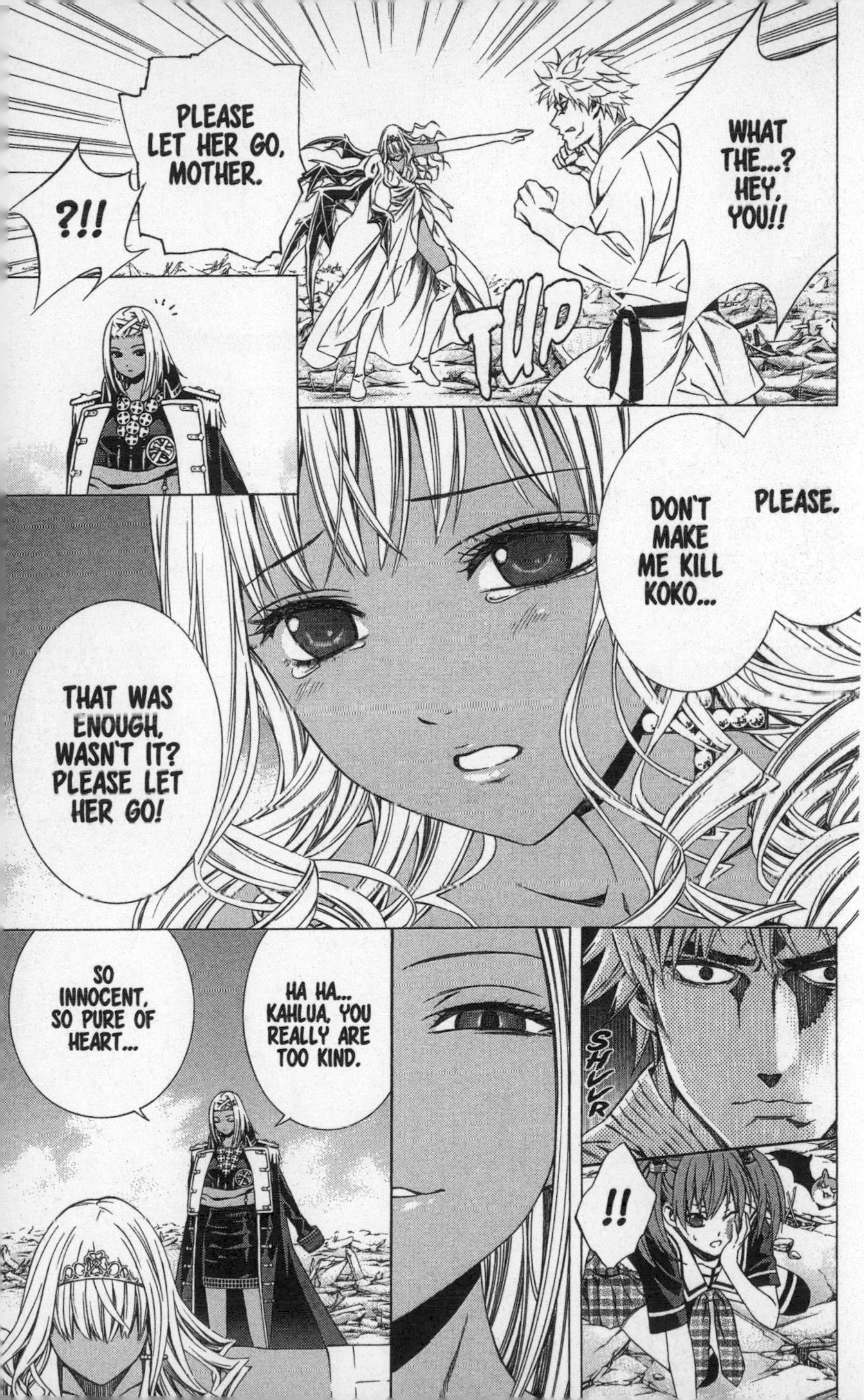
WHAT THE...? HEY, YOU!!
PLEASE LET HER GO, MOTHER.
TUP
?!!
PLEASE.
DON'T MAKE ME KILL KOKO...
THAT WAS ENOUGH, WASN'T IT? PLEASE LET HER GO!
SHUUR
!!
HA HA... KAHLUA, YOU REALLY ARE TOO KIND.
SO INNOCENT, SO PURE OF HEART...

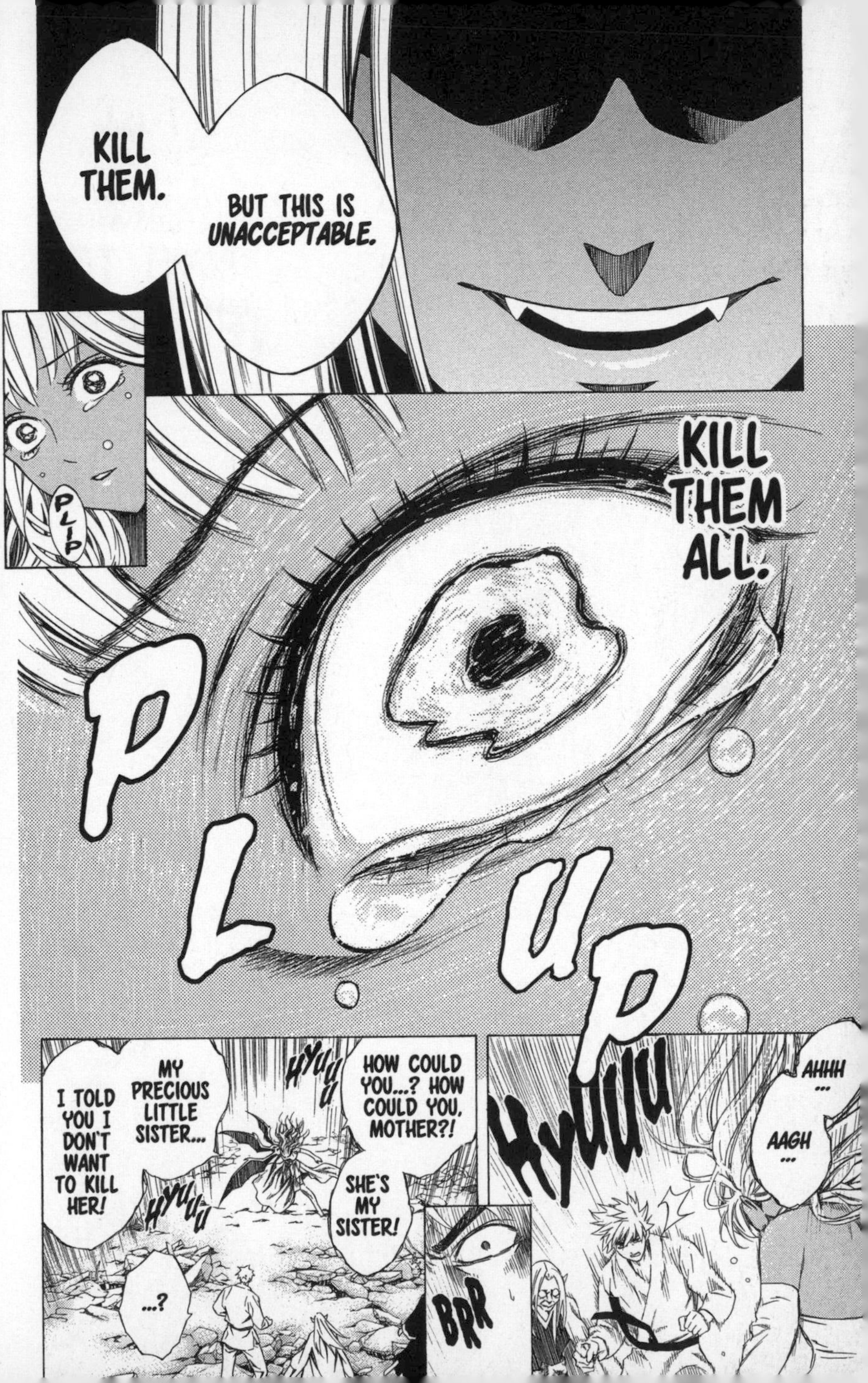
BUT THIS IS UNACCEPTABLE.
KILL THEM.
KILL THEM ALL.
PLUP
PLIP
AHHH...
AAGH...
HYUUU
BRR
HOW COULD YOU...? HOW COULD YOU, MOTHER?!
SHE'S MY SISTER!
HYUUU
MY PRECIOUS LITTLE SISTER...
I TOLD YOU I DON'T WANT TO KILL HER!
HYUUU
...?

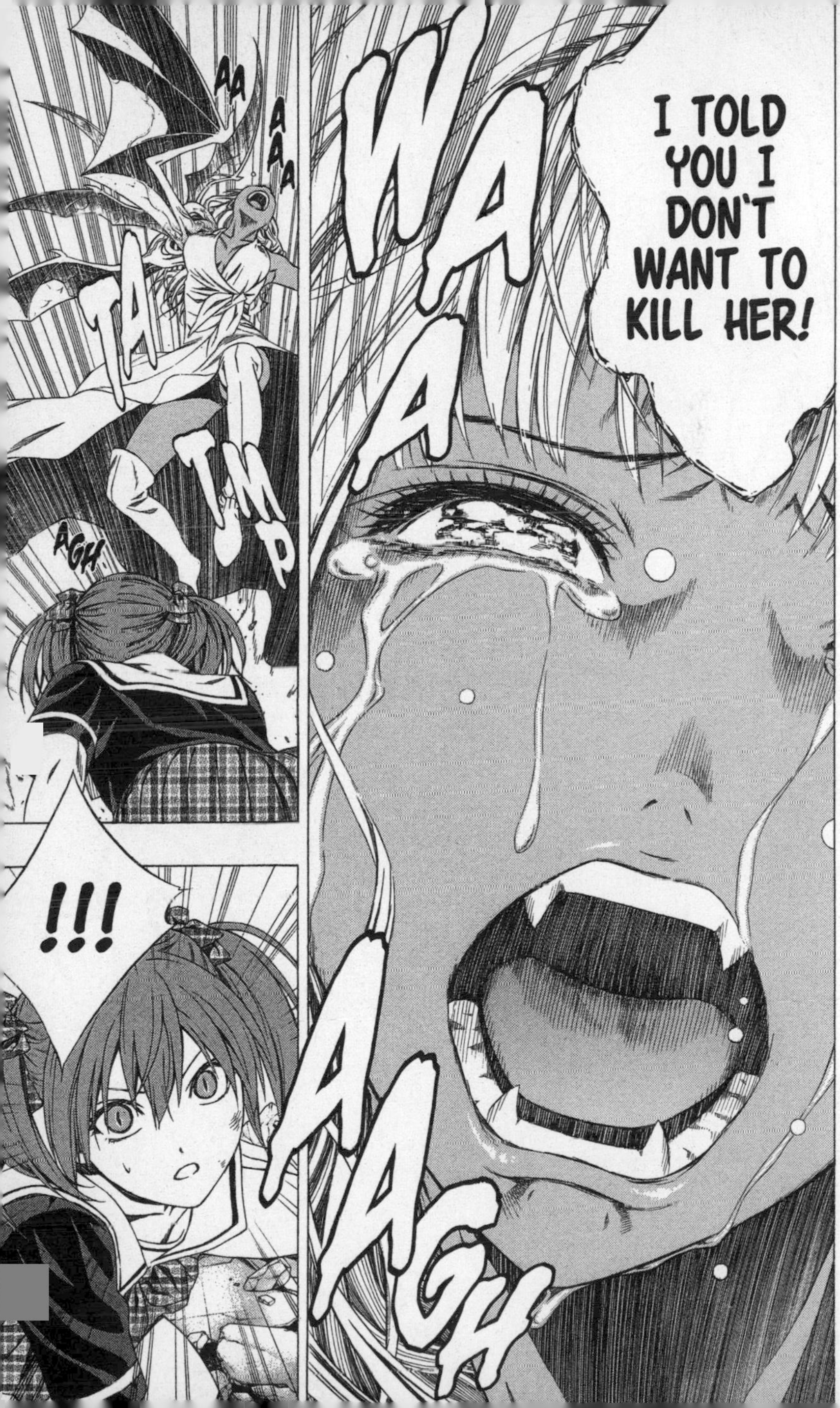
I TOLD YOU I DON'T WANT TO KILL HER!
WAAAAGH
AAAAA
TA
TMP
AGH
!!!

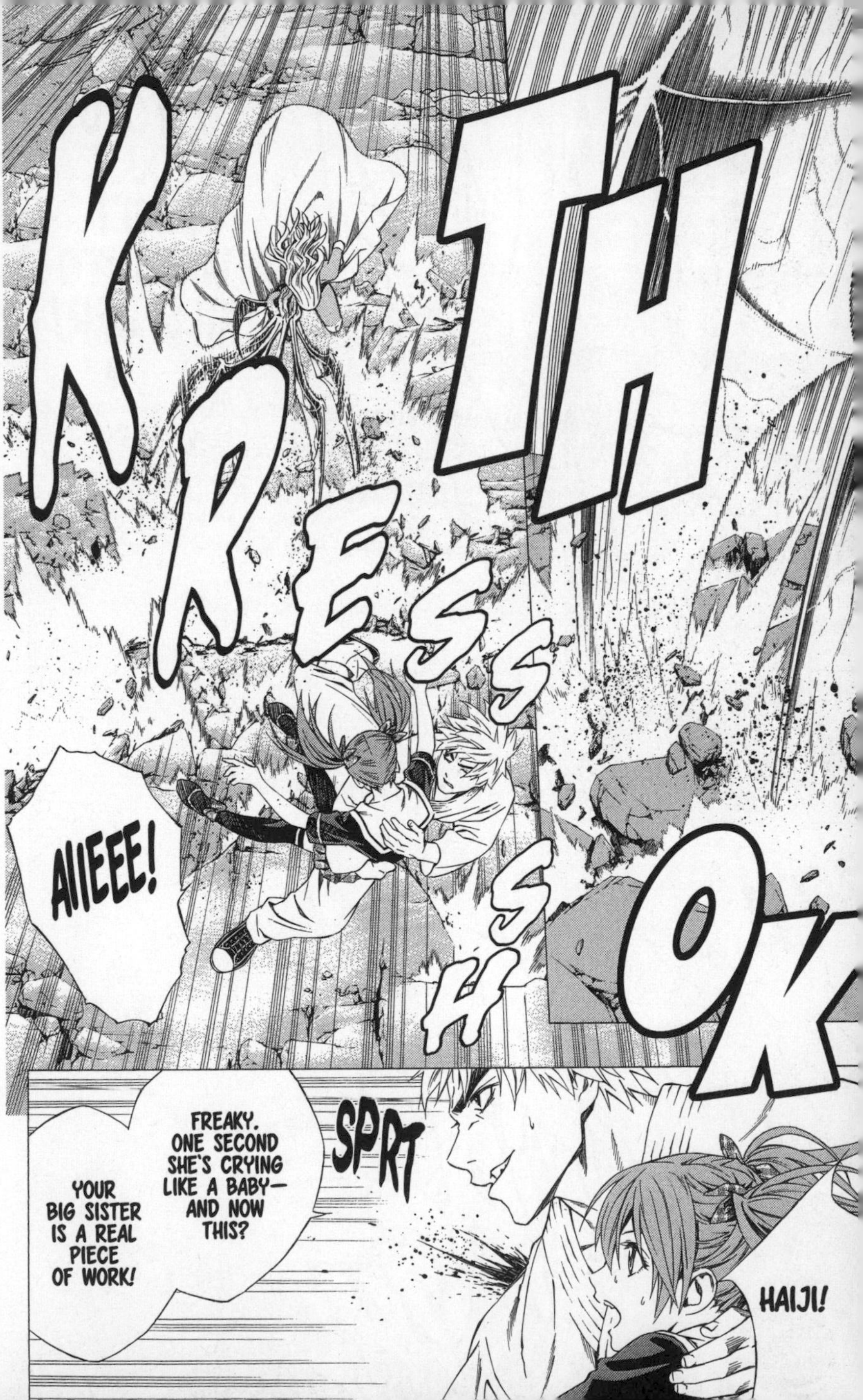
THOK
KRESSSSH
AIIEEE!
HAIJI!
SPRT
FREAKY. ONE SECOND SHE'S CRYING LIKE A BABY— AND NOW THIS?
YOUR BIG SISTER IS A REAL PIECE OF WORK!

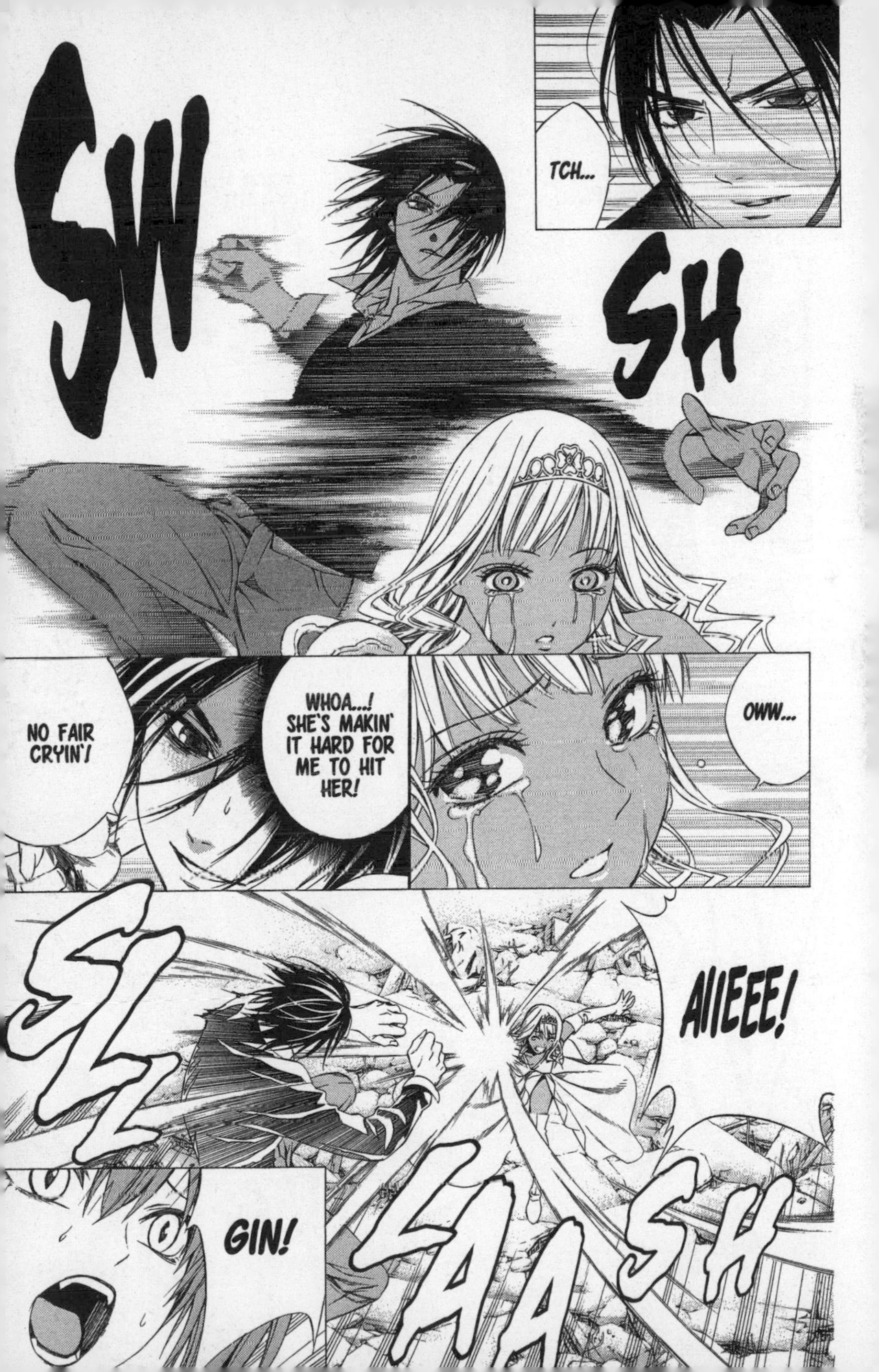
TCH...
SW
SH
OWW...
WHOA...! SHE'S MAKIN' IT HARD FOR ME TO HIT HER!
NO FAIR CRYIN'!
AIIEEE!
SZZ
LAASH
GIN!

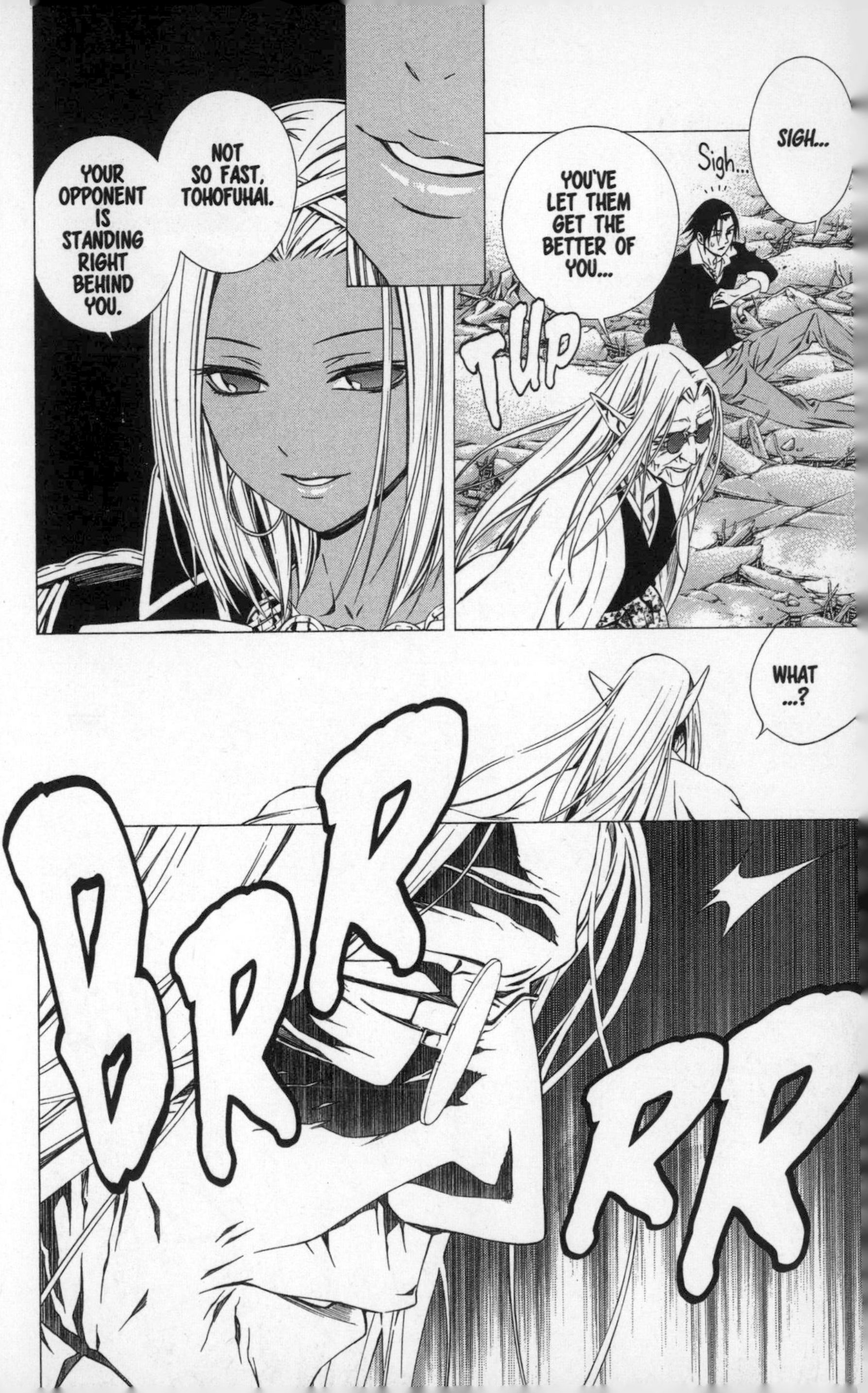
SIGH...
Sigh...
YOU'VE LET THEM GET THE BETTER OF YOU...
TUP
NOT SO FAST, TOHOFUHAI.
YOUR OPPONENT IS STANDING RIGHT BEHIND YOU.
WHAT ...?
BRRRR

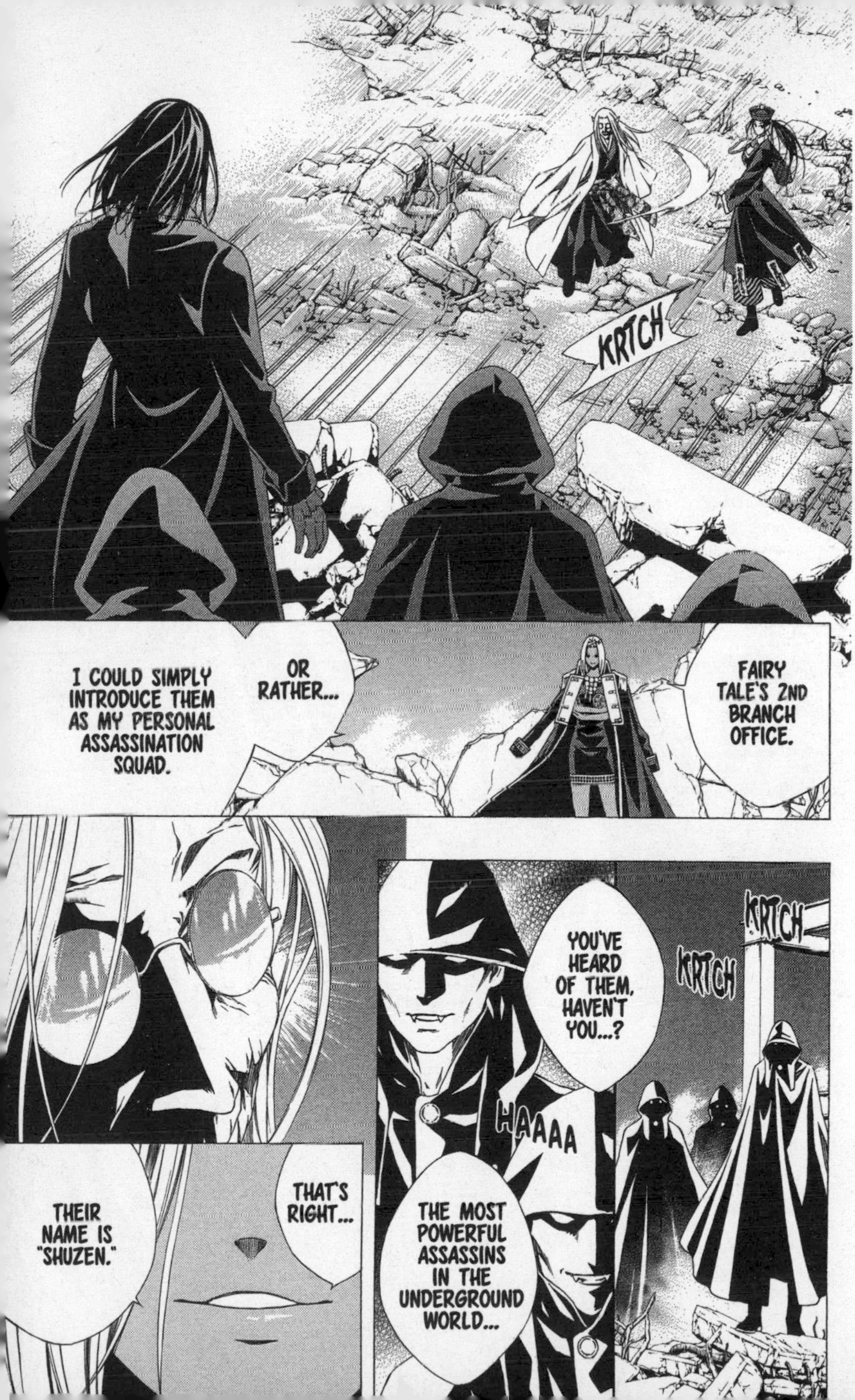
KRTCH
FAIRY TALE'S 2ND BRANCH OFFICE.
OR RATHER...
I COULD SIMPLY INTRODUCE THEM AS MY PERSONAL ASSASSINATION SQUAD.
KRTCH
KRTCH
YOU'VE HEARD OF THEM, HAVEN'T YOU...?
HAAAA
THE MOST POWERFUL ASSASSINS IN THE UNDERGROUND WORLD...
THAT'S RIGHT...
THEIR NAME IS "SHUZEN."

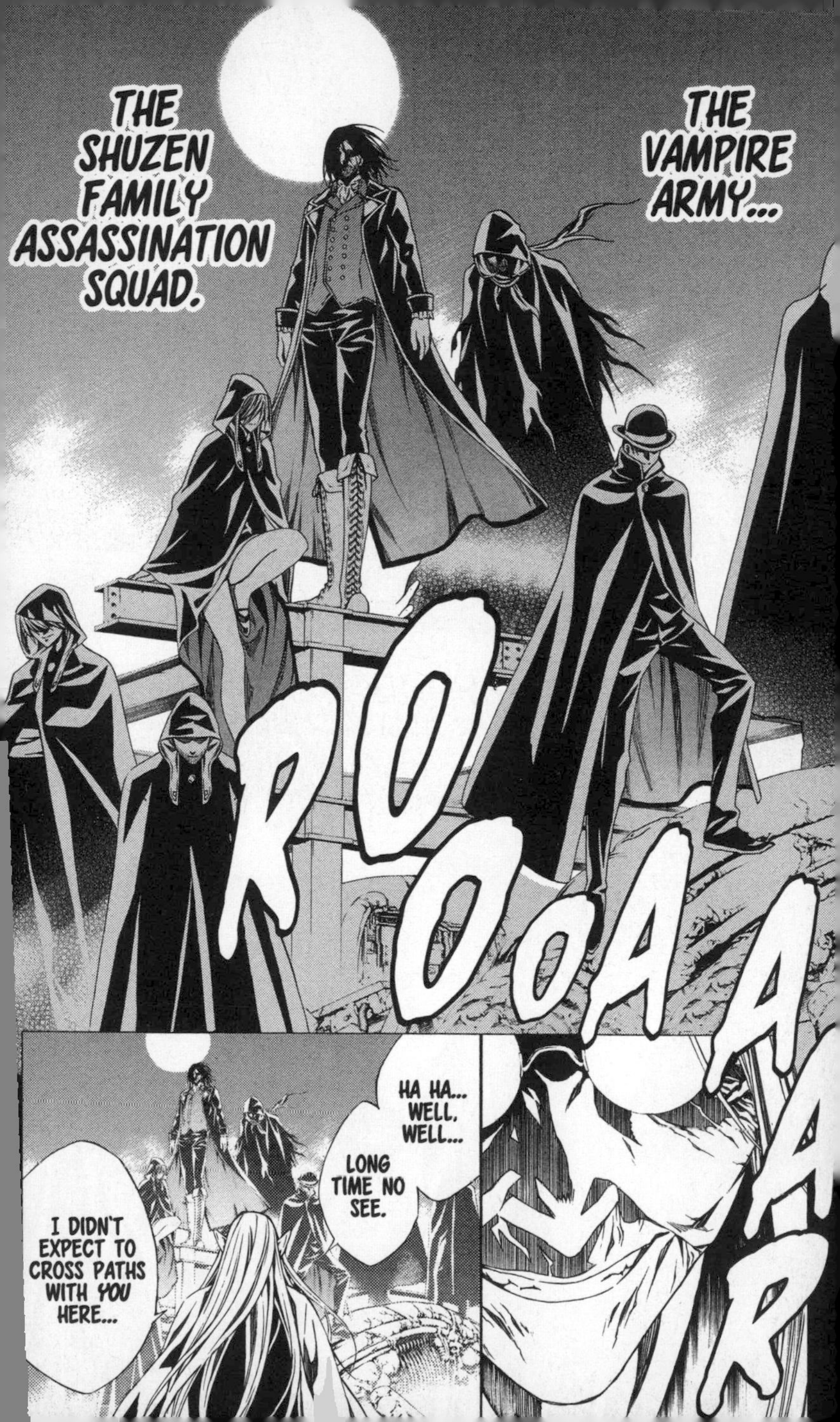
THE VAMPIRE ARMY...
THE SHUZEN FAMILY ASSASSINATION SQUAD.
ROOOOAAAAR
HA HA... WELL, WELL...
LONG TIME NO SEE.
I DIDN'T EXPECT TO CROSS PATHS WITH YOU HERE...

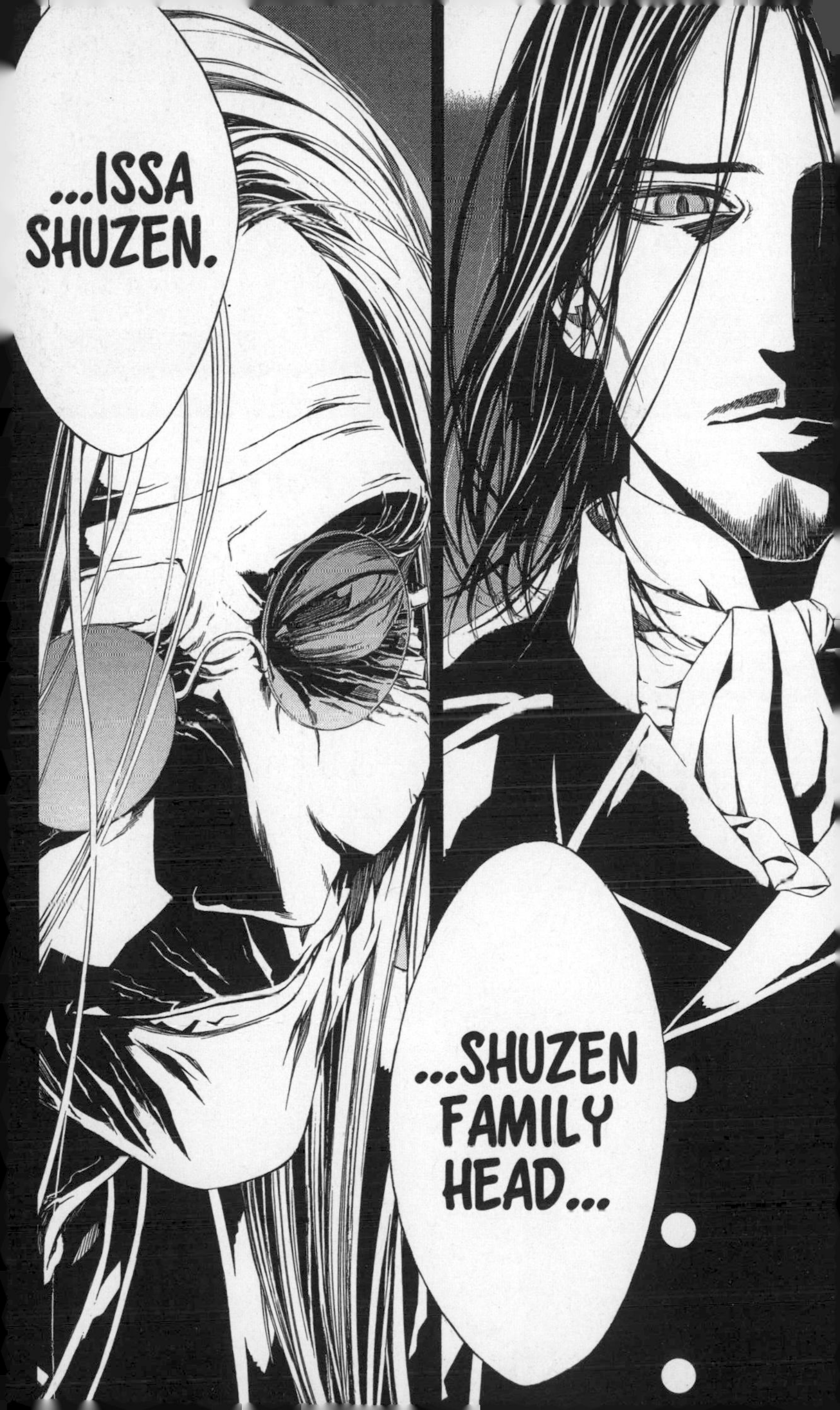
...SHUZEN FAMILY HEAD...
...ISSA SHUZEN.

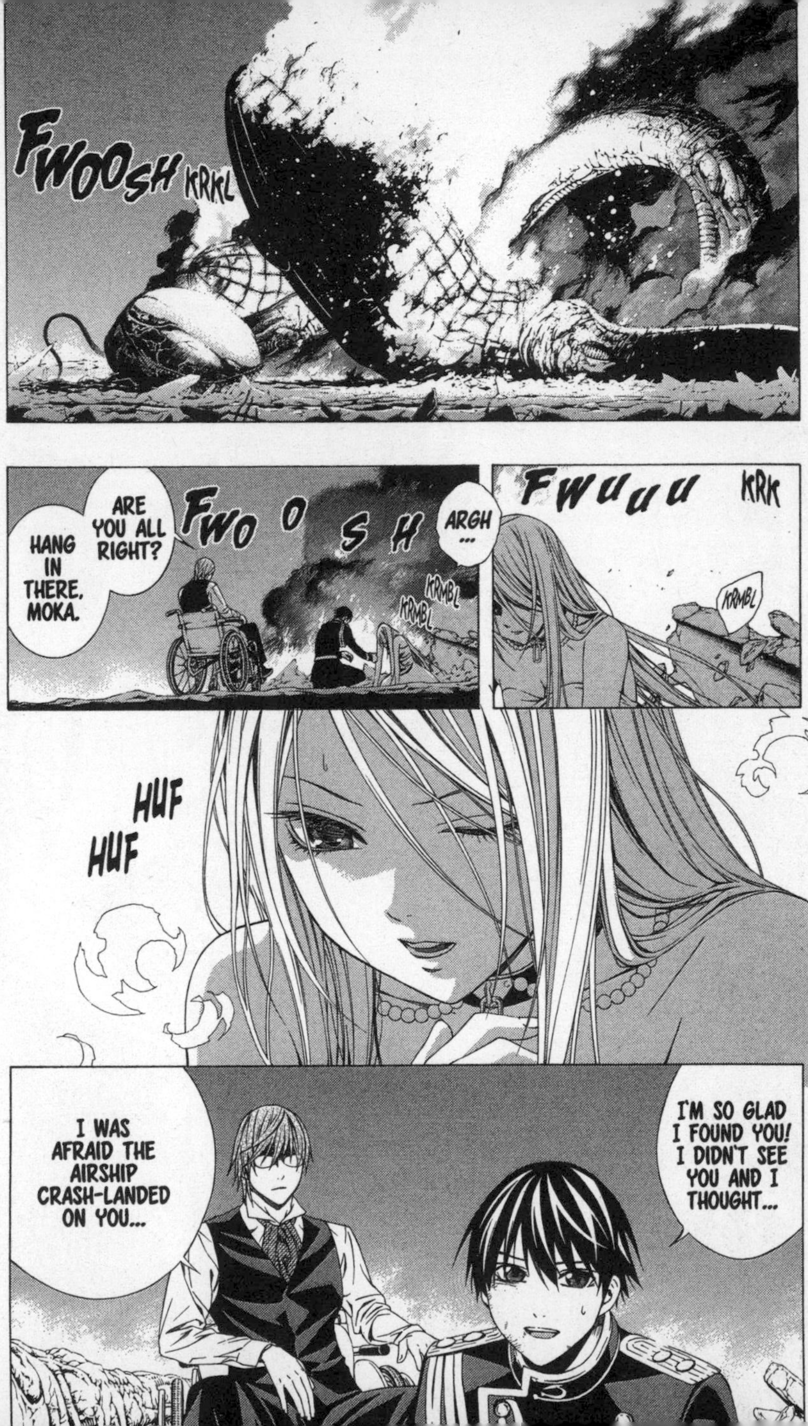
FWOOSH
KRKL
FWUUUU
KRK
ARGH...
KRMBL
ARE YOU ALL RIGHT?
HANG IN THERE, MOKA.
FWOOSH
KRMBL
KRMBL
HUF
HUF
I'M SO GLAD I FOUND YOU! I DIDN'T SEE YOU AND I THOUGHT...
I WAS AFRAID THE AIRSHIP CRASH-LANDED ON YOU...

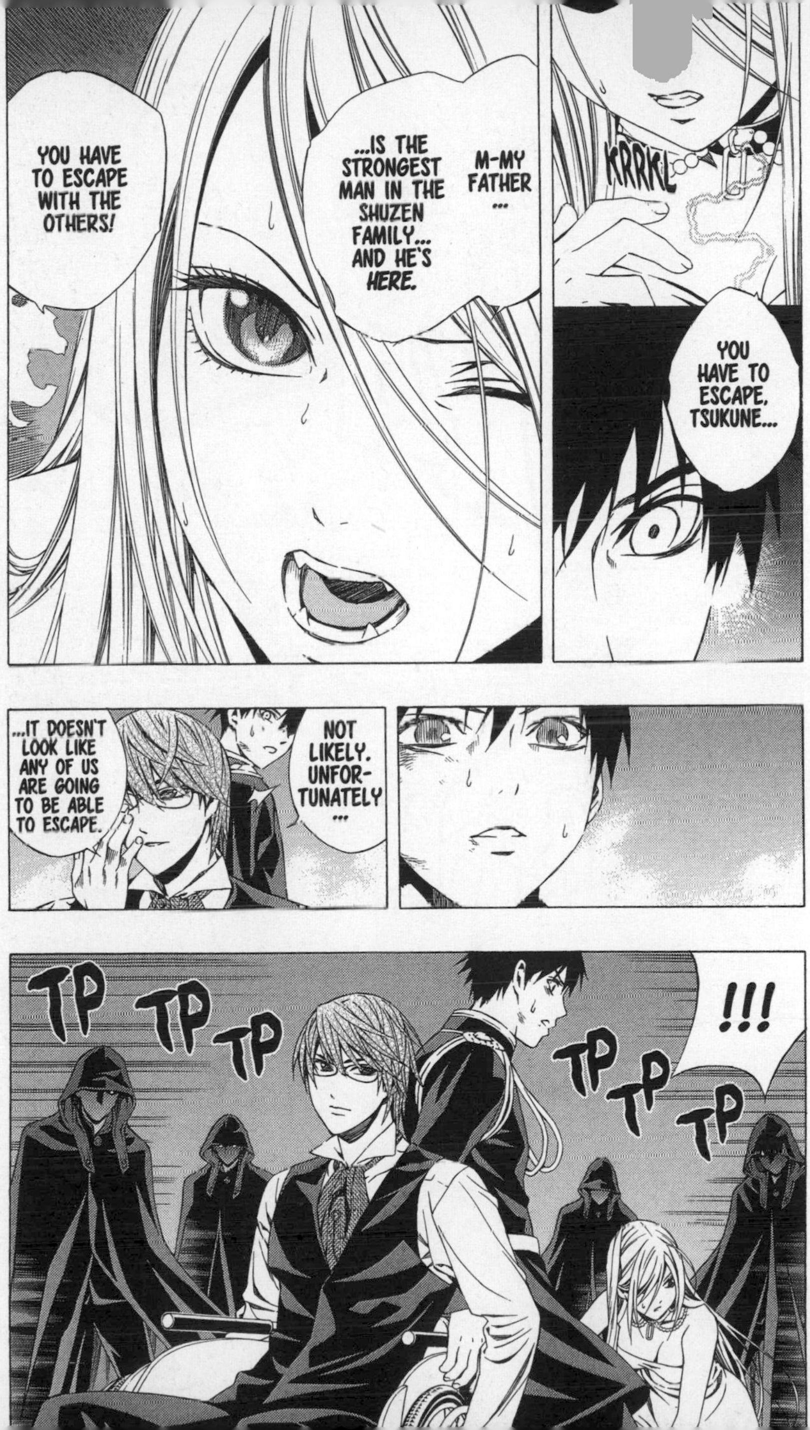
KRRKL
YOU HAVE TO ESCAPE, TSUKUNE...
M-MY FATHER...
...IS THE STRONGEST MAN IN THE SHUZEN FAMILY... AND HE'S HERE.
YOU HAVE TO ESCAPE WITH THE OTHERS!
NOT LIKELY. UNFORTUNATELY...
...IT DOESN'T LOOK LIKE ANY OF US ARE GOING TO BE ABLE TO ESCAPE.
!!!
TP TP TP
TP TP TP

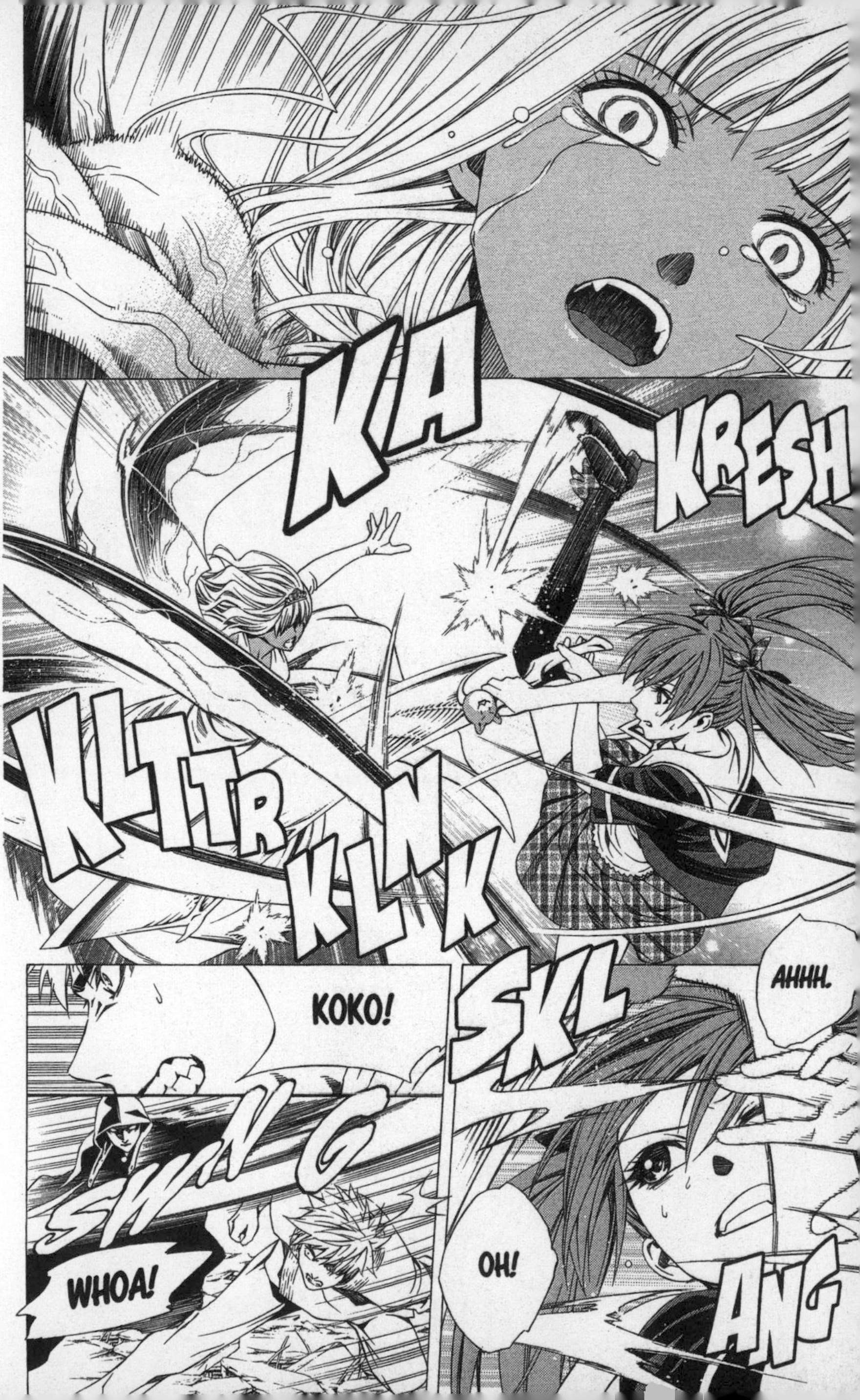
KA
KRESH
KLTTR
KLNK
SKL
AHHH.
OH!
ANG
KOKO!
SHING
WHOA!

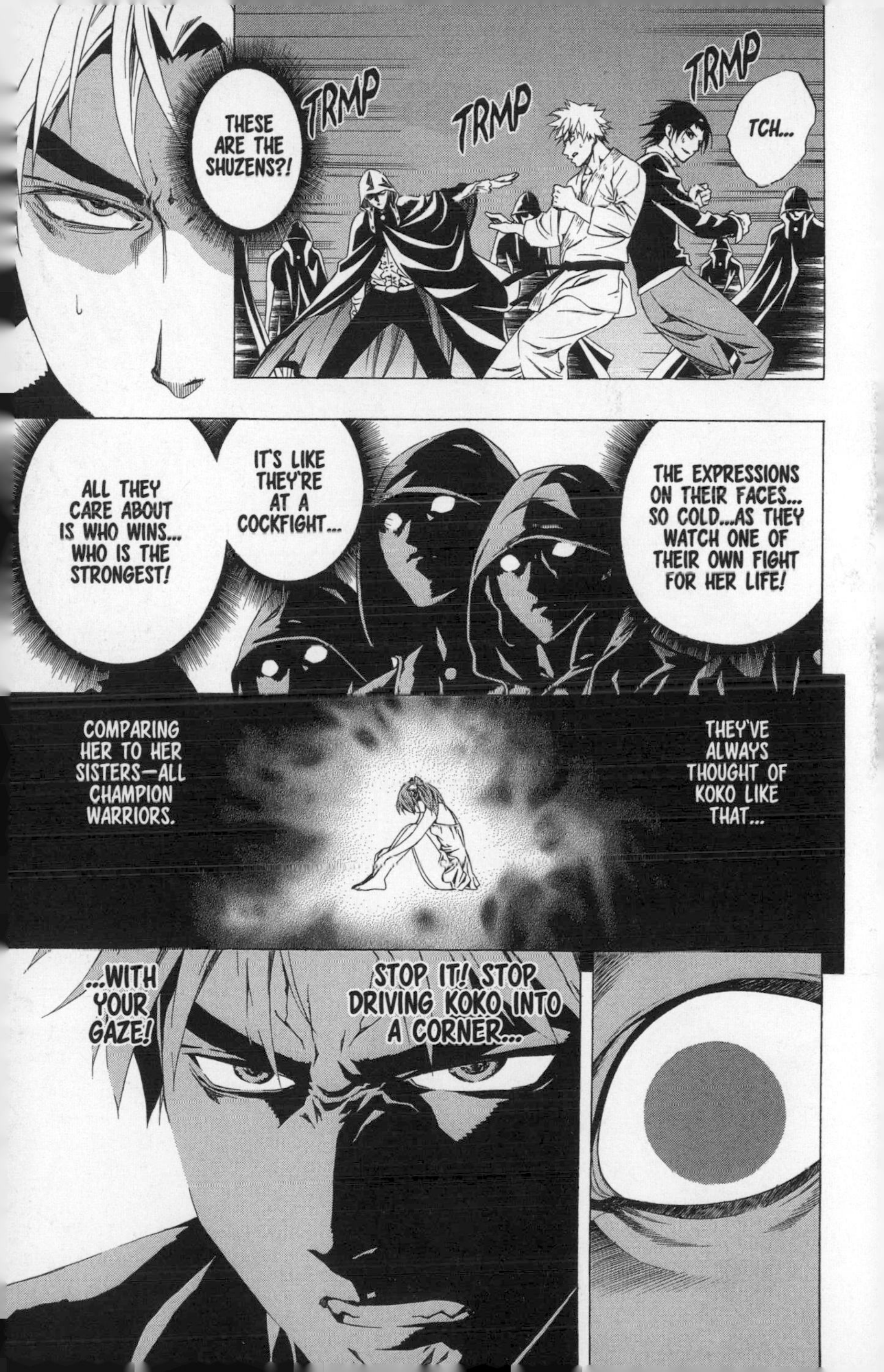
TRMP
TCH...
TRMP
TRMP
THESE ARE THE SHUZENS?!
THE EXPRESSIONS ON THEIR FACES... SO COLD...AS THEY WATCH ONE OF THEIR OWN FIGHT FOR HER LIFE!
IT'S LIKE THEY'RE AT A COCKFIGHT...
ALL THEY CARE ABOUT IS WHO WINS... WHO IS THE STRONGEST!
THEY'VE ALWAYS THOUGHT OF KOKO LIKE THAT...
COMPARING HER TO HER SISTERS—ALL CHAMPION WARRIORS.
STOP IT! STOP DRIVING KOKO INTO A CORNER...
...WITH YOUR GAZE!

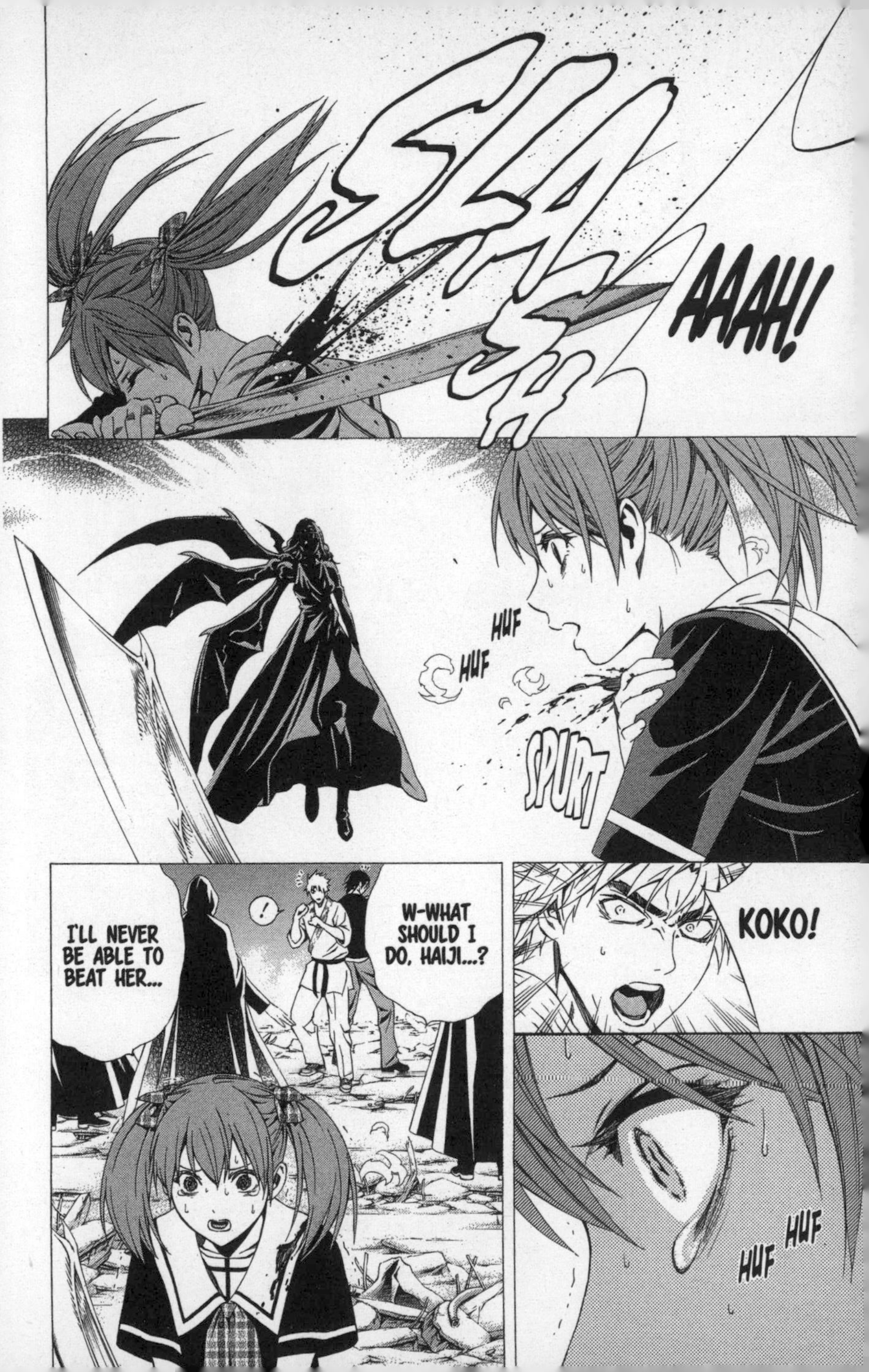
AAAH!
HUF
HUF
SPURT
KOKO!
HUF
HUF
W-WHAT SHOULD I DO, HAIJI...?
!
I'LL NEVER BE ABLE TO BEAT HER...

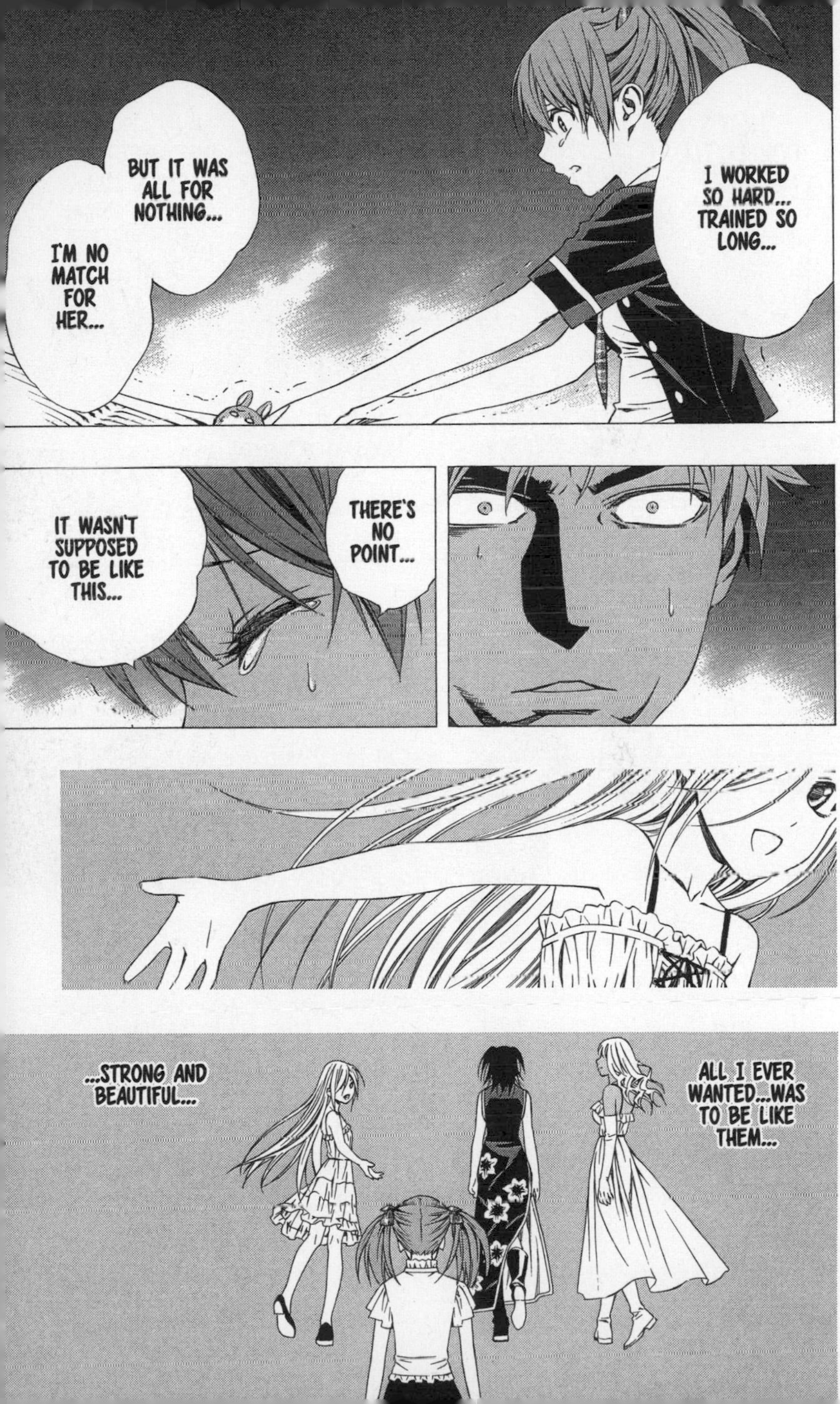
I WORKED SO HARD... TRAINED SO LONG...
BUT IT WAS ALL FOR NOTHING...
I'M NO MATCH FOR HER...
THERE'S NO POINT...
IT WASN'T SUPPOSED TO BE LIKE THIS...
ALL I EVER WANTED...WAS TO BE LIKE THEM...
...STRONG AND BEAUTIFUL...

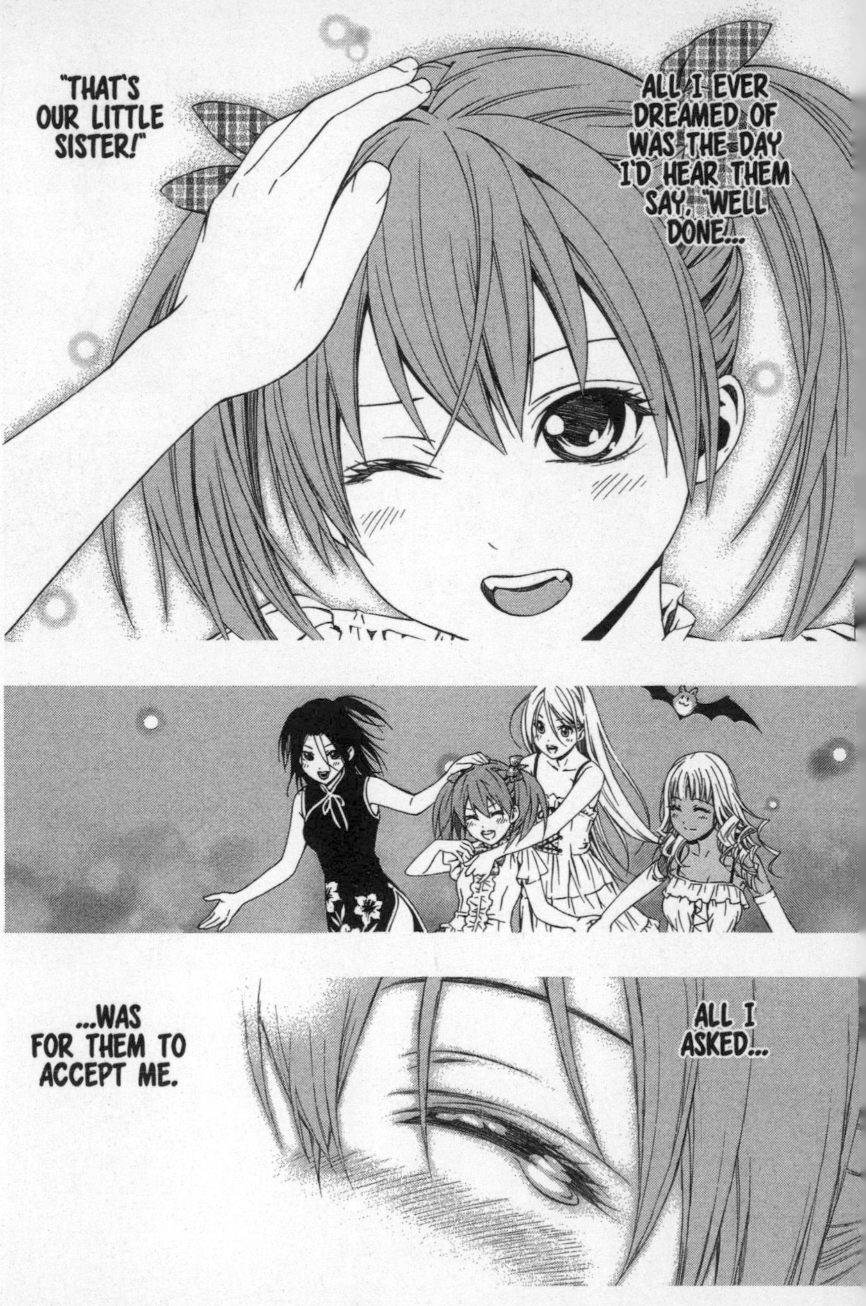
ALL I EVER DREAMED OF WAS THE DAY I'D HEAR THEM SAY, "WELL DONE...
"THAT'S OUR LITTLE SISTER!"
ALL I ASKED...
...WAS FOR THEM TO ACCEPT ME.

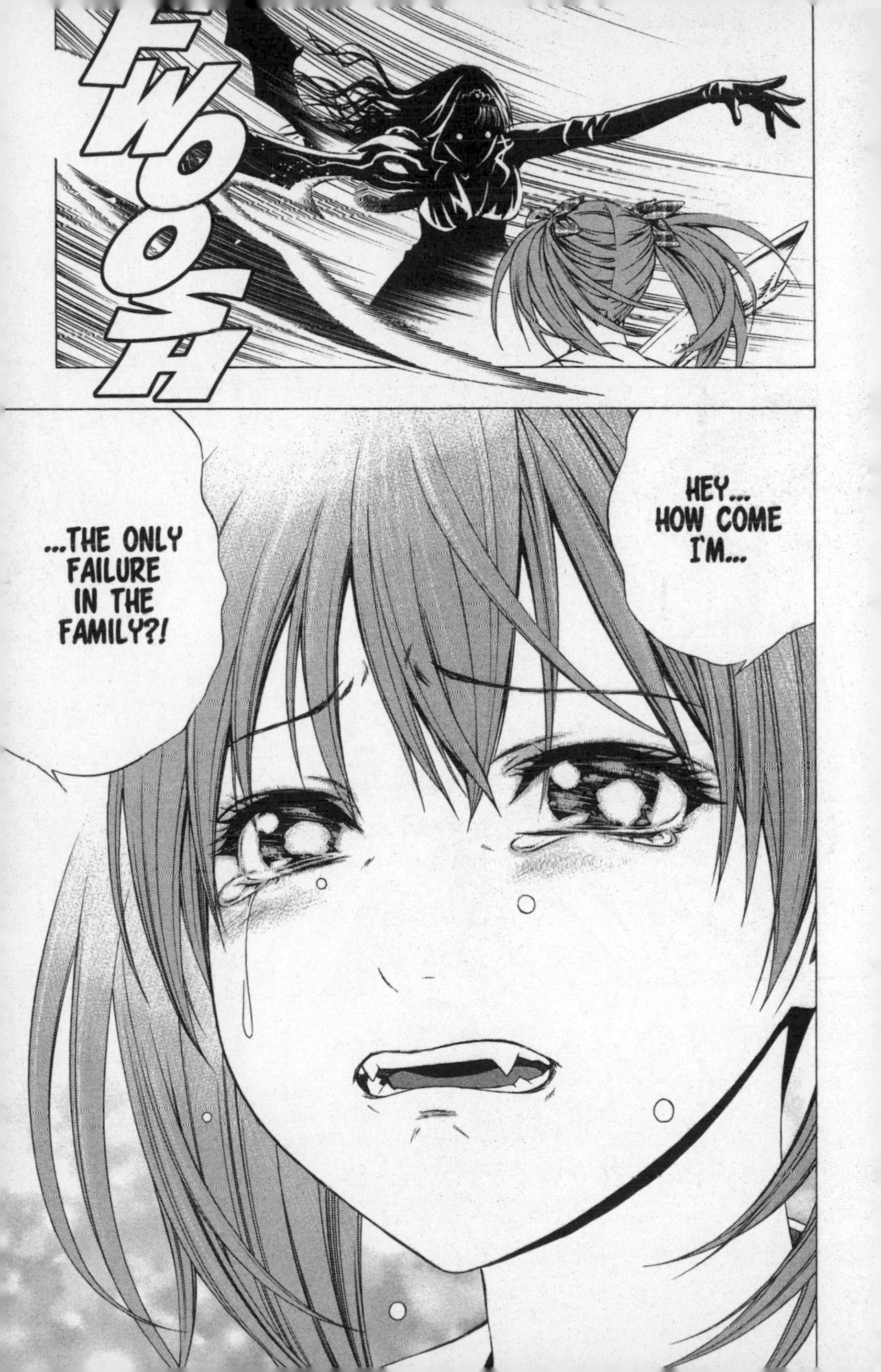
FWOOSH
HEY... HOW COME I'M...
...THE ONLY FAILURE IN THE FAMILY?!

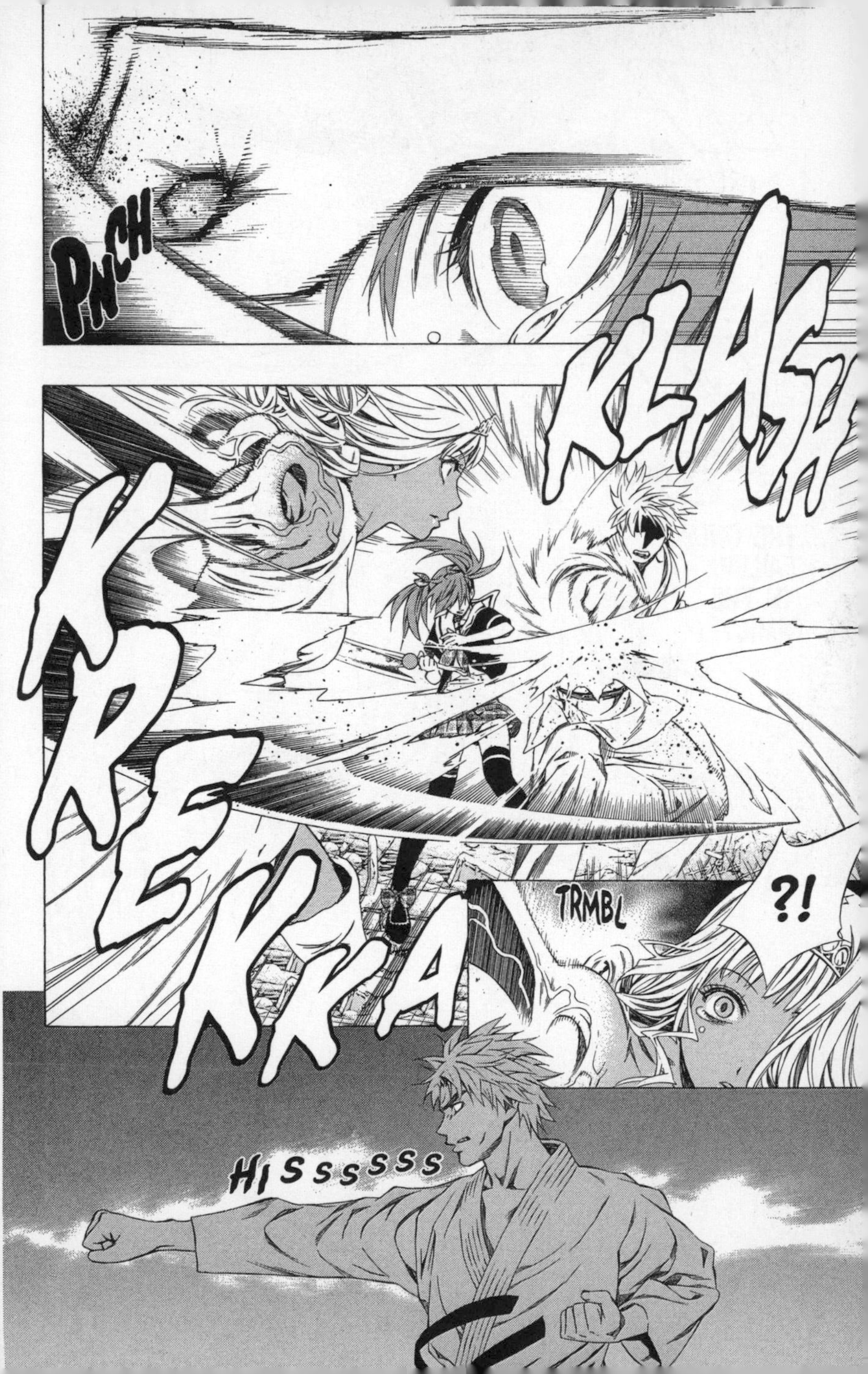
PNCH
KLASH
KRENKA
?!
TRMBL
HISSSSSS

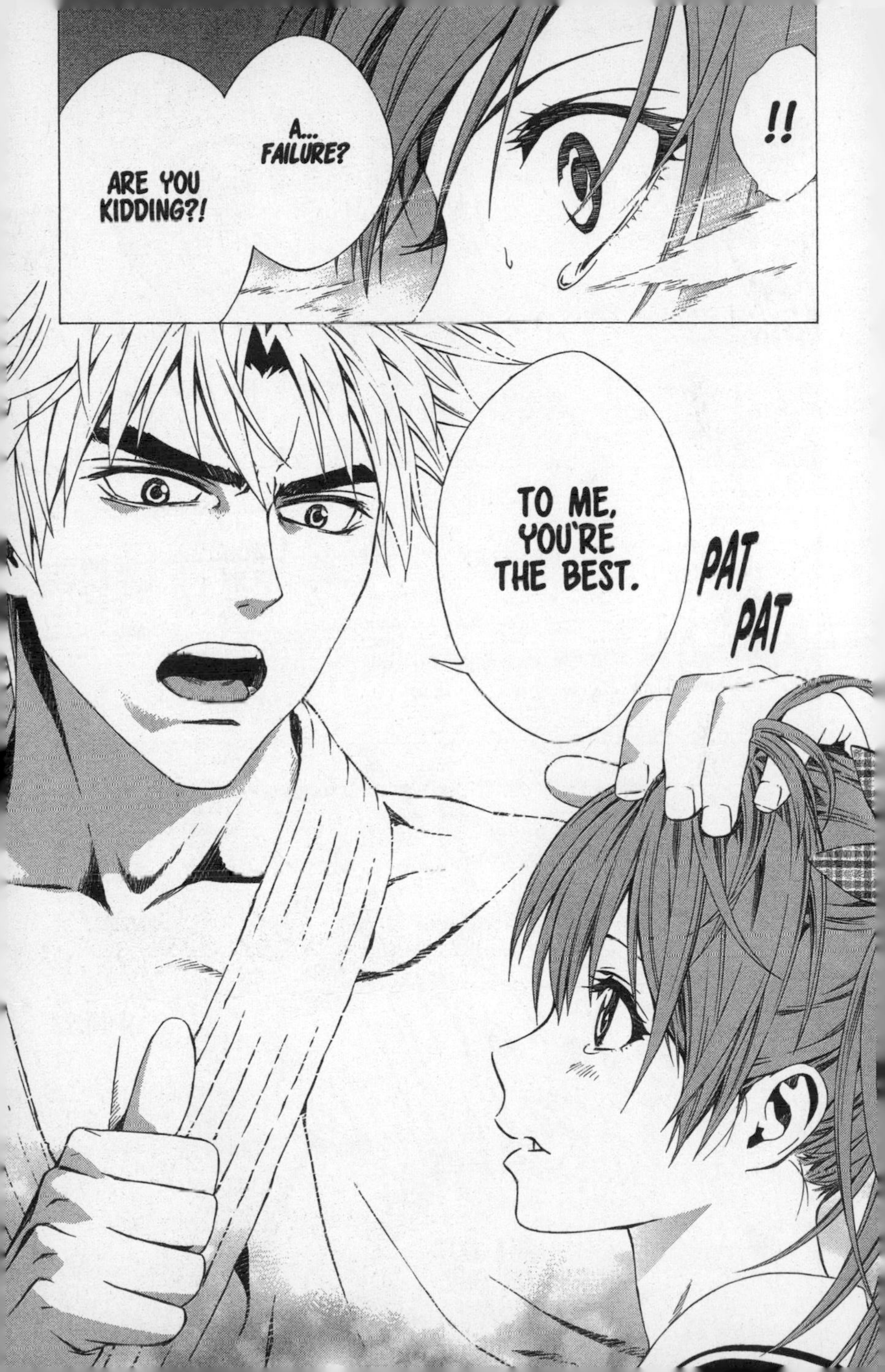
!!
A... FAILURE?
ARE YOU KIDDING?!
TO ME, YOU'RE THE BEST.
PAT PAT

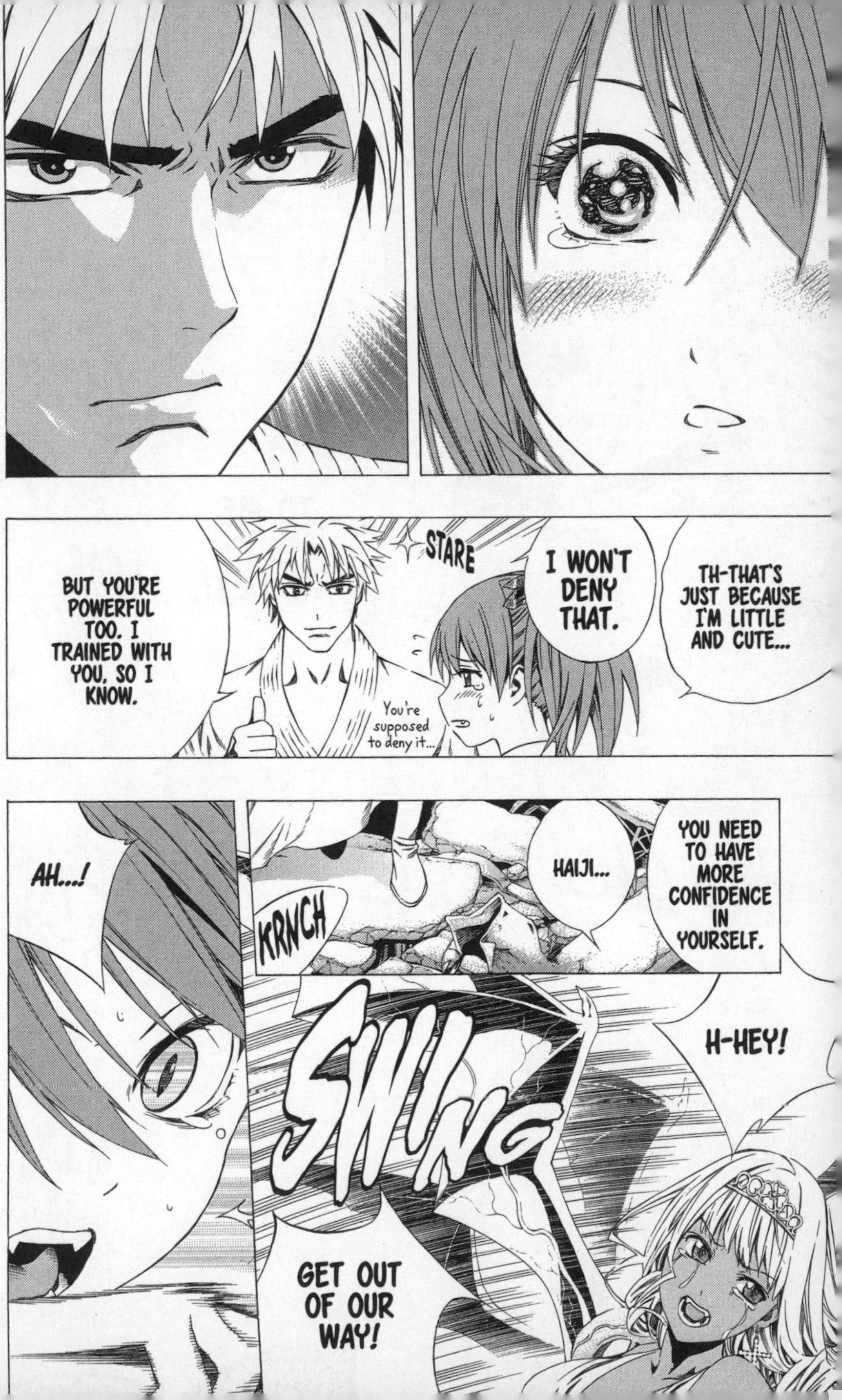
TH-THAT'S JUST BECAUSE I'M LITTLE AND CUTE...
I WON'T DENY THAT.
STARE
BUT YOU'RE POWERFUL TOO. I TRAINED WITH YOU, SO I KNOW.
You're supposed to deny it...
YOU NEED TO HAVE MORE CONFIDENCE IN YOURSELF.
HAIJI...
KRNCH
H-HEY!
SWING
GET OUT OF OUR WAY!
AH...!

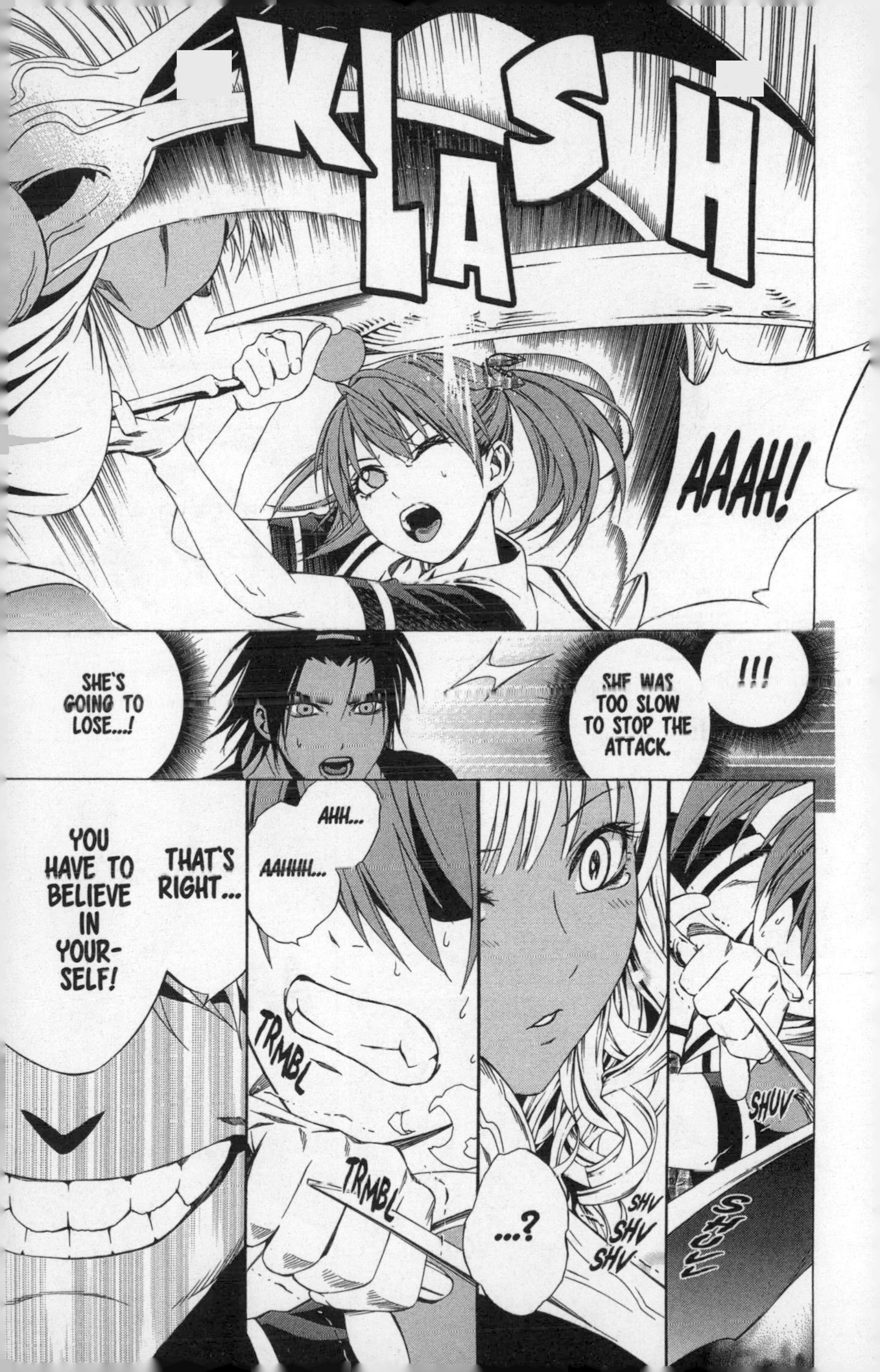
KLASH
AAAH!
!!!
SHE WAS TOO SLOW TO STOP THE ATTACK.
SHE'S GOING TO LOSE...!
SHUV
SHV SHV SHV
...?
AHH...
AAHHH...
TRMBL
TRMBL
THAT'S RIGHT...
YOU HAVE TO BELIEVE IN YOUR-SELF!

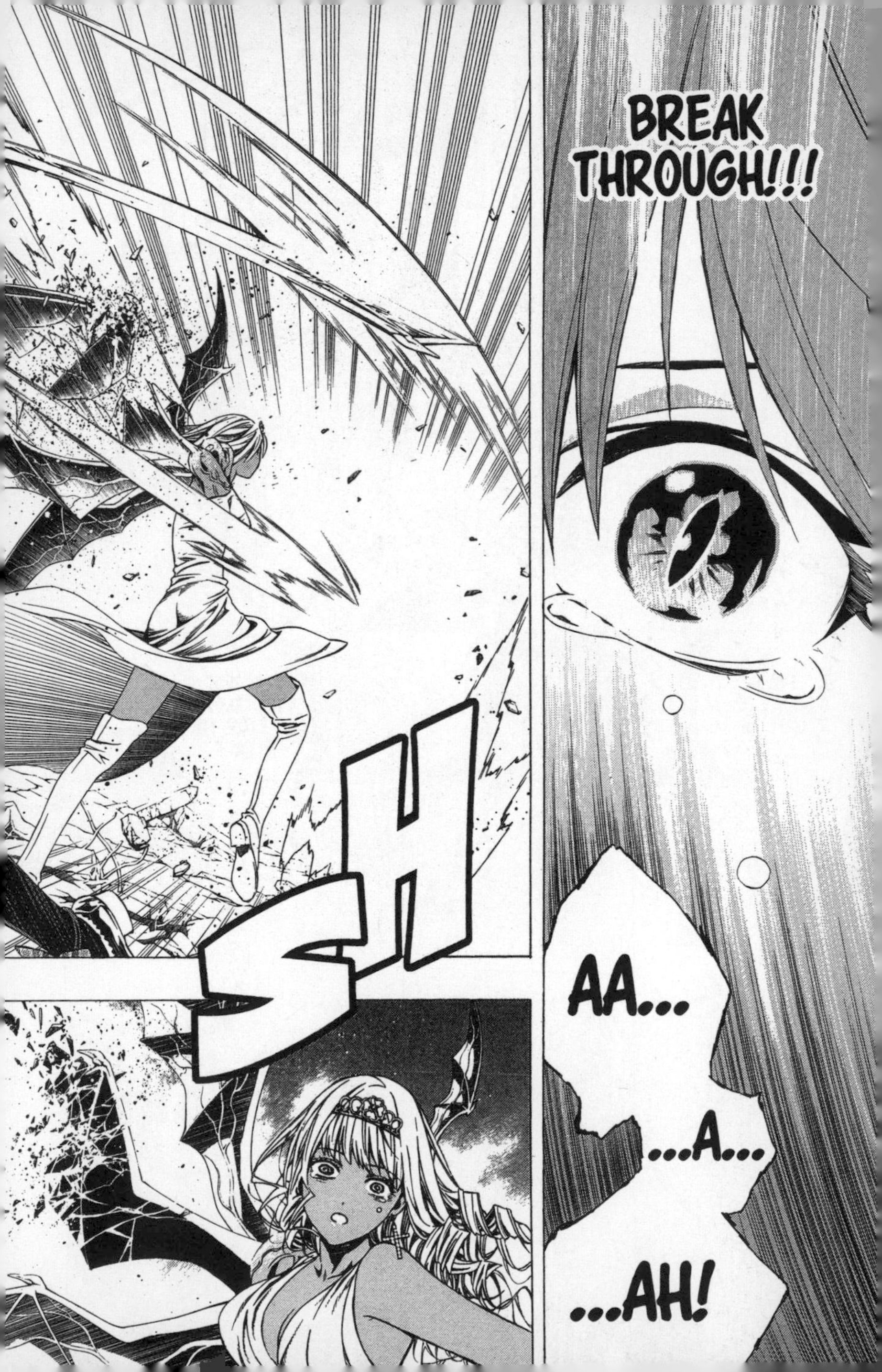
BREAK THROUGH!!!
SH
AA...
...A...
...AH!

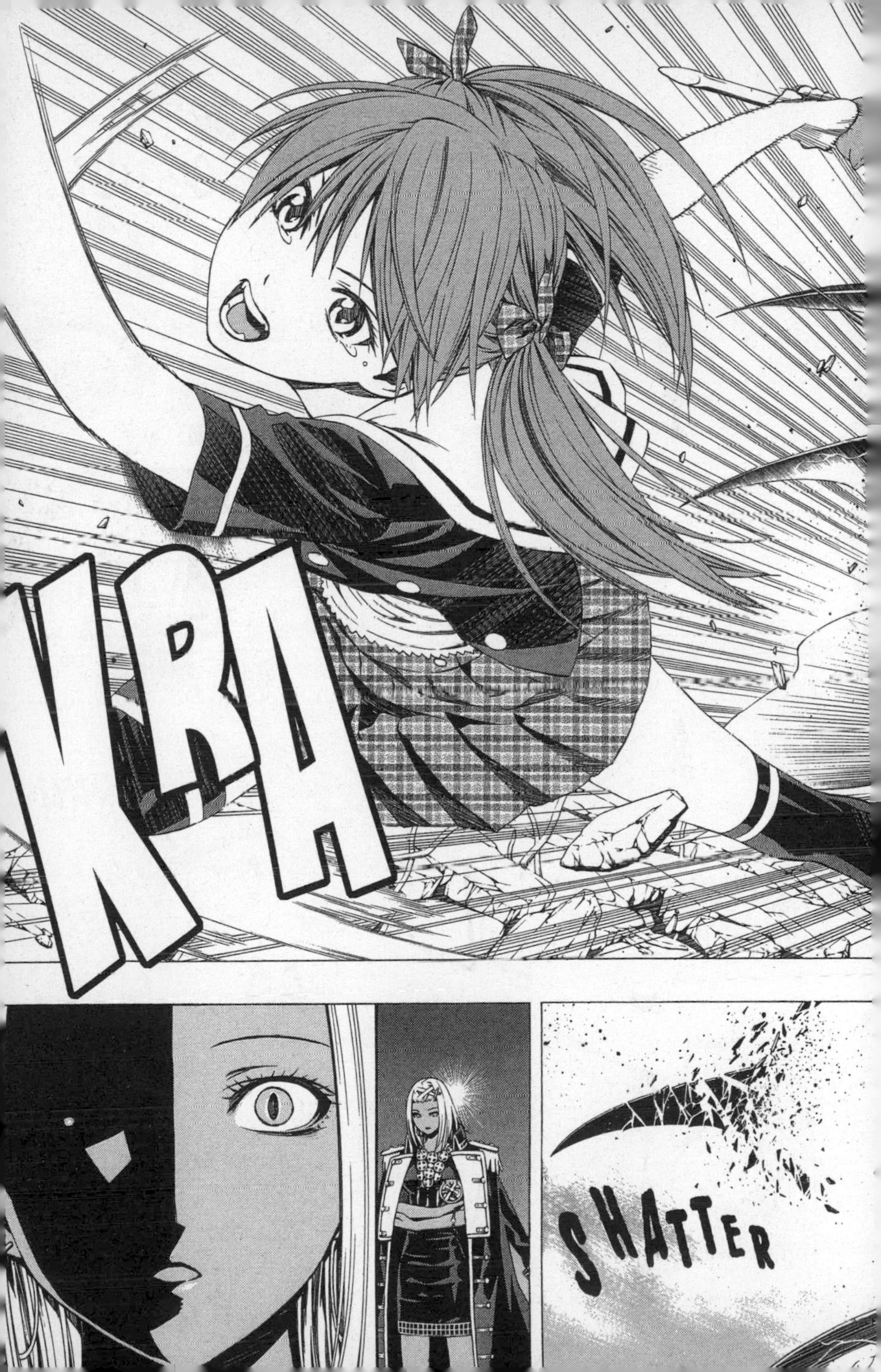
KRA
SHATTER

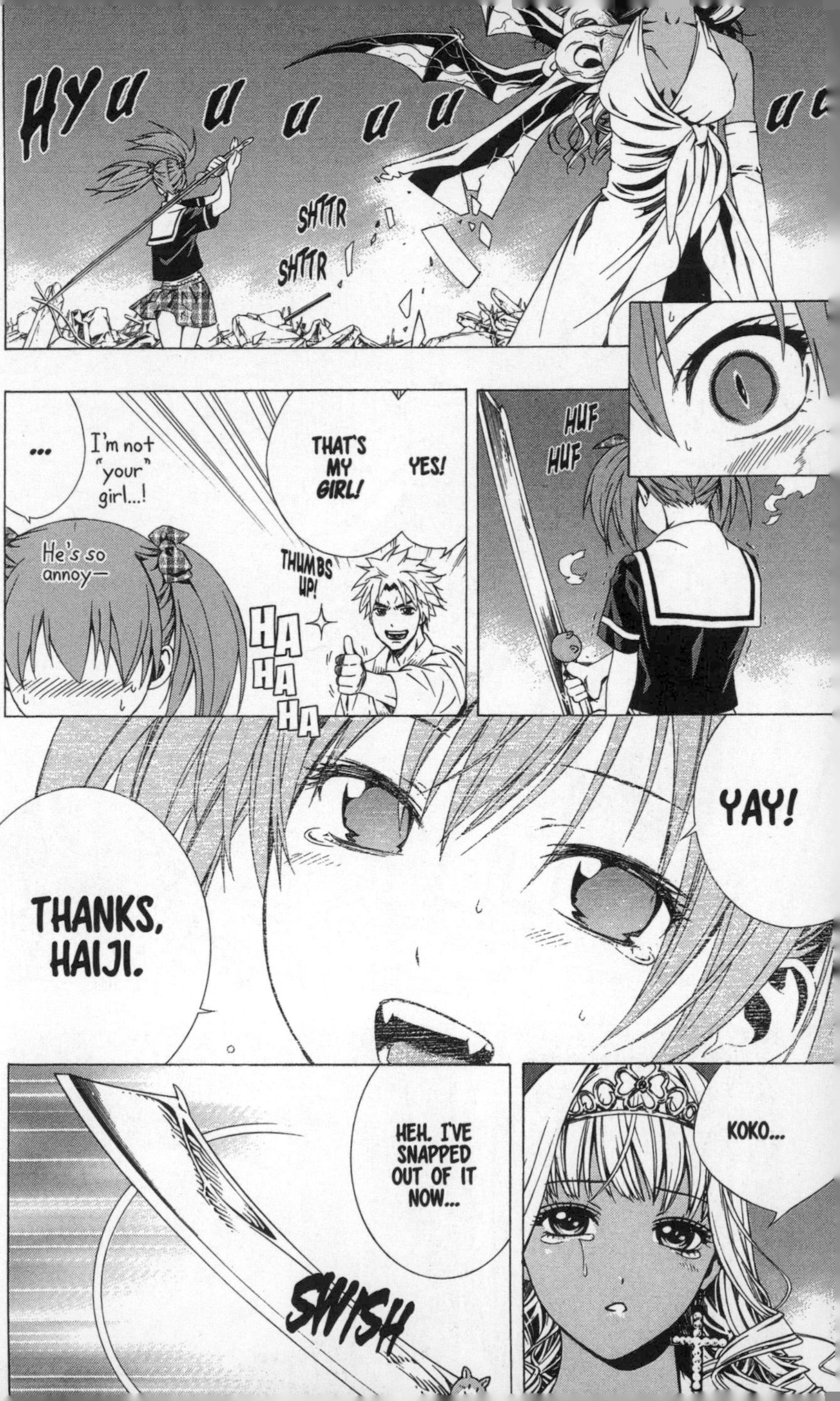
HYU U U U U UU
SHTTR
SHTTR
HUF
HUF
YES!
THAT'S MY GIRL!
...
I'm not "your" girl...!
THUMBS UP!
HA HA HA HA
He's so annoy—
YAY!
THANKS, HAIJI.
KOKO...
HEH. I'VE SNAPPED OUT OF IT NOW...
SWISH

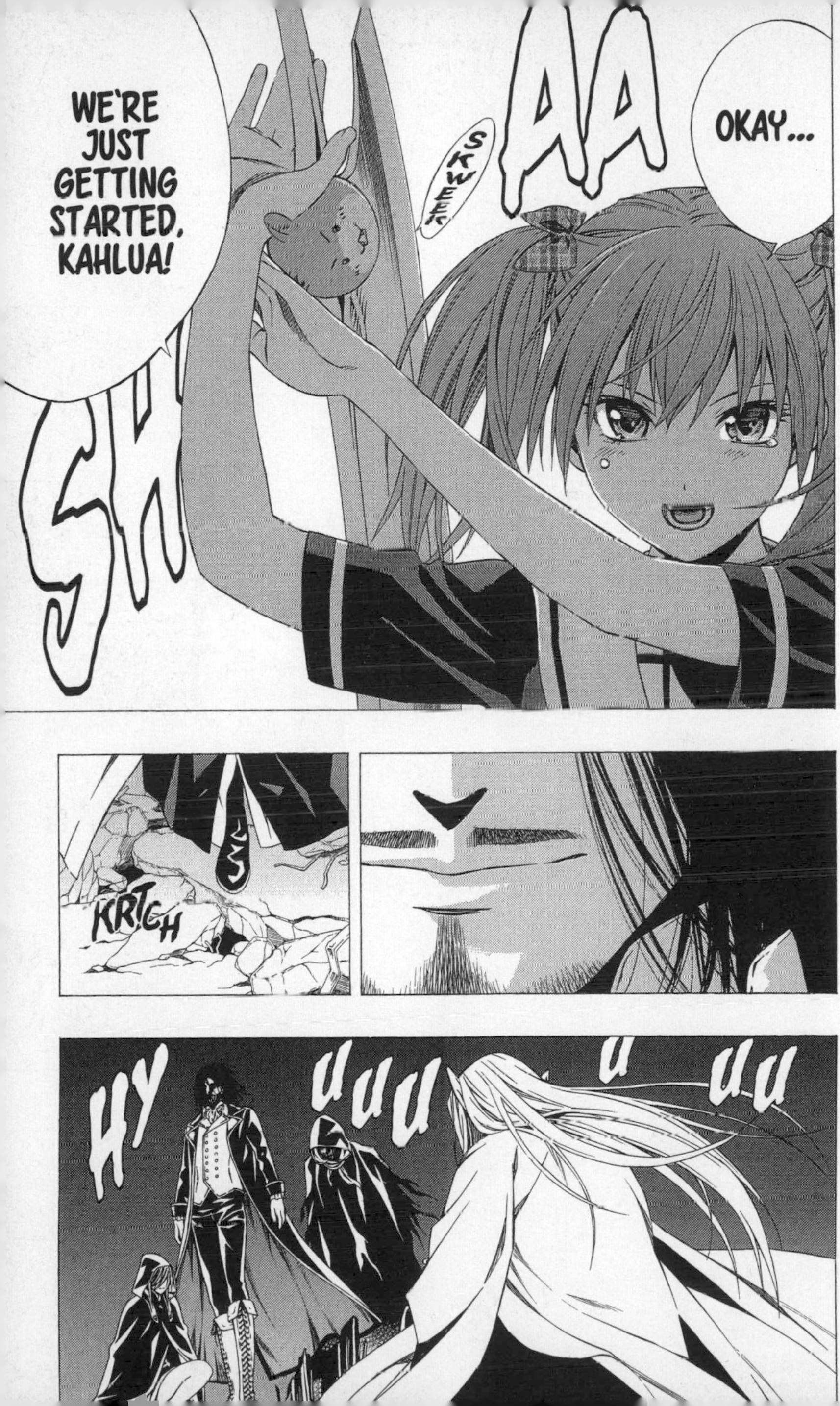
OKAY...
SKWEEK
SHAA
WE'RE JUST GETTING STARTED, KAHLUA!
KRTCH
HYUUUUUU

58: Rock 'n' Roll #2

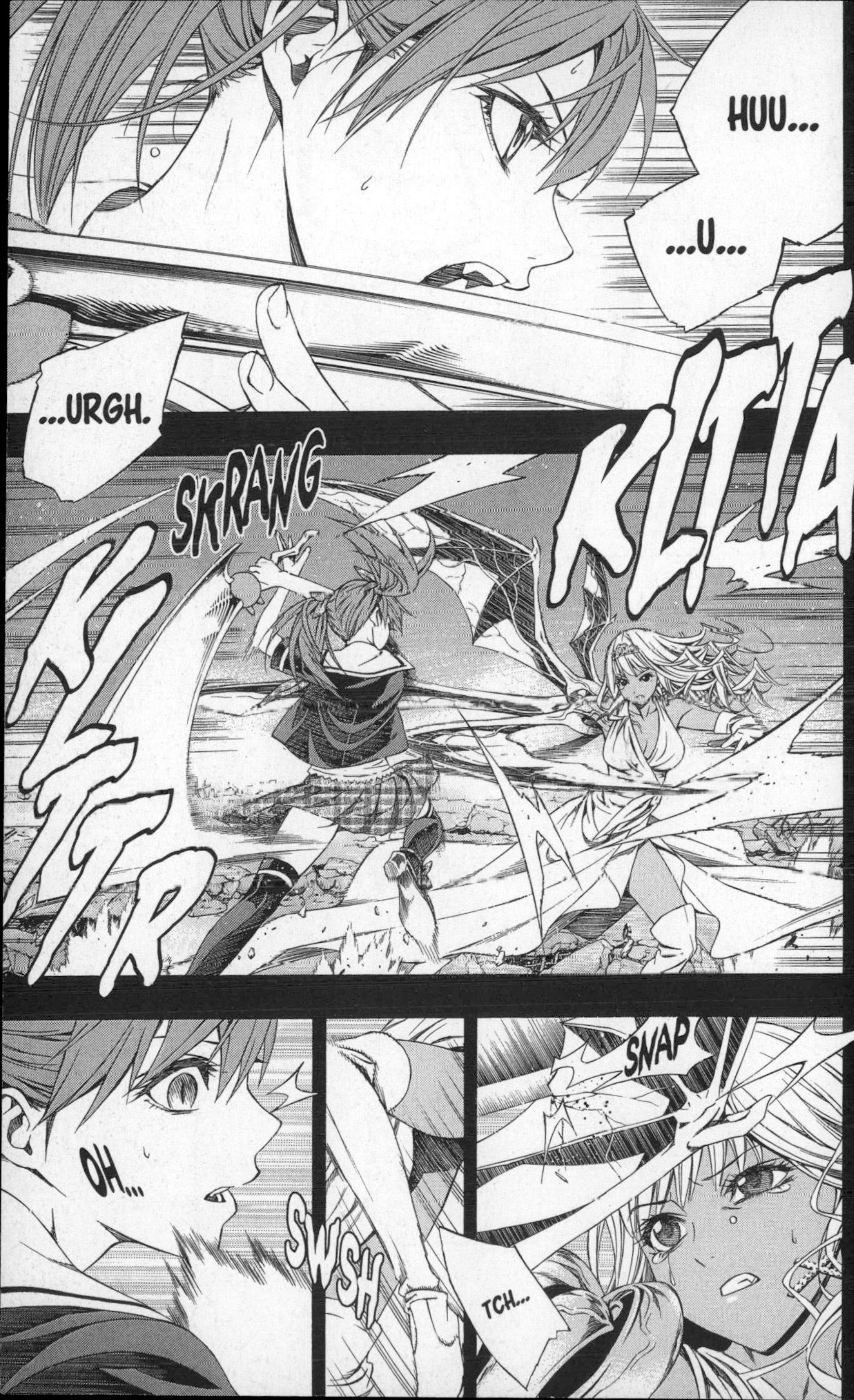
HUU...
...U...
...URGH.
SKRANG
SNAP
TCH...
SWSH
OH...

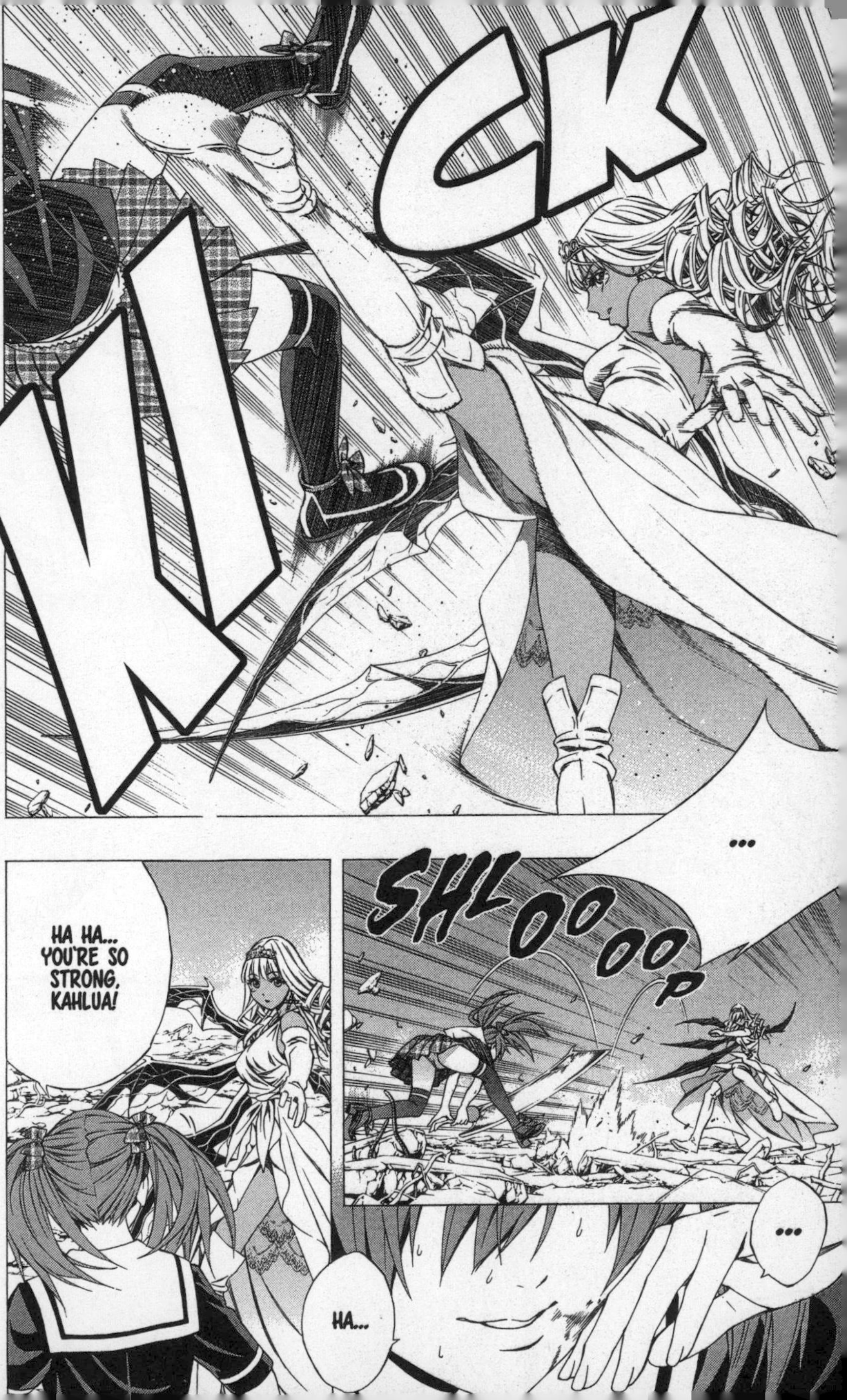
CK
...
SHLOOOOOP
HA HA... YOU'RE SO STRONG, KAHLUA!
...
HA...

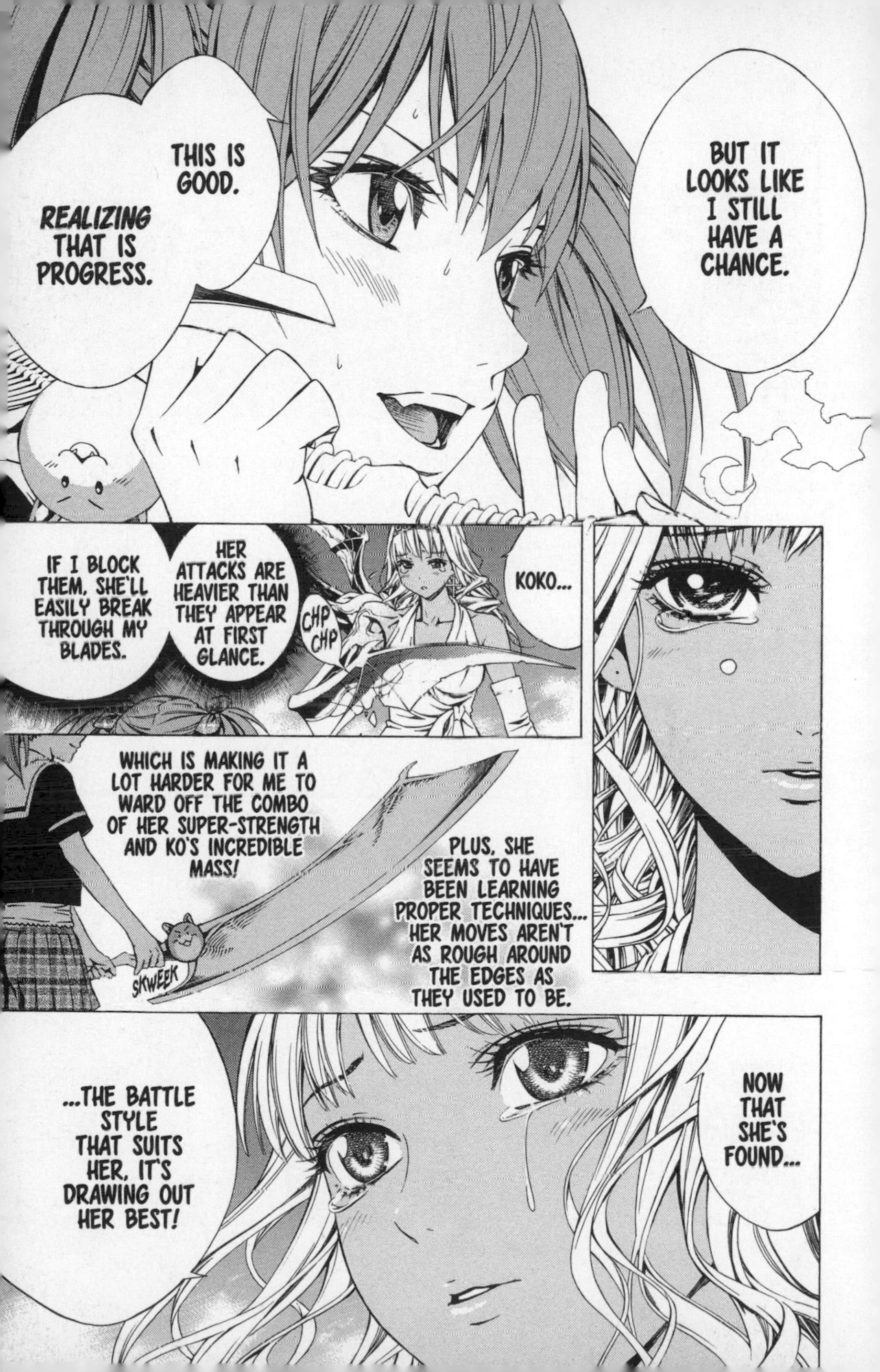
BUT IT LOOKS LIKE I STILL HAVE A CHANCE.
THIS IS GOOD.
REALIZING THAT IS PROGRESS.
KOKO...
CHP CHP
HER ATTACKS ARE HEAVIER THAN THEY APPEAR AT FIRST GLANCE.
IF I BLOCK THEM, SHE'LL EASILY BREAK THROUGH MY BLADES.
PLUS, SHE SEEMS TO HAVE BEEN LEARNING PROPER TECHNIQUES... HER MOVES AREN'T AS ROUGH AROUND THE EDGES AS THEY USED TO BE.
WHICH IS MAKING IT A LOT HARDER FOR ME TO WARD OFF THE COMBO OF HER SUPER-STRENGTH AND KO'S INCREDIBLE MASS!
SKWEEK
NOW THAT SHE'S FOUND...
...THE BATTLE STYLE THAT SUITS HER, IT'S DRAWING OUT HER BEST!

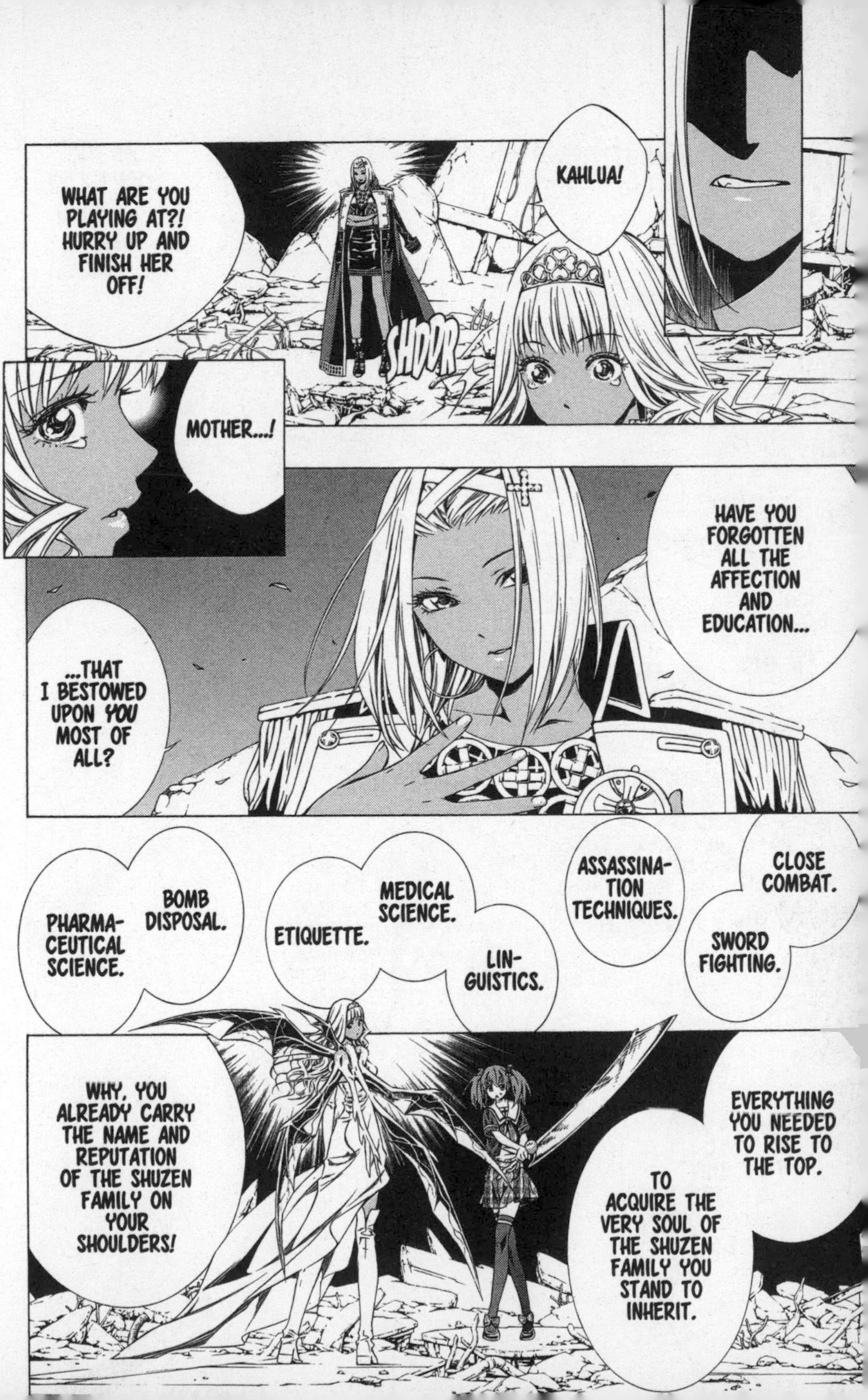
KAHLUA!
WHAT ARE YOU PLAYING AT?! HURRY UP AND FINISH HER OFF!
SHOOR
MOTHER...!
HAVE YOU FORGOTTEN ALL THE AFFECTION AND EDUCATION...
...THAT I BESTOWED UPON YOU MOST OF ALL?
CLOSE COMBAT.
SWORD FIGHTING.
ASSASSINATION TECHNIQUES.
MEDICAL SCIENCE.
LINGUISTICS.
ETIQUETTE.
BOMB DISPOSAL.
PHARMACEUTICAL SCIENCE.
EVERYTHING YOU NEEDED TO RISE TO THE TOP.
TO ACQUIRE THE VERY SOUL OF THE SHUZEN FAMILY YOU STAND TO INHERIT.
WHY, YOU ALREADY CARRY THE NAME AND REPUTATION OF THE SHUZEN FAMILY ON YOUR SHOULDERS!

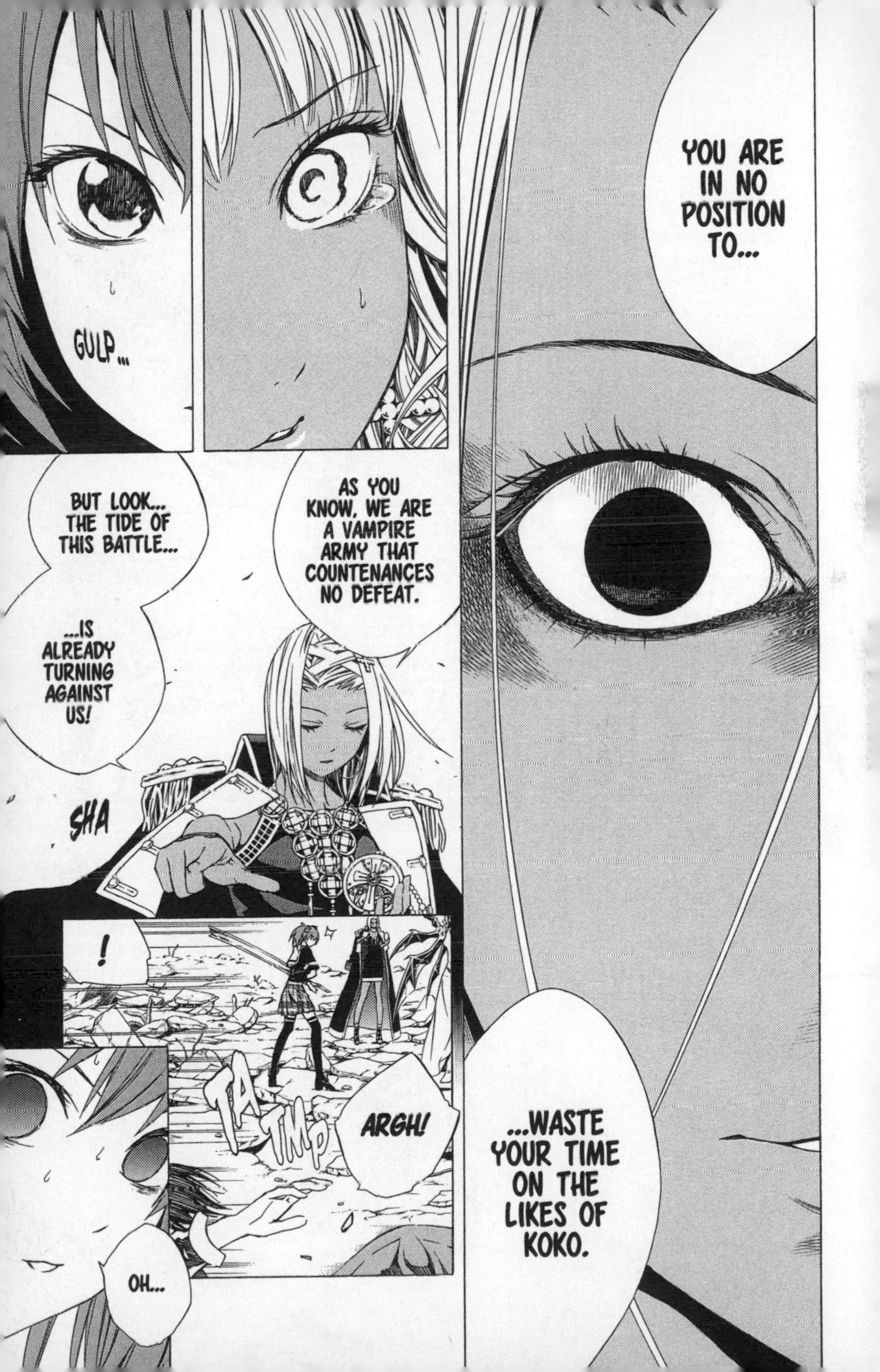
YOU ARE IN NO POSITION TO...
...WASTE YOUR TIME ON THE LIKES OF KOKO.
GULP...
AS YOU KNOW, WE ARE A VAMPIRE ARMY THAT COUNTENANCES NO DEFEAT.
BUT LOOK... THE TIDE OF THIS BATTLE...
...IS ALREADY TURNING AGAINST US!
SHA
!
TA
TMP
ARGH!
OH...

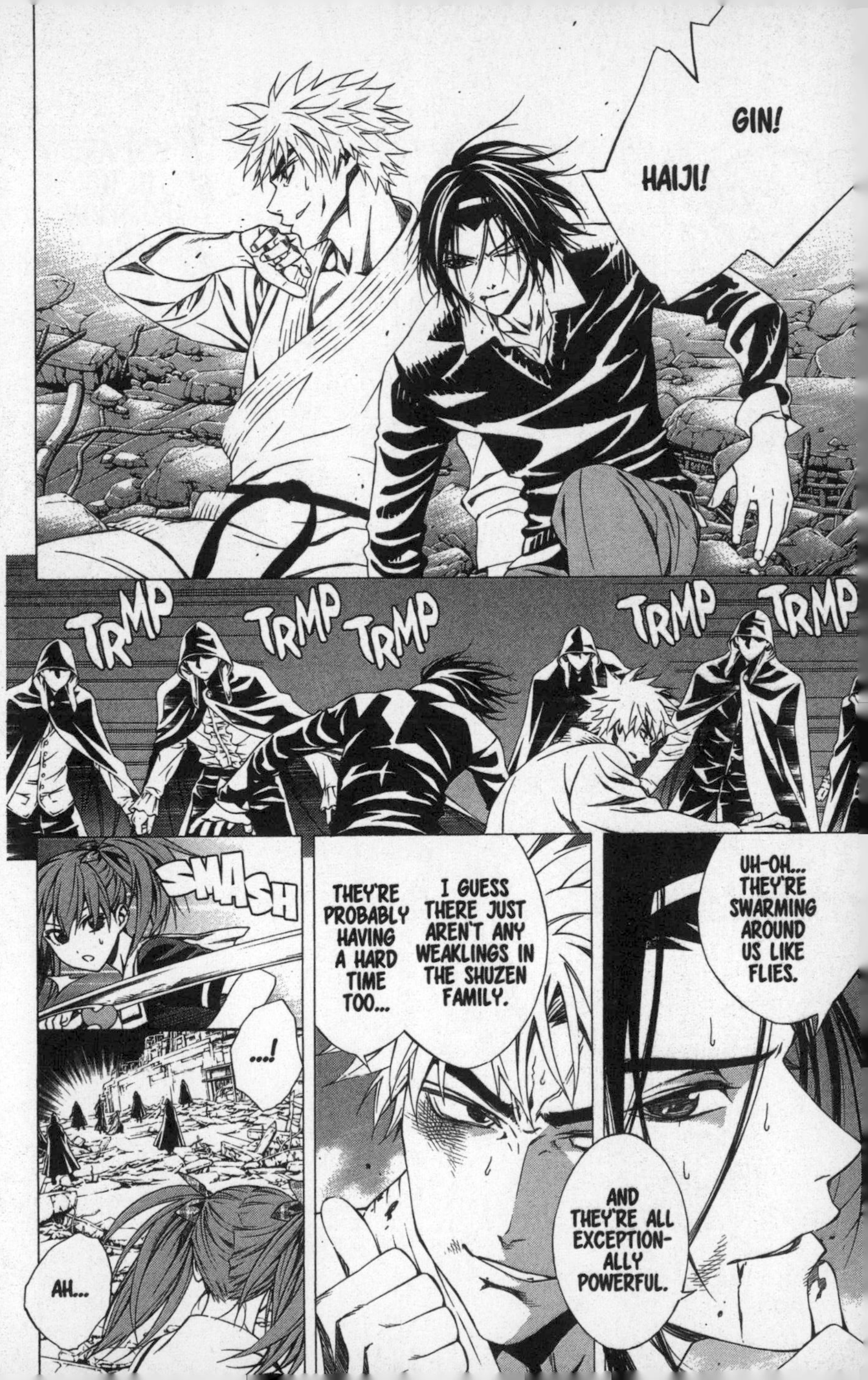
GIN!
HAIJI!
TRMP
TRMP
TRMP
TRMP
TRMP
UH-OH... THEY'RE SWARMING AROUND US LIKE FLIES.
I GUESS THERE JUST AREN'T ANY WEAKLINGS IN THE SHUZEN FAMILY.
AND THEY'RE ALL EXCEPTION- ALLY POWERFUL.
THEY'RE PROBABLY HAVING A HARD TIME TOO...
SMASH
...!
AH...

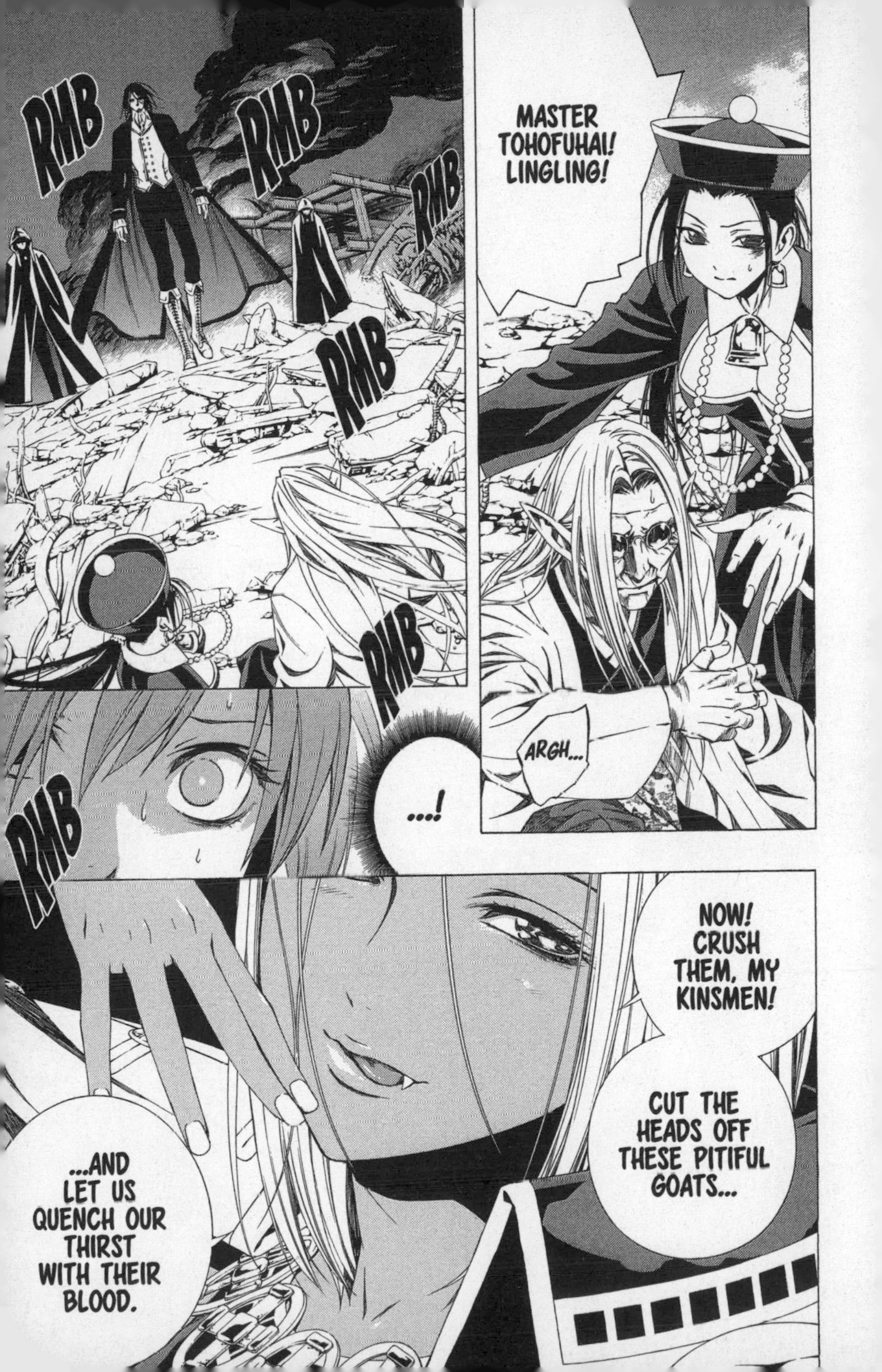
MASTER TOHOFUHAI! LINGLING!
ARGH...
RMB
RMB
RMB
RMB
RMB
...!
RMB
NOW! CRUSH THEM, MY KINSMEN!
CUT THE HEADS OFF THESE PITIFUL GOATS...
...AND LET US QUENCH OUR THIRST WITH THEIR BLOOD.

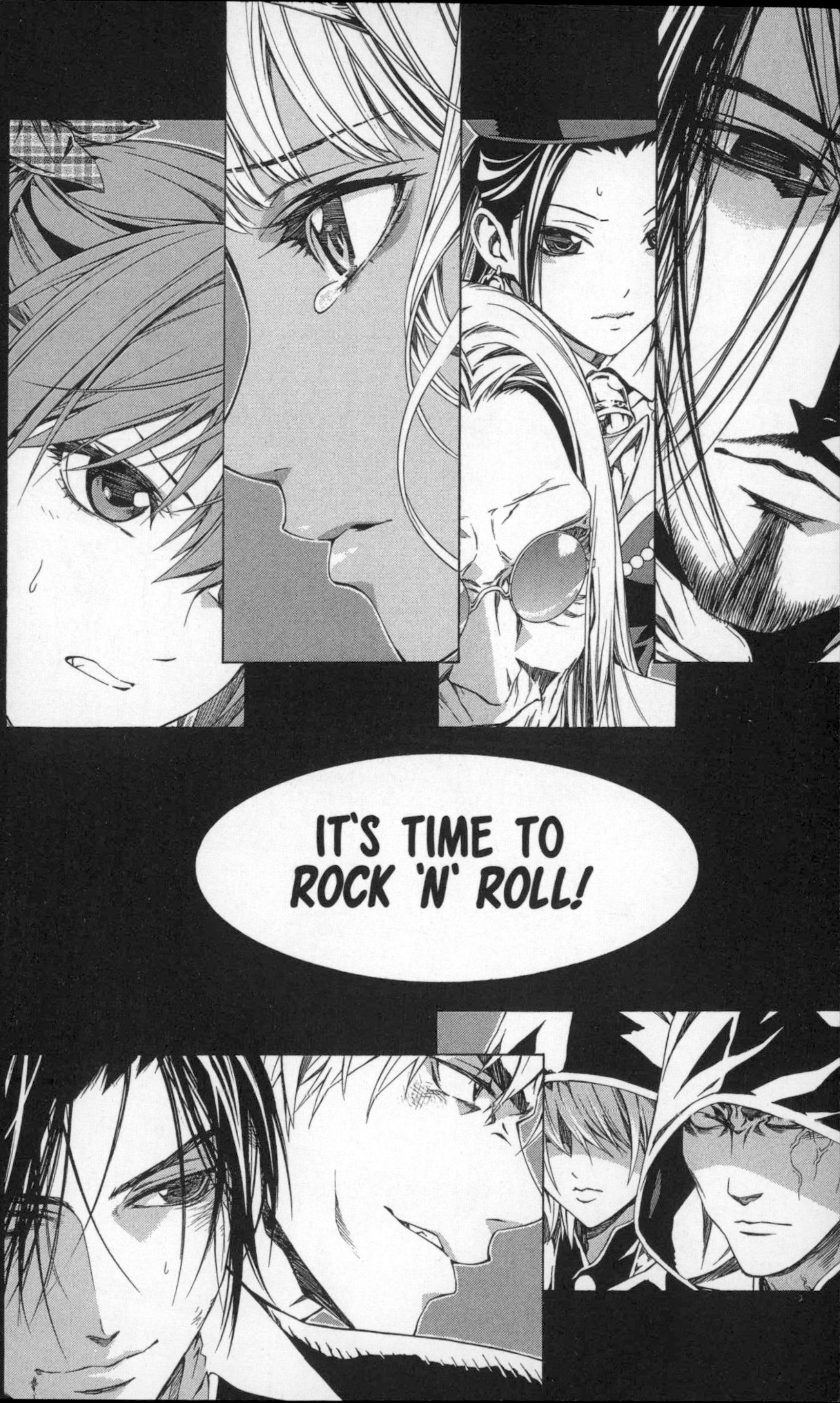
IT'S TIME TO ROCK 'N' ROLL!

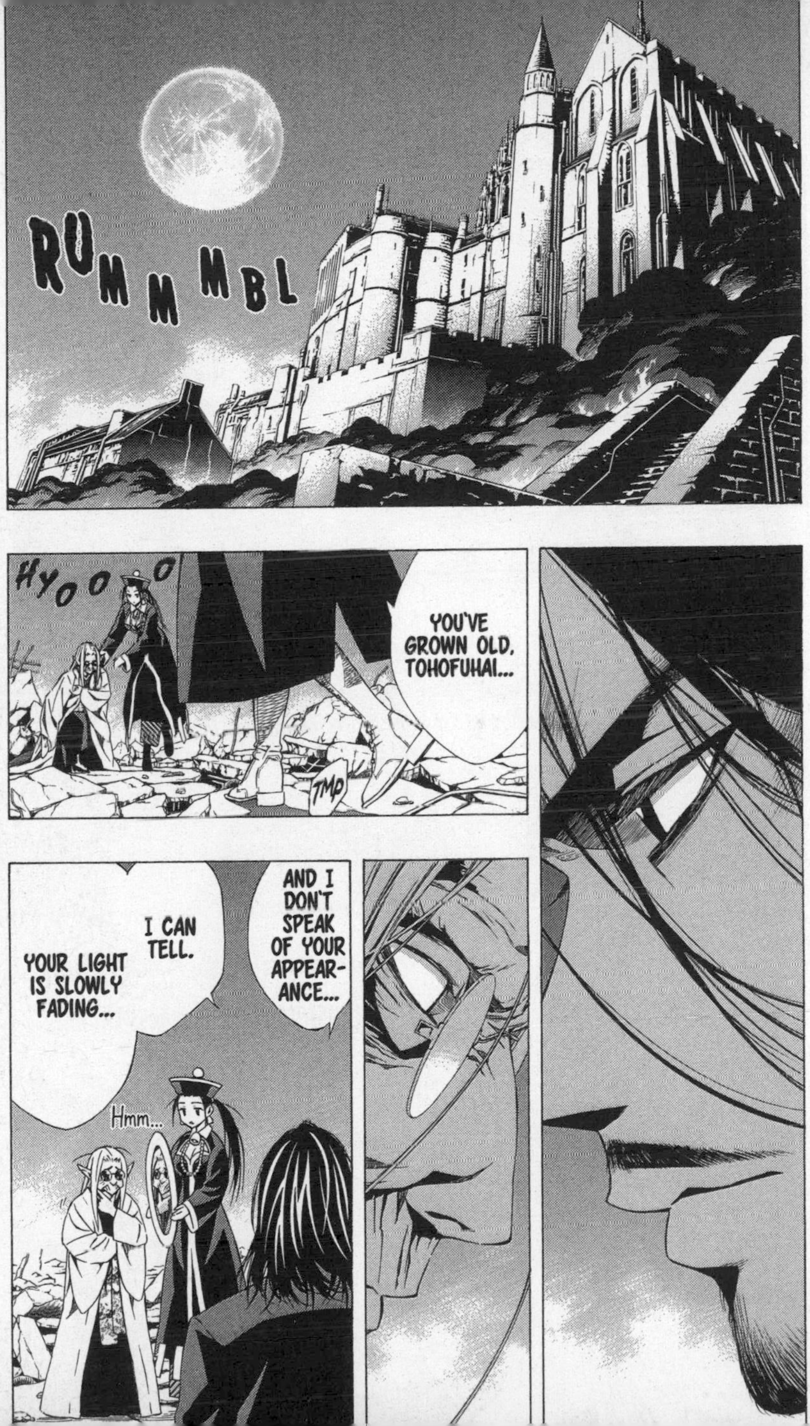
RUMMMBL
YOU'VE GROWN OLD, TOHOFUHAI...
HYOOOO
TMP
AND I DON'T SPEAK OF YOUR APPEARANCE...
I CAN TELL.
YOUR LIGHT IS SLOWLY FADING...
Hmm...

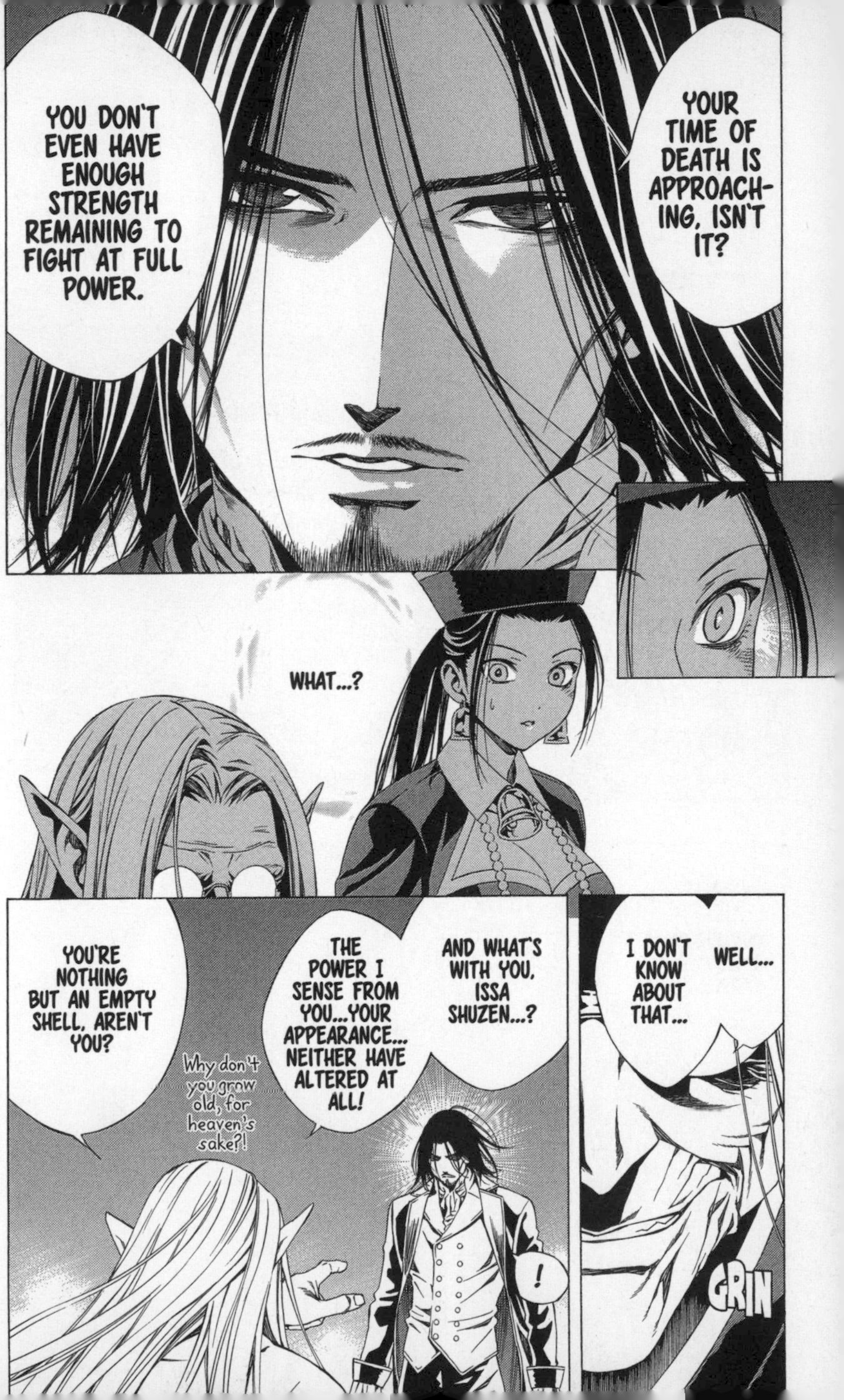
YOUR TIME OF DEATH IS APPROACHING, ISN'T IT?
YOU DON'T EVEN HAVE ENOUGH STRENGTH REMAINING TO FIGHT AT FULL POWER.
WHAT...?
WELL...
I DON'T KNOW ABOUT THAT...
GRIN
AND WHAT'S WITH YOU, ISSA SHUZEN...?
THE POWER I SENSE FROM YOU...YOUR APPEARANCE... NEITHER HAVE ALTERED AT ALL!
YOU'RE NOTHING BUT AN EMPTY SHELL, AREN'T YOU?
Why don't you grow old, for heaven's sake?!
!

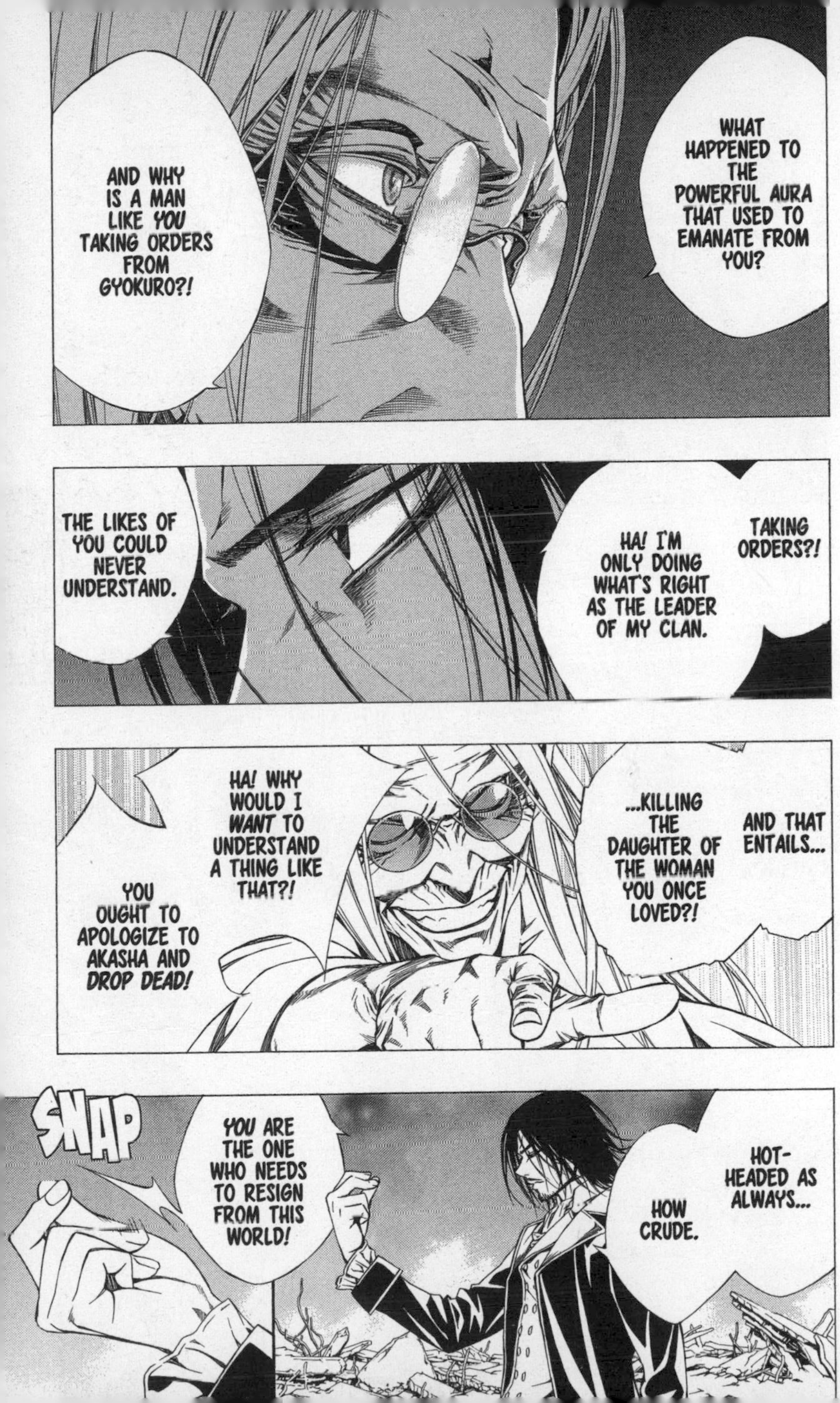
WHAT HAPPENED TO THE POWERFUL AURA THAT USED TO EMANATE FROM YOU?
AND WHY IS A MAN LIKE *YOU* TAKING ORDERS FROM GYOKURO?!
TAKING ORDERS?!
HA! I'M ONLY DOING WHAT'S RIGHT AS THE LEADER OF MY CLAN.
THE LIKES OF YOU COULD NEVER UNDERSTAND.
AND THAT ENTAILS...
...KILLING THE DAUGHTER OF THE WOMAN YOU ONCE LOVED?!
HA! WHY WOULD I *WANT* TO UNDERSTAND A THING LIKE THAT?!
YOU OUGHT TO APOLOGIZE TO AKASHA AND *DROP DEAD!*
HOT-HEADED AS ALWAYS...
HOW CRUDE.
YOU ARE THE ONE WHO NEEDS TO RESIGN FROM THIS WORLD!
SNAP

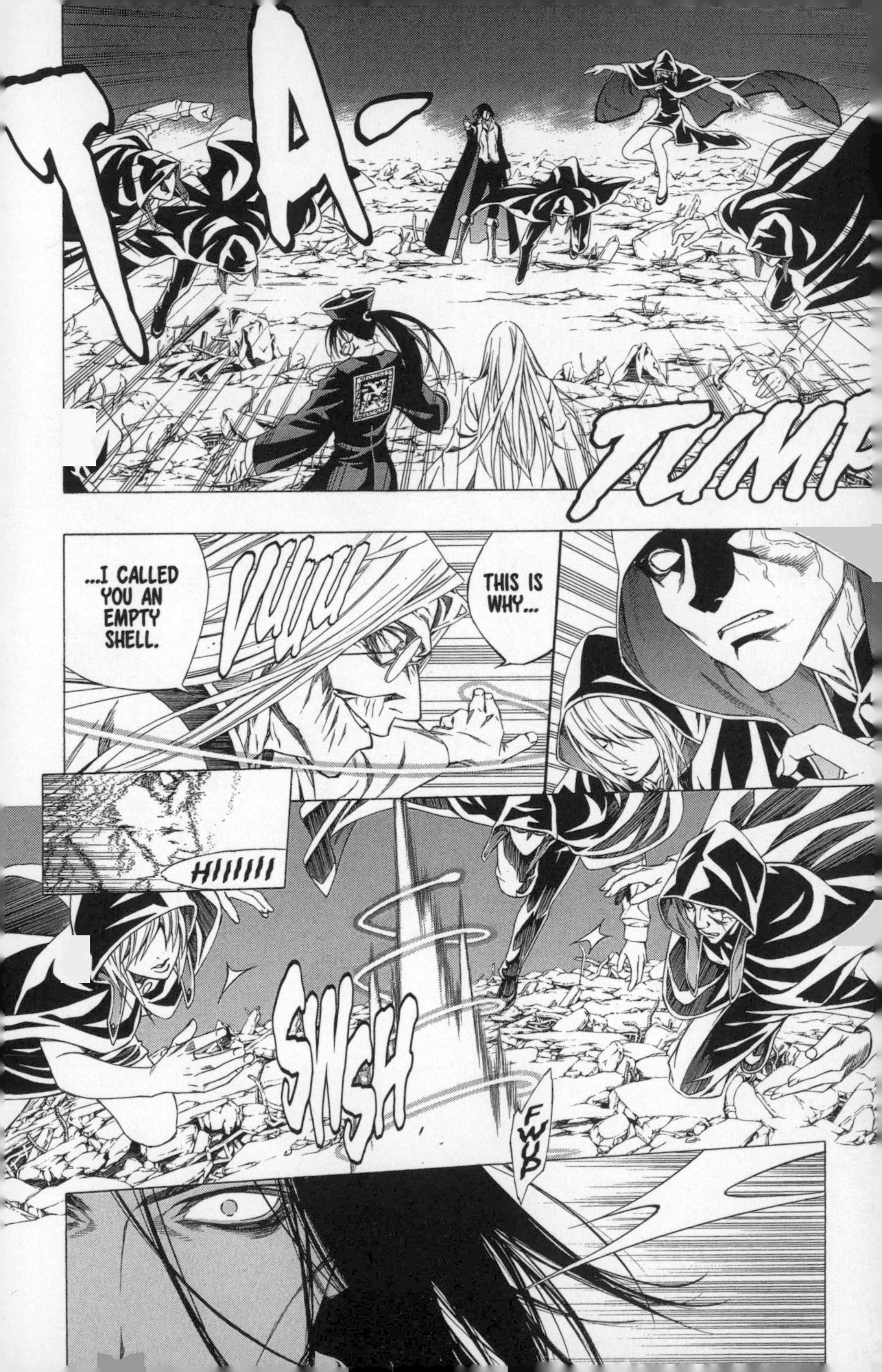
TA-
TUMP
THIS IS WHY...
...I CALLED YOU AN EMPTY SHELL.
HIIIIII
SWSH
FWUP

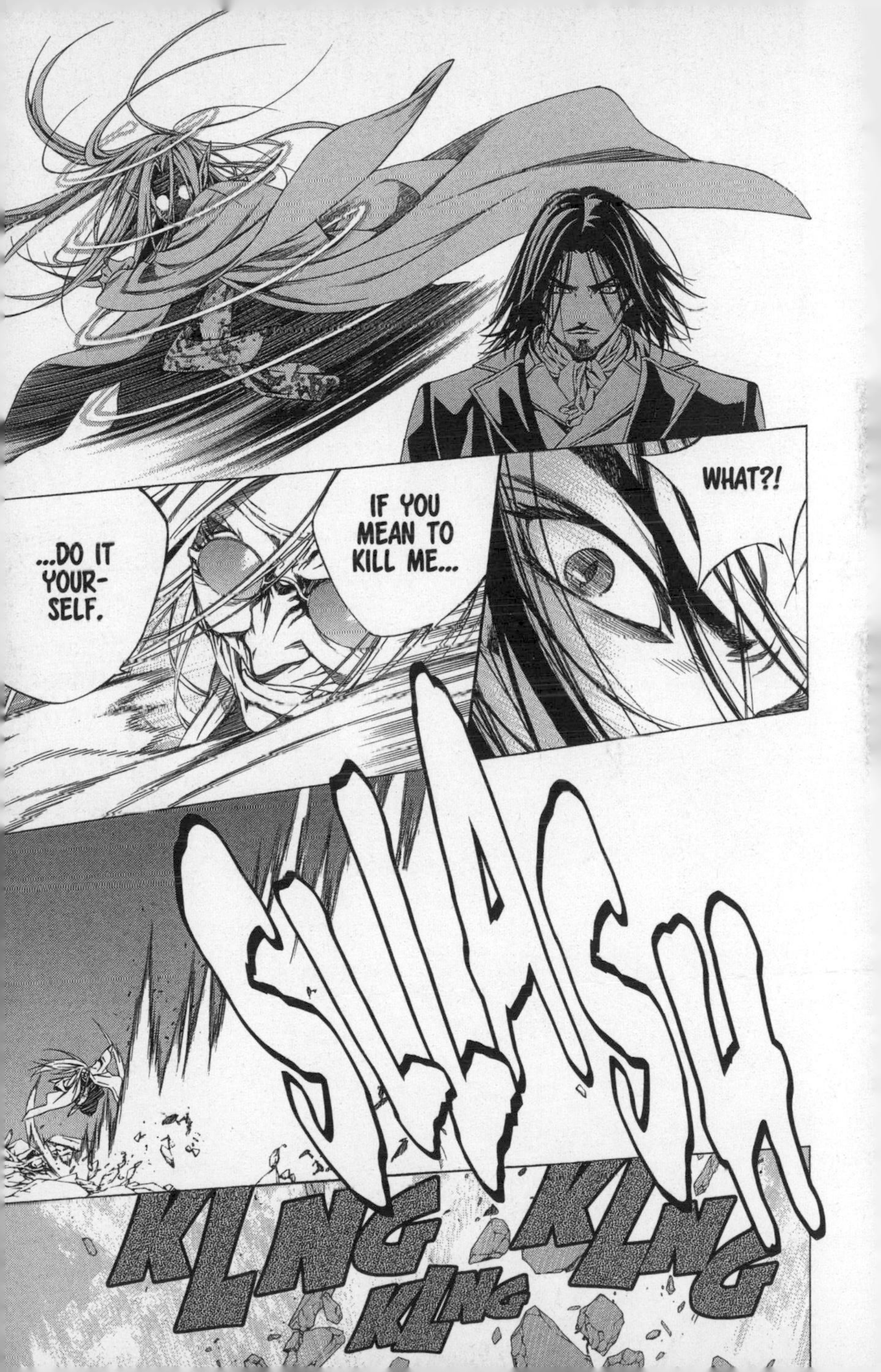
WHAT?!
IF YOU MEAN TO KILL ME...
...DO IT YOURSELF.
SWASH
KLING KLING KLING

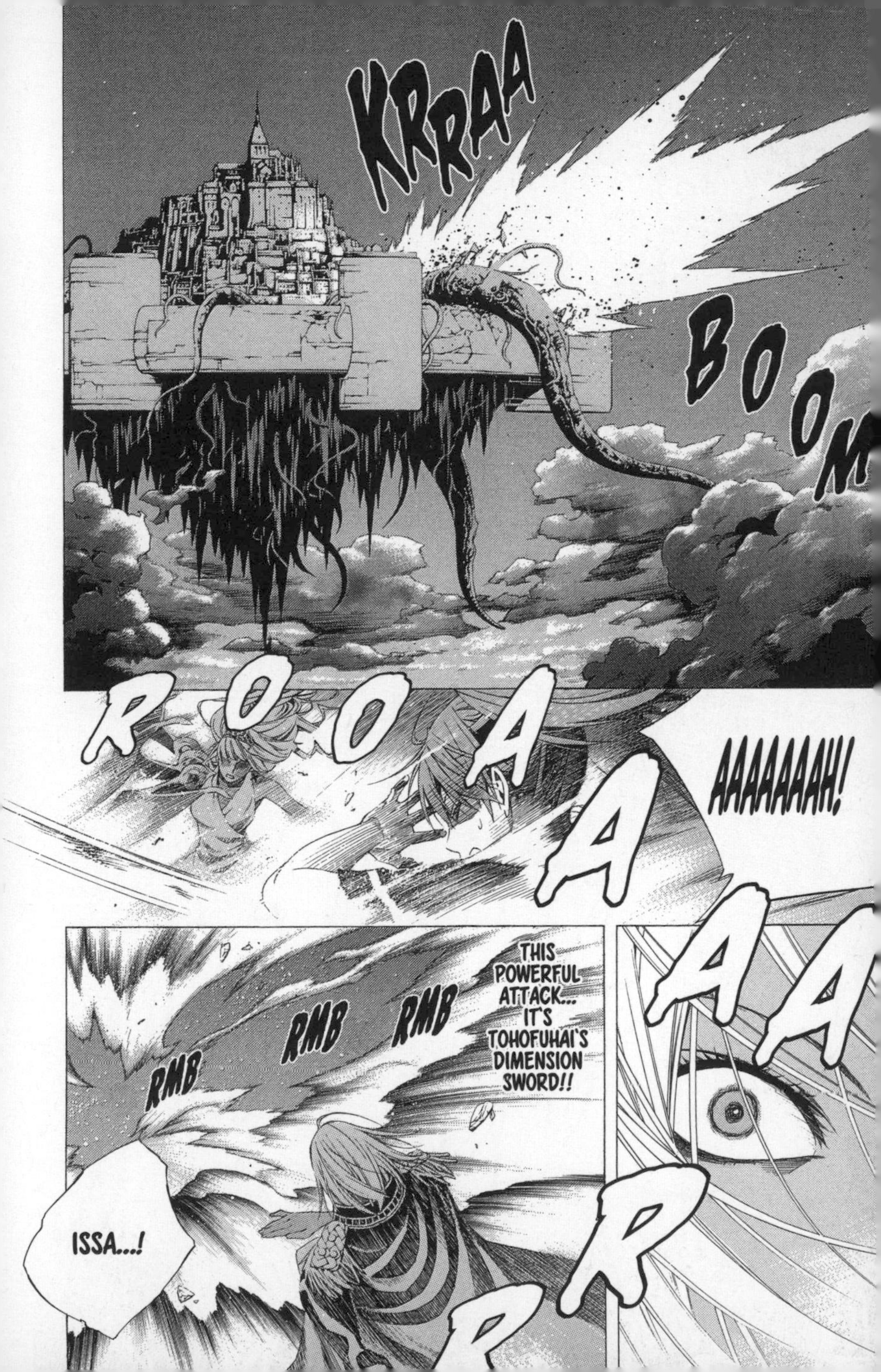
KRRAA
BOOM
ROOAAAARR
AAAAAAH!
RMB
RMB
RMB
THIS POWERFUL ATTACK... IT'S TOHOFUHAI'S DIMENSION SWORD!!
ISSA...!

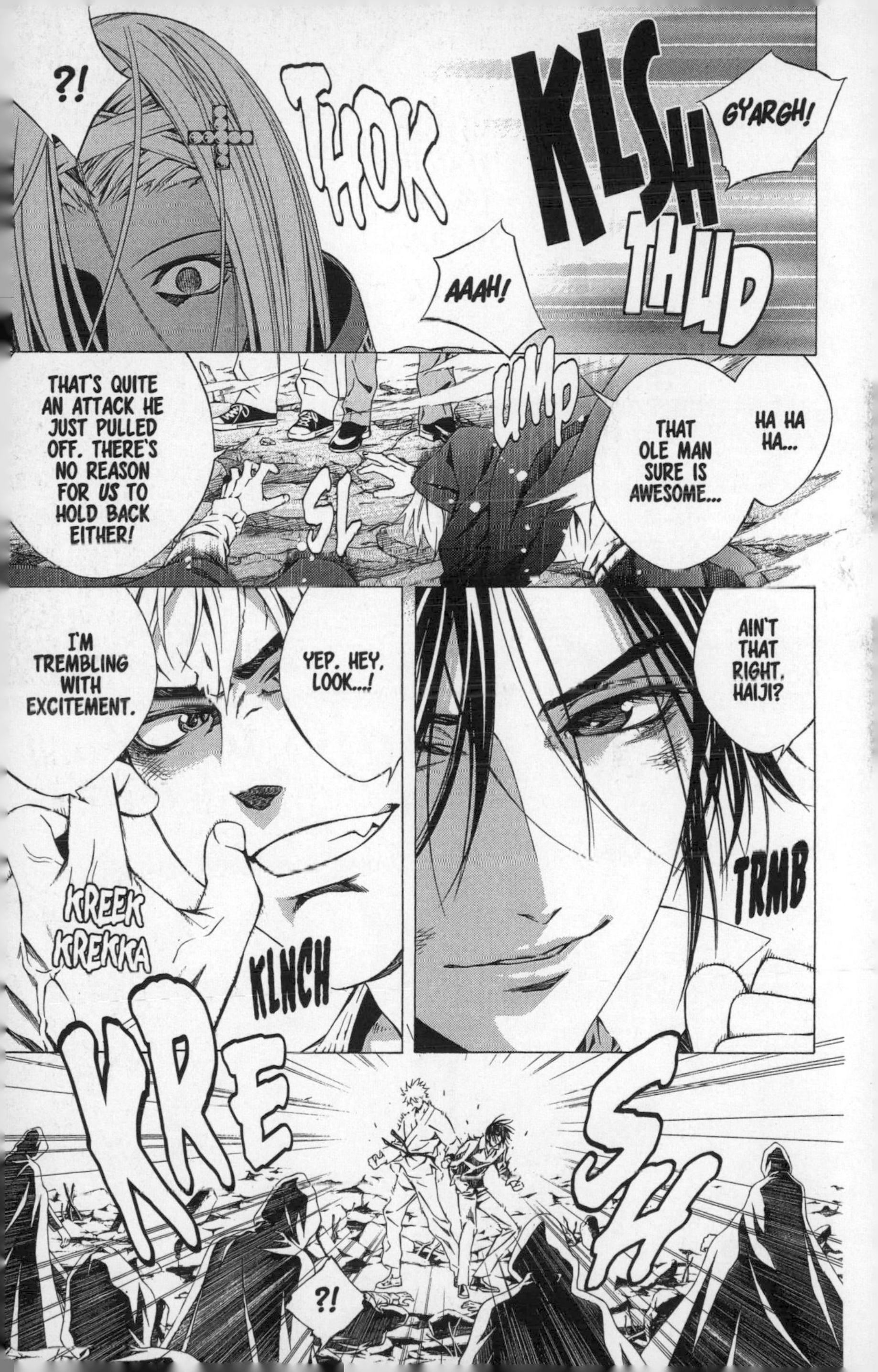
GYARGH!
KLSH
THOK
?!
THUD
AAAH!
HA HA HA...
THAT OLE MAN SURE IS AWESOME...
UMP
THAT'S QUITE AN ATTACK HE JUST PULLED OFF. THERE'S NO REASON FOR US TO HOLD BACK EITHER!
SL
AIN'T THAT RIGHT, HAIJI?
TRMB
YEP. HEY, LOOK...!
I'M TREMBLING WITH EXCITEMENT.
KREEK KREKKA
KLNCH
VRESH
?!

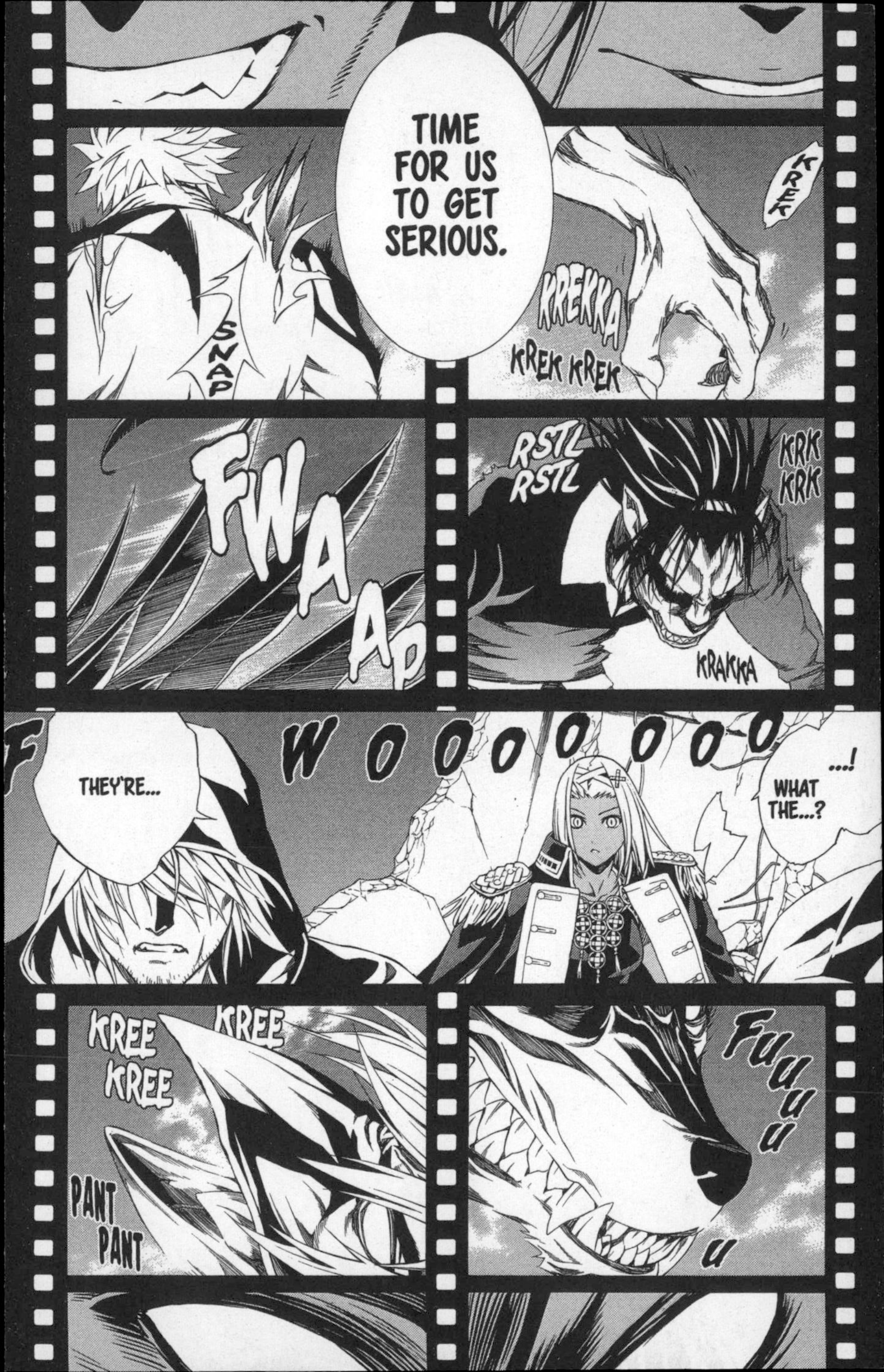

TIME FOR US TO GET SERIOUS.
KREK
KREKKA
KREK KREK
SNAP
KRK KRK
RSTL RSTL
KRAKKA
FWAAP
...!
WHAT THE...?
WOOOOOOOO
THEY'RE...
Fuuuuuu
KREE
KREE KREE
PANT PANT

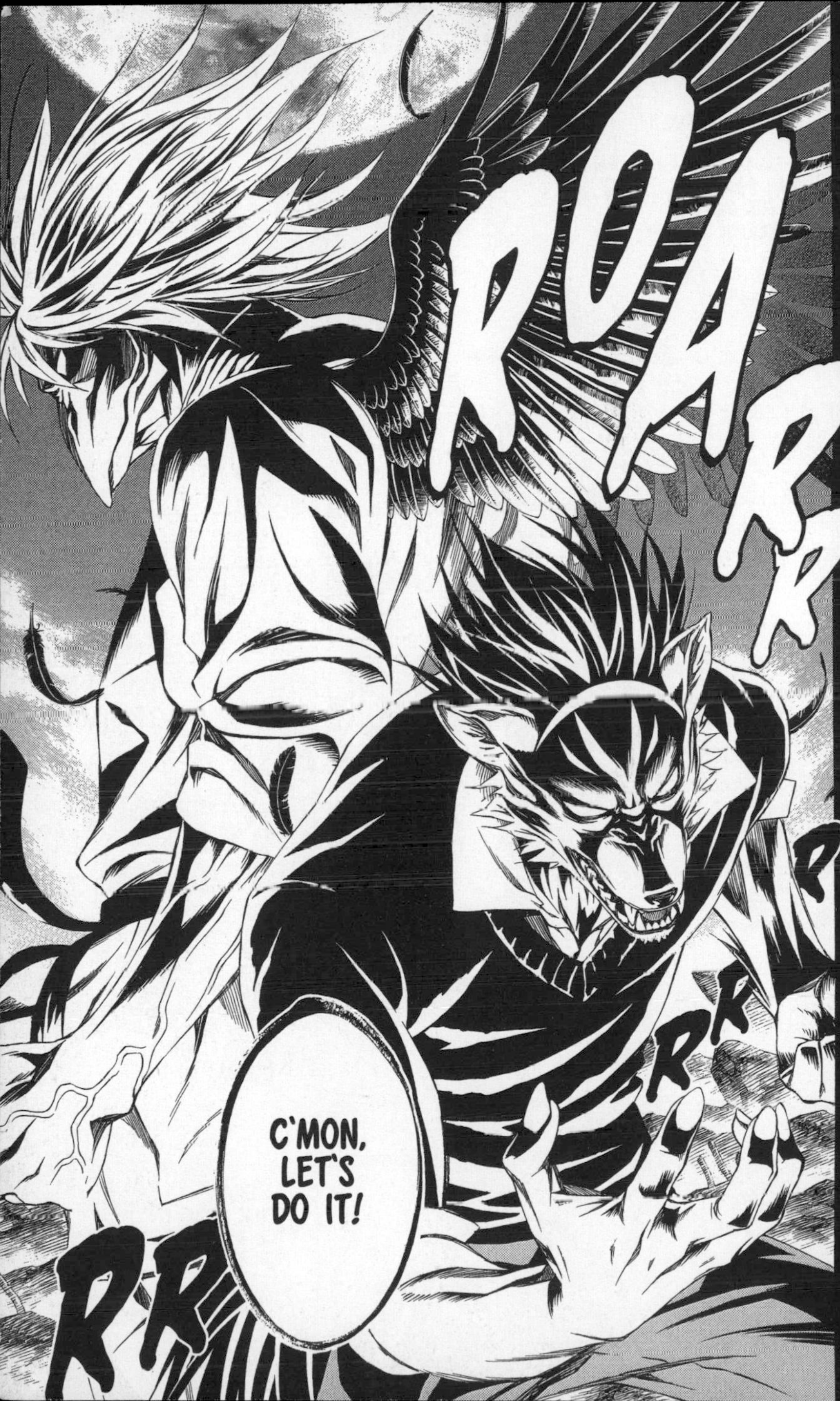
ROAR
C'MON, LET'S DO IT!
RR

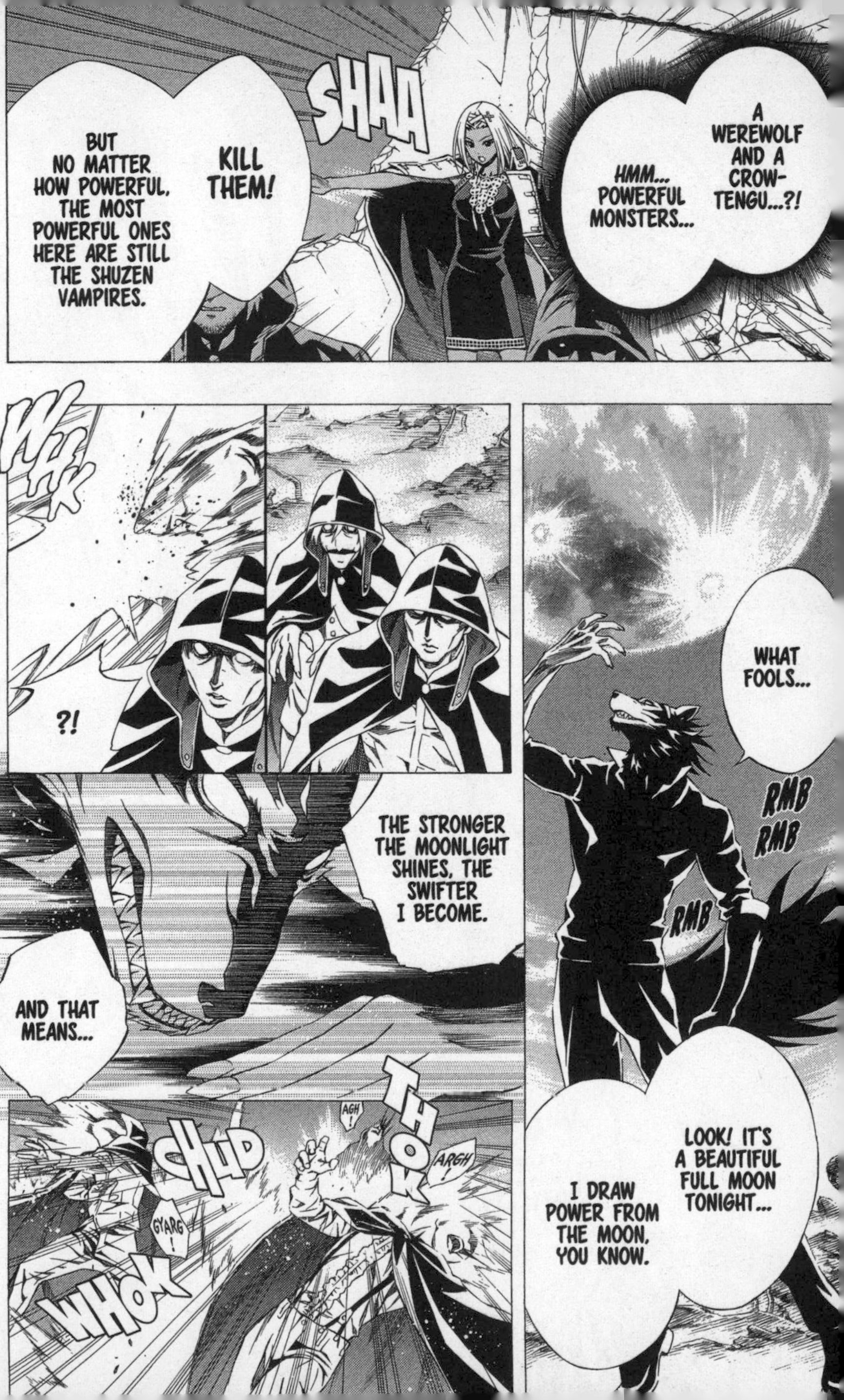
A WEREWOLF AND A CROW-TENGU...?!
HMM... POWERFUL MONSTERS...
SHAA
KILL THEM!
BUT NO MATTER HOW POWERFUL, THE MOST POWERFUL ONES HERE ARE STILL THE SHUZEN VAMPIRES.
WHAT FOOLS...
RMB RMB
RMB
LOOK! IT'S A BEAUTIFUL FULL MOON TONIGHT...
I DRAW POWER FROM THE MOON, YOU KNOW.
WHAK
?!
THE STRONGER THE MOONLIGHT SHINES, THE SWIFTER I BECOME.
AND THAT MEANS...
THOOK
AGH!
ARGH!
CHUD
GYARG!
WHOK

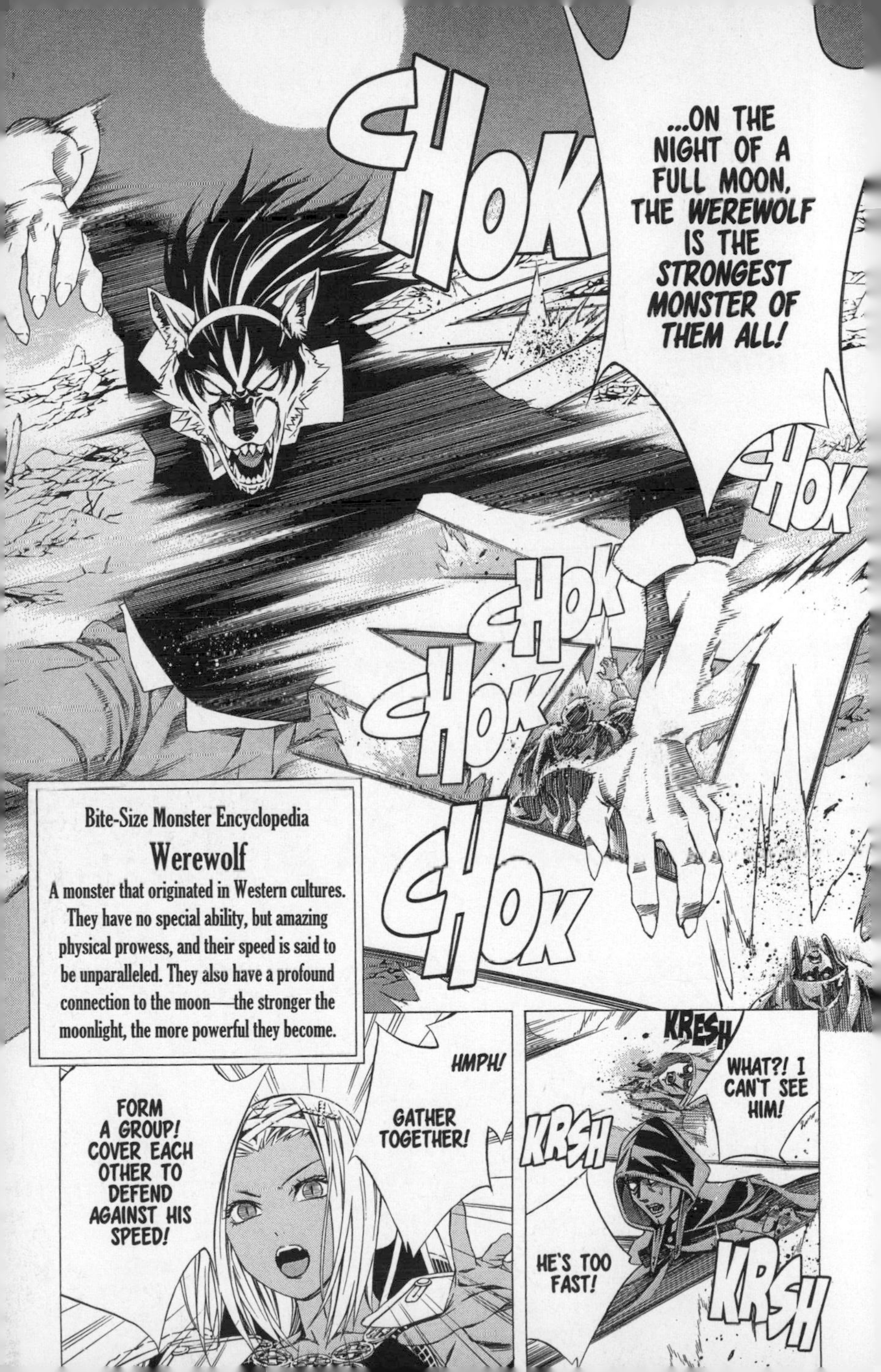
CHOK
...ON THE NIGHT OF A FULL MOON, THE WEREWOLF IS THE STRONGEST MONSTER OF THEM ALL!
CHOK
CHOK
CHOK
CHOK
Bite-Size Monster Encyclopedia
Werewolf
A monster that originated in Western cultures. They have no special ability, but amazing physical prowess, and their speed is said to be unparalleled. They also have a profound connection to the moon—the stronger the moonlight, the more powerful they become.
KRESH
WHAT?! I CAN'T SEE HIM!
KRSH
HE'S TOO FAST!
KRSH
HMPH!
GATHER TOGETHER!
FORM A GROUP! COVER EACH OTHER TO DEFEND AGAINST HIS SPEED!

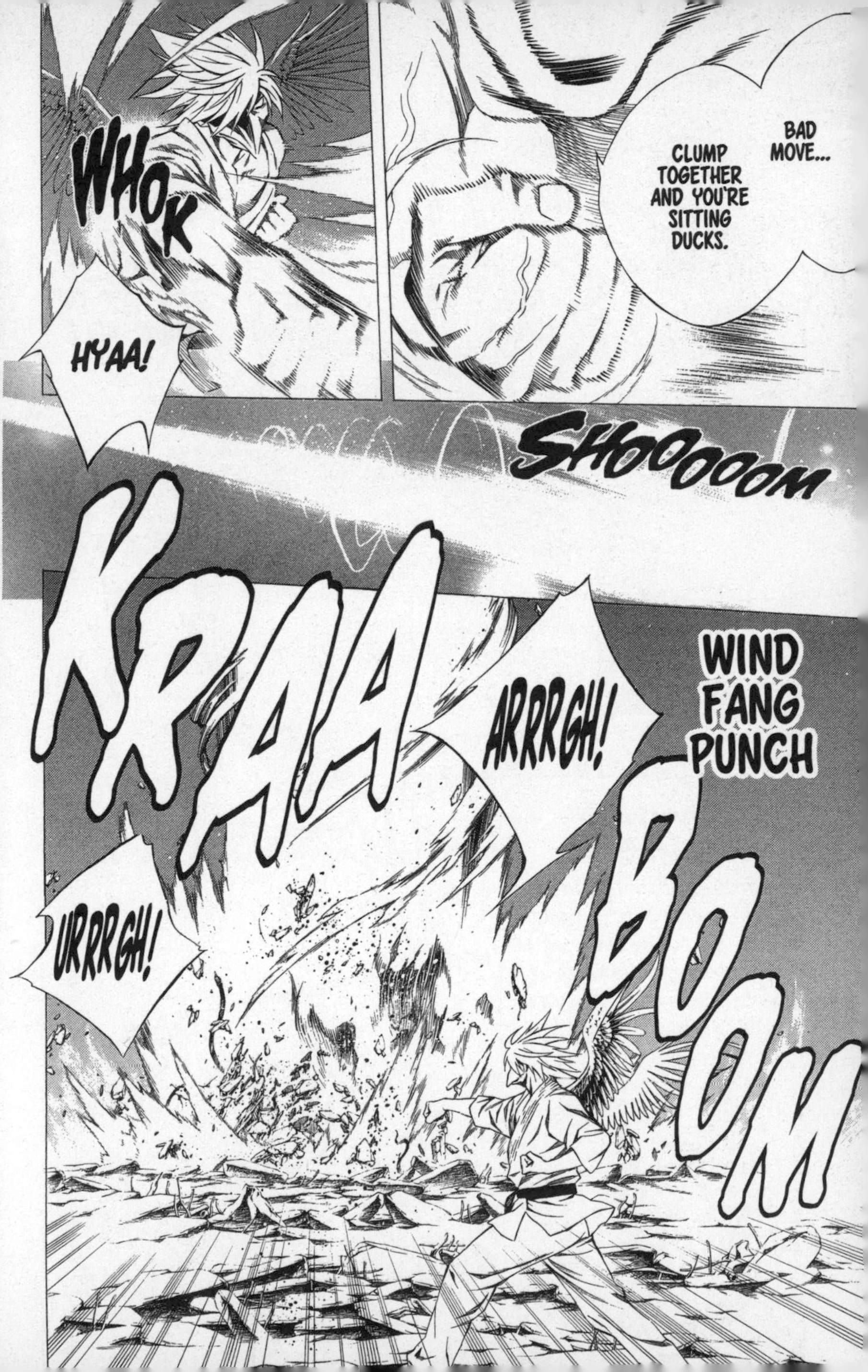
BAD MOVE...
CLUMP TOGETHER AND YOU'RE SITTING DUCKS.
WHOK
HYAA!
SHOOOOOOM
WIND FANG PUNCH
ARRRGH!
KRAA
BOOM
URRRGH!

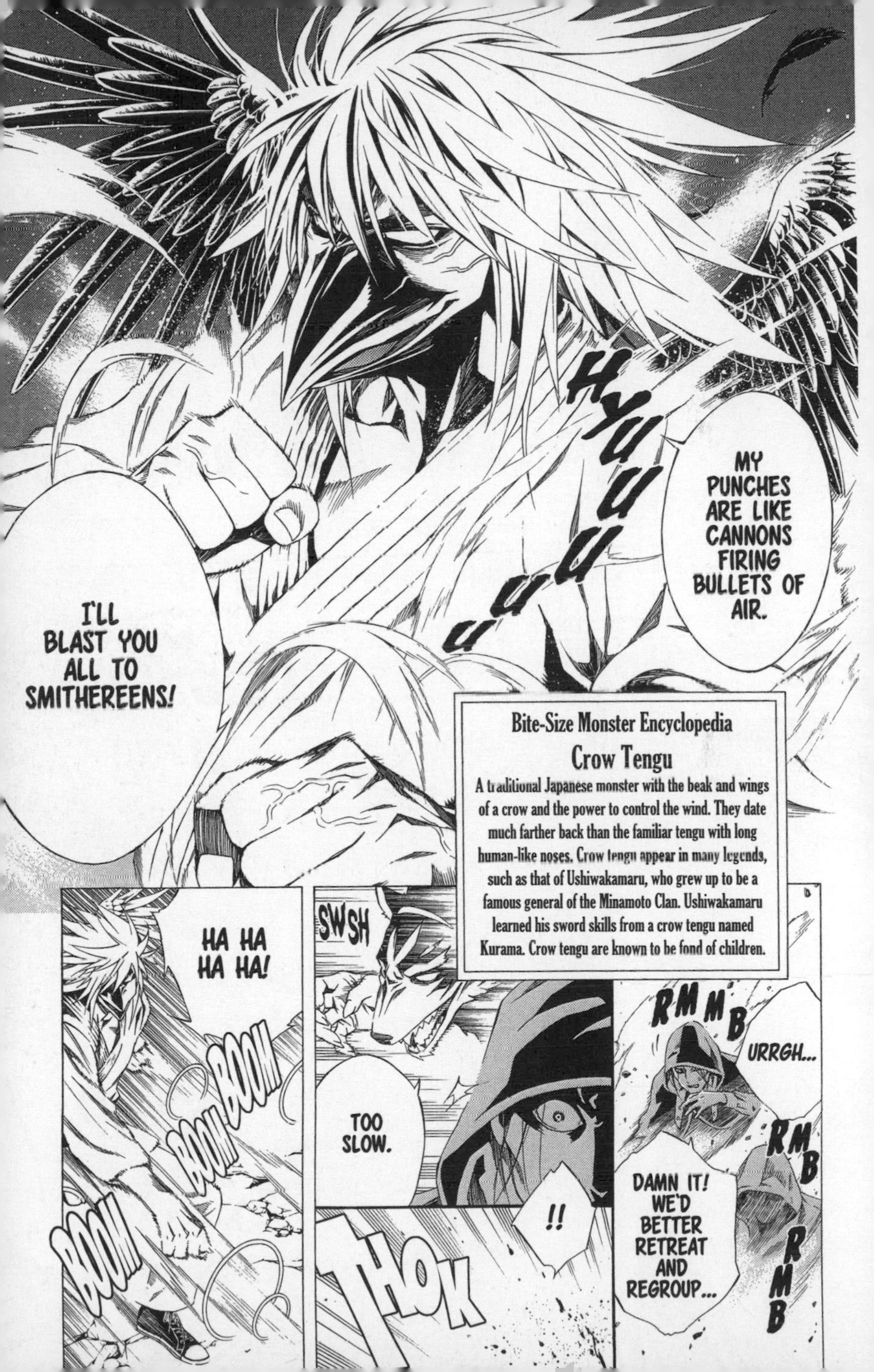
MY PUNCHES ARE LIKE CANNONS FIRING BULLETS OF AIR.
HYUUUUUU
I'LL BLAST YOU ALL TO SMITHEREENS!
Bite-Size Monster Encyclopedia
Crow Tengu
A traditional Japanese monster with the beak and wings of a crow and the power to control the wind. They date much farther back than the familiar tengu with long human-like noses. Crow tengu appear in many legends, such as that of Ushiwakamaru, who grew up to be a famous general of the Minamoto Clan. Ushiwakamaru learned his sword skills from a crow tengu named Kurama. Crow tengu are known to be fond of children.
RMMB
URRGH...
RMB
DAMN IT! WE'D BETTER RETREAT AND REGROUP...
RMB
SWSH
TOO SLOW.
!!
THOK
HA HA HA HA!
BOOM BOOM BOOM
BOOM

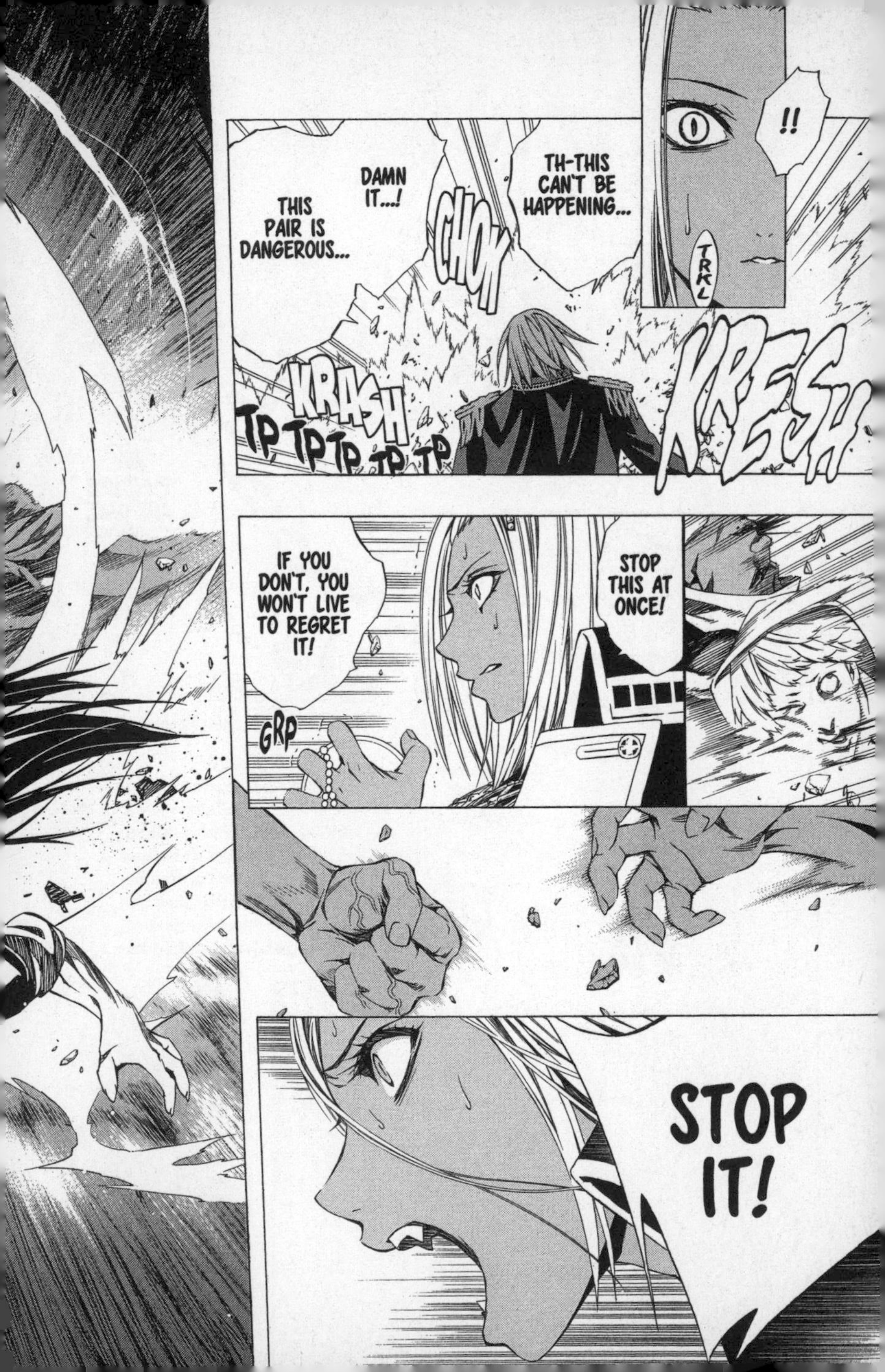
!!
TRKL
TH-THIS CAN'T BE HAPPENING...
CHOK
DAMN IT...!
THIS PAIR IS DANGEROUS...
KRESH
KRASH
TP TP TP TP TP
STOP THIS AT ONCE!
IF YOU DON'T, YOU WON'T LIVE TO REGRET IT!
GRP
STOP IT!

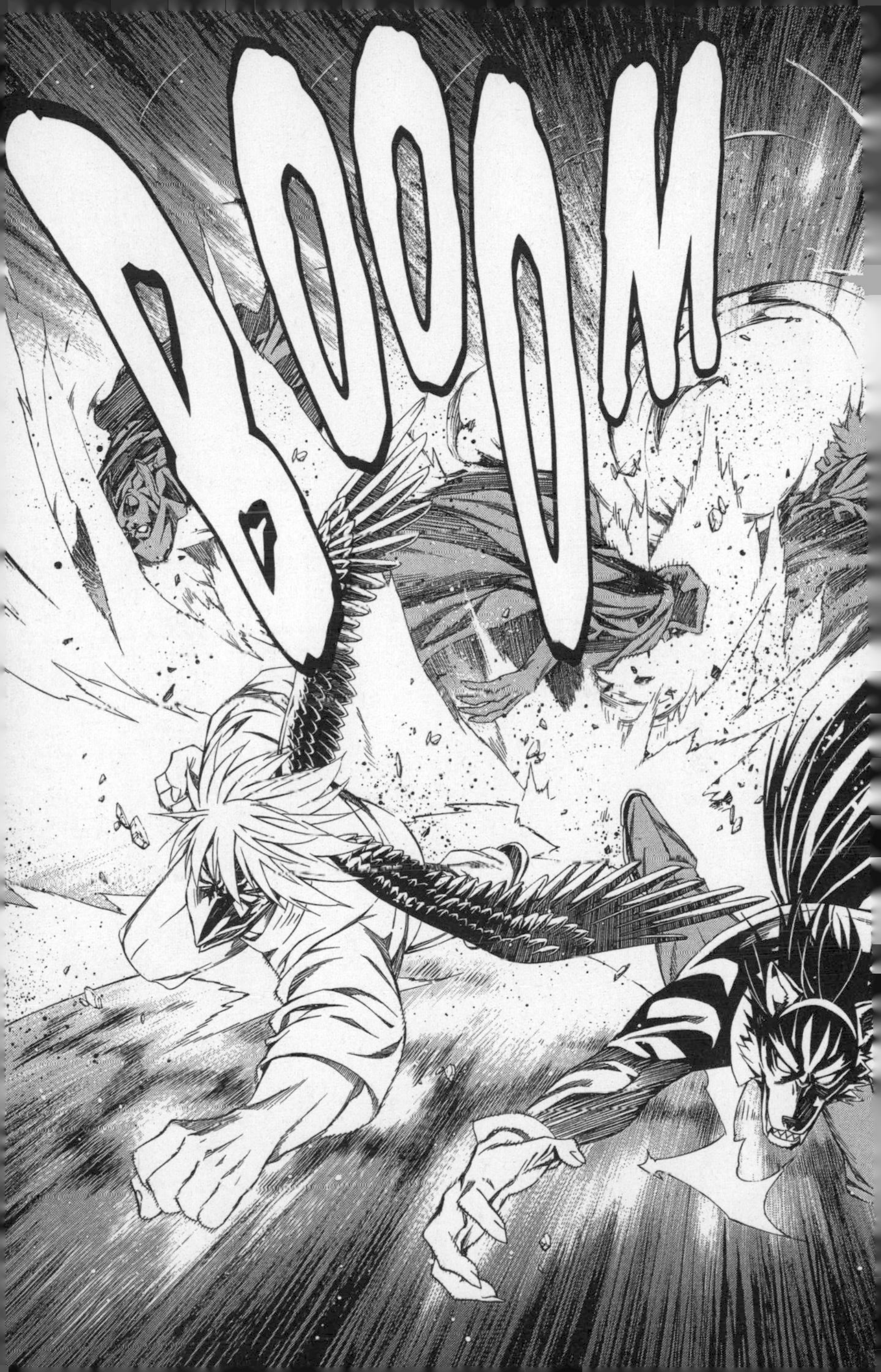
BOOOM

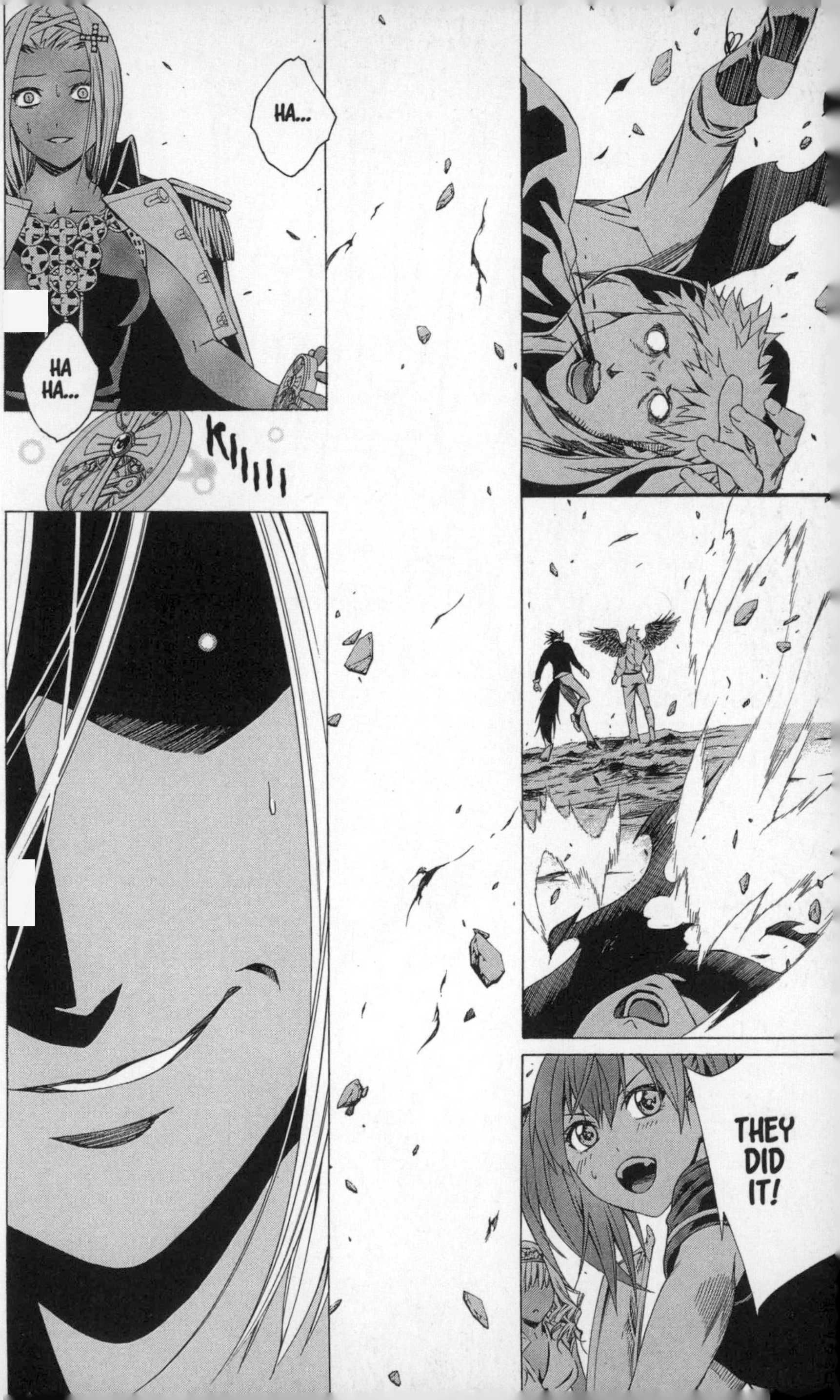
THEY DID IT!
HA...
HA HA...
KIIIIII

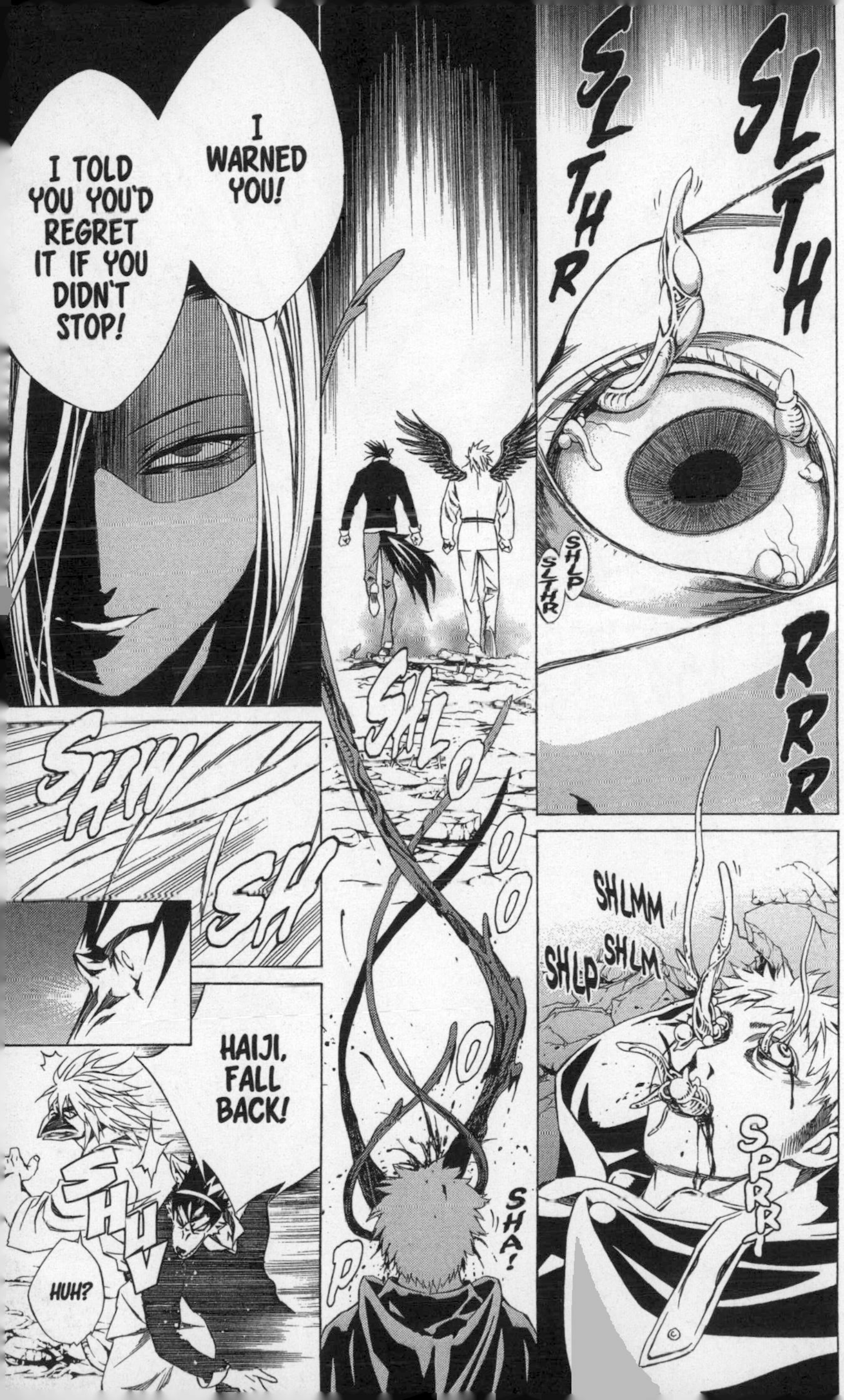
SLTH
SLTHR
SHLP SLTHR
RRR
I WARNED YOU!
I TOLD YOU YOU'D REGRET IT IF YOU DIDN'T STOP!
SHLMM SHLM
SHLP
SPRRT
SHLOOOOOO
SHA!
P
SHW
SH
HAIJI, FALL BACK!
SHUV
HUH?

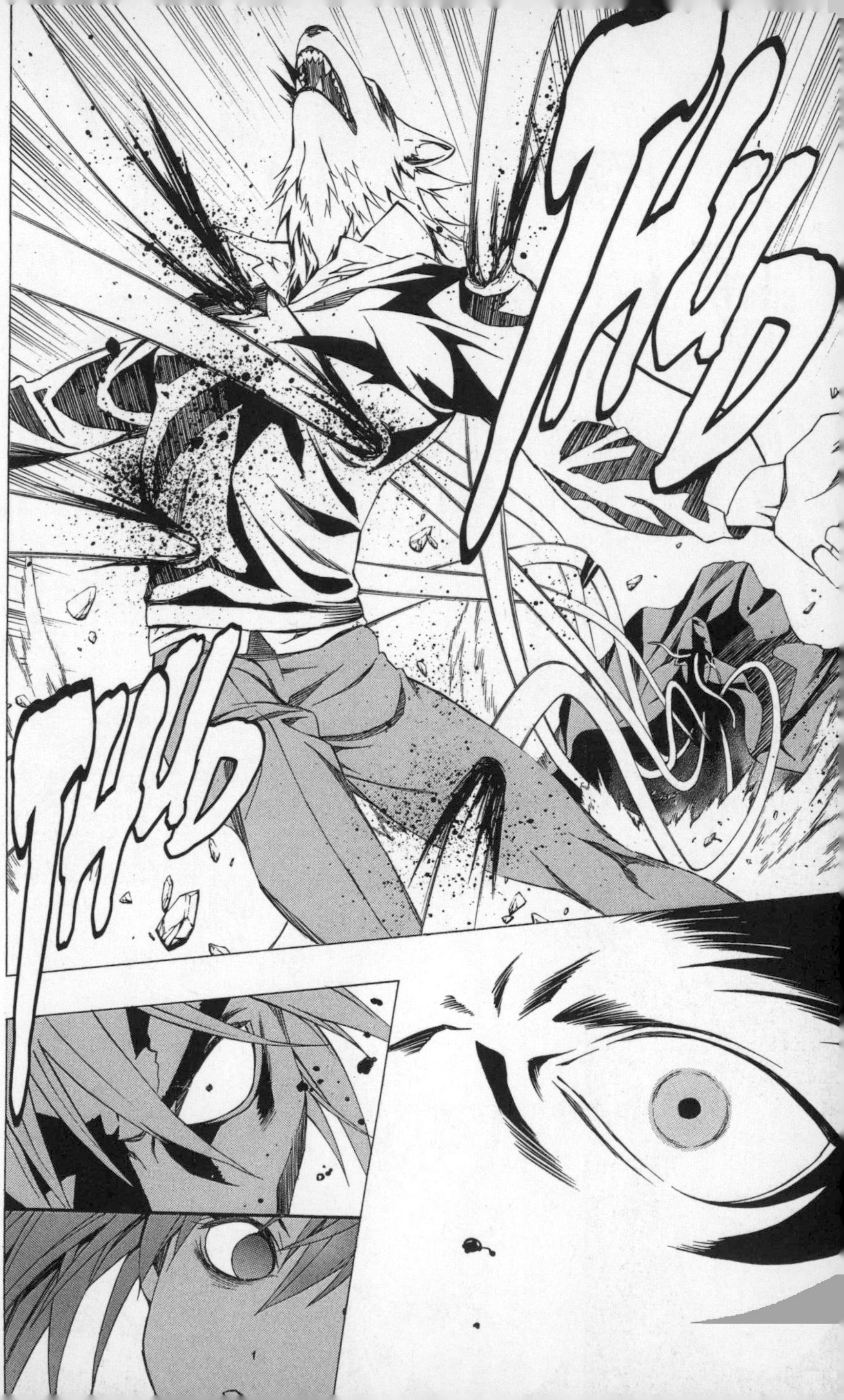
THUD
THUD

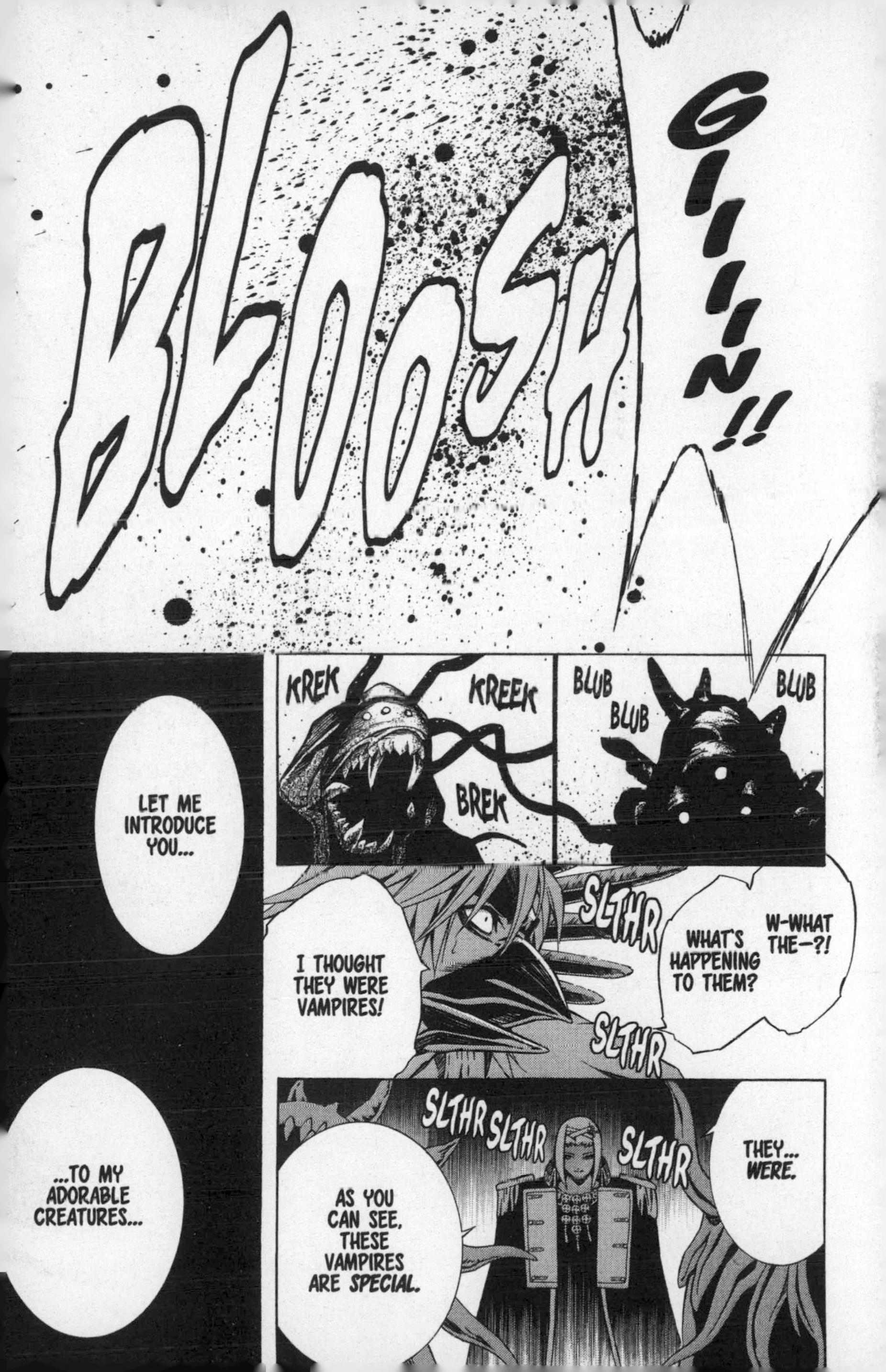
GIIIIN!!
BLOOSH
BLUB
BLUB
BLUB
KREEK
KREK
BREK
W-WHAT THE–?!
WHAT'S HAPPENING TO THEM?
SLTHR
I THOUGHT THEY WERE VAMPIRES!
SLTHR
THEY... WERE.
SLTHR
SLTHR
SLTHR
AS YOU CAN SEE, THESE VAMPIRES ARE *SPECIAL*.
LET ME INTRODUCE YOU...
...TO MY ADORABLE CREATURES...

59: The Black Parade

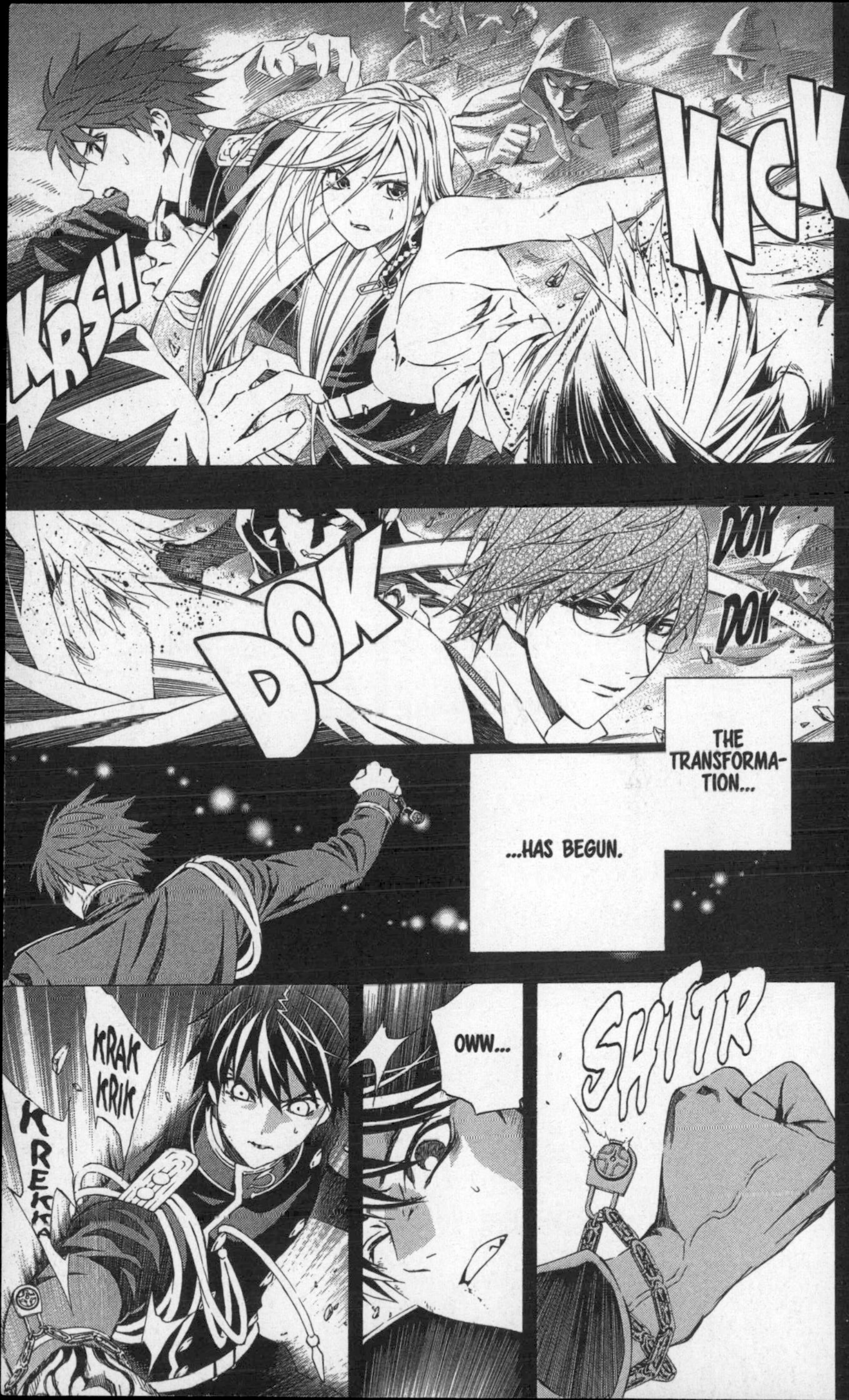
KICK
KRSH
DOK
DOK
DOK
THE TRANSFORMA-TION...
...HAS BEGUN.
SHTTR
OWW...
KRAK KRIK
KREKKA

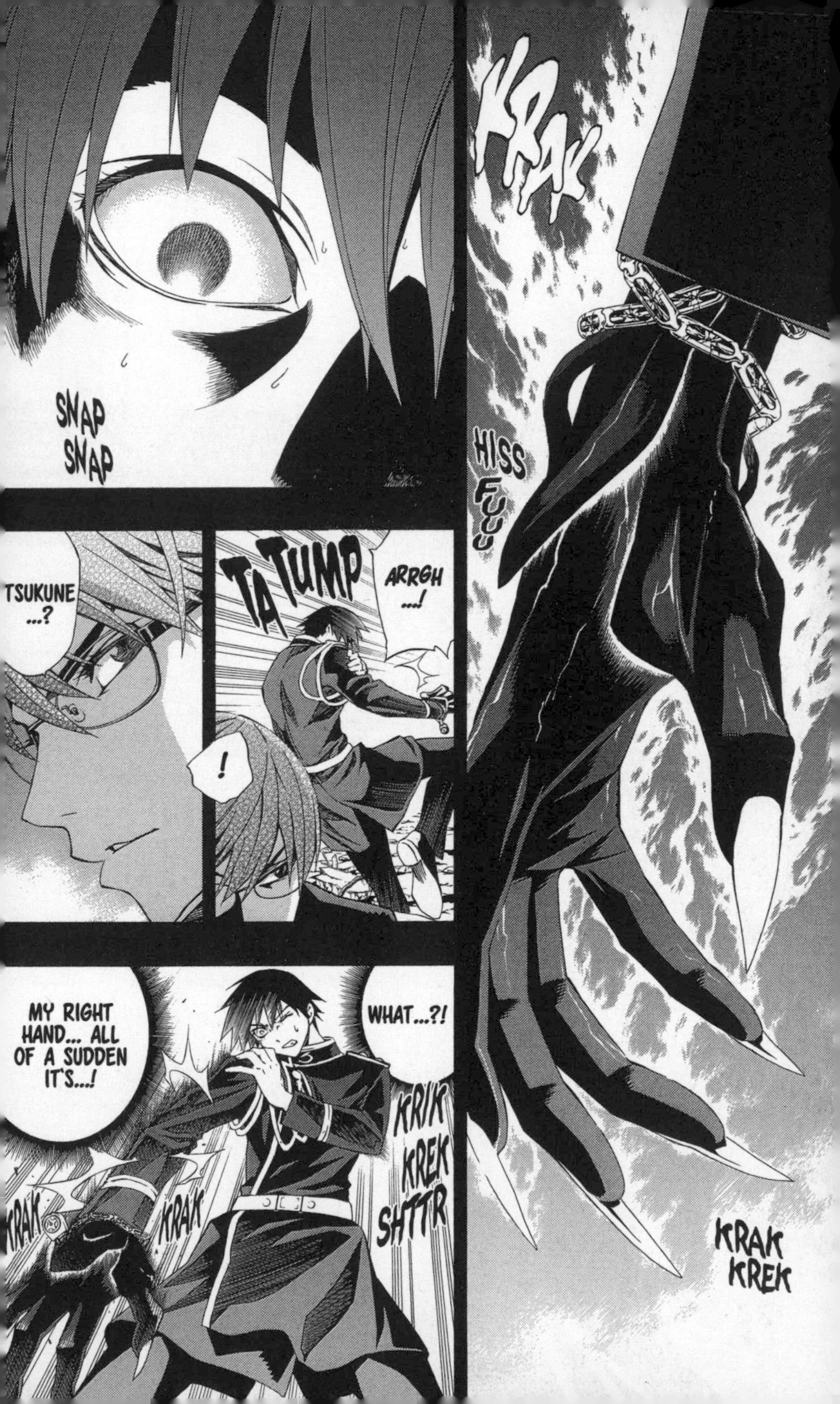
KRAK
HISS
FUUU
KRAK
KREK
SNAP
SNAP
ARRGH ...!
TA TUMP
!
TSUKUNE ...?
WHAT...?!
MY RIGHT HAND... ALL OF A SUDDEN IT'S...!
KRIK
KREK
SHTTR
KRAK
KRAK

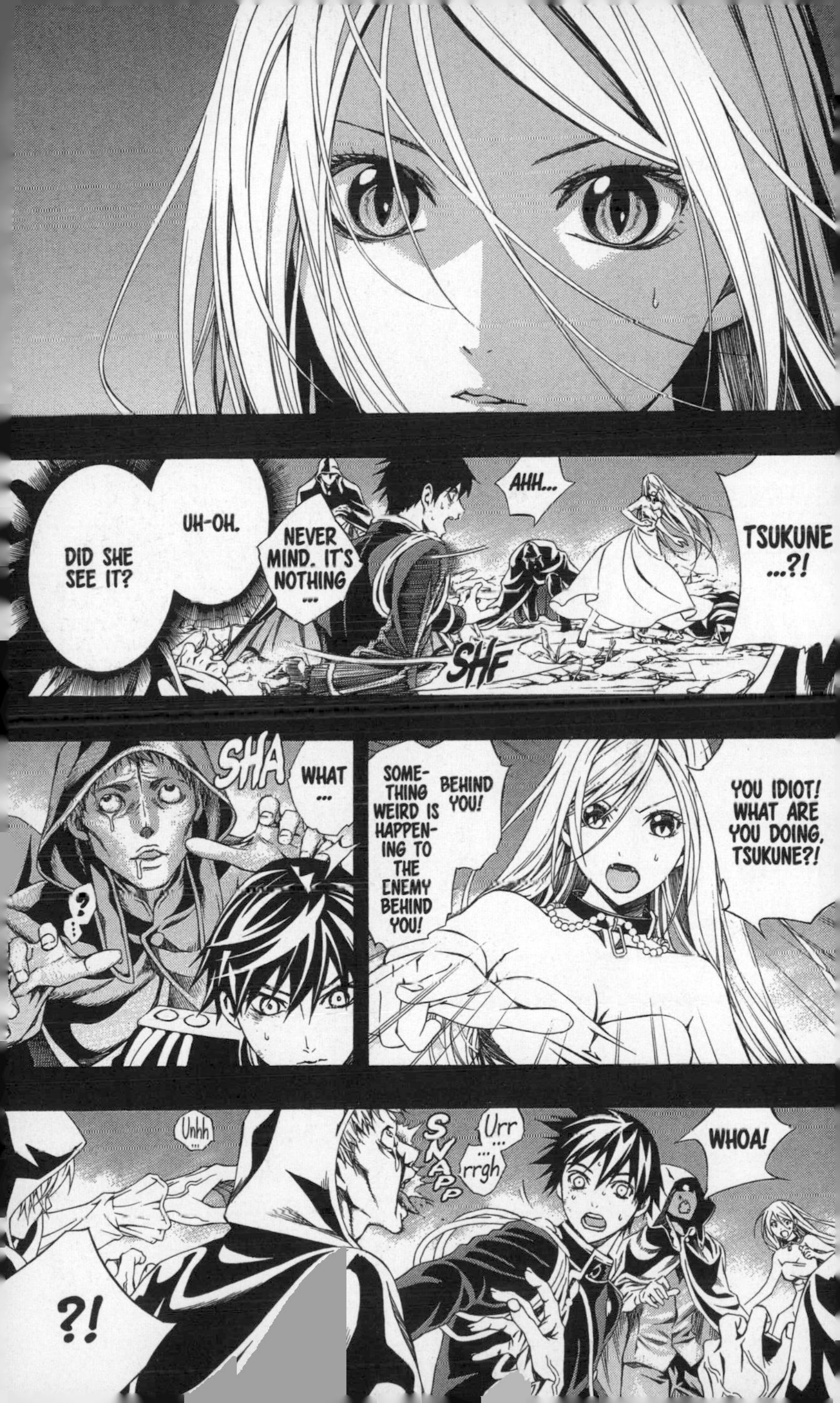
TSUKUNE ...?!
AHH...
NEVER MIND. IT'S NOTHING ...
UH-OH.
DID SHE SEE IT?
SHF
YOU IDIOT! WHAT ARE YOU DOING, TSUKUNE?!
BEHIND YOU!
SOMETHING WEIRD IS HAPPENING TO THE ENEMY BEHIND YOU!
WHAT ...
SHA
?
WHOA!
Urr ... rrgh
SNAPP
Unhh ...
?!

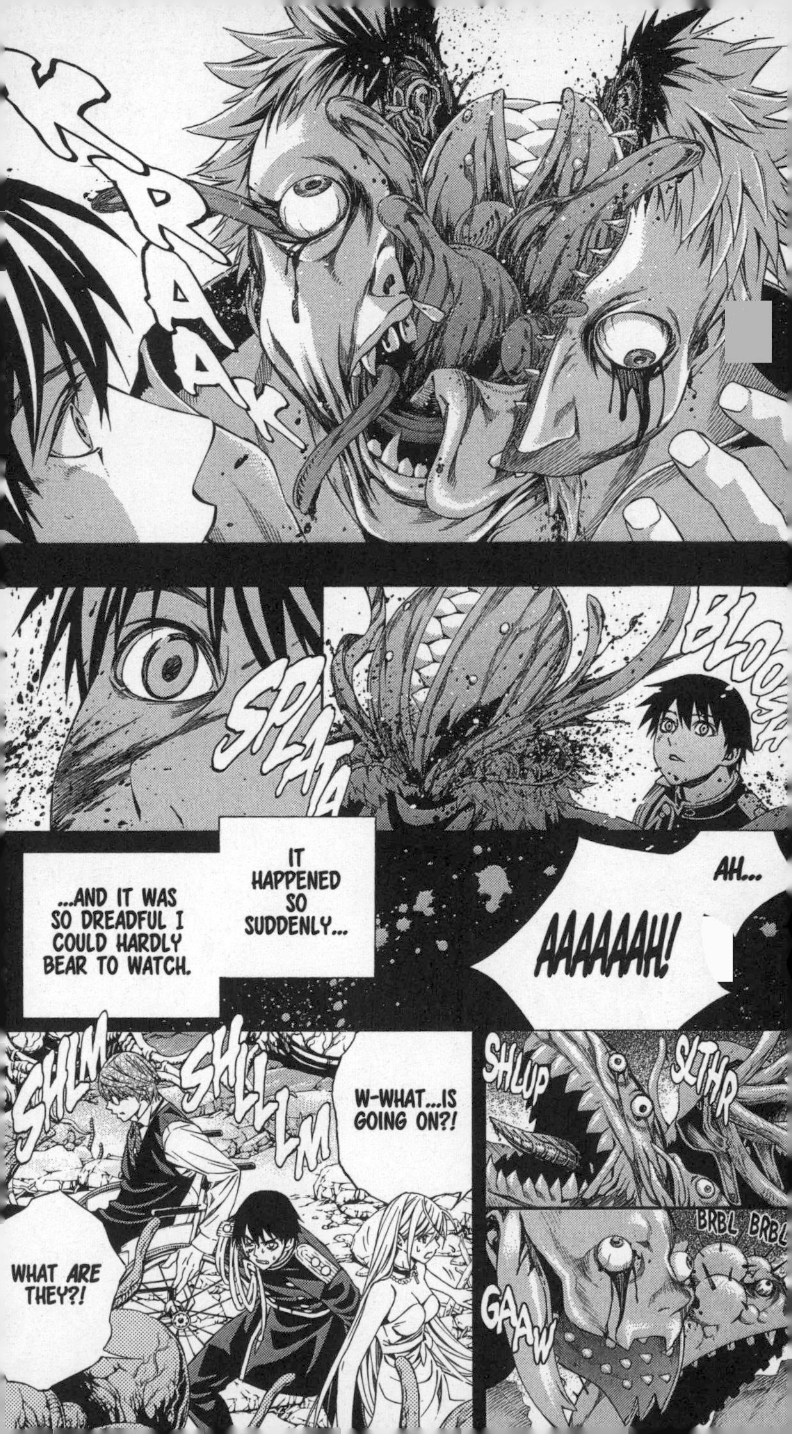
KRAK
BLOOSH
SPLATA
AH...
AAAAAAH!
IT HAPPENED SO SUDDENLY...
...AND IT WAS SO DREADFUL I COULD HARDLY BEAR TO WATCH.
SLTHR
SHLUP
BRBL BRBL
GAAW
W-WHAT...IS GOING ON?!
SHLLLM
SHLM
WHAT ARE THEY?!

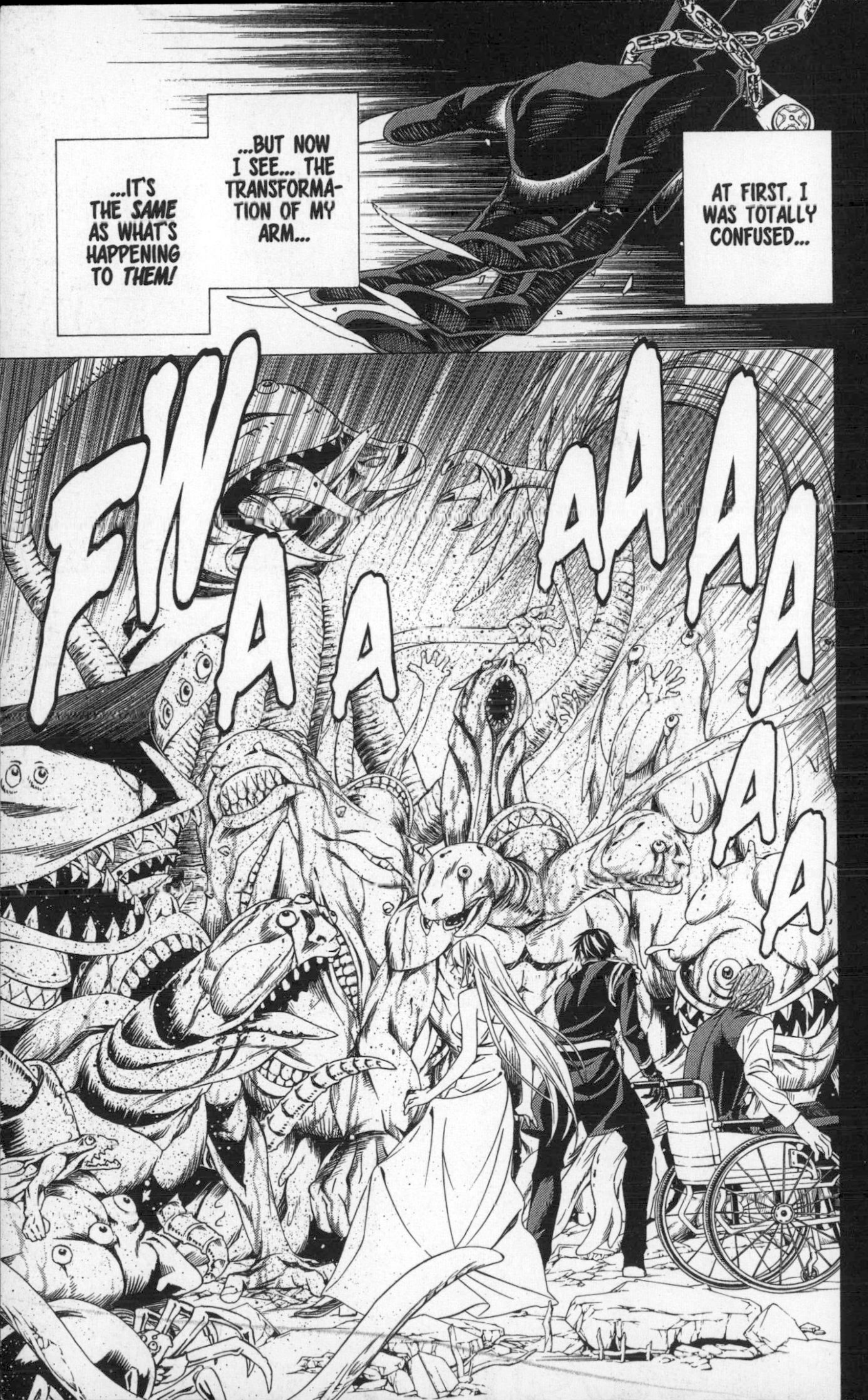
AT FIRST, I WAS TOTALLY CONFUSED...
...BUT NOW I SEE... THE TRANSFORMATION OF MY ARM...
...IT'S THE SAME AS WHAT'S HAPPENING TO THEM!
FWAAAAAAAAA

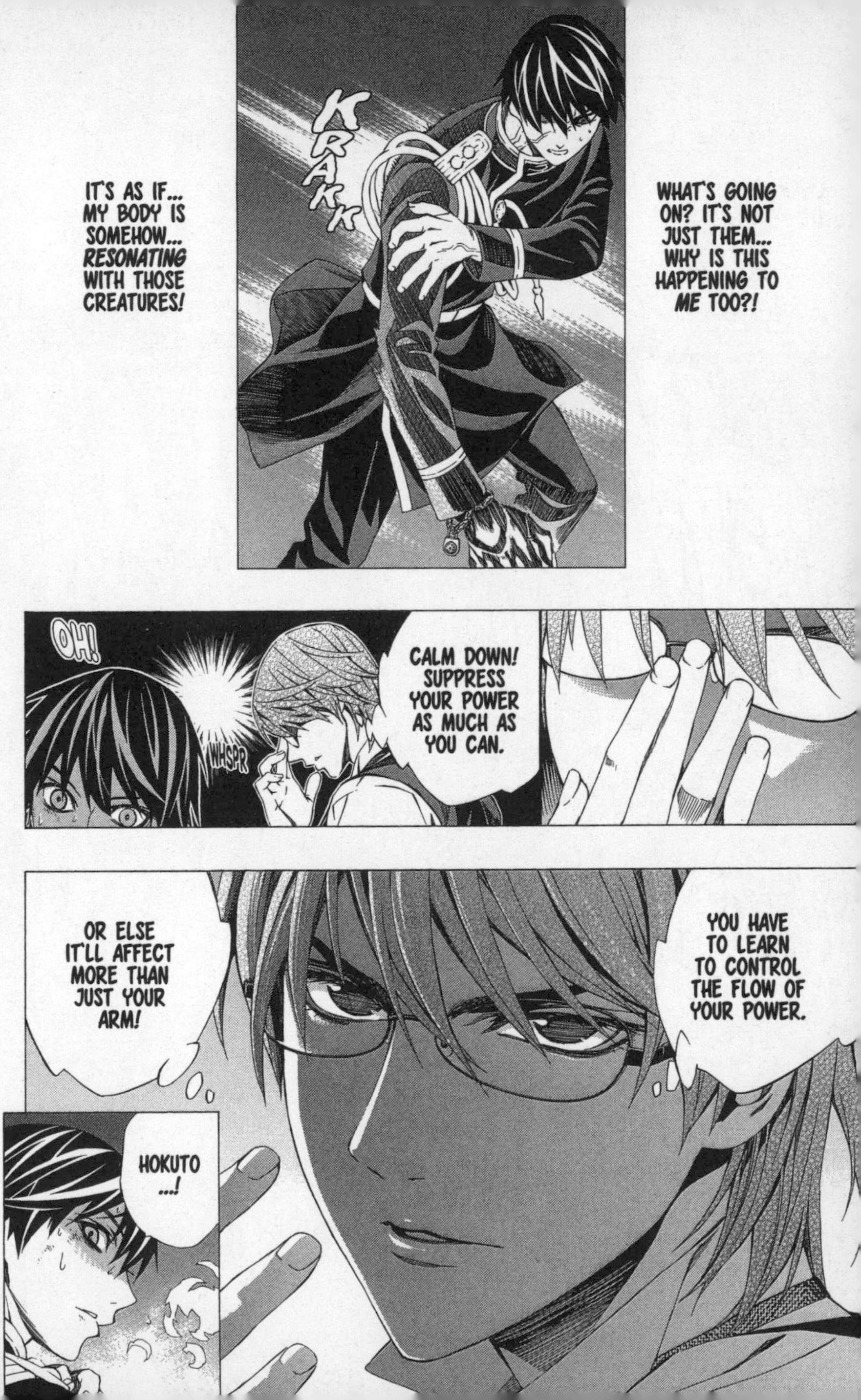
WHAT'S GOING ON? IT'S NOT JUST THEM... WHY IS THIS HAPPENING TO *ME* TOO?!
KRAKK
IT'S AS IF... MY BODY IS SOMEHOW... *RESONATING* WITH THOSE CREATURES!
CALM DOWN! SUPPRESS YOUR POWER AS MUCH AS YOU CAN.
WHSPR
OH!
YOU HAVE TO LEARN TO CONTROL THE FLOW OF YOUR POWER.
OR ELSE IT'LL AFFECT MORE THAN JUST YOUR ARM!
HOKUTO ...!

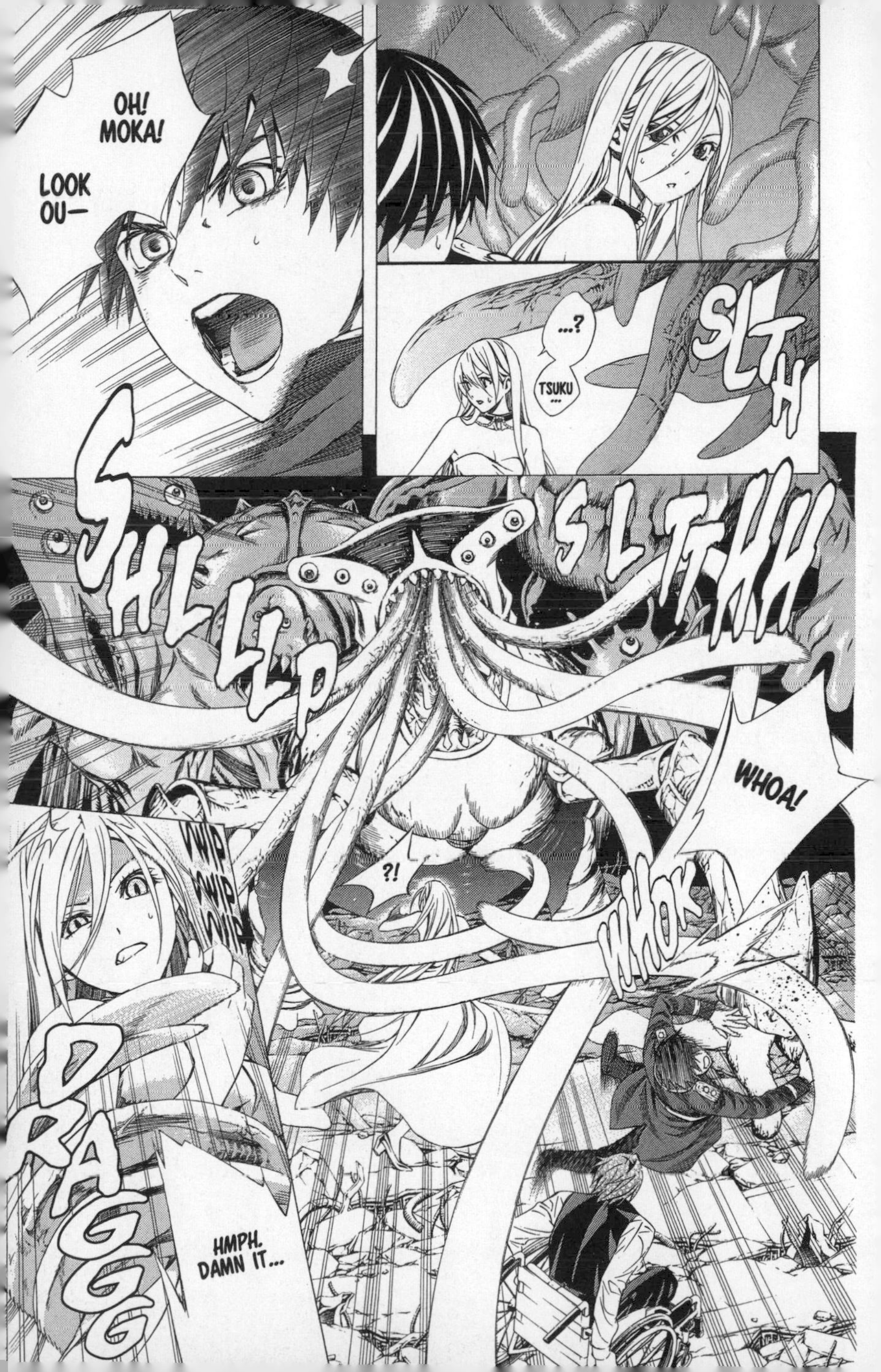
...?
TSUKU...
SLTH
OH! MOKA!
LOOK OU—
SHLLP
SLTHH
WHOA!
WHOK
?!
VWIP VWIP VWIP
DRAGG
HMPH. DAMN IT...

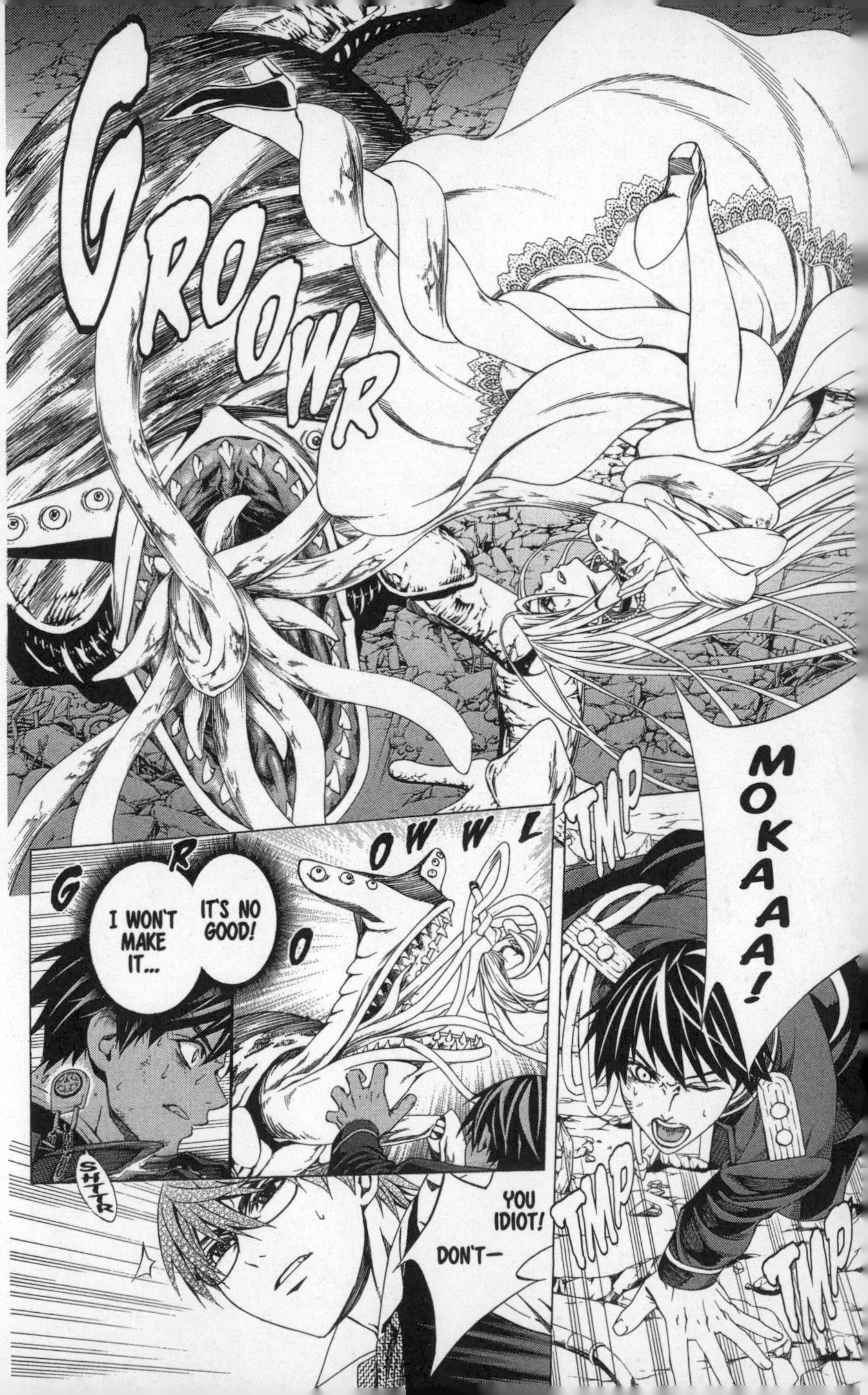
GROOWR
MOKAAAA!
TMP
GROOWWL
IT'S NO GOOD!
I WON'T MAKE IT...
SHTTR
TMP
TMP
YOU IDIOT!
DON'T—

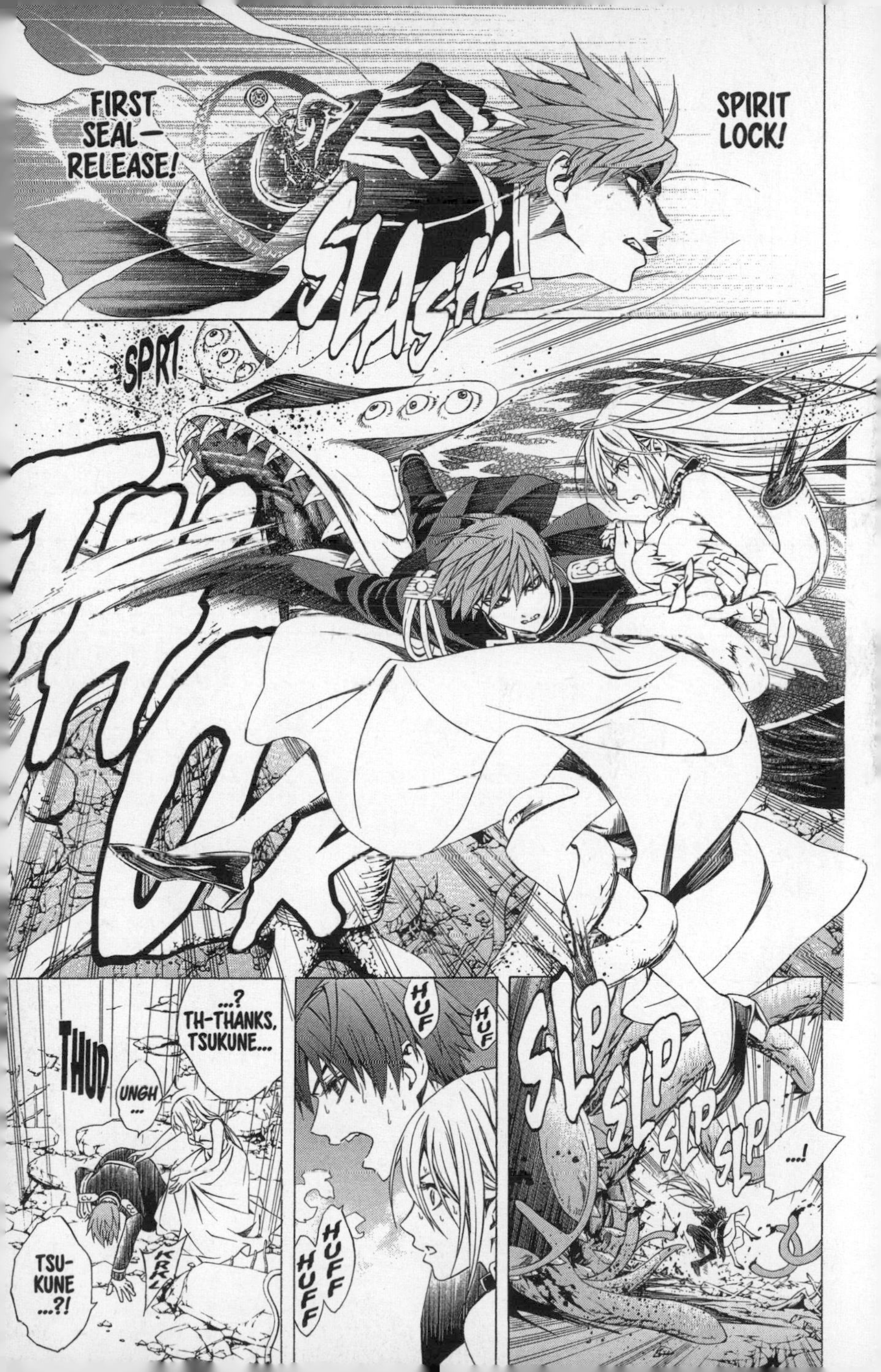
SPIRIT LOCK!
FIRST SEAL—RELEASE!
SLASH
SPRT
SLP SLP SLP SLP SLP
...!
HUF HUF
HUFF HUFF
...? TH-THANKS, TSUKUNE...
THUD
UNGH ...
KRK
TSU-KUNE ...?!

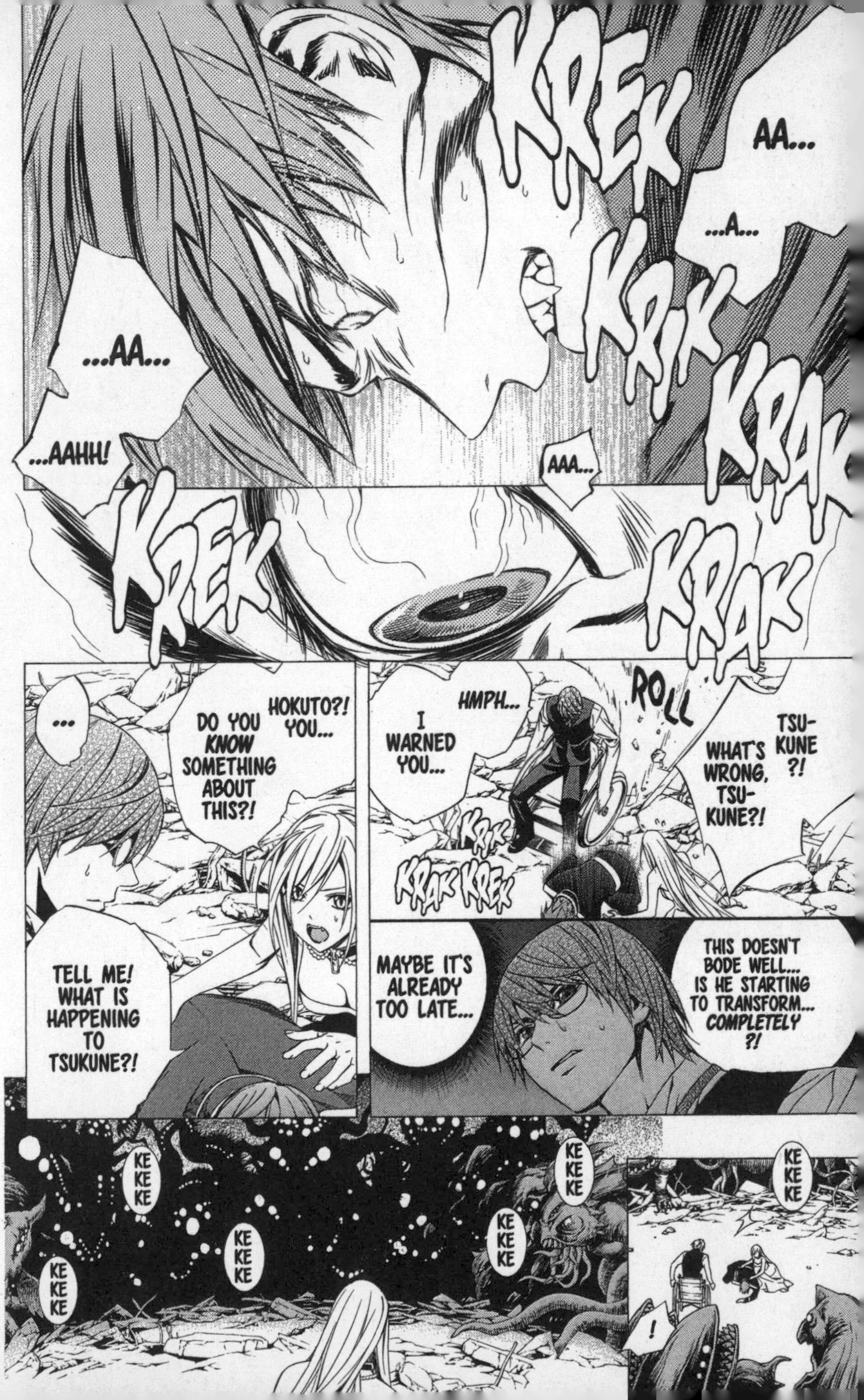
KREK
AA...
...A...
KRIK
KRAK
AAA...
...AA...
...AAHH!
KRAK
KREK
TSU-KUNE?!
WHAT'S WRONG, TSU-KUNE?!
ROLL
HMPH...
I WARNED YOU...
KRIK
KRAK KREK
HOKUTO?! YOU...
DO YOU KNOW SOMETHING ABOUT THIS?!
...
TELL ME! WHAT IS HAPPENING TO TSUKUNE?!
THIS DOESN'T BODE WELL... IS HE STARTING TO TRANSFORM... COMPLETELY?!
MAYBE IT'S ALREADY TOO LATE...
KE KE KE
!
KE KE KE
KE KE KE
KE KE KE
KE KE KE

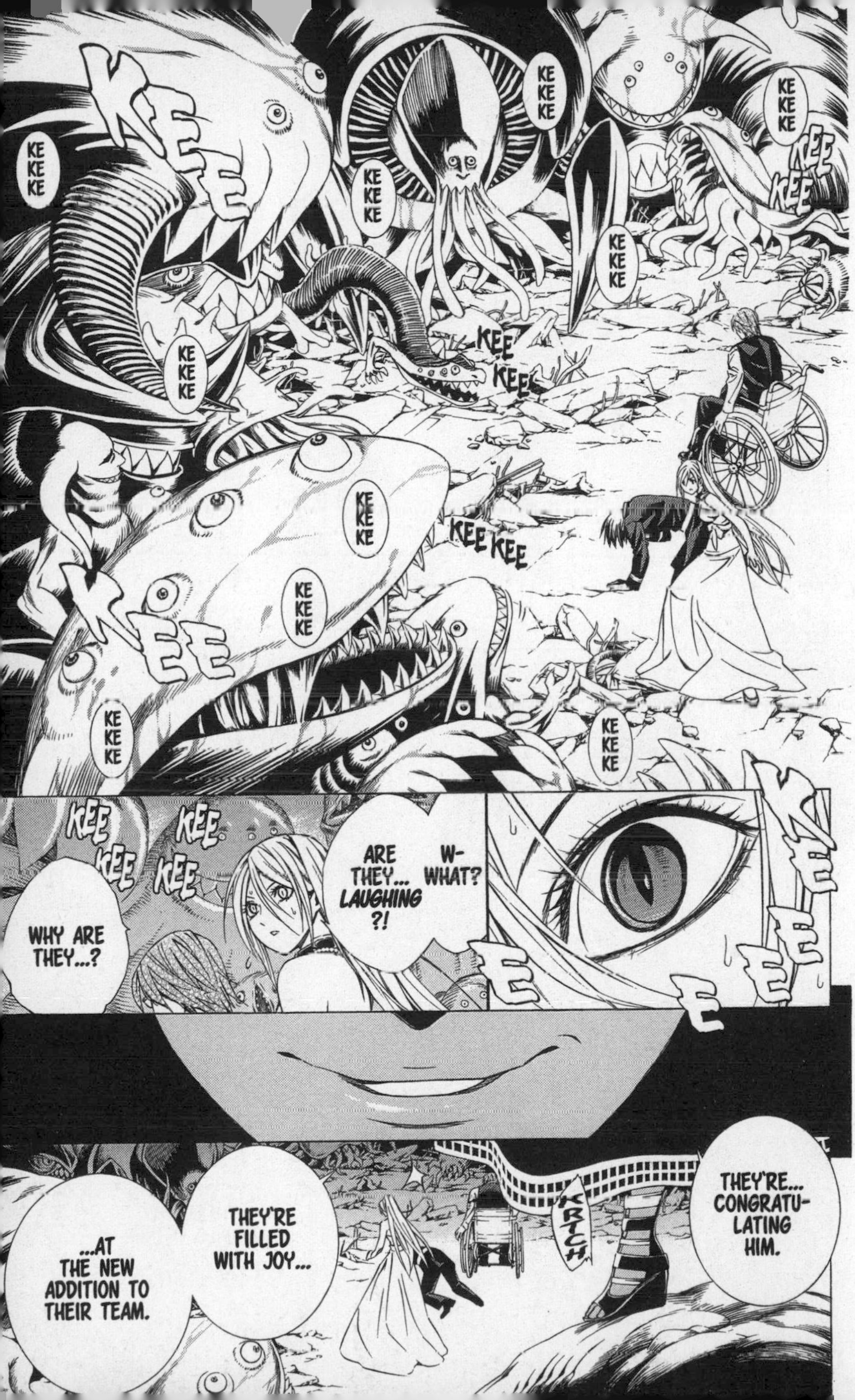
KE KE KE
KEE KEE
KE KE KE
KEE
KE KE KE
KE KE KE
KE KE KE
KEE KEE
KE KE KE
KE KE KE
KEE KEE
KE KE KE
KEE
KE KE KE
KE KE KE
KEEEEE
W- WHAT?
ARE THEY... LAUGHING?!
KEE KEE KEE KEE
WHY ARE THEY...?
THEY'RE... CONGRATU-LATING HIM.
KRTCH
THEY'RE FILLED WITH JOY...
...AT THE NEW ADDITION TO THEIR TEAM.

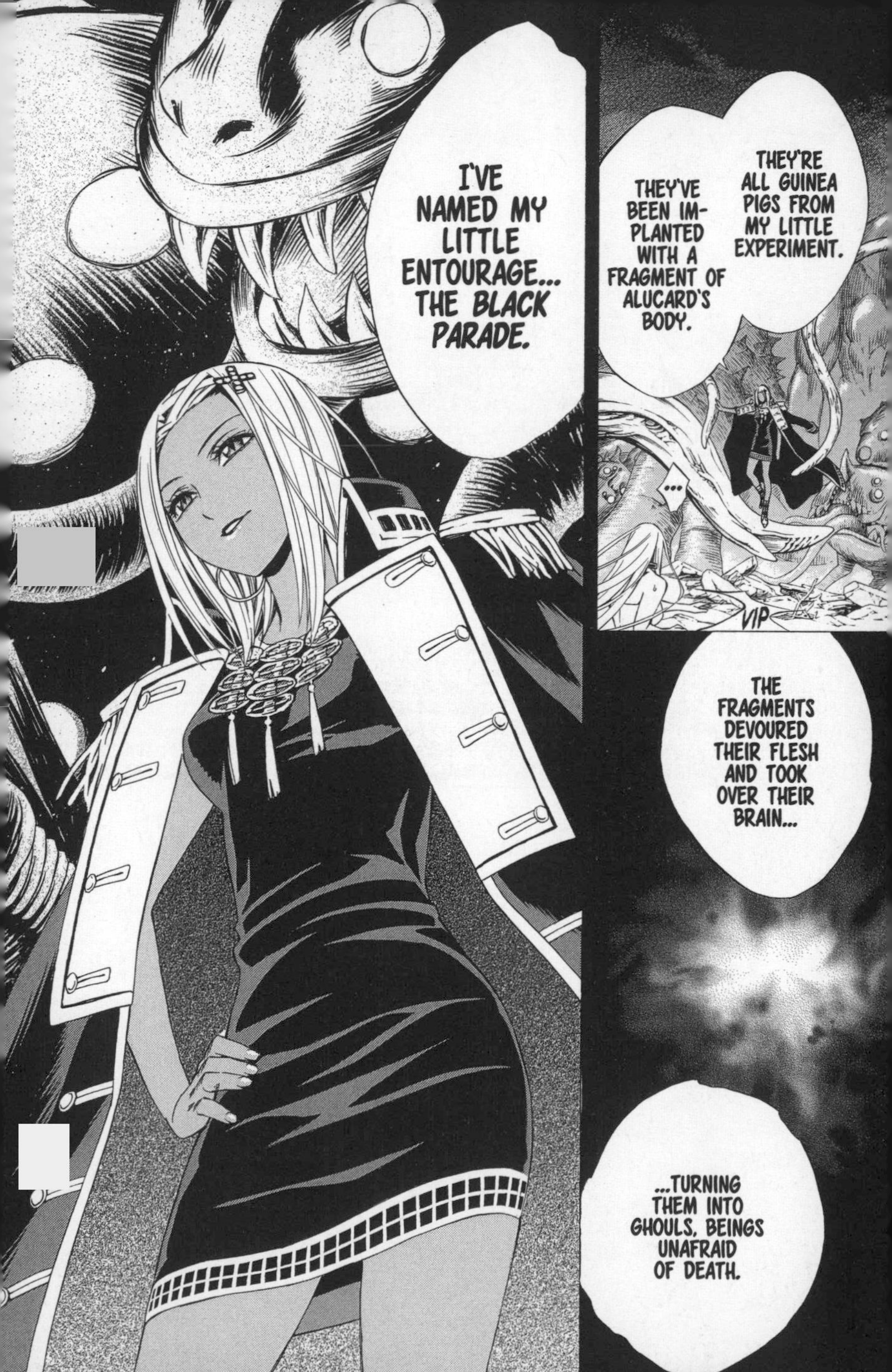
THEY'RE ALL GUINEA PIGS FROM MY LITTLE EXPERIMENT.
THEY'VE BEEN IM-PLANTED WITH A FRAGMENT OF ALUCARD'S BODY.
...
VIP
THE FRAGMENTS DEVOURED THEIR FLESH AND TOOK OVER THEIR BRAIN...
...TURNING THEM INTO GHOULS, BEINGS UNAFRAID OF DEATH.
I'VE NAMED MY LITTLE ENTOURAGE... THE *BLACK PARADE*.

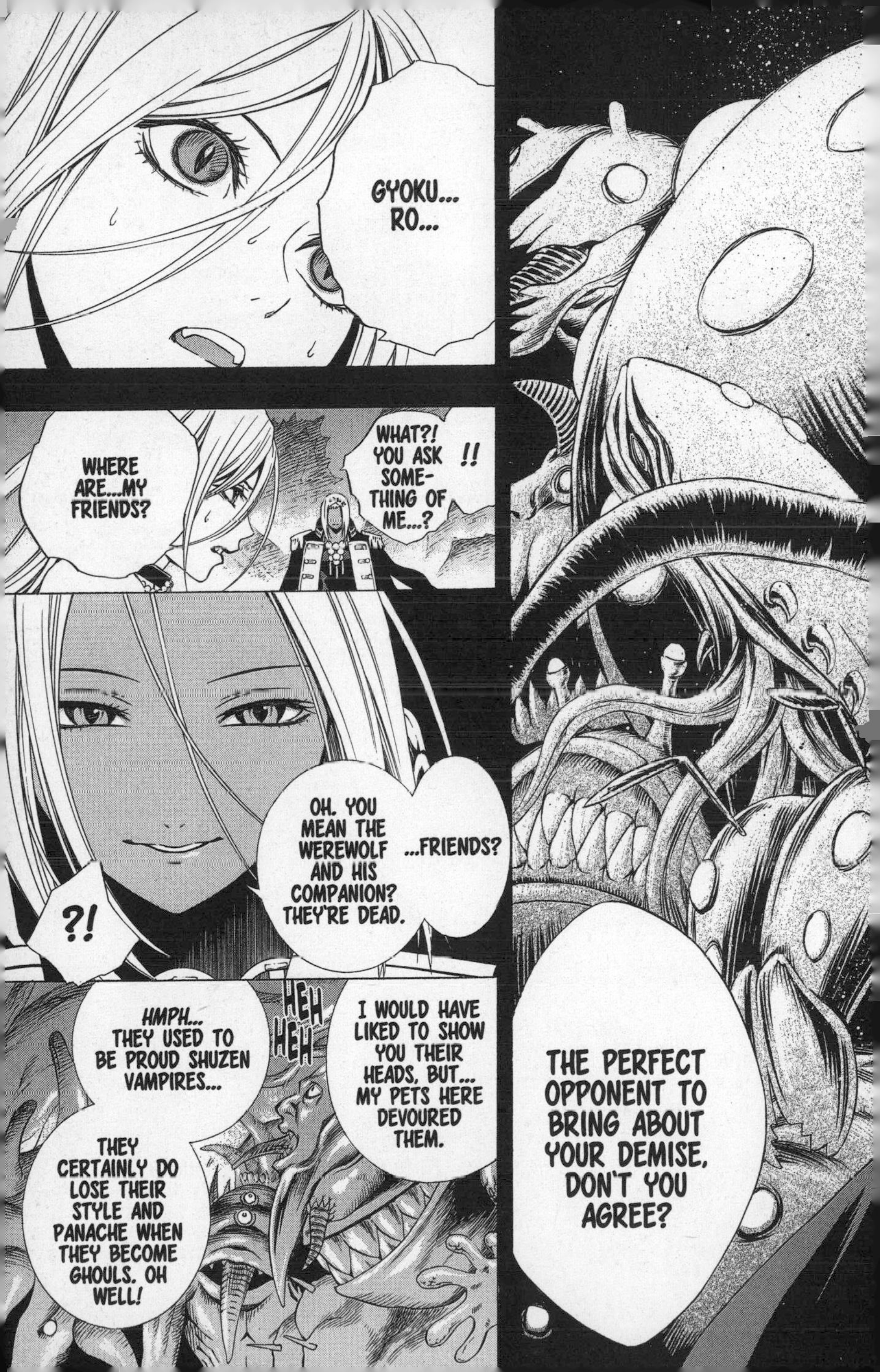
GYOKU... RO...
WHERE ARE...MY FRIENDS?
!!
WHAT?! YOU ASK SOME-THING OF ME...?
...FRIENDS?
OH. YOU MEAN THE WEREWOLF AND HIS COMPANION? THEY'RE DEAD.
?!
I WOULD HAVE LIKED TO SHOW YOU THEIR HEADS, BUT... MY PETS HERE DEVOURED THEM.
HEH HEH
HMPH... THEY USED TO BE PROUD SHUZEN VAMPIRES...
THEY CERTAINLY DO LOSE THEIR STYLE AND PANACHE WHEN THEY BECOME GHOULS. OH WELL!
THE PERFECT OPPONENT TO BRING ABOUT YOUR DEMISE, DON'T YOU AGREE?

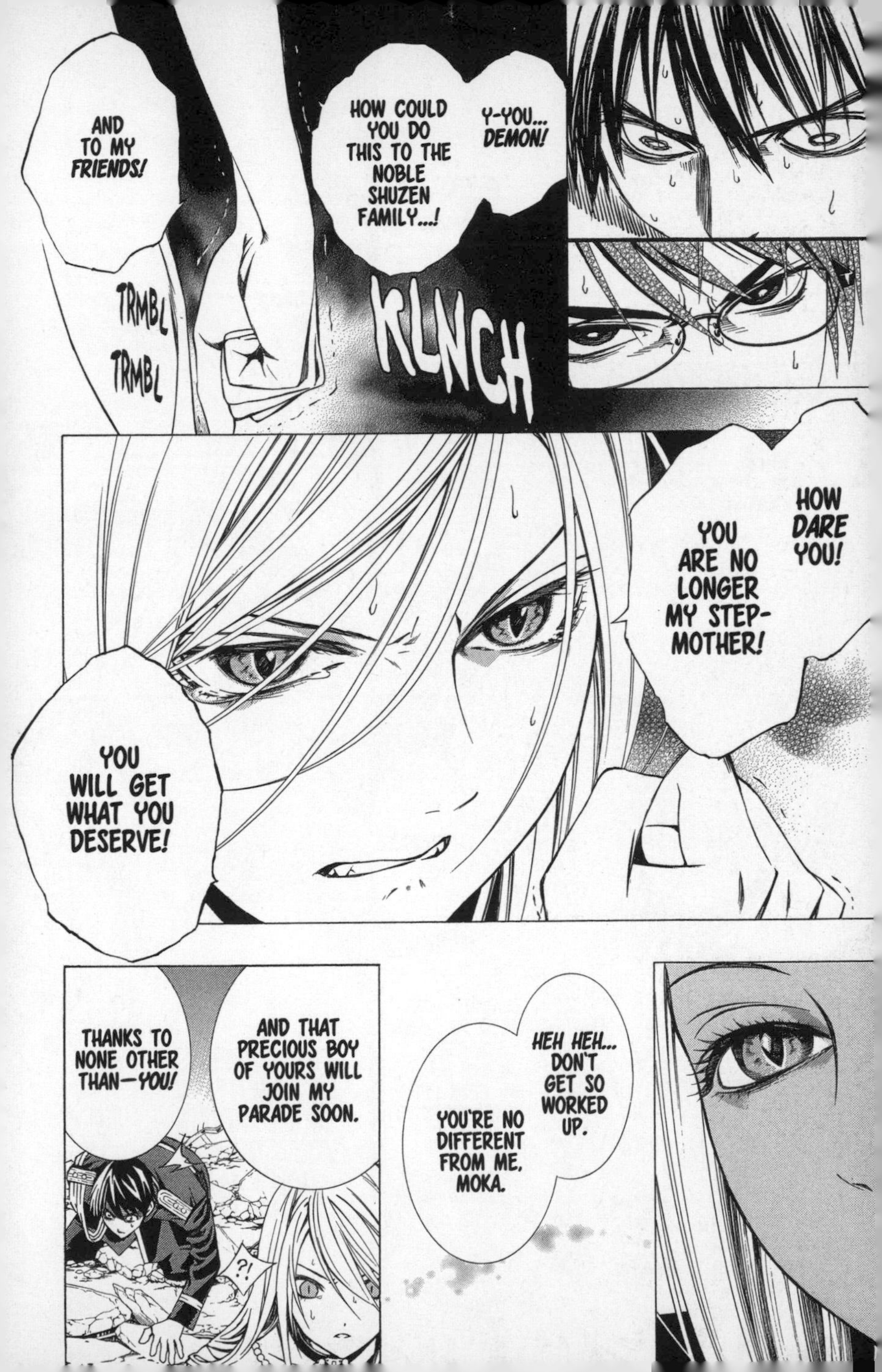
Y-YOU... DEMON!
HOW COULD YOU DO THIS TO THE NOBLE SHUZEN FAMILY...!
AND TO MY FRIENDS!
KLNCH
TRMBL
TRMBL
HOW DARE YOU!
YOU ARE NO LONGER MY STEP-MOTHER!
YOU WILL GET WHAT YOU DESERVE!
HEH HEH... DON'T GET SO WORKED UP.
YOU'RE NO DIFFERENT FROM ME, MOKA.
AND THAT PRECIOUS BOY OF YOURS WILL JOIN MY PARADE SOON.
THANKS TO NONE OTHER THAN—YOU!
?!

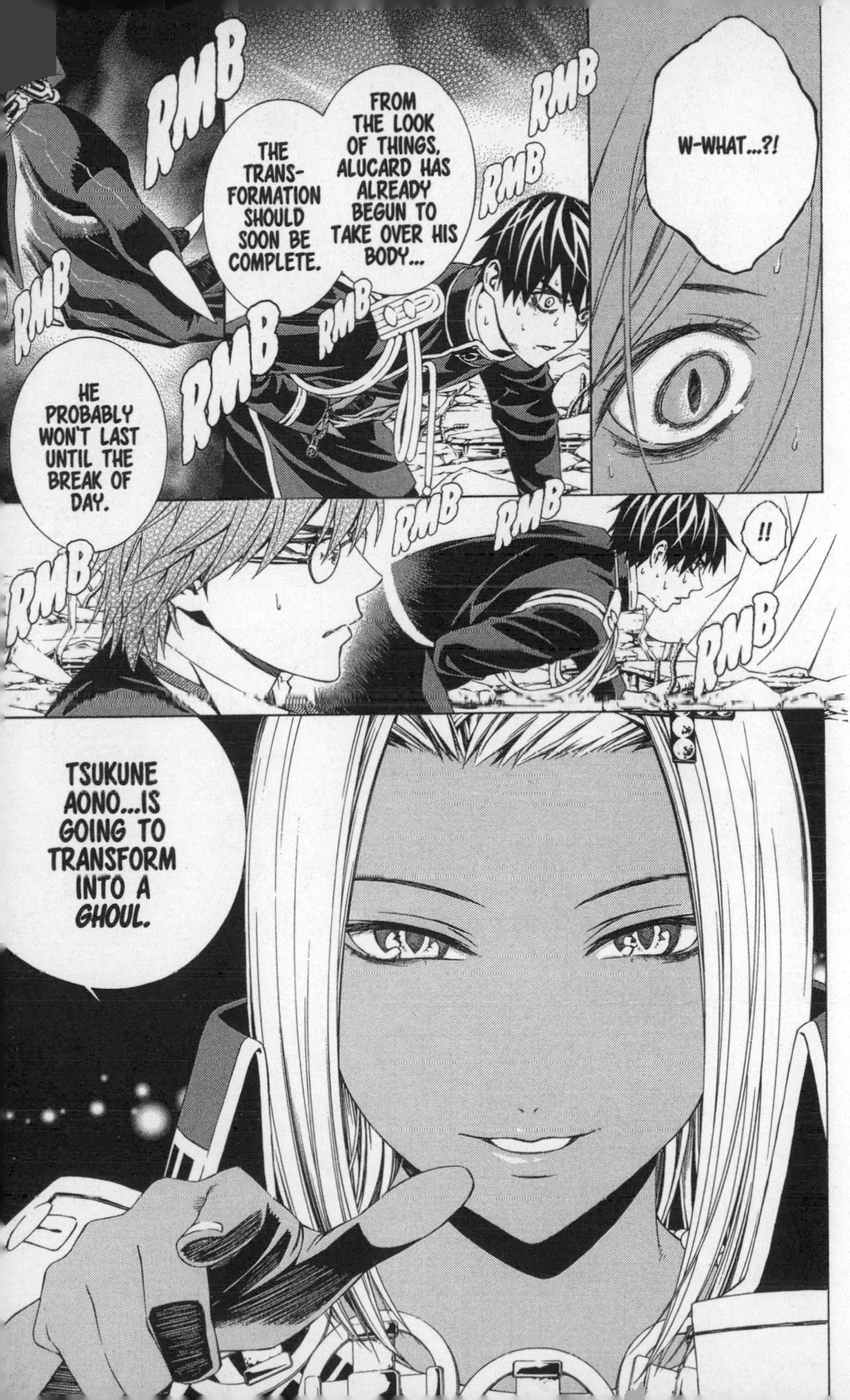
W-WHAT...?!
RMB
RMB
RMB
FROM THE LOOK OF THINGS, ALUCARD HAS ALREADY BEGUN TO TAKE OVER HIS BODY...
RMB
THE TRANS-FORMATION SHOULD SOON BE COMPLETE.
RMB
RMB
RMB
RMB
HE PROBABLY WON'T LAST UNTIL THE BREAK OF DAY.
!!
RMB
RMB
RMB
RMB
TSUKUNE AONO...IS GOING TO TRANSFORM INTO A GHOUL.

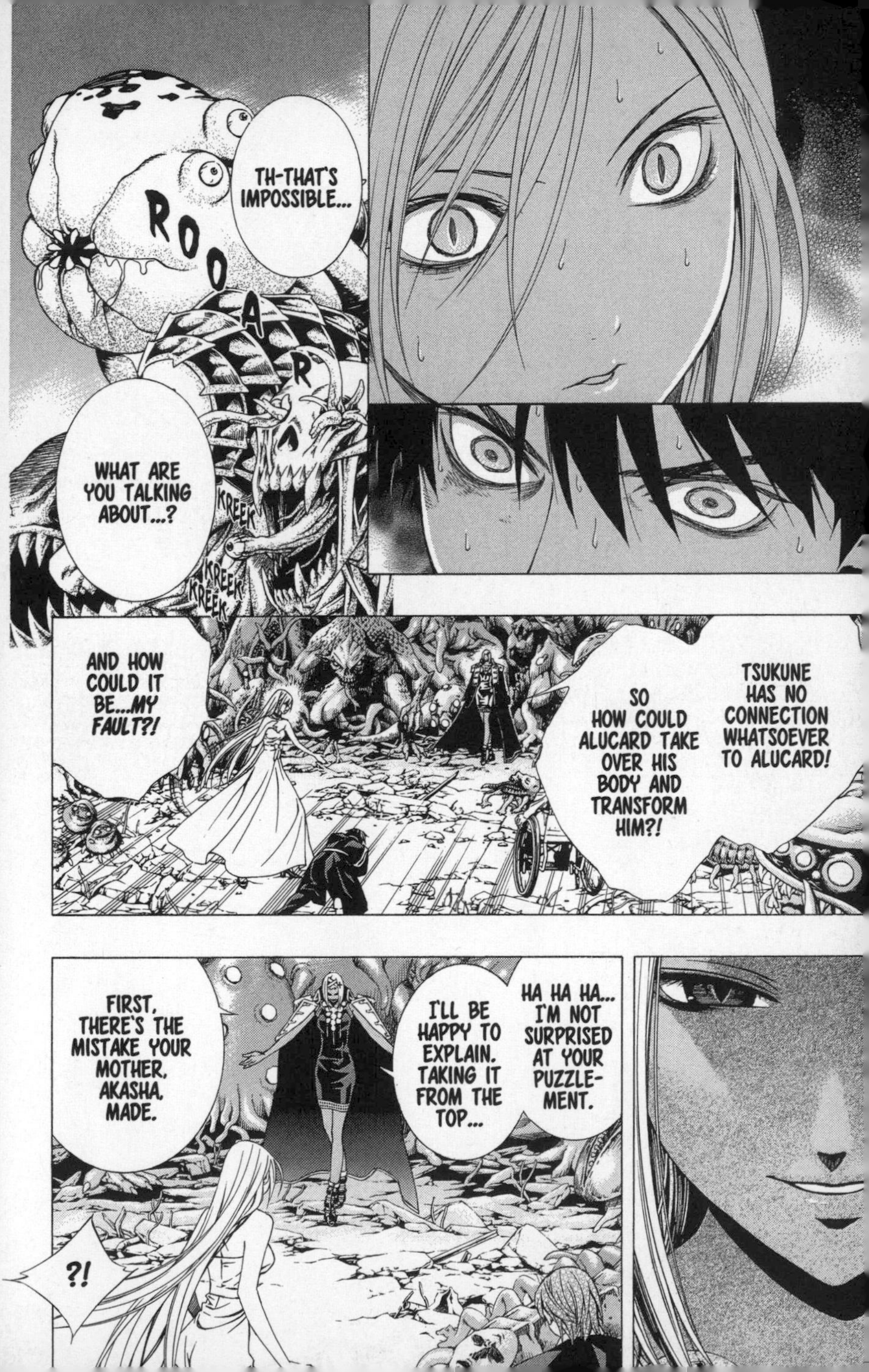
ROOOAR
TH-THAT'S IMPOSSIBLE...
WHAT ARE YOU TALKING ABOUT...?
KREEK KREEK KREEK KREEK
TSUKUNE HAS NO CONNECTION WHATSOEVER TO ALUCARD!
SO HOW COULD ALUCARD TAKE OVER HIS BODY AND TRANSFORM HIM?!
AND HOW COULD IT BE...MY FAULT?!
HA HA HA... I'M NOT SURPRISED AT YOUR PUZZLEMENT.
I'LL BE HAPPY TO EXPLAIN. TAKING IT FROM THE TOP...
FIRST, THERE'S THE MISTAKE YOUR MOTHER, AKASHA, MADE.
?!

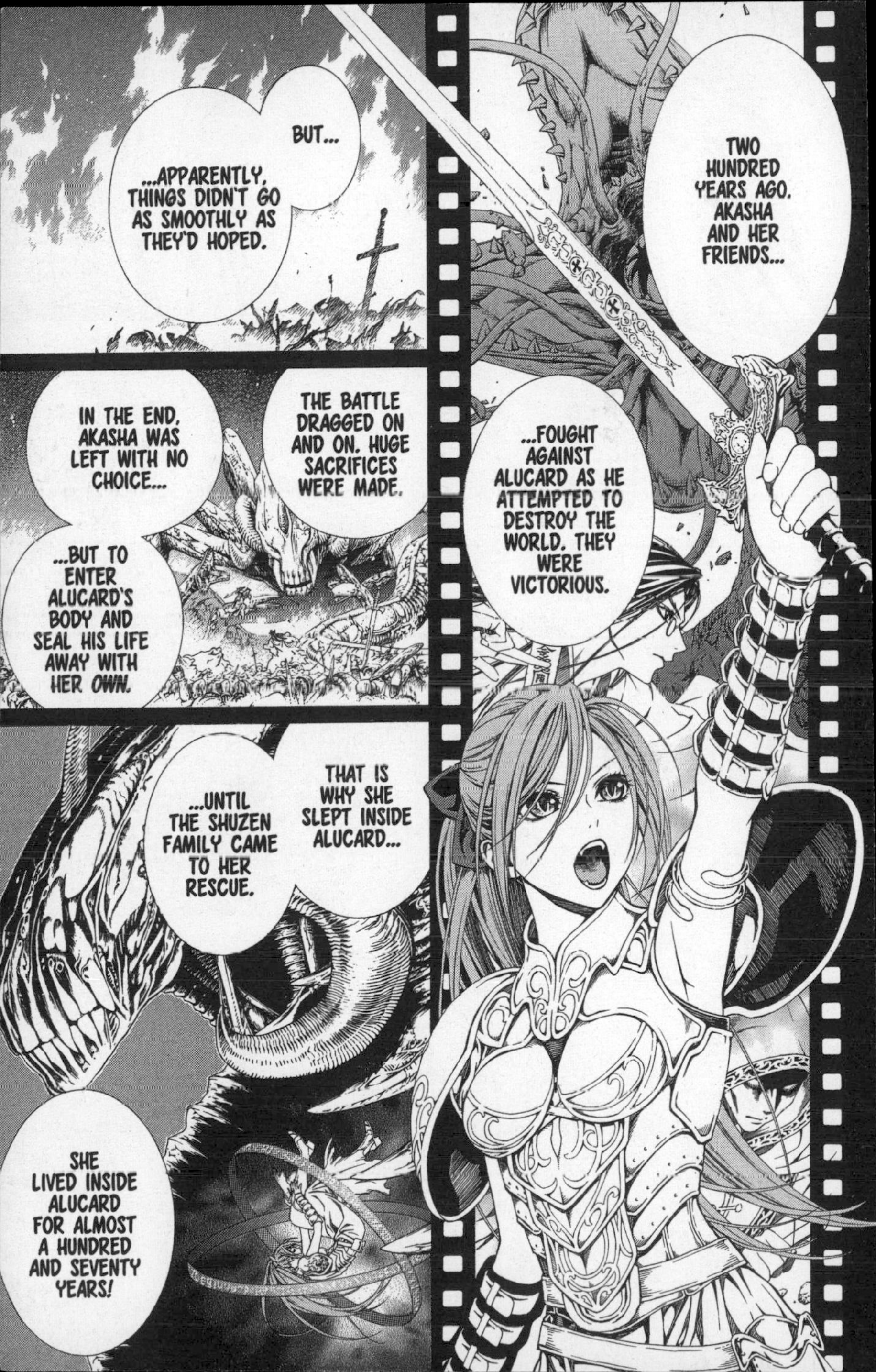
TWO HUNDRED YEARS AGO. AKASHA AND HER FRIENDS...
...FOUGHT AGAINST ALUCARD AS HE ATTEMPTED TO DESTROY THE WORLD. THEY WERE VICTORIOUS.
BUT...
...APPARENTLY, THINGS DIDN'T GO AS SMOOTHLY AS THEY'D HOPED.
THE BATTLE DRAGGED ON AND ON. HUGE SACRIFICES WERE MADE.
IN THE END, AKASHA WAS LEFT WITH NO CHOICE...
...BUT TO ENTER ALUCARD'S BODY AND SEAL HIS LIFE AWAY WITH HER OWN.
THAT IS WHY SHE SLEPT INSIDE ALUCARD...
...UNTIL THE SHUZEN FAMILY CAME TO HER RESCUE.
SHE LIVED INSIDE ALUCARD FOR ALMOST A HUNDRED AND SEVENTY YEARS!

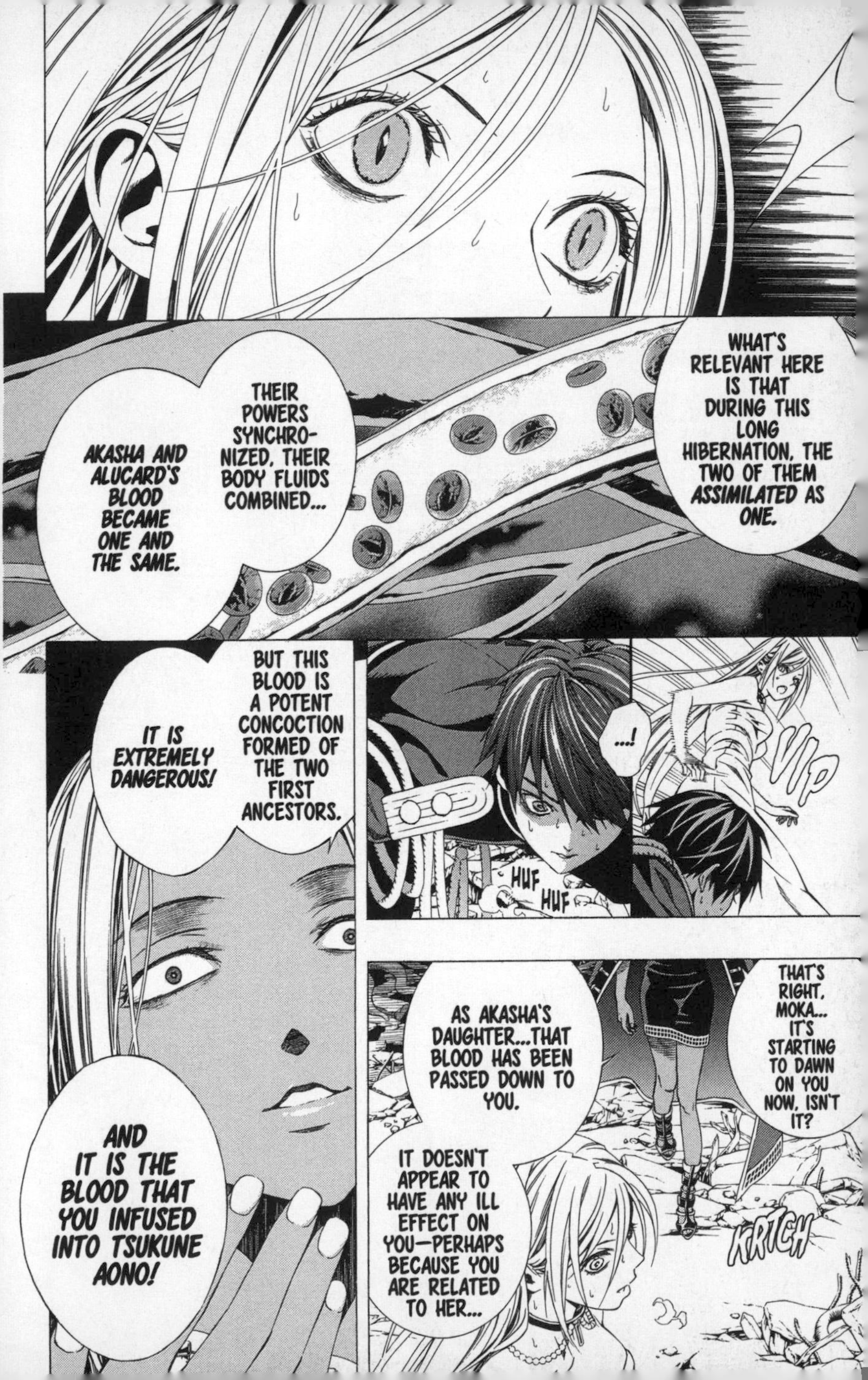
WHAT'S RELEVANT HERE IS THAT DURING THIS LONG HIBERNATION, THE TWO OF THEM ASSIMILATED AS ONE.
THEIR POWERS SYNCHRONIZED, THEIR BODY FLUIDS COMBINED...
AKASHA AND ALUCARD'S BLOOD BECAME ONE AND THE SAME.
VIP
...!
HUF HUF
THAT'S RIGHT, MOKA... IT'S STARTING TO DAWN ON YOU NOW, ISN'T IT?
AS AKASHA'S DAUGHTER...THAT BLOOD HAS BEEN PASSED DOWN TO YOU.
IT DOESN'T APPEAR TO HAVE ANY ILL EFFECT ON YOU—PERHAPS BECAUSE YOU ARE RELATED TO HER...
KRTCH
BUT THIS BLOOD IS A POTENT CONCOCTION FORMED OF THE TWO FIRST ANCESTORS.
IT IS EXTREMELY DANGEROUS!
AND IT IS THE BLOOD THAT YOU INFUSED INTO TSUKUNE AONO!

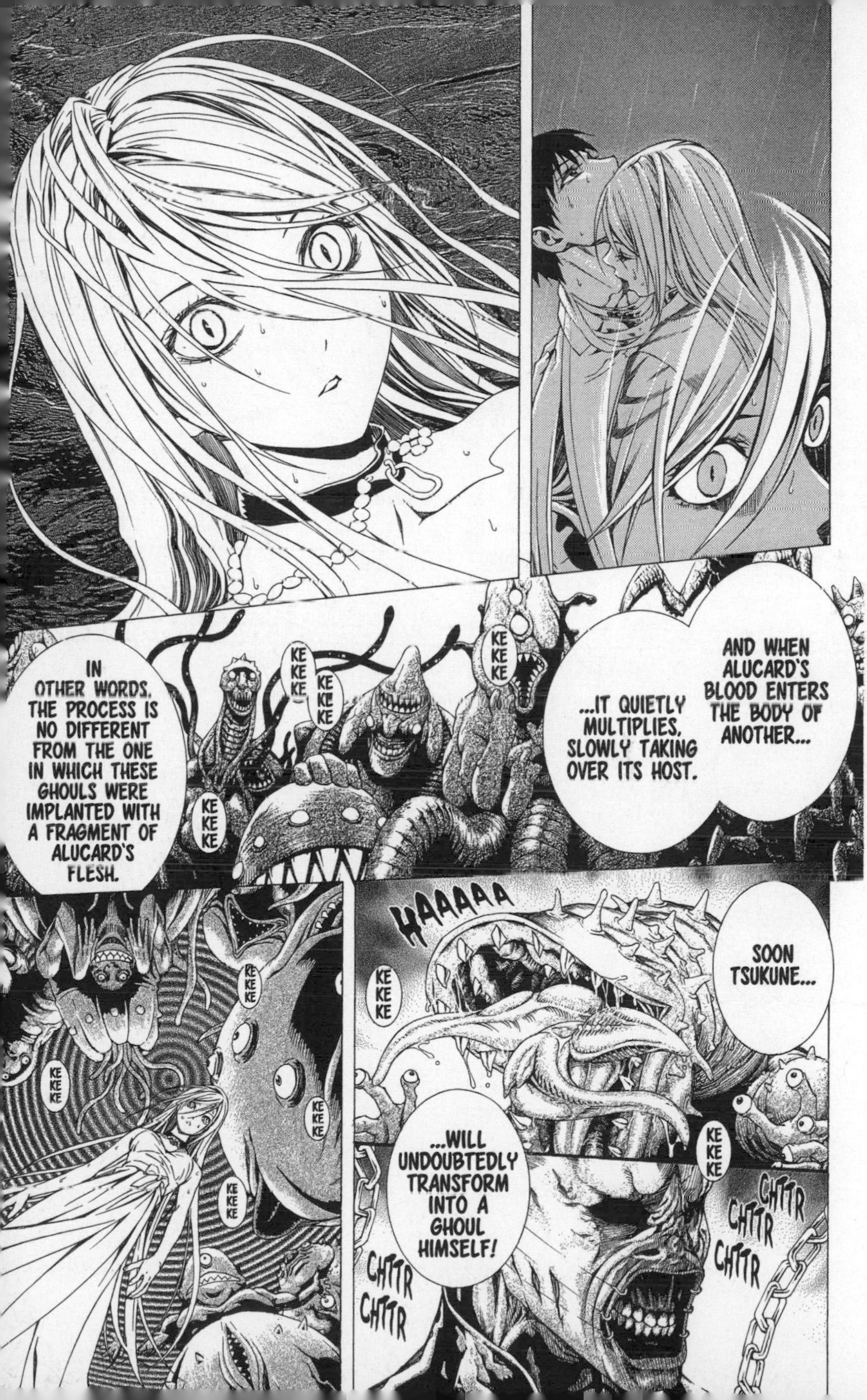
AND WHEN ALUCARD'S BLOOD ENTERS THE BODY OF ANOTHER...
...IT QUIETLY MULTIPLIES, SLOWLY TAKING OVER ITS HOST.
KE KE KE
KE KE KE
KE KE KE
KE KE KE
IN OTHER WORDS, THE PROCESS IS NO DIFFERENT FROM THE ONE IN WHICH THESE GHOULS WERE IMPLANTED WITH A FRAGMENT OF ALUCARD'S FLESH.
SOON TSUKUNE...
HAAAAA
KE KE KE
...WILL UNDOUBTEDLY TRANSFORM INTO A GHOUL HIMSELF!
KE KE KE
CHTTR CHTTR CHTTR
CHTTR CHTTR
KE KE KE
KE KE KE
KE KE KE
KE KE KE

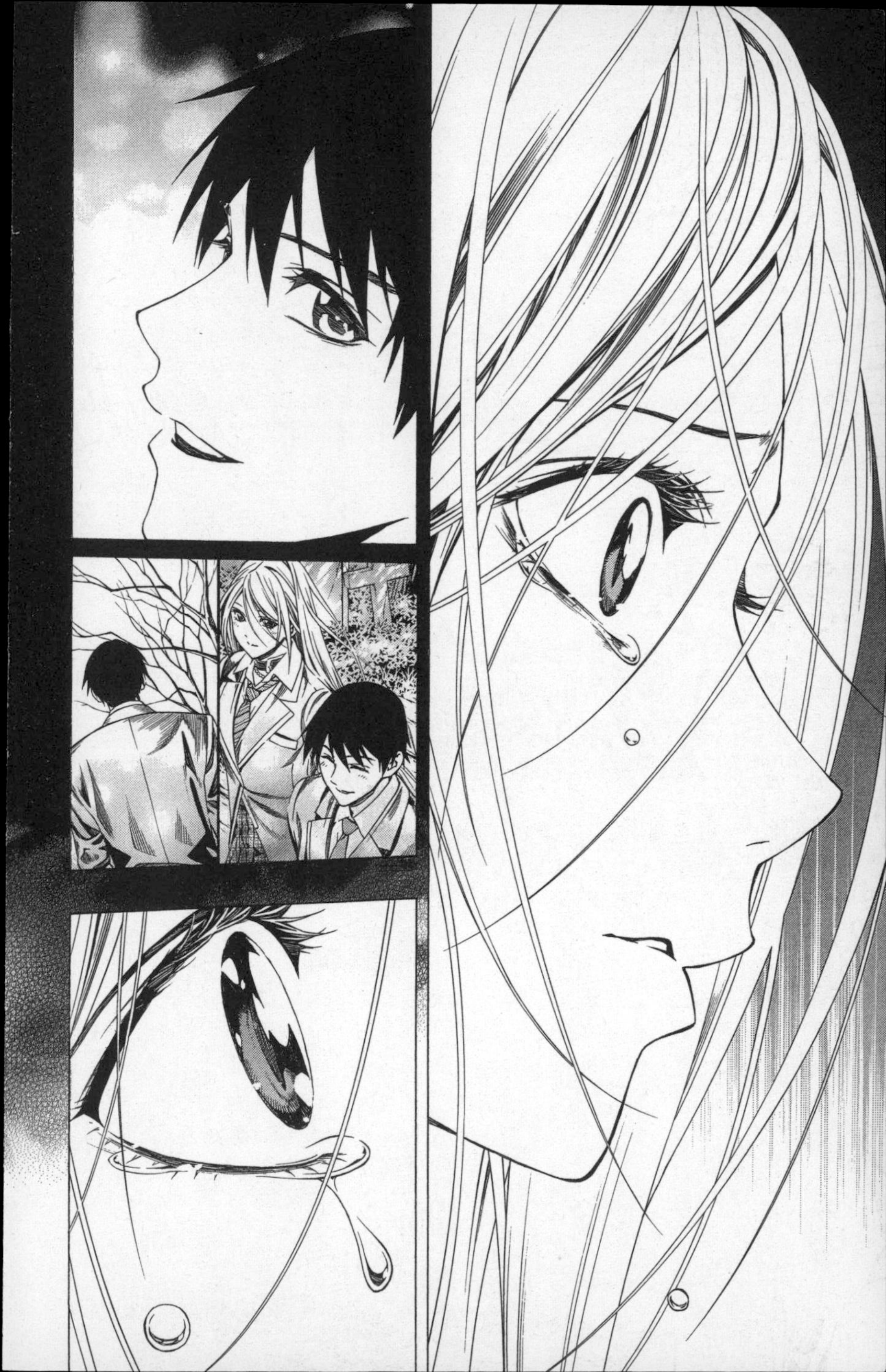

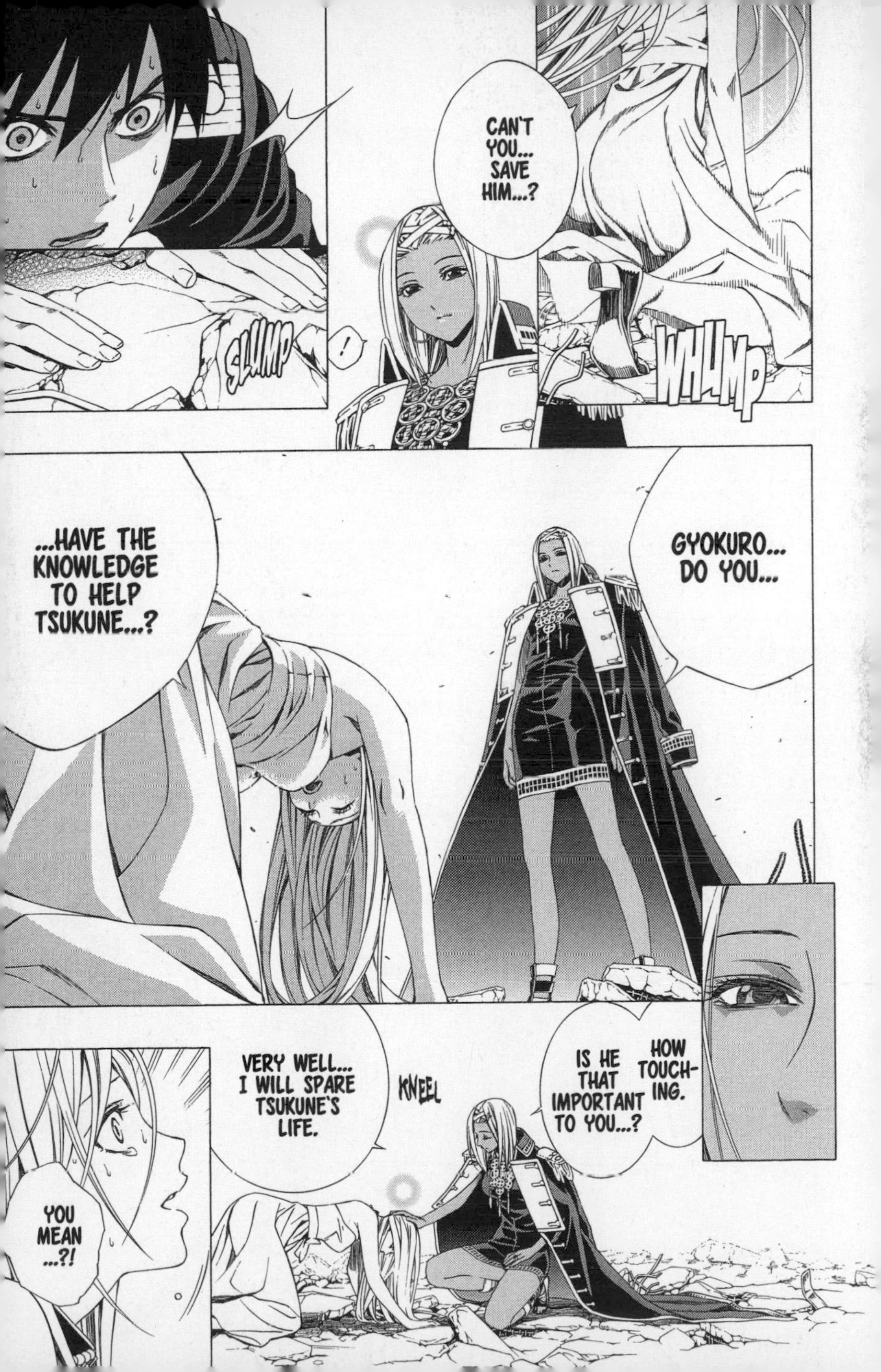
WHUMP
CAN'T YOU... SAVE HIM...?
!
SLUMP
GYOKURO... DO YOU...
...HAVE THE KNOWLEDGE TO HELP TSUKUNE...?
HOW TOUCHING.
IS HE THAT IMPORTANT TO YOU...?
KNEEL
VERY WELL... I WILL SPARE TSUKUNE'S LIFE.
YOU MEAN ...?!

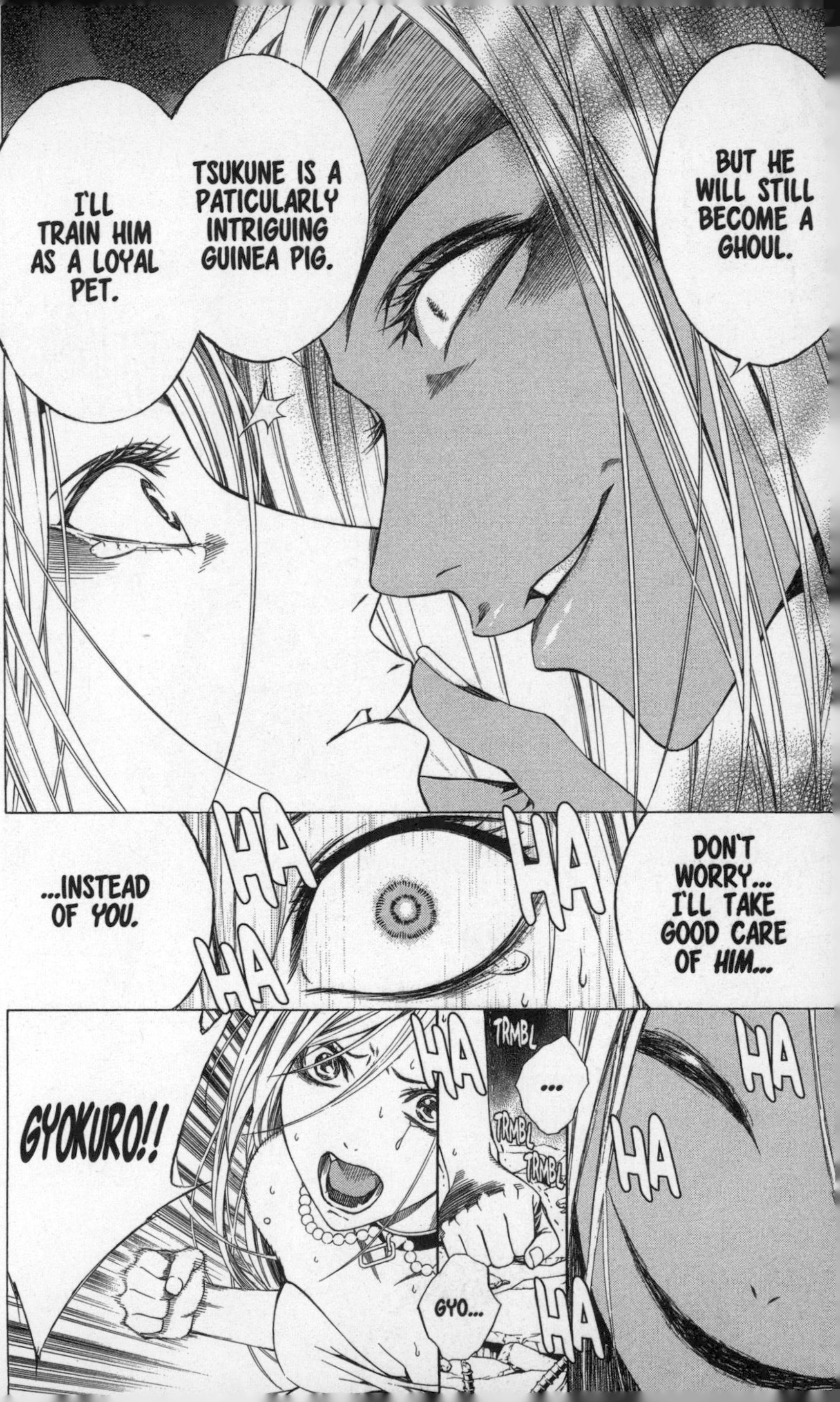
BUT HE WILL STILL BECOME A GHOUL.
TSUKUNE IS A PATICULARLY INTRIGUING GUINEA PIG.
I'LL TRAIN HIM AS A LOYAL PET.
DON'T WORRY... I'LL TAKE GOOD CARE OF HIM...
HA HA HA
...INSTEAD OF YOU.
HA HA HA HA
TRMBL
...
TRMBL TRMBL
GYO...
HA
GYOKURO!!

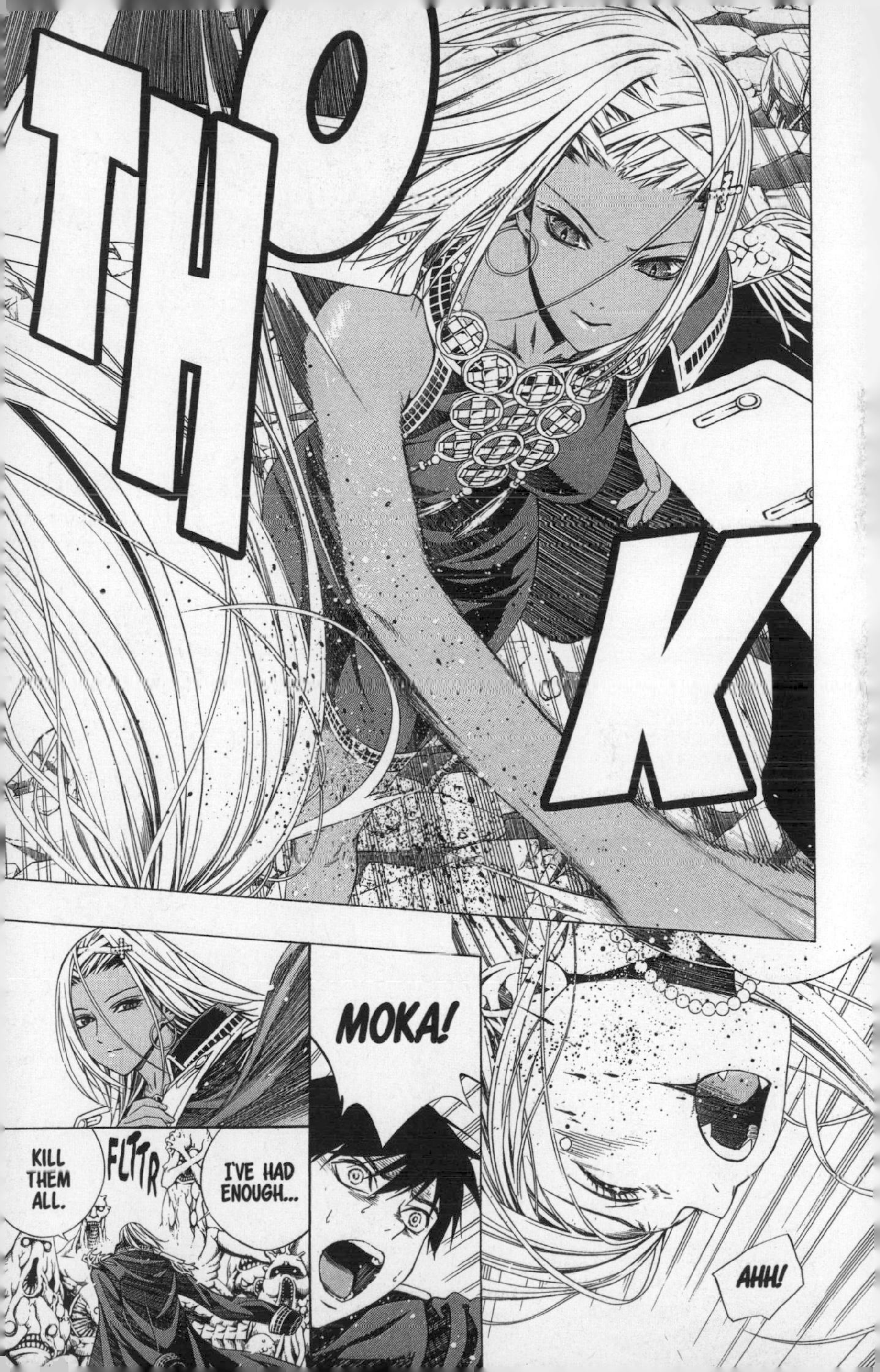
THOK
AHH!
MOKA!
I'VE HAD ENOUGH...
FLTTR
KILL THEM ALL.

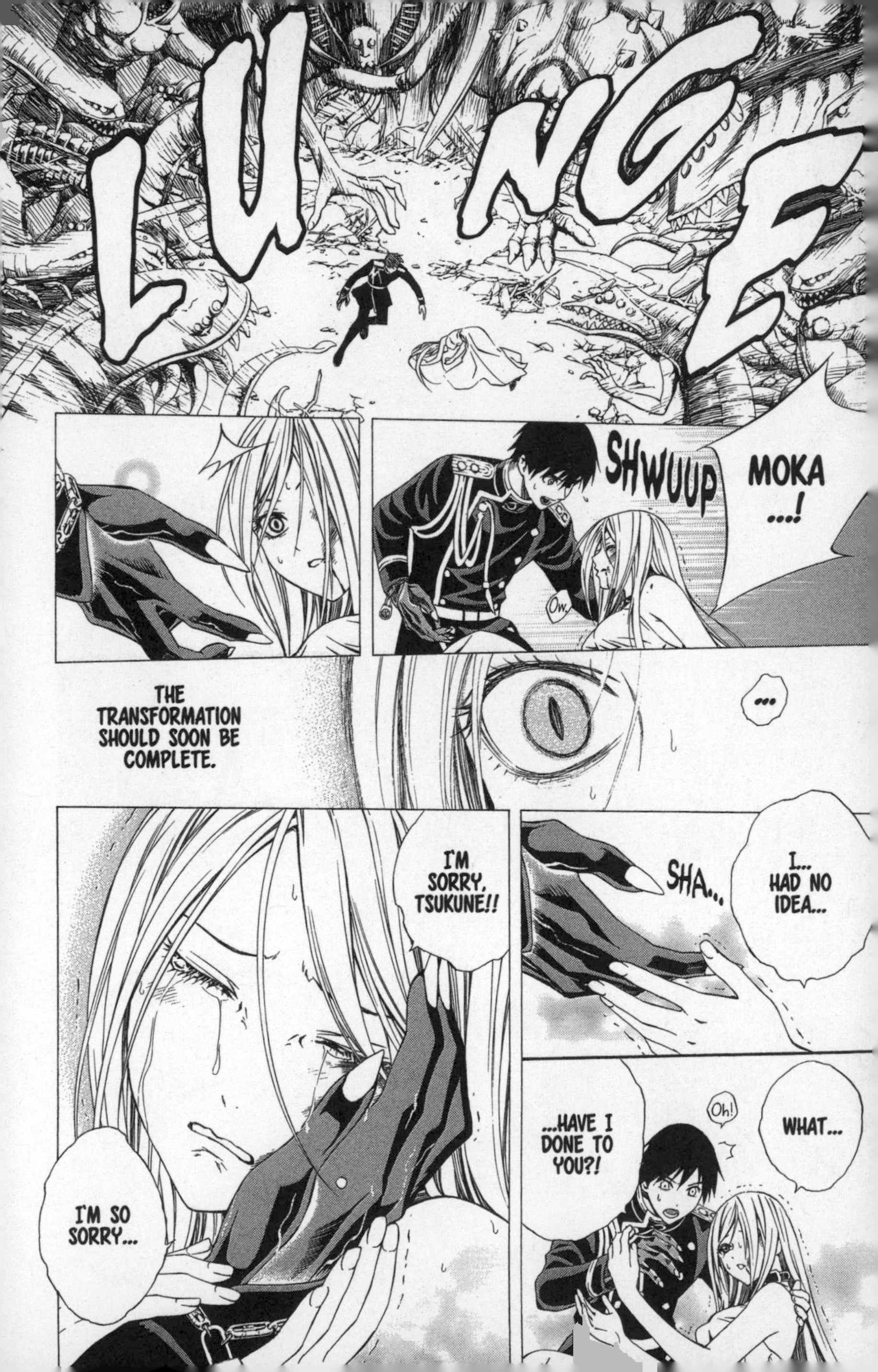
LUNGE
MOKA ...!
SHWUUP
Ow.
...
THE TRANSFORMATION SHOULD SOON BE COMPLETE.
I... HAD NO IDEA...
SHA..
WHAT...
Oh!
...HAVE I DONE TO YOU?!
I'M SORRY, TSUKUNE!!
I'M SO SORRY...

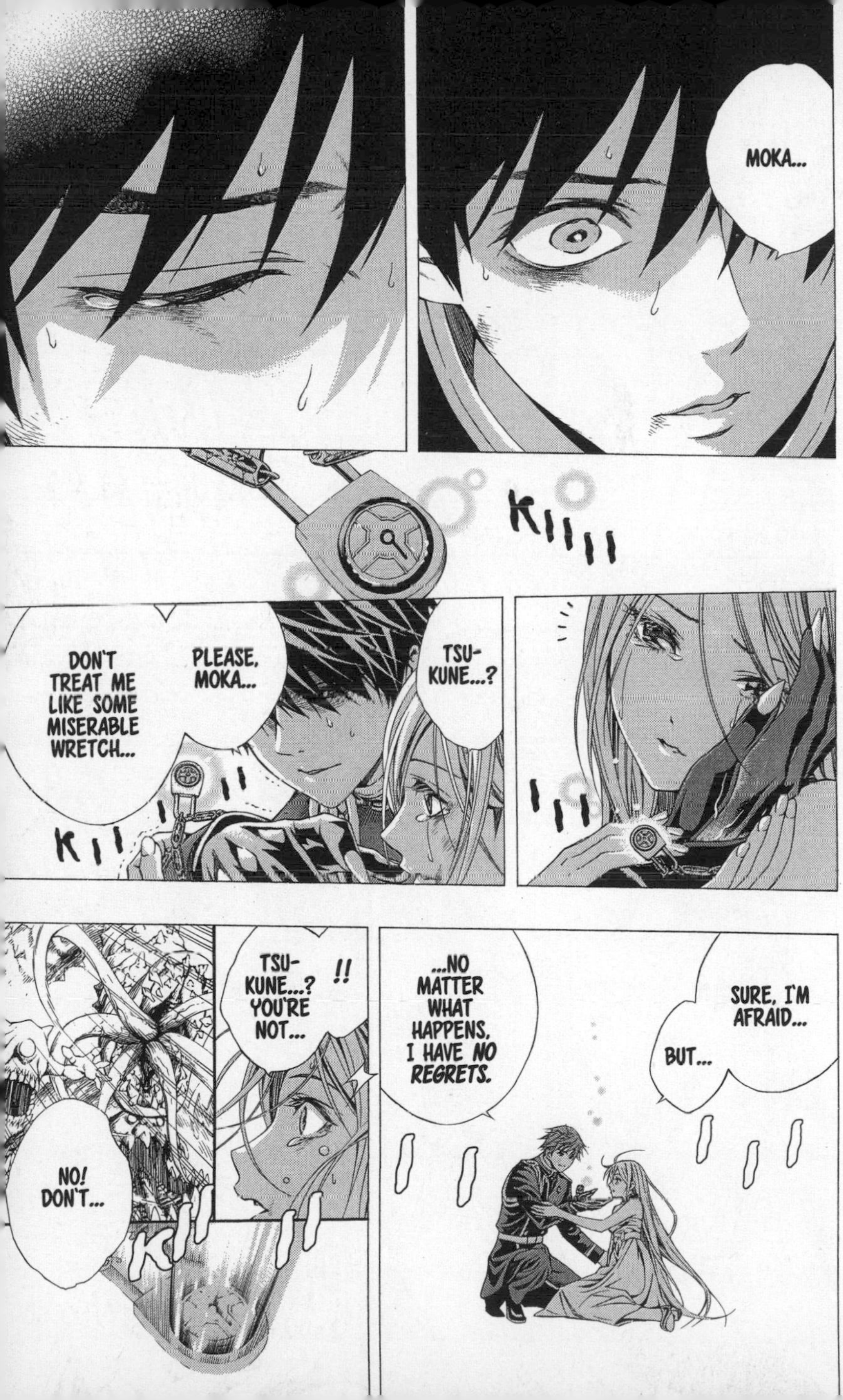
MOKA...
KIIII
TSU-KUNE...?
PLEASE, MOKA...
DON'T TREAT ME LIKE SOME MISERABLE WRETCH...
KII
SURE, I'M AFRAID...
BUT...
...NO MATTER WHAT HAPPENS, I HAVE NO REGRETS.
TSU-KUNE...? YOU'RE NOT...
!!
NO! DON'T...
KIII

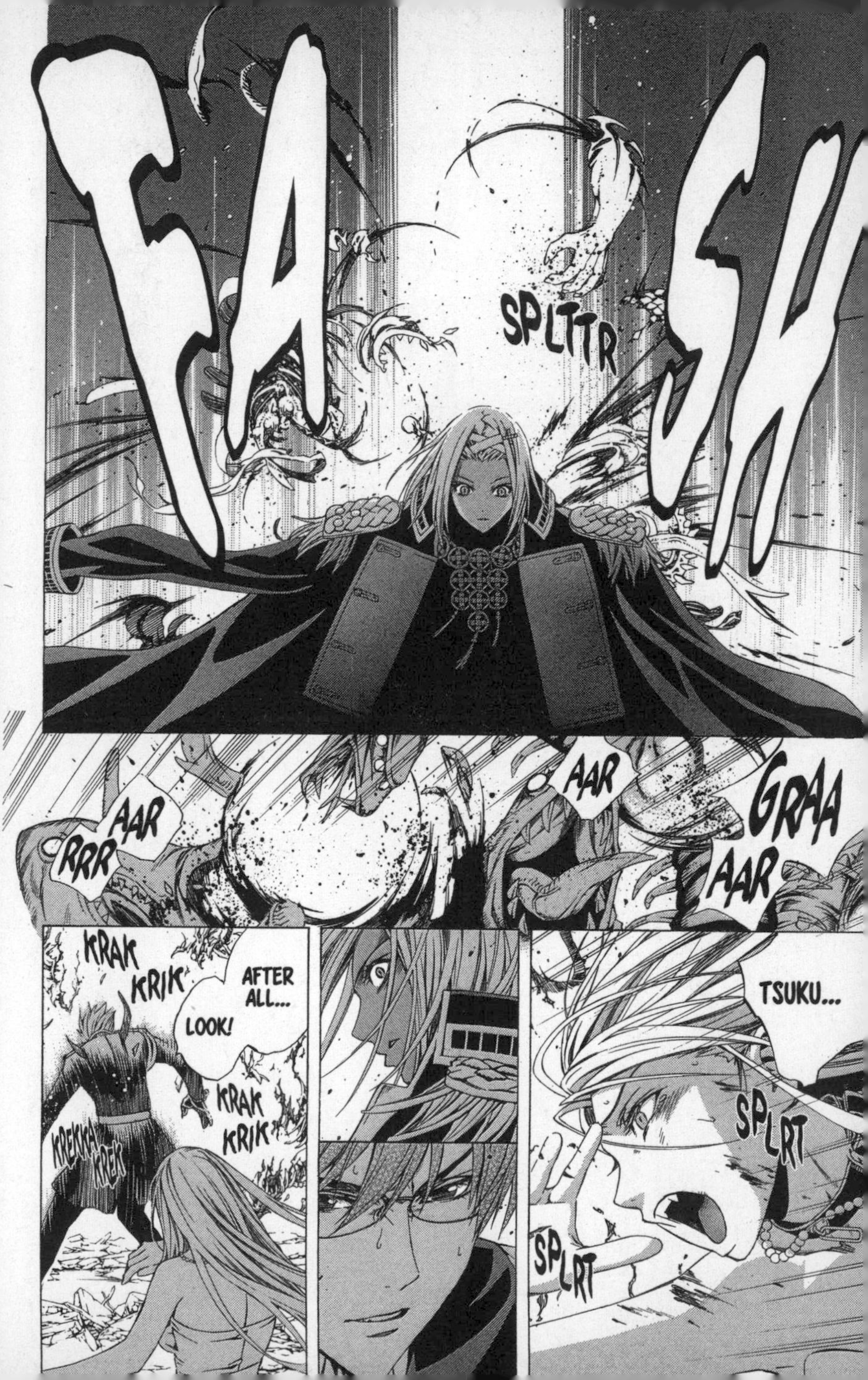

FASH
SPLTTR
GRAA AAR
AAR
AAR RRR
TSUKU...
SPLRT
SPLRT
AFTER ALL...
LOOK!
KRAK KRIK
KRAK KRIK
KREKKA KREK

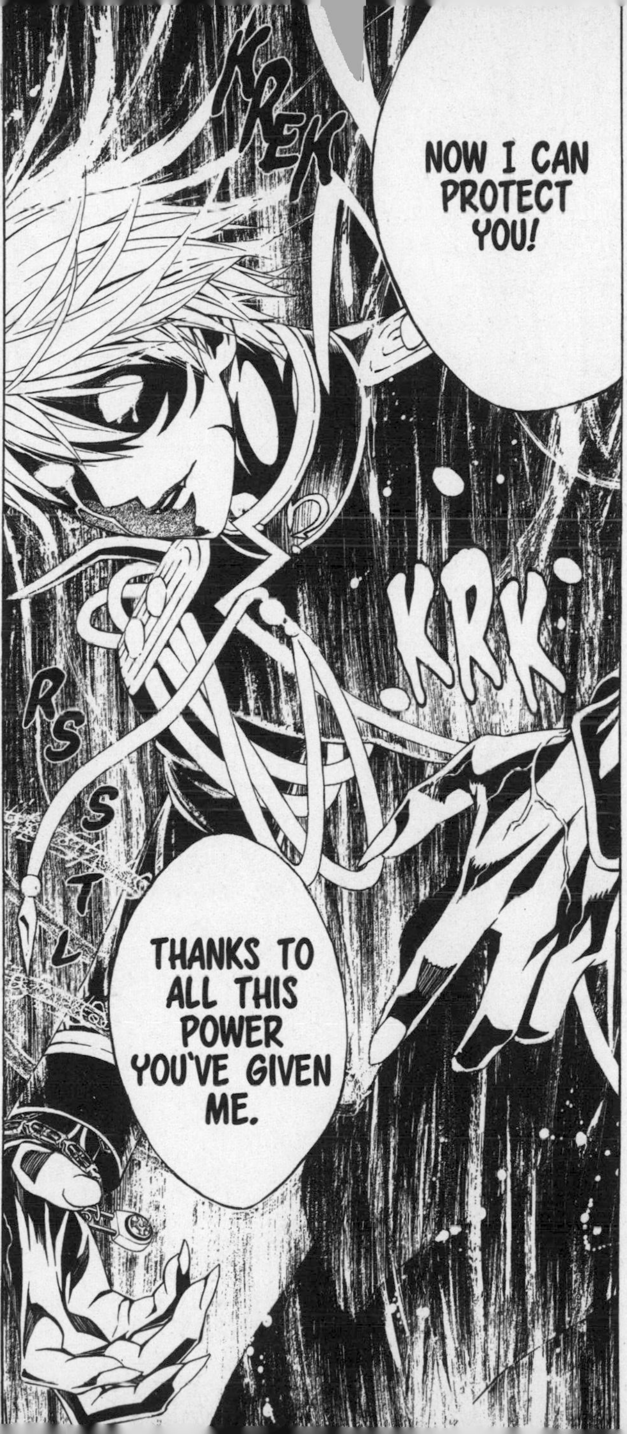

SPIRIT LOCK, SECOND SEAL... *RELEASE!*

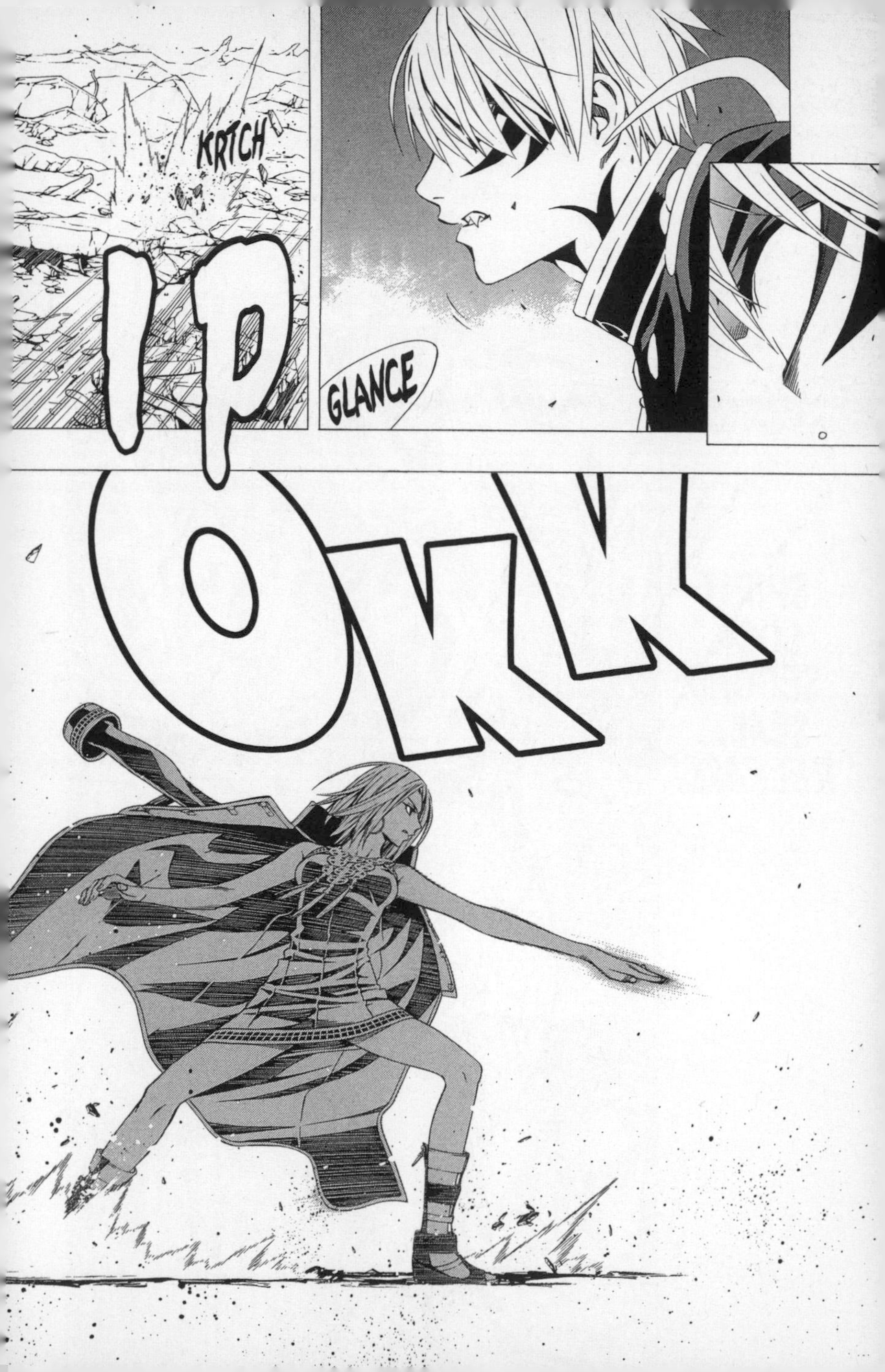
GLANCE
KRTCH

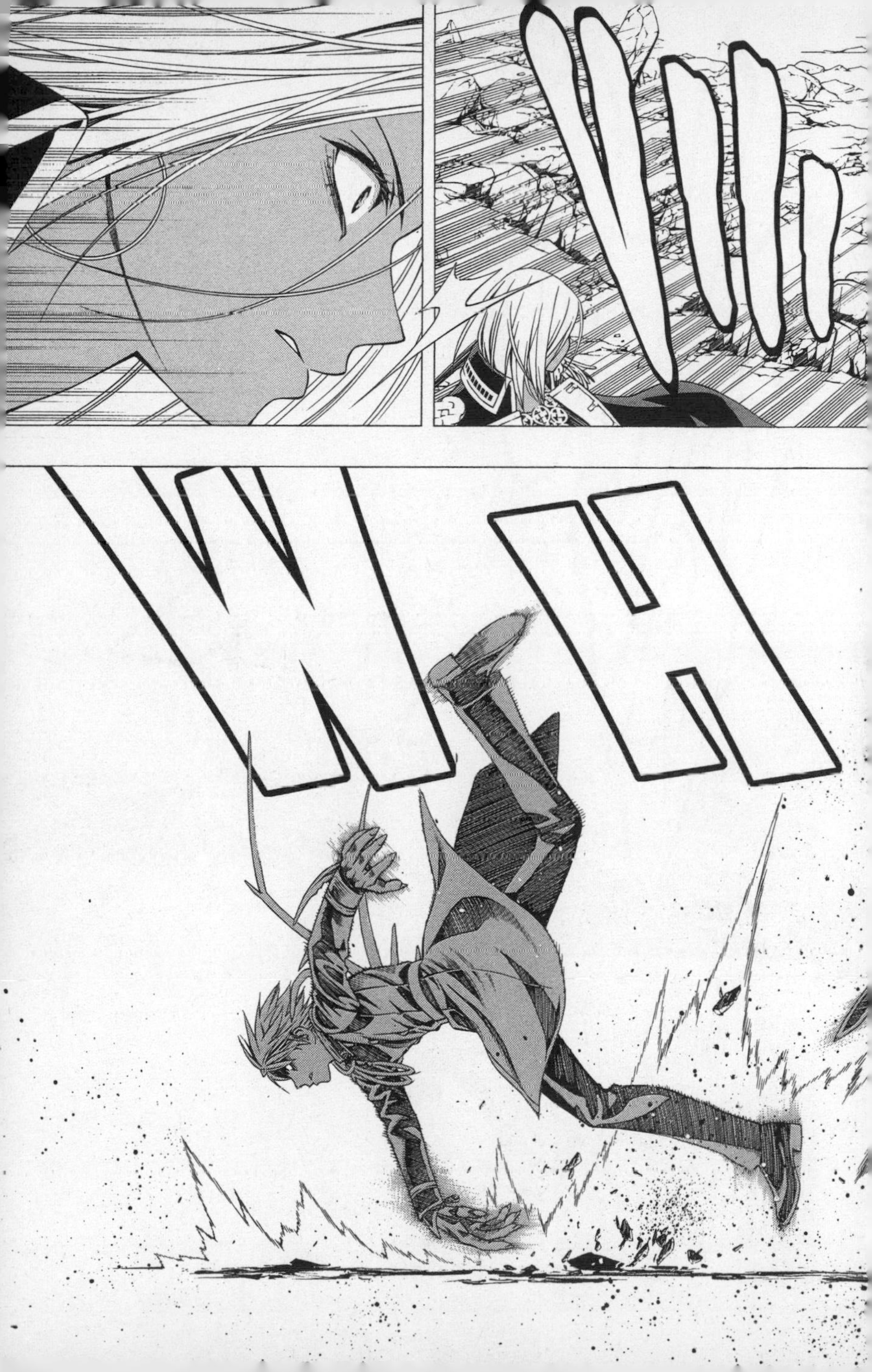

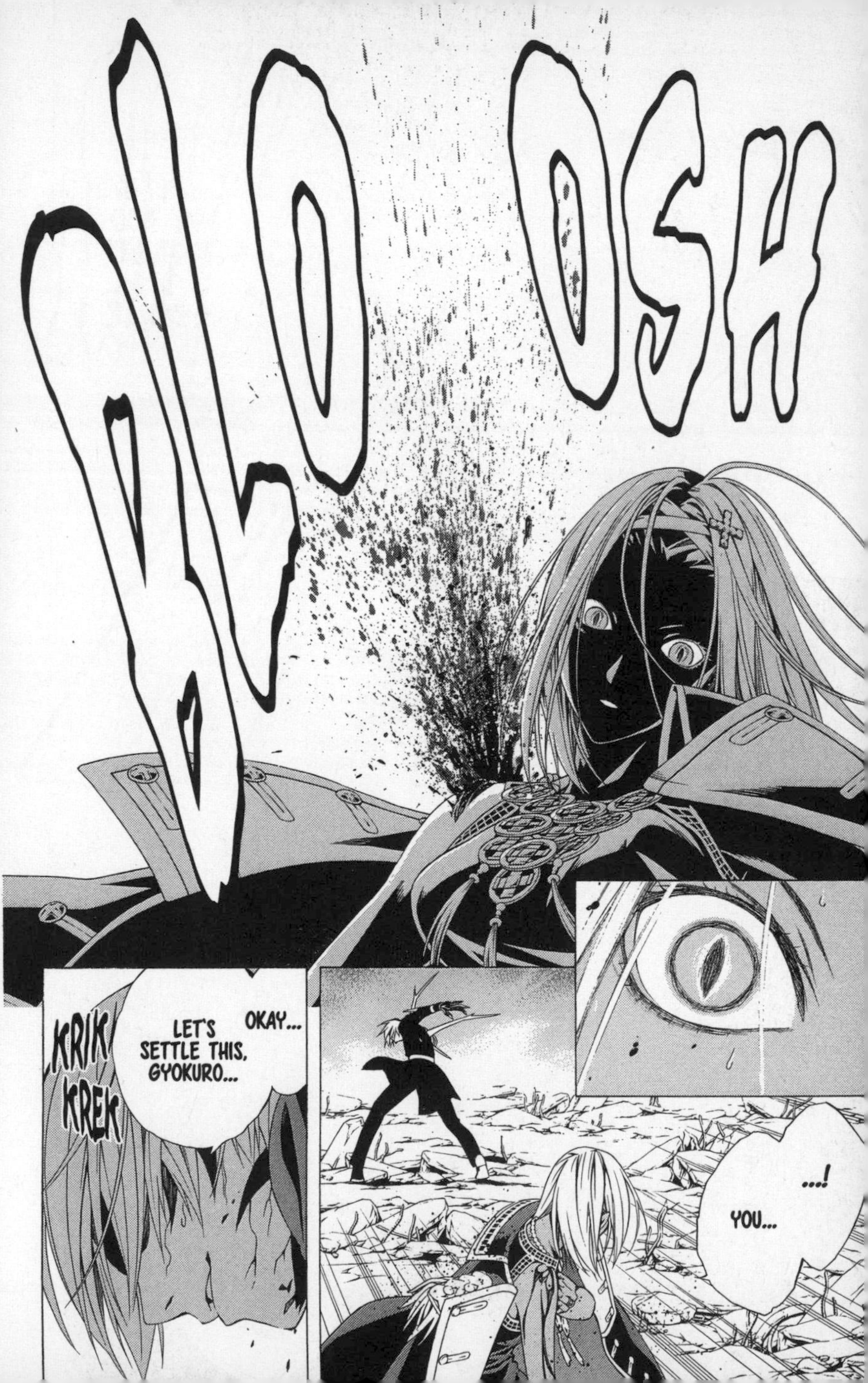
BLOOSH
...! YOU...
OKAY... LET'S SETTLE THIS, GYOKURO...
KRIK KREK

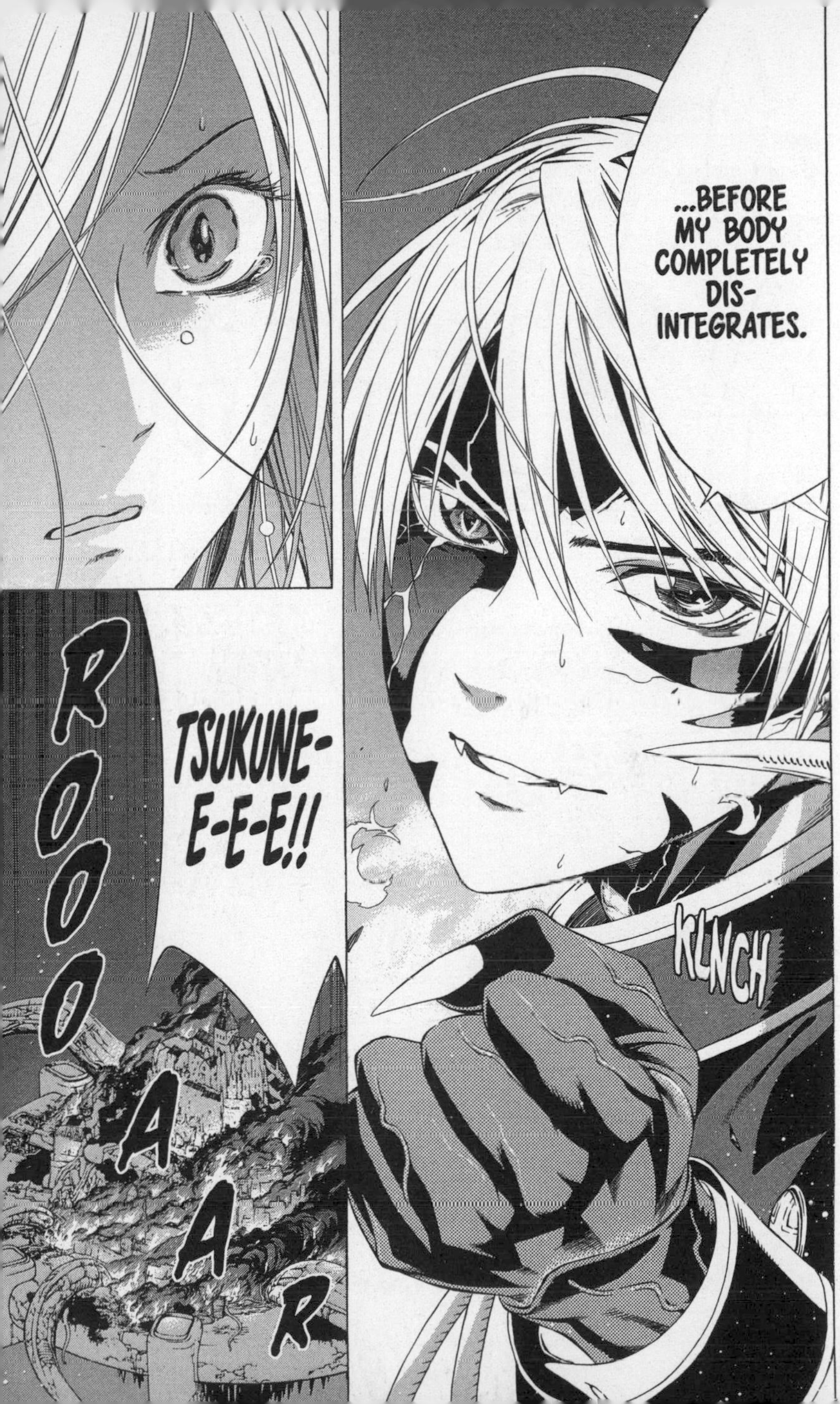
...BEFORE MY BODY COMPLETELY DIS-INTEGRATES.
KLNCH
TSUKUNE-E-E-E!!
ROOOOAAR

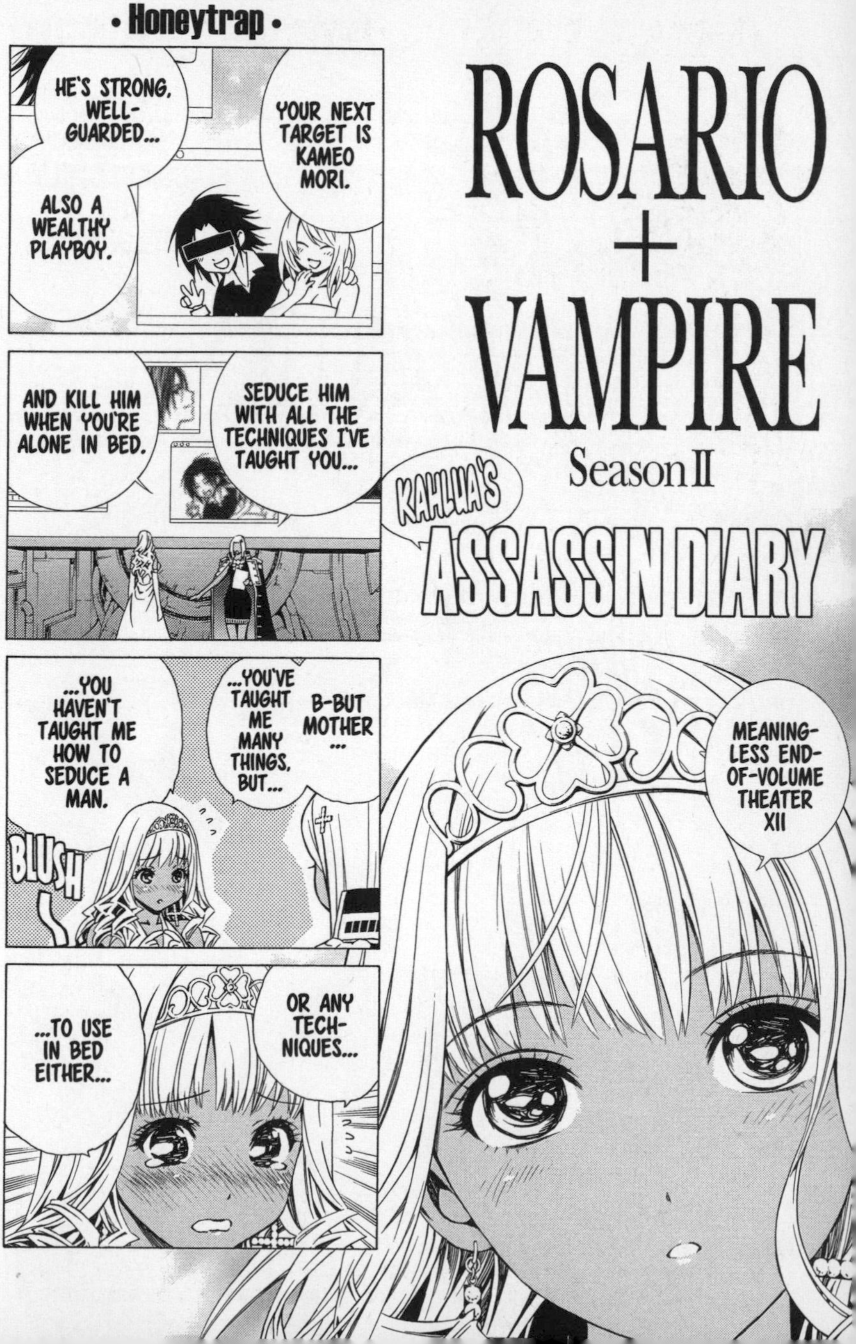
ROSARIO + VAMPIRE
Season II
KAHLUA'S
ASSASSIN DIARY
MEANINGLESS END-OF-VOLUME THEATER XII
• Honeytrap •
YOUR NEXT TARGET IS KAMEO MORI.
HE'S STRONG, WELL-GUARDED...
ALSO A WEALTHY PLAYBOY.
SEDUCE HIM WITH ALL THE TECHNIQUES I'VE TAUGHT YOU...
AND KILL HIM WHEN YOU'RE ALONE IN BED.
B-BUT MOTHER...
...YOU'VE TAUGHT ME MANY THINGS, BUT...
...YOU HAVEN'T TAUGHT ME HOW TO SEDUCE A MAN.
BLUSH
OR ANY TECHNIQUES...
...TO USE IN BED EITHER...

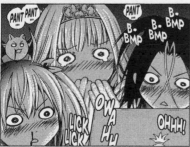

• Source: Branch Office Leaders •

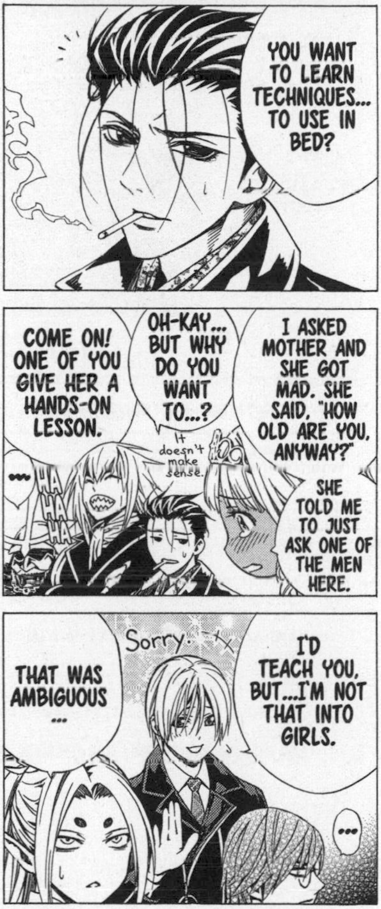
YOU WANT TO LEARN TECHNIQUES... TO USE IN BED?
I ASKED MOTHER AND SHE GOT MAD. SHE SAID, "HOW OLD ARE YOU, ANYWAY?"
SHE TOLD ME TO JUST ASK ONE OF THE MEN HERE.
OH-KAY... BUT WHY DO YOU WANT TO...?
It doesn't make sense.
COME ON! ONE OF YOU GIVE HER A HANDS-ON LESSON.
HA HA HA HA
...
I'D TEACH YOU, BUT...I'M NOT THAT INTO GIRLS.
Sorry.
THAT WAS AMBIGUOUS...
...
UNFORTUNATELY, I'M STILL A VIR—
I CAN TEACH YOU SOME S+M TECHNIQUES...
HOW OLD ARE THESE GUYS...?
PUNCH

• Source: The Internet •

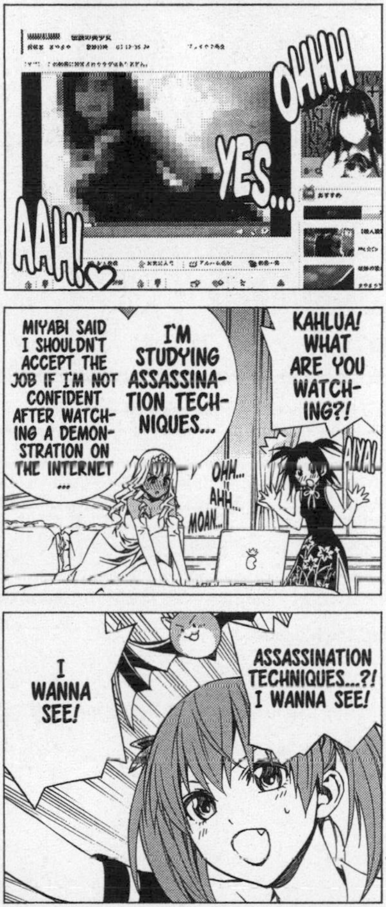
OHHH
YES...
AAH!
KAHLUA! WHAT ARE YOU WATCHING?!
AIYA!
I'M STUDYING ASSASSINATION TECHNIQUES...
MIYABI SAID I SHOULDN'T ACCEPT THE JOB IF I'M NOT CONFIDENT AFTER WATCHING A DEMONSTRATION ON THE INTERNET...
OHH... AHH...
MOAN...
ASSASSINATION TECHNIQUES...?! I WANNA SEE!
I WANNA SEE!
PANT...
B-BMP
B-BMP
B-BMP
PANT PANT...
OWAHH
OHHH!
LICK LICK

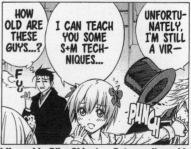

Staff: Akihisa Ikeda • Makoto Saito • Nobuyuki Hayashi • Rika Shirota • Tetsuya Hayashi
Help: Yosuke Takeda • Fumi Tanaka   Editor: Takuya Ogawa   Comic: Kenju Noro

AKIHISA IKEDA

To put it bluntly, I think it's impossible for a nice guy to be super popular with girls. (*laugh*)

He's kind but weak...and in the end, girls protect him.

But then he gains experience through his battles and changes from the protected to the protector... And now, he's very close to reaching his goal.

I wonder if Tsukune has managed to acquire the charm he needs to be the main character of this series. I think I'll leave that question for you to answer.

Akihisa Ikeda was born in 1976 in Miyazaki. He debuted as a mangaka with the four-volume magical warrior fantasy series *Kiruto* in 2002, which was serialized in *Monthly Shonen Jump*. *Rosario+Vampire* debuted in *Monthly Shonen Jump* in March of 2004 and is continuing in the magazine *Jump Square (Jump SQ)* as *Rosario+Vampire: Season II*. In Japan, *Rosario+Vampire* is also available as a drama CD. In 2008, the story was released as an anime. Season II is also available as an anime now. And in Japan, there is a Nintendo DS game based on the series.

Ikeda has been a huge fan of vampires and monsters since he was a little kid. He says one of the perks of being a manga artist is being able to go for walks during the day when everybody else is stuck in the office.

ROSARIO+VAMPIRE: Season II
12
SHONEN JUMP ADVANCED Manga Edition

STORY & ART BY AKIHISA IKEDA

Translation/Tetsuichiro Miyaki
English Adaptation/Annette Roman
Touch-up Art & Lettering/Stephen Dutro
Cover & Interior Design/Ronnie Casson
Editor/Annette Roman

ROSARIO + VAMPIRE SEASON II © 2007 by Akihisa Ikeda
All rights reserved. First published in Japan in 2007 by SHUEISHA Inc.,
Tokyo. English translation rights arranged by SHUEISHA Inc.

The stories, characters and incidents mentioned in this publication are
entirely fictional.

No portion of this book may be reproduced or transmitted in any form or
by any means without written permission from the copyright holders.

Printed in the U.S.A.

Published by VIZ Media, LLC
P.O. Box 77010
San Francisco, CA 94107

10 9 8 7 6 5 4 3 2 1
First printing, October 2013

www.viz.com

www.shonenjump.com

PARENTAL ADVISORY
ROSARIO+VAMPIRE is rated T+ for Older Teen and is
recommended for ages 16 and up. It contains suggestive
situations and violence.

ratings.viz.com

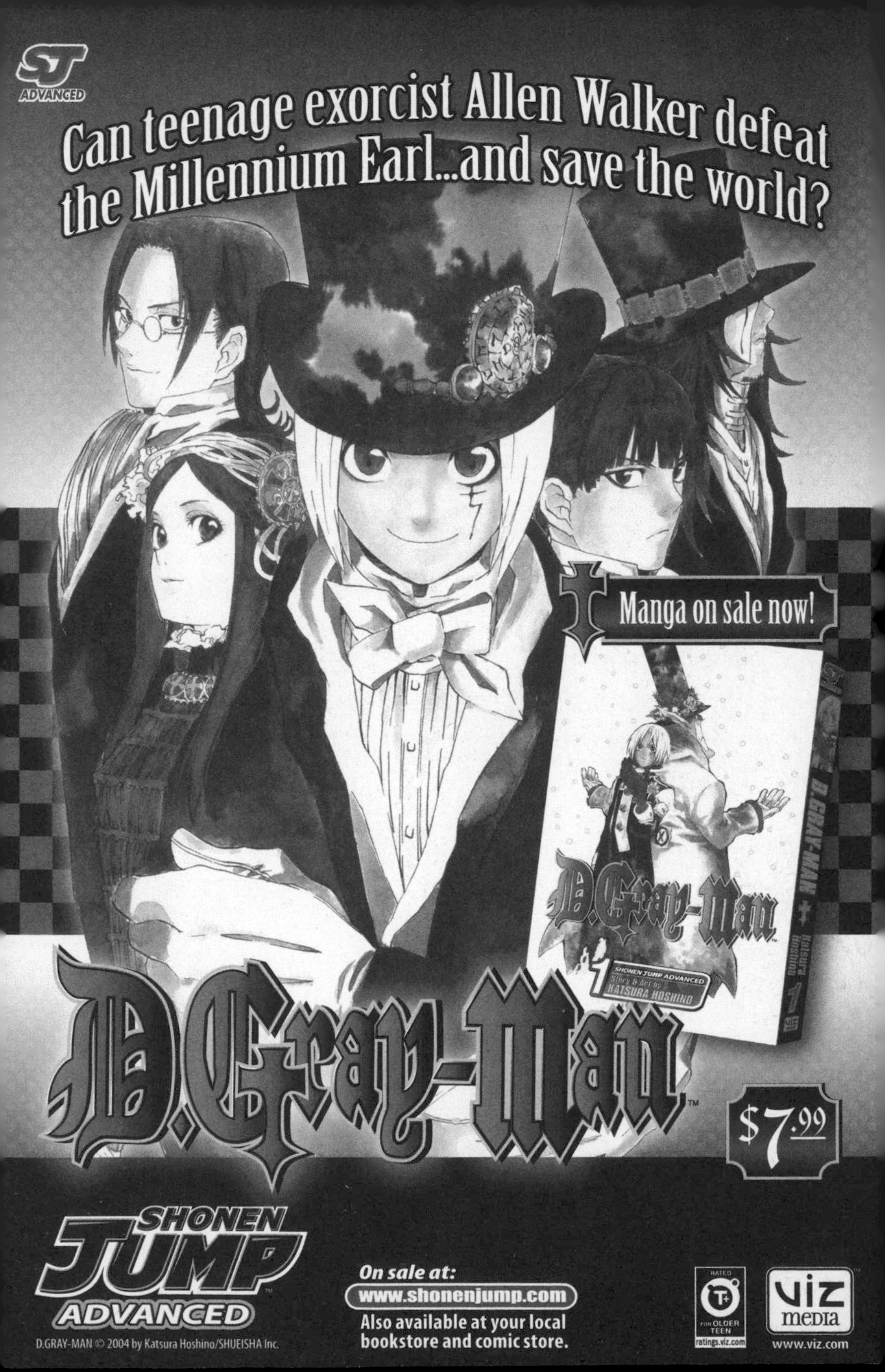
SJ ADVANCED
Can teenage exorcist Allen Walker defeat the Millennium Earl...and save the world?
Manga on sale now!
D.Gray-man
SHONEN JUMP ADVANCED
Story & Art by KATSURA HOSHINO
D.Gray-man™
$7.99
SHONEN JUMP ADVANCED
On sale at:
www.shonenjump.com
Also available at your local bookstore and comic store.
D.GRAY-MAN © 2004 by Katsura Hoshino/SHUEISHA Inc.
RATED T+ FOR OLDER TEEN
ratings.viz.com
VIZ media
www.viz.com

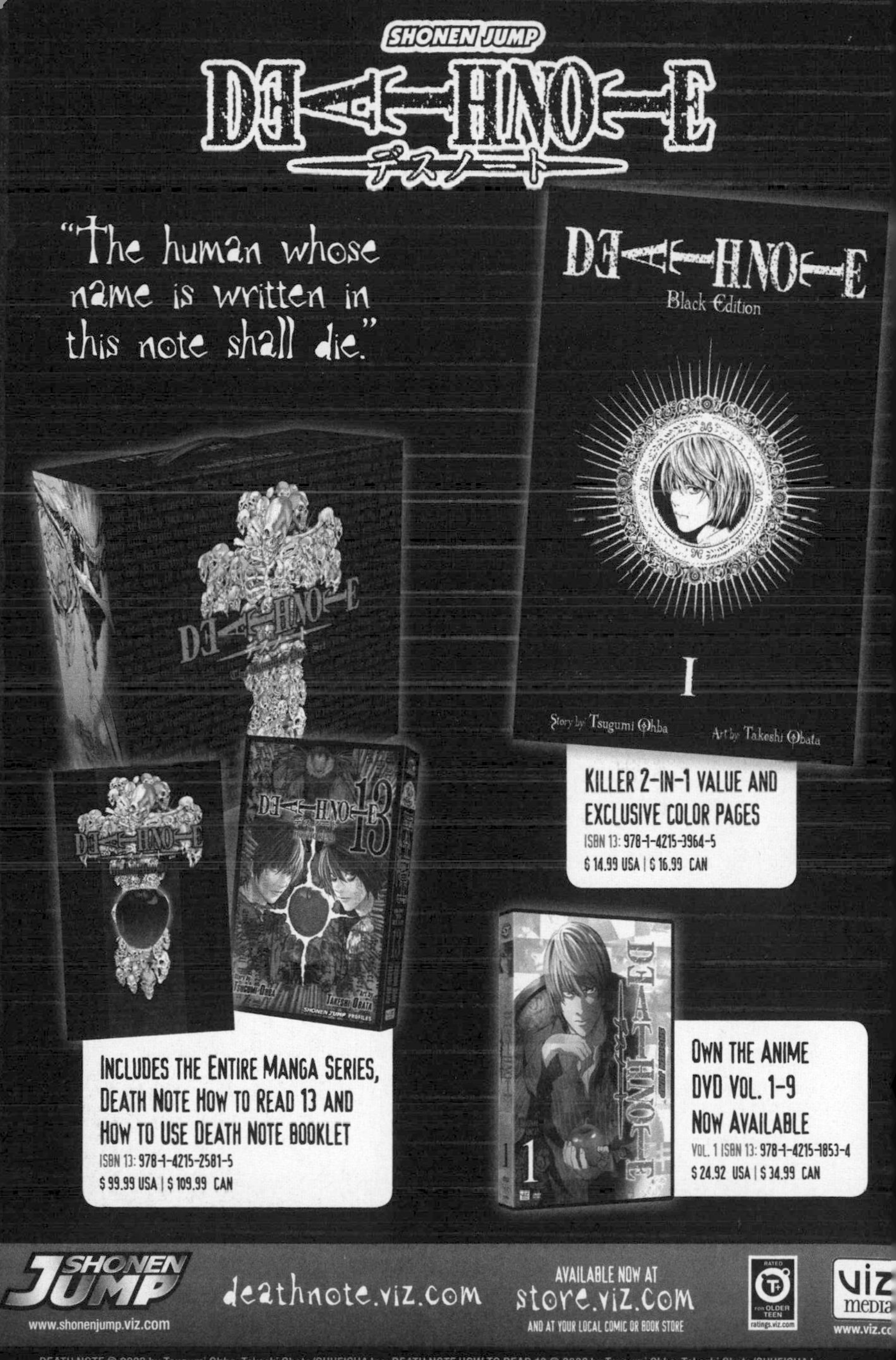
SHONEN JUMP
DEATH NOTE
デスノート
"The human whose name is written in this note shall die."
DEATH NOTE
Black Edition
1
Story by: Tsugumi Ohba
Art by: Takeshi Obata
KILLER 2-IN-1 VALUE AND EXCLUSIVE COLOR PAGES
ISBN 13: 978-1-4215-3964-5
$ 14.99 USA | $ 16.99 CAN
DEATH NOTE
DEATH NOTE 13
INCLUDES THE ENTIRE MANGA SERIES, DEATH NOTE HOW TO READ 13 AND HOW TO USE DEATH NOTE BOOKLET
ISBN 13: 978-1-4215-2581-5
$ 99.99 USA | $ 109.99 CAN
DEATH NOTE
1
OWN THE ANIME DVD VOL. 1-9 NOW AVAILABLE
VOL. 1 ISBN 13: 978-1-4215-1853-4
$ 24.92 USA | $ 34.99 CAN
SHONEN JUMP
www.shonenjump.viz.com
deathnote.viz.com
AVAILABLE NOW AT
store.viz.com
AND AT YOUR LOCAL COMIC OR BOOK STORE
RATED T+ FOR OLDER TEEN
ratings.viz.com
viz media
www.viz.co

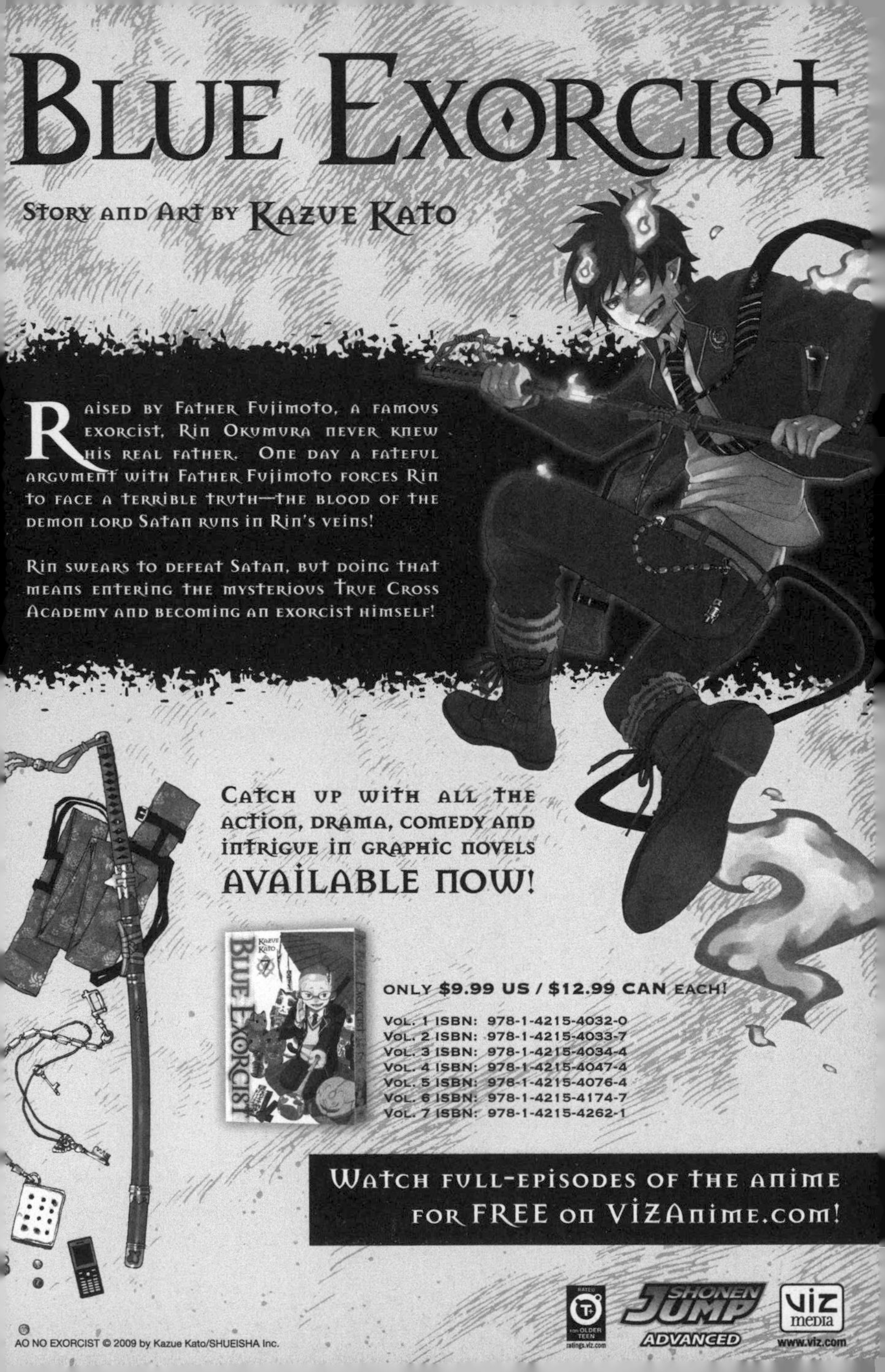
BLUE EXORCIST
STORY AND ART BY KAZUE KATO
RAISED BY FATHER FUJIMOTO, A FAMOUS EXORCIST, RIN OKUMURA NEVER KNEW HIS REAL FATHER. ONE DAY A FATEFUL ARGUMENT WITH FATHER FUJIMOTO FORCES RIN TO FACE A TERRIBLE TRUTH—THE BLOOD OF THE DEMON LORD SATAN RUNS IN RIN'S VEINS!
RIN SWEARS TO DEFEAT SATAN, BUT DOING THAT MEANS ENTERING THE MYSTERIOUS TRUE CROSS ACADEMY AND BECOMING AN EXORCIST HIMSELF!
CATCH UP WITH ALL THE ACTION, DRAMA, COMEDY AND INTRIGUE IN GRAPHIC NOVELS AVAILABLE NOW!
ONLY $9.99 US / $12.99 CAN EACH!
VOL. 1 ISBN: 978-1-4215-4032-0
VOL. 2 ISBN: 978-1-4215-4033-7
VOL. 3 ISBN: 978-1-4215-4034-4
VOL. 4 ISBN: 978-1-4215-4047-4
VOL. 5 ISBN: 978-1-4215-4076-4
VOL. 6 ISBN: 978-1-4215-4174-7
VOL. 7 ISBN: 978-1-4215-4262-1
WATCH FULL-EPISODES OF THE ANIME FOR FREE ON VIZANIME.COM!
RATED T+ FOR OLDER TEEN ratings.viz.com
SHONEN JUMP ADVANCED
VIZ MEDIA
www.viz.com
AO NO EXORCIST © 2009 by Kazue Kato/SHUEISHA Inc.

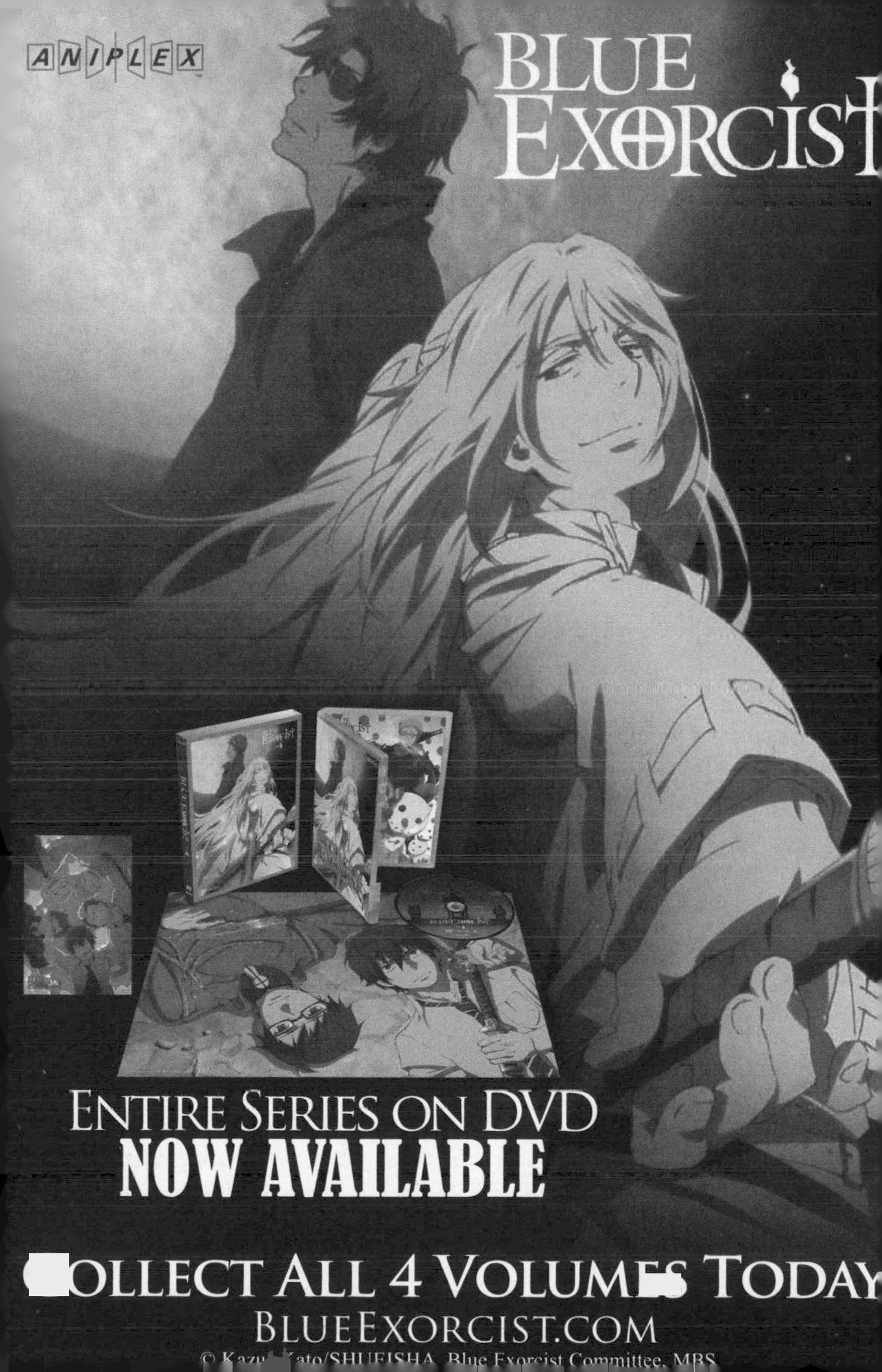

ANIPLEX
BLUE EXORCIST
ENTIRE SERIES ON DVD
NOW AVAILABLE
COLLECT ALL 4 VOLUMES TODAY
BLUEEXORCIST.COM
© Kazue Kato/SHUEISHA, Blue Exorcist Committee, MBS

VIZMANGA
Read manga anytime, anywhere!

From our newest hit series to the classics you know and love, the best manga in the world is now available digitally. Buy a volume* of digital manga for your:

- iOS device (**iPad®, iPhone®, iPod® touch**) through the **VIZ Manga app**
- Android-powered device (**phone or tablet**) with a browser by visiting VIZManga.com
- **Mac or PC computer** by visiting VIZManga.com

VIZ Digital has loads to offer:

- 500+ ready-to-read volumes
- New volumes each week
- FREE previews
- Access on multiple devices! Create a log-in through the app so you buy a book once, and read it on your device of choice!*

To learn more, visit www.viz.com/apps

* Some series may not be available for multiple devices.
  Check the app on your device to find out what's available.

DEATH NOTE © 2003 by Tsugumi Ohba, Takeshi Obata/SHUEISHA Inc.
NURARIHYON NO MAGO © 2008 by Hiroshi Shiibashi/SHUEISHA Inc.
ONE PIECE © 1997 by Eiichiro Oda/SHUEISHA Inc.